EXCHANGE
PRICES, AND PRODUCTION
IN HYPER-INFLATION:
GERMANY, 1920-1923

BY

FRANK D. GRAHAM

Professor of Economics
in Princeton University

FOREWORD

THIS study is the first of a series to be published under the auspices of the International Finance Section of the Department of Economics and Social Institutions in Princeton University. This section was established as a memorial to the late James Theodore Walker, Princeton 1927, with funds largely provided by members of Mr. Walker's family. The function of the Section is research, advanced teaching and public service in the field of international finance.

Since German reparations furnish perhaps the most important present problems in this field it seemed fitting that this volume on the German currency débâcle in the immediate post-war years—a phenomenon closely associated with reparations—should inaugurate the series. It is the intention of the Section on International Finance to develop the fundamental rather than the ephemeral aspects of the subjects with which it deals and the student of monetary problems will find matter in the theoretical and statistical chapters of this book which will, I am sure, be of permanent interest to scientific economists. At the same time the careful analysis which Professor Graham has made of the effects of inflation on German national economic life should engage the attention of men of affairs. The rapidity of German recovery since 1924 has frequently been remarked. If, as Professor Graham suggests, the patient was not as sick in 1924 as appearances indicated, and had in fact slowly been improving since the end of the war, prevailing ideas should be readjusted along two lines. In the first place, it is improbable that the relative prosperity of Germany since 1924 is the flash in the pan that many people have been disposed to regard it and, in the second, prosperity, though real, has not been as rapid as surface phenomena would lead one to believe. The synthesis of these conclusions points to a tempered optimism for the future.

E. W. KEMMERER.

PREFACE

CLIFFE-LESLIE once remarked that in social matters the greatest scientific progress is made when economic disorders raise vexing questions as to their causes. In the study of social phenomena, disorder is, it is true, the sole substitute for the controlled experiments of the natural sciences. But it sometimes happens that, in the midst of disorder, events move so rapidly that we are not able properly to observe them; disorder may be excessive even to the most detached of scientists. The course of inflation in Germany in the first post-war quinquennium had so much of this character that it has seemed to many to be incapable of throwing any light upon monetary problems. This most striking of monetary experiences has, in consequence, evoked a minimum of scientific curiosity.[1] In spite of the fact that statistics— those notes of process on which the social scientist must so heavily rely— were for some phenomena abandoned in Germany in this period and for others are open to grave objection on the score of accuracy, it has seemed to me that such an attitude implies an unwarranted surrender in the face of difficulties which might with perseverance be surmounted. This book is an attempt, therefore, to discover what actually happened in Germany and either to bring the observed phenomena within the fold of accepted theory or else so to modify that theory as to give it a more catholic character. The actual course of events during inflation has not merely an historical and scientific interest but is of considerable practical importance. Germany's present position as a nation with heavy international obligations has led to apprehension, both within and without the Reich, as to the future in international finance. The fears of such German competition as may issue out of the debtor status may be dismissed as but thinly-veiled mercantilism but the question as to the possibility of ultimate transfer of the large sums involved in reparations and interest payments must, perhaps, be treated with more respect. The ability of the German economy to provide, within Germany, the funds required, is, on the other hand, no longer seriously doubted. It is hoped

---

[1] cf. *Foreign Banking Systems*, H. P. Willis and B. H. Beckhart, editors, Chap. VIII, "The Banking System of Germany." Paul Quittner, Henry Holt and Company, New York, 1929, p. 632, where it is declared that it would be useless to try to connect the development of the German currency system from 1919 to 1923 with any theories of money.

that the sequel will throw some light on the disappearance of the latter doubt as also on the prospect of future transfers undisturbed by any serious economic friction.

The subjects toward which inquiry has been directed involve the status of Germany as a national unit only. Practically no attempt has been made to deal with such changes in the distribution of wealth and income among German nationals as arose out of inflation. These changes were of great, perhaps of extreme, significance, but justice to this topic requires the work of a social philosopher rather than that of a mere economist.

The present book owes much to the financial and clerical assistance provided by the International Finance Section of the Department of Economics and Social Institutions in Princeton University, and to that given by the John Simon Guggenheim Memorial Foundation, under the auspices of which the author spent part of the years 1928 and 1929 in Germany. It is based very largely on official German statistics as published by the Statistische Reichsamt and the Institut für Konjunkturforschung. These statistics, for the period studied, are, no doubt, far from perfect,[2] but nothing is gained by attempting to go behind them and there is no reason to suppose that such alternative sources as are available are at all superior.[2] The hope is cherished, perhaps not without justification, that such errors as are involved do not vitiate the conclusions reached. The immense nominal magnitudes attained by all -monetary phenomena in Germany in the inflation-time tend to dwarf the influence of even very considerable imperfections in the statistics. I am far from supposing, nevertheless, that the results obtained are to be taken as clearly proven and I trust that the reader will be no more credulous. They are merely hypotheses.

The publications of the Statistische Reichsamt which have been principally used are : Statistisches Jahrbuch für das deutsche Reich, Statistik des deutschen Reichs, Wirtschaft und Statistik, Monatliche Nachweise über den auswärtigen Handel Deutschlands, Zahlen zur Geldentwertung in Deutschland 1914 bis 1923, *and* Germany's Economy, Currency and Finance.[3] *Sparing use has been made of forms of statistics already avail-*

---

[2] In the matter of mark exchange rates, for instance, sizable differences developed, in the later stages of inflation, between the Berlin and other markets. These were due to the obstruction of arbitrage transactions. At the time that this occurred, however, the Berlin rate was alone of much significance. The Berlin rates have therefore been used throughout. In the matter of prices the alternative sources are the indices of the *Berliner Tageblatt,* the *Frankfurter Zeitung,* and the *Industrie- und Handelszeitung.*

[3] The latter compilation was published in English, as well as in German, for use by the Committees of Experts of the Reparations Commission.

able in these sources and, where tables are given in the text, they are, in nearly all cases, the result of computations from the original data.

To get these data into usable and significant form was a very laborious task and, more than that, it called for ingenuity and technical skill of a high order. To Miss Mabel S. Lewis, research assistant in the International Finance Section at Princeton University, I am indebted for all of this work. It was rendered not only with unremitting diligence but with a cheerfulness which, in view of my frequent vacillations, was extraordinary. Miss Lewis has also drawn all the charts.

I can but briefly express my appreciation of the unfailing courtesy and assistance which came to me from many other sources. I should like, however, to mention specifically Dr. Ernst Wagemann and the staff of the Statistische Reichsamt, especially Dr. Otto Nathan; Dr. Hjalmar Schacht and the staff of the statistical division of the Reichsbank; Mr. F. W. Allport, American Commercial Attaché in Berlin; Mr. J. H. Riddle, formerly of the staff of the Agent-General for Reparations Payments; the former German under-Secretary of State, Julius Hirsch; Professor Melchior Palyi of the Handelshochschule, Berlin; Dr. Carl Köttgen, Director-General of the Siemens-Schuckertwerke, Berlin; Dr. E. W. Schmidt of the Diskontogesellschaft, Berlin; Dr. Ernst Jäckh of the Deutsche Hochschule für Politik, Berlin; Mr. Magnus W. Alexander of the National Industrial Conference Board, New York; and Sir Arthur Salter and the staff of the League of Nations Library in Geneva.

The manuscript was read by Mr. H. C. Kuthe and by Professors F. W. Fetter and C. R. Whittlesey of Princeton University and Chapter VII was read by Professor J. G. Smith of the same institution. They are, of course, by no means necessarily committed to the views here expressed but their comments were most valuable. My wife has devoted much of her time and attention to the work of revision, has criticized generously, and has brought many obscurities into the realm of the intelligible.

Princeton, New Jersey   F. D. G.
October 25, 1930.

CONTENTS

Part II will be of most interest to the student of monetary phenomena and Part III will appeal, perhaps, to the statistically-minded. The general reader may prefer to omit these parts and this may be done without much loss of continuity.

LIST OF TABLES

LIST OF CHARTS

PART I

HISTORICAL BACKGROUND

CHAPTER I

INTRODUCTION

§ SCOPE AND CHARACTER OF GERMAN INFLATION

GERMANY, in common with other warring countries, departed from the gold standard at the outbreak of hostilities in 1914. On November 20, 1923, the German paper mark, after having fallen to an infinitesimal fraction of its former value, was made redeemable in the newly introduced rentenmark at a trillion to one.[1] The rentenmark, after a short but honorable existence during which its gold value remained substantially stable at that of the original gold mark, was supplanted by the present standard reichsmark.[2] The latter is also of equal gold value with the German pre-war currency unit and is convertible, in practice, into dollar exchange at the old rate.[3]

The régime of inconvertible and depreciating paper money thus ran for a little less than a decade. The progress of depreciation was, however, very unevenly distributed over these ten years. During most of the war-period the exchange value of the mark did not fall greatly from par

[1] A trillion according to American and French nomenclature, a billion according to English and German. American usage will be adhered to throughout. The following notation will help to keep the reader clear if he is accustomed to the English and German usage.

NUMBER	AMERICAN AND FRENCH NOMENCLATURE	ENGLISH AND GERMAN NOMENCLATURE
1,000,000	Million	Million
1,000,000,000	Billion or Milliard	Milliard
1,000,000,000,000	Trillion	Billion
1,000,000,000,000,000	Quadrillion	Thousand Billion
1,000,000,000,000,000,000	Quintillion	Trillion
1,000,000,000,000,000,000,000	Sextillion	Thousand Trillion
1,000,000,000,000,000,000,000,000	Septillion	Quadrillion

[2] The rentenmark was supplanted only in its capacity as the standard currency unit. Rentenmarks still circulate alongside the standard reichsmark but are gradually being retired.

[3] 1 gold mark = 23.82 American cents.
4.198 gold marks = $1.00.

with the dollar and if, when the issue of the conflict was no longer in doubt, it sank heavily, it was still quoted in December 1918 at more than twelve American cents. During the peace negotiations, however, German exchange continued to fall fast. This downward movement persisted till February 1920 when the descent was checked at just a shade below one cent per mark, that is, at about 1/24 of its pre-war value. A quick recovery then set in which carried the rate to nearly 3c in May. Though there was some reaction from this figure relative stability at a level of from 1½ to 2c was attained in June. By early 1920 the period of immediate adjustment to post-war conditions may therefore be considered to have been completed. Not until September 1921 did the value of the mark again fall below one American cent and as late as June 1922 it still sold for about 1/3 of a cent. From then onward the decline was vertiginous till the final collapse in November 1923. At the latter date forty-two billion (42,000,000,000) marks were worth but a single American cent. Without a complete ouster of the currency concerned, no corresponding depreciation appears in the long and varied annals of monetary history. Never before had a paper money fallen at so rapid a rate over such an extended period. In 1913 the mark was solidly based on gold; in 1923 its value was, as one writer has said, something more ridiculous than zero.

Not only in magnitude of depreciation was the German currency experience unique. Its quality was also peculiar. In this respect the most informative comparison is not so much with other times as with other countries at the same time. Many of the phenomena which occurred in Germany were, it is true, more or less closely paralleled in neighboring countries the currencies of which were undergoing contemporaneous depreciation. But the degree of deviation of exchange rates from the course of internal prices was much greater in Germany than elsewhere and this resulted in domestic business being carried on at a price level very largely divorced from that of the outside world. The extent of governmental intervention in external commercial and financial transactions, as well as in the domestic markets, was greater than in any other country organized on a capitalistic basis. Upon no other country was foreign tribute assessed on anything like the same scale and no other country was forced to pay any sizable sum on this account. The difficulty of securing foreign or domestic loans in any measure adequate to the need found no parallel in any other land with the possible exception of the Succession States and Russia. Finally, the will to check depreciation in Germany was much weaker than in other countries since the Germans were convinced, by no means without justification, that improvement in the public finances would lead to still more severe exactions on the part of the victors in the war. All these forces combined to give to the inflation of the mark a peculiar character the features of which it will be the task of the ensuing chapters to examine.

§ FINANCIAL POSITION OF GERMANY AT THE END OF THE WAR

The cessation of war found Germany in a financial position not markedly inferior to that of most of the other countries involved in the struggle. The far-reaching alterations in the Reichsbankgesetz in 1914 had permitted the suspension of specie payments, had removed the tax on excess Reichsbank note issues, had permitted the Reichsbank to use discounted Treasury bills in lieu of commercial bills as the non-cash cover for Reichsbank notes, and had made Reichskassenscheine[4] and Darlehns-kassenscheine[5] available to meet the "cash" reserve requirements. (The distinction between cash and non-cash cover was abolished in 1921.) This war legislation paved the way for all the coming currency difficulties but it did not differ very greatly from that adopted at the same time in practically all the countries then engaged in hostilities, nor did inflation in Germany, up to the time of the Armistice, much surpass that of some of the principal Entente Allies. The total circulation (including coin other than Reichsbank reserves) in the middle of 1914 is estimated to have been approximately six billions of marks;[6] at the end of 1918 it was something more than five times as much, 32,936,-700,000 marks.[7] The total monetary circulation in Great Britain was about £180,000,000 when war broke out[8] while four and a half years later the total of outstanding notes was more than double that sum and stood at approximately £394,000,000. Bank deposits, which in

[4] Treasury notes, a fiduciary currency. These were, however, issued rather sparingly. The maximum issue was 356 million marks. Reichskassenscheine had been legal as cash cover in pre-war days but their issue had been closely restricted and few had been available. These Treasury *notes* are to be carefully distinguished from Treasury *bills*, a short-term security not used as money.

[5] A form of currency issued by officially established Loan Bureaus against the pledge of securities (or commodities) by borrowers other than the government and the larger banks and business concerns. During the war these notes formed an important share of the circulating medium but thereafter remained comparatively stable in absolute figures (7 to 14 billion marks) and were of constantly declining relative importance. They played but a slight rôle from 1921 onward.

[6] *Germany's Economic and Financial Situation*, Statistisches Reichsamt, Zentral-verlag G.m.b.H., Berlin, 1923, p. 28.

[7] *Zahlen zur Geldentwertung in Deutschland* 1914 *bis* 1923, Statistisches Reichsamt, Verlag von Reimar Hobbing, Berlin, 1925, p. 46.

[8] *Committee on Currency and Foreign Exchanges After the War (Cunliffe Committee) First Interim Report*, H. M. Stationery Office, London, 1924, p. 5.

England are a more important index of inflation, had grown in about the same proportion.[9] The total circulation in France (excluding reserves of the Bank of France) in mid-1914 was something over 8,000,-000,000 francs (6.5 billion francs in gold and silver, less 4 billion Bank of France reserves, plus 5.8 billion in notes of the Bank of France[10]) while at the end of 1918 the note circulation of the Bank of France amouted to over 30,000,000,000 francs[10] or not quite four times the total pre-war volume of currency. By this date all the gold formerly in circulation had of course disappeared.

Wholesale prices in Germany, Great Britain and France at the end of 1918 were respectively 2.45, 2.30 and 3.53 times their pre-war height.[11] In the United States they were just about twice their 1913 level.

The public finances of Germany had of course been adversely affected by the war and, under the illusion of an early victory, loans had been too heavily relied upon. But the German debt in 1918 was not disproportionately large in comparison with that of any other of the principal belligerents. Measured in terms of the actual values of their respective currencies as expressed in wholesale price levels, the obligations of the four chief financial Powers engaged in the war, Great Britain, France, Germany and the United States, showed indeed, a close equivalence at its close. It is true that the domestic short-time floating debt in Germany, even at this time, formed an unduly large part of the total, but the German situation in this respect was not materially worse than the French.

As a result of inability to purchase abroad in any large measure during the war Germany had no long-term *foreign* debt, and short-term foreign obligations, the amount of which is not definitely ascertainable, probably did not exceed three or four billion gold marks. Most of this was paid off in the early post-war years. So far as inflation and government finances are concerned, therefore, the end of the war found the Reich in a position by no means hopeless. The situation at that time may be envisaged from the subjoined Tables I and II giving data on government finance and currency up to the close of 1918.

Granted a respite from abnormal burdens there is no reason to believe that the administration could not have brought the federal finances

[9] Total bank deposits, exclusive of those of small private banks, were £716 million on June 30, 1914, and £1361 million on June 30, 1919. *European Currency and Finance*, United States Senate Commission of Gold and Silver Inquiry, Serial 9, Vol. I, Government Printing Office, Washington, 1925, pp. 277, 278.

[10] *ibid.*, Vol. I, pp. 308, 470.

[11] *ibid.*, Vol. I, pp. 534, 477, 455.

into order. In fact, early in 1920, it succeeded in balancing non-reparation expenditures with receipts other than loans. This favorable progress did not, however, continue. Nevertheless, even as late as the spring of 1922, when inflation was far advanced, a similar position was again temporarily attained.

TABLE I

EXPENDITURES, REVENUES OTHER THAN FROM SHORT-TERM BORROWING,
AND DEFICITS OF THE REICH; 1914–1919

(Billions of marks)

FISCAL YEAR (APRIL 1–MARCH 31)	EXPENDITURES	REVENUES OTHER THAN FROM SHORT-TERM BORROWING	DEFICITS (COVERED BY SHORT-TERM BORROWING)
1914–1915	9.6	8.2	1.4
1915–1916	26.7	24.0	2.7
1916–1917	28.8	24.6	4.2
1917–1918	53.3	37.1	16.2
1918–1919	45.5	34.2	11.3
Totals	163.9	128.1[12]	35.8

[12] Of this amount approximately 97 billion marks had been obtained through long-term loans.

Sources of data: (1) *Statistisches Jahrbuch* 1919, Verlag von Puttkamer und Mühlbrecht, Berlin, 1919, *passim.* (2) *Verwaltungsbericht der Reichsbank* 1918, Reichsdruckerei, Berlin, 1919, p. 11.

TABLE II

NATIONAL DEBT OF GERMANY, ISSUES OF PAPER CURRENCY, INDEX OF WHOLESALE PRICES, AND INDEX OF DOLLAR EXCHANGE RATES AGAINST PAPER MARKS; 1914–1918

(Value figures in millions of marks)

YEAR	TOTAL DEBT (END OF MARCH OF THE SUCCEEDING YEAR)	TOTAL ISSUES OF PAPER CURRENCY (EXCEPT EMERGENCY MONEY) (END OF YEAR)	INDEX OF WHOLESALE PRICES 1913=1 (END OF YEAR)	INDEX OF DOLLAR EXCHANGE RATES IN BERLIN 1913=1 (END OF YEAR)
1914	5,158	5,862	1.25	1.07
1915	16,955	8,360	1.48	1.23
1916	39,856	11,438	1.51	1.36
1917	69,211	18,245	2.03	1.35
1918	105,304	32,937	2.45	1.97

Sources of data: (1) *European Currency and Finance*, Vol. I, pp. 533-5, 540. (2) *Zahlen zur Geldentwertung in Deutschland* 1914 *bis* 1923, pp. 6, 45.

§ EFFECT OF REPARATIONS

The burdens laid upon Germany by the Treaty of Versailles went far to establish the difference between success and failure in the restoration of financial order. The health of the state finances was largely conditioned by the course of foreign exchange rates and of prices. The latter in turn were driven upward by the failure of the Reich to cover its obligations without inflation. The relation of cause and effect in the vicious circle of movements of exchange rates, prices, the status of government finance, and note issues has been much disputed not only in the German but in many similar cases. Whatever it may have been in other countries the situation in Germany was such as to make the movement of exchange rates of peculiar and preeminent importance. At regular intervals the administration had to procure, for reparations purposes, fixed sums of foreign exchange. The mark cost of this exchange was dependent on the rate prevailing at the time of purchase and was increased by the depreciation attendant upon the purchases themselves. It was, consequently, not only impossible for the government of the Reich to estimate the probable burden on the budget and so to plan in a rational manner in advance, but, in the absence of any other form of government credit, any sharp rise in the cost of foreign currency practically forced the administration to have recourse to the Reichsbank for loans. An enlarged issue of Reichsbank notes was then the inevitable result.

Reparations affected the situation in two ways. In the first place the failure of the Allied Powers to fix a total sum till May 1921, and the magnitude of that total when fixed (132,000,000,000 gold marks), destroyed whatever credit the German government might otherwise have had. But more important than the total amount of reparations was the demand for large immediate payments. Given time for adjustment, there is probably no limit to the possibility of transferring abroad any excess of production over the bare minimum of subsistence, provided such excess can be collected at home. But time is of the essence of the matter. Transfers cannot be made *instanter* since the necessary volume of goods is not available in transportable form. The requisite foreign exchange can therefore not be acquired by the immediate export of commodities. Having no credit abroad on the basis of which foreign exchange might have been obtained without a present excess of commodity exports, Germany's attempt to make large cash reparation payments was bound to depress the exchange value of the mark relative to its purchasing power at home, and it would have done so regardless of the volume of issues of paper currency. The amount of such issues, on the other hand, was, in the manner above described, inevitably increased by a fall in the exchange value of the mark.

The fact of reparations, therefore, sharply distinguishes the German inflationary experience from that of other countries. In most cases an inconvertible and fluctuating currency was avoidable however poor the country which was employing it might be. Poverty is no excuse for bad money. Government outlay is conditioned by income and monetary disorder does not improve the situation. If the outlays are within the control of the government concerned all can be made well. But if ineluctable demands for cash payments outside its own borders be made upon a state, and if these demands be in excess of current national cash assets, resort to sales of capital or to loans must first be had, and when these fail, disorder is inevitable. Without such demands the currency can always be kept convertible into gold, or substantially stable in exchange value, by a sufficiently rigorous policy of taxation. When such demands are present it cannot be done. This fact must be kept constantly in mind in a consideration of the causes of the collapse of the German monetary unit. In Germany's case alone was the depreciation of the currency in large part due to pressure from outside; for Germany alone could it be reasonably maintained that, so long as reparations demands were insatiable, stabilization was a matter beyond her own control.

The climax in the reparations conflict came with the invasion of the Ruhr, an action which had no support from some of the creditor Powers.[13] Much as the invasion is to be regretted or condemned, however foolish it may have been as a method of collecting payment, and however evil its immediate results, it was the thunderclap that cleared the air. It showed the obdurate creditors how little could be obtained by a policy of force and, on the other hand, it brought such distress to Germany as to convince even the stoutest opponent of the policy of fulfilment (and they were many and powerful) that it was better to accept a moderated burden of payments which, in spite of strong convictions to the contrary, it might be possible for the country to carry, than to continue in an attitude of stubborn intransigence.

When force had led to disaster, the repercussions of which affected the creditors as well as the debtors,[14] the way was at last open to men of conciliatory spirit, and a solution of the problem, or at any rate a working compromise, could be reached. The invasion was a tragic but triumphant vindication of the policy of moderation, and it led to sympathetic, even if selfish, efforts on the part of the creditor Powers to re-

[13] The occupation, by French and Belgian troops, took place in the early days of January 1923. The British government of the day adopted an attitude of passive disapproval and Italy, while assenting to the measures taken, refused to participate actively in the occupation.

[14] The exchange value of French currency, for instance, was brought very low when it became apparent that the French fisc could not count on any large receipts from Germany.

habilitate the economy and finances of the Reich. Once order had been restored progress was possible.

But order came only through chaos. The Germans had decided upon a policy of passive resistance to the French and Belgians. The financing of the program was a costly process and was carried out almost entirely with the proceeds of discounted treasury bills. The consequent enormous issues of paper currency gave the *coup de grace* to the mark. During January 1923 its dollar value fell to 1/7 of what it had been at the beginning of the month. The effort officially made in the next few months to influence the foreign exchange markets was but temporarily successful. Thereafter it was merely a question of how long the currency unit could retain any value at all. The pace of depreciation was constantly accelerated. Within each of the months of May and June, 1923, the price of the dollar in paper marks doubled. Such increases were by no means unprecedented but in July the mark price of dollars was multiplied 7 times, in August 10 times, in September 17 times, and in October 400 times. By this date resort to other means of payment was general and almost the sole determinant of the value of the existing monetary unit were guesses at the rate at which conversion into the rentenmark currency, which was presently to be established, would take place.

§ DOMESTIC COMPLACENCY TOWARD INFLATION

While the payments of cash reparations in 1921 undoubtedly played an important part in promoting the decline in the currency, and while the sanctions imposed on Germany in 1923 led to the ultimate collapse, this is, of course, by no means the whole story. Reparations gravely affected public finances but the fiscal difficulties were far from being solely due to this cause. It is true that, if a more soundly conceived and executed reparations policy had been adopted by the creditor Powers, inflation of the currency might perhaps have been stayed by the vigorous measures of reform of the public finances initiated in Germany in 1920. But inflation had none the less proceeded far before any cash reparations whatever had been paid and it was accelerated after they had been entirely suspended. Its roots went back into the early war period and it was, in many German quarters, nurtured rather than repressed. The war administration, for instance, with Vice-Chancellor Helfferich holding the Treasury portfolio, had looked with a much too friendly eye on inflationary policies. The initial impetus thus given was never checked and long after the war was over the Reichsbank, where Helfferich again was influential and its President, Havenstein, ineffectual, was entirely too pliable in its attitude toward both governmental and private borrowing.

The attitude of the Reichsbank was but one aspect of a fairly general complacency toward currency depreciation. The burden of the great internal government debt, piled up during and immediately after the war, meant exceedingly high taxes unless it should be lightened by a decline in the value of the counters in which it was expressed. Though currency depreciation meant confiscation of the property of holders of the government debt it was the line of least resistance for the Treasury and was thus not unwelcome in official circles. The policy of inflation had, in addition, powerful support from influential private quarters. Many of the leaders of business were convinced that inflation was necessary to the rehabilitation of the German industrial organization; that only through a falling exchange value of the mark could essential foreign markets be regained; that the business profits which it promised, and indeed produced, were a prerequisite to the restoration of a sound peacetime economy; that the demands of the war victors were outrageous and might be made to react upon those victors' own heads if German exchange should fall so far as to lead to ruinous competition in foreign trade.

Inflation was therefore combated but half-heartedly at best. Though several of the administrations of the years 1920 to 1923 made valiant attempts to arrest its progress they could not summon the sustained powers necessary to success. All of their efforts came to naught, largely through the apathy or active opposition of powerful business groups who were disposed neither to aid their government in imposing regular taxation nor to cooperate with it in carrying out its obligations under the Treaty of Versailles.[15] Whatever might have been possible to a government backed by a people determined to have no further traffic with inflation, the will to establish a stable standard was lacking until the drama had run its course. It may well be doubted whether a stable standard could in any case have been set up while immense reparations debts were plaguing the situation. But this must remain an open question. So long as wealth and income were being merely transferred by the decline in the value of the monetary unit and not, as a sum, diminished, so long as scapegoats could be found to assume the burdens and

[15] When the administration proposed a capital levy to meet the burdens imposed, the industrialists countered with the offer of a *loan* of one billion gold marks. But, as negotiations proceeded, the industrialists demanded a remission of future taxes and the turning over to them of the state railroads. The government properly refused and resorted to a *forced* loan which, however, yielded only 50 million gold marks.

yield of their substance to those who knew how to profit from the situation, projects of reform were treated cavalierly. It was only when enterprisers, instead of surely profiting from inflation as they long did, were suddenly plunged into a sea of uncertainties, only when business activity passed from the stage of exhilaration to panic, only when resistance to a further assumption of losses on the part of the public at large became general, that influential opinion veered to a conviction of the necessity of restoring a stable standard. The pass to which matters had then come is shown in Table III.

§ RESTORATION OF CURRENCY STABILITY

The successful introduction of the rentenmark in November 1923, a currency without gold backing and, indeed, nothing more than a new tenor of inconvertible paper,[16] with the monetary stabilization thus effected, has been hailed as a miracle. It was certainly a remarkable achievement and bears strong witness to the steadfastness of the German character.[17] The time was ripe but extremely unpropitious. The people had lost all confidence in their currency and in the possibility of its reform. Foreign troops were in possession of their chief industrial districts and the coercive measures adopted by the occupying powers had paralyzed the industrial life of the country. The masses of the urban population were living from hand to mouth, nay, had nothing in their hands but worthless bits of paper which the farmers would no longer accept in exchange for grain. Food riots were general. Political dissolution was in imminent prospect and armed revolt had already raised its head. Affairs were indeed so black that it is clear, in retrospect, that they actually facilitated the reform by imbuing the people with the resolution of despair. The conduct of currency matters was given to Dr. Hjalmar Schacht[18] who possessed the temperament necessary to the situation. His powers were presently enlarged by his election to the Presidency of the Reichsbank. The former President Havenstein had died on the very day that conversion of the old currency into the new was undertaken, a demise which cannot be thought of as other than opportune.

---

[16] The provisions for redemption in "rentenbank certificates" and the mortgage cover provided had, as all students of monetary phenomena will recognize, but a psychological value. The success of the rentenmark was due entirely to the rigid limitations on issue.

[17] The reform was carried out without foreign assistance of any sort. Rather was there covert opposition from certain powerful foreign groups who would have welcomed the threatened political, as well as financial, dissolution of the Reich.

[18] Dr. Schacht has written an excellent account of the reform in his *Stabilization of the Mark*, George Allen and Unwin Ltd., London, 1927.

TREASURY BILLS DISCOUNTED BY THE REICH, ISSUES OF PAPER CURRENCY, INDEX OF WHOLESALE PRICES, AND INDEX OF DOLLAR EXCHANGE RATES AGAINST PAPER MARKS; 1919-1923

(Value figures in millions of marks)

END OF MONTH	TOTAL AMOUNT OF TREASURY BILLS DISCOUNTED BY THE REICH[19]	TOTAL ISSUES OF PAPER CURRENCY (EXCEPT EMERGENCY CURRENCY)	INDEX OF WHOLESALE PRICES[20] 1913=1	INDEX OF DOLLAR EXCHANGE RATES IN BERLIN[21] 1913=1
1919 Dec.	86,400	50,065	8.03	11.14
1920 June	113,200	68,154	13.82	9.17
Dec.	152,800	81,387	14.40	17.48
1921 June	185,100	84,556	13.66	17.90
Dec.	247,100	122,497	34.87	43.83
1922 June	295,200	180,169	70.30	89.21
July	308,000	202,626	100.59	159.60
Aug.	331,600	252,212	192.00	410.91
Sept.	451,100	331,876	287.00	393.04
Oct.	603,800	484,685	566.00	1,071.94
Nov.	839,100	769,500	1,154.00	1,822.30
Dec.	1,495,200	1,295,228	1,475.00	1,750.83
1923 Jan.	2,081,800	1,999,600	3,286.00	11,672.00
Feb.	3,588,000	3,536,300	5,257.00	5,407.00
Mar.	6,601,300	5,542,900	4,827.00	4,996.00
April	8,442,300	6,581,200	5,738.00	7,099.00
May	10,275,000	8,609,700	9,034.00	16,556.00
June	22,019,800	17,340,500	24,618.00	36,803.00
July	57,848,900	43,813,500	183,510.00	262,030.00
Aug.	1,196,294,700	668,702,600	1,695,109.00	2,454,000.00
Sept.	46,716,616,400	28,244,405,800	36,223,771.00	38,113,000.00
Oct.	6,907,511,102,800	2,504,955,700,000	18,700,000,000.00	17,270,000,000.00
Nov.	191,580,465,422,100[19]	400,338,326,400,000	1,422,900,000,000.00	1,000,000,000,000.00
Dec.	1,232,679,853,100	496,585,345,990,000	1,200,400,000,000.00	1,000,000,000,000.00

[19] Practically all government borrowing after 1919 was in the form of discounted Treasury bills. The figure for November 1923 is as of the 15th of that month.

[20] In the index number of wholesale prices from December 1919 to December 1922 inclusive, the figures represent monthly averages. From January to June, 1923, statistics are available for specific days three times a month, and from July to December, 1923, weekly. The figures in the table are for the latest available date in each month.

[21] The December 1919 figure for the index number of exchange rates is a monthly average. All other figures for this index are end-of-month quotations.

Sources of data: (1) *Zahlen zur Geldentwertung in Deutschland 1914 bis 1923*; Statistisches Reichsamt, Verlag von Reimar Hobbing, Berlin, 1925, pp. 6-10, 16-18, 46-7. (2) *Germany's Economy, Currency and Finance*, Zentral-Verlag G.m.b.H., Berlin, 1924, p. 63.

Under Dr. Schacht's firm grip it was but a short time before financial order was restored. The permanent success of Schacht's measures was assured through the work of Chancellor Stresemann and Finance Minister Luther.[22] The government balanced its budget, reparations were presently put upon a practicable basis with the adoption of the Dawes Plan in 1924, and German finances were once again given a solid footing.

§ RESULTS OF THE CURRENCY COLLAPSE

Inflation had shaken the social structure to its roots. The changes of status which it caused were profound. No such shifting of property rights, in time of peace, had ever before taken place. Great numbers of families of long established wealth and position were reduced to beggary at the very time that new or additional fortunes of staggering magnitude were being accumulated. The old middle class wellnigh disappeared and a new group came into prominence. There was less change in the condition of the masses—they had not so much to lose—but the wiping out of savings, insurance, and pensions pressed heavily upon the worker even if his losses did not parallel those of some of the better-to-do social classes.

The drama, and particularly the tragedy, of the time have left an indelible impression of the evils of inflation on the minds of the generation which lived through it. The most striking effects were in the realm of the distribution of wealth rather than in production but there were periods, principally in the final stages of depreciation, when the great majority of the population was in extreme want and perhaps even more distressing uncertainty. When prices were rising hourly by leaps and bounds, when the purchasing power of present and prospective receipts of money was vanishing before it could be spent, or would even be acquired, the population of a so highly specialized exchange society as Germany, was subjected to a wellnigh intolerable strain.

But though suffering was widespread and terrible, though the blow to *morale* was devastating, though imponderable psychological assets withered, the material losses, from the national point of view at any rate, were largely ephemeral, and the obvious evils were in large part compensated by benefits which only later came to light. Much of the distress attributed to the depreciation of the currency was due to other causes, such as the decline in productive capacity on both the material and human side which was a legacy of the war, and the invasion of the Ruhr in 1923. Inflation worked with blind injustice but was not otherwise an

[22] Shortly after the inauguration of the reform Stresemann was followed by Marx as Chancellor, but Stresemann remained in the Cabinet.

essentially destructive force. The common analogy likening inflation to a drug is only half true. Currency depreciation acted as a stimulant for years; there was then a short period of prostration, a rather quick recovery, and no indisputable permanent weakening of the body economic. It has been maintained, indeed, that the reverse was true, that Germany came out strengthened rather than enfeebled. The facts would seem to be that, aside from its revolutionary effects on the distribution of wealth and income, about which little will be said in this book, inflation influenced the national welfare in diverse ways, some favorable, some the reverse. The net material result is in some degree susceptible of measurement and an attempt will therefore be made to follow the process, to assess the material gains and losses, and to cast up the accounts without benefit of advocates of one view or the other.

CHAPTER II

FACTORS IN INFLATION

§ OUTLINE

T HE relative importance of external pressure on the Germans, and of their internal lack of cohesion, as causes of the decline and dissolution of the mark is disputable. The external pressure, especially as applied in 1923, was combated with more spirit than intelligence, and the struggle with foreign Powers stirred rather than allayed the centrifugal tendencies at home. Nevertheless, it is not improbable that had the external burden not been crushing, the government would have been able to marshal such support of its efforts to establish sound public finance as to have insured success. In this chapter the several factors in inflation will be examined, not in the order of their presumed importance, but rather as they fit into a more or less logical and chronological scheme. The effects of the German war- and treaty-losses will first be appraised and this will be followed by estimates of the influence of reparations, of fiscal policy and status, of speculation, of banking operations, and of military sanctions. Under some one of these heads all of the important causes of inflation may, it is submitted, be subsumed.

I. EFFECTS OF THE WAR- AND TREATY-LOSSES

§ GERMANY'S COMPARATIVE ECONOMIC STATUS AFTER THE WAR

All of the countries engaged in the war from the beginning suffered an immense impairment of productive powers. Though, except for a small area in East Prussia, German territory was not devastated, it is none the less probable that the decline in the productive capacity of that country was greater than in the case of any other of the principal combatants. The shortage of important materials occasioned by the practical cessation of imports in the war years and the somewhat more complete organization of production for the purpose of immediate yield, and therefore without regard for repairs and replacements, led to an extreme deterioration in equipment of all types. On the human side, the losses in killed and wounded were proportionately not very unequal as between Germany and the other principal Powers engaged, but the much greater deficiency in foodstuffs in Germany had sapped the strength of the population and had induced a persistent lassitude which affected the output not only of the then adult workers but of the generation which was adolescent when peace was concluded.

The exactions under the Armistice and the Treaty of Versailles considerably increased any discrepancy in relative productive powers which may have existed between Germany and the victor nations at the end of the conflict and made the task of restoring order to currency and finance more difficult for the Reich and somewhat easier for its adversaries. That Germany's failure to prevent a financial *débâcle* was directly or indirectly due to the losses of territory, resources, and capital imposed by the victor nations has, indeed, freely been asserted. It is doubtful, however, whether such losses played any great part. The effect of cash reparations (and other recurring cash payments) on mark exchange, on the budget, and on the whole financial structure was great, but this is much less true of the capital goods delivered once and for all in 1918 and 1919, and it is scarcely true at all of the cession of land.

§ CONTRAST BETWEEN THE POLITICAL AND ECONOMIC EFFECTS OF LOSS OF TERRITORY

Politically considered Germany's losses were certainly staggering. About 1/8 of the area in Europe, as well as all the colonies, and 1/10 of the population was transferred to other flags. Much of this area was well supplied with basic minerals, was industrially advanced, or, to the extent that it was agricultural, was of better than average fertility. But from the economic, as distinguished from the political point of view, this cession of territory and transfer of population is, in itself, a matter of indifference. There is no *inherent* reason why the people either of the ceded or remaining territory should have been one whit the worse for the shifting of boundary lines. This will be clear enough when it is pointed out that, in the absence of later political interference, it would have been possible to carry on industry and trade within and across the new borders in the identical manner in which it had taken place before the severance occurred. The German nation was smaller after this territory was taken away but by no means necessarily poorer.[1]

Though, under certain conditions, the cession of territory might thus have no adverse economic effects upon the ceding country, the German economy was in fact subjected to an increase in *per capita* burdens

---

[1] The national wealth as a whole would, of course, be less. But this has almost no meaning apart from population. Per capita wealth might well be the same as before or it might be greater or less. Individual wealth would tend to remain unchanged except as affected by further political action.

through the loss of districts in the West and East. In so far as the German people as a unit, rather than as individuals, were under obligation to make payments to foreign governments or private persons (and in this matter recurring reparations were of dominating import), the per capita burden on the smaller population would be increased in equal proportion with the loss in numbers and in total wealth and income. Further than this, a large real loss was occasioned by the dislocation to industry consequent upon the general adoption of political measures running counter to economic sense. This was of special significance in Alsace-Lorraine and in Upper Silesia where the most advantageous use of coal and iron in conjunction, or as factors in the production of finished goods requiring either or both as raw materials, was disturbed by the fact that the separate natural deposits, or the mines and the finishing industries, were no longer within the same political unit.[2] Economic organization was consequently subject to distortion by tariffs, or other forms of administrative control, in the supposed interest of the levying country and certainly to the harm of Germany. But though this latter loss was real it may very easily be overestimated. It is confined to the difference between the use of equipment and resources in the most, and in a less, advantageous manner and is similar in scope to the burden which any protective tariff may at any time impose both upon the levying and on other countries.[3]

§ SLIGHT INFLUENCE OF TERRITORIAL LOSSES ON TRADE,
EXCHANGE, AND CURRENCY

The shrinkage in total German area, wealth, and numbers did materially reduce the base of taxation at the very time that heavy external burdens were being laid upon the German fisc and this was a factor retarding the rehabilitation of the national finance. But the notion that Germany's foreign trade balance, and with it foreign exchange rates and the domestic value of the currency, was acutely affected by the separation of territory is erroneous. Because, in the pre-war era, Germany had failed to provide sufficient food for her own population, the surrender of the agricultural districts, Posen and West Prussia, which

[2] Much of the iron ore for the Ruhr industry had, however, always come from France.

[3] Germany was compelled to admit free of duty, for five years, raw materials and manufactured goods from Alsace-Lorraine and, for three years, all imports from those parts of Poland which had formerly been German. Unilateral most-favored-nation treatment had to be accorded, for five years, to all imports from the Allied and Associated States. It is doubtful whether these impositions were harmful to Germany however discriminatory they may have been. The real harm came from the duties levied against German goods imported.

had always furnished a surplus of foodstuffs above their own consumption, has quite generally been supposed to have been of peculiar significance. The abstraction of this territory from the Reich compelled an even greater resort to foreign supplies than had hitherto been necessary and so, it has been alleged, increased the unfavorable balance of trade. In addition to this, the loss of the industrial export of Alsace-Lorraine and Upper Silesia is generally regarded as having still further widened the spread between exports and imports. Such reasoning fails to take account of the true nature of trade and forgets that production is offset by consumption. If, in the pre-Armistice period, Posen and West Prussia contributed agricultural products to the remainder of Germany they took industrial products in exchange.[4] Solely as a result of the division of territory the post-Armistice Germany might therefore show a greater total foreign trade than did the larger pre-war unit, since, without any change in the volume and character of trading, the smaller political unit would tend to have greater imports of foodstuffs and greater exports of manufactured goods than did its larger predecessor. The export of foodstuffs by Posen and West Prussia to the present German territories would, after the separation, count as German imports, though they did not do so before the Peace of Versailles, and conversely, the export of manufactured goods from the present German territories to Posen and West Prussia would count as German exports. On the other hand, neither exports nor imports of Posen and West Prussia to and from the non-German world would appear in German post-war foreign trade figures. If, instead of assuming that the volume and direction of trade remained unaltered, it be supposed that Posen and West Prussia no longer trade with post-war Germany, or trade in less degree than formerly, the increased German import of foodstuffs from other sources would presumably be paid for by the export to other lands of the very commodities, or their equivalents, which had formerly gone to Posen and West Prussia. In whatever degree trade between these former German provinces and the Reich was affected by the separation there would thus be no tendency to alter the *balance* of international transactions.

With industrial Alsace-Lorraine and Upper Silesia the case is similar.

---

[4] This is the general situation. Part of the export of agricultural products from Posen and West Prussia to the other pre-war German territory may, of course, have been as payment of interest on investments or other "invisible" items. The same is true of other territories later discussed. Unless the private property concerned was confiscated, a matter to which attention will presently be given, the argument here advanced is not affected. The territory in which investment was made will still pay interest to that from which the capital was drawn, just as it always did.

In so far as these districts exported their products to foreign countries in the pre-war period, such exports then counting as part of the German export trade, they must have drawn on foreign countries, or on the remainder of Germany, for imports in exchange.[5] If they drew on foreign countries, both exports and imports of the present German territory would be diminished in equal degree provided no change in the total volume or in the direction of transactions occurred. Similar conclusions hold if it be supposed that they drew for imports on the rest of Germany since, with the identical trade, exports from the present German territory would now, on the one hand, be increased by so much of the volume of German shipments to Alsace-Lorraine and Upper Silesia as was necessary to balance the excess of exports of those territories to the outside world and, on the other, would be reduced by an equivalent amount owing to the fact that Alsace-Lorraine and Upper Silesia are no longer part of Germany and their exports no longer German exports. In neither case would the German balance of trade be disturbed. Nor would it be disturbed if Alsace-Lorraine and Upper Silesia should no longer trade with Germany on the old scale. This will be clear from the examples given for Posen and West Prussia.

So far as *total* German foreign trade is concerned the separation of parts of the old territory from the main body might thus operate either to increase or diminish it. This would depend upon the relation between the foreign trade of the separate units of the original territory and their trade with one another.[6] Before the severance, the foreign trade (both imports and exports) of any one of the separated units appeared in the foreign trade statistics of the Reich, while its trade with other units of the original political federation did not. After the severance, that part of the trade of any of the separated areas which formerly counted as German foreign trade no longer appeared in the import and export statistics of the reduced Germany, but, on the other hand, its trade with such units of the old federation as remained within the Reich, trade

[5] If Alsace-Lorraine and Upper Silesia formerly drew on the remainder of Germany for imports they would offer in payment the foreign exchange proceeds of their exports abroad. This would have been used to finance imports from foreign countries into the present German territory.

[6] It may be worth while to indicate the limits of variation. They are:

1. If *all* the external trade of the severed unit is, and always was, done with the original political entity, the foreign trade of this truncated entity will be *increased* by the amount of trade between the two units.

2. If *none* of the external trade of the severed unit is, or ever was, done with the remaining part of the original political entity, the foreign trade of the latter will be *less* than that of the full original territory by the amount of the foreign trade of the severed part.

which formerly counted as domestic, was now classified as German foreign commerce. Since the trade between the separated territories and the rest of Germany was probably considerably greater than the trade of those territories with the outside world, there would be a tendency, so far as the old commercial connections were maintained, for the total imports and exports of the smaller post-war Germany to be greater than for the larger pre-war area. But whether or not old commercial connections were kept up, and whether or not total German foreign trade was larger or smaller as a result of the changes, there would be no effect on the *balance* of imports and exports nor any tendency, from this source, toward an adverse movement of exchange rates.

Similar reasoning is applicable to the German colonies in Africa and the Pacific. Fiscally considered the cession of these colonies was a gain rather than a loss since more was spent on them than was ever received and any economies from trade with their former possessions are, in most cases, as open to the Germans now as they ever were. So far as foreign exchange is concerned, the commerce of the colonies with the home country had always been foreign trade, and its status is therefore unchanged.

§ LOSS OF NATURAL RESOURCES OTHER THAN LAND

If now we turn to resources other than the land itself, and especially to the raw materials of industry, there is no reason to believe that the transfer to other jurisdictions of the *locus* of certain raw materials, whether in or outside of Europe, would in itself have any adverse effect on the prosperity of the transferred or the remaining territory or on rates of exchange. It is improbable that these or competing raw materials will now cost the German economy any more than if they had remained under German control, and they will be paid for, as they always have been, by an exchange of products between the territory producing more raw materials and less manufactured goods, and the territory producing more manufactured goods and less raw materials, than they respectively consume. The total wealth of Germany will be less by reason of the "loss" solely because its area and population will be smaller than they would otherwise have been. *Per capita* wealth,[7] productivity, general prosperity, total foreign trade, and foreign exchange rates suffer no necessary or probable impairment.

---

[7] This is a matter of the relative *per capita* productivity in the separated and remaining territory. The probabilities are that they were approximately equal though this cannot be proven. Competition within a given political unit, however, is normally free enough to bring value productivity of workers, and their returns, into something like equality.

§ LOSSES OF PROPERTY VS. LOSS OF SUZERAINTY

Changes of suzerainty affected only the *per capita* weight of future reparations charges and, aside from this, were of no economic significance, but, on the other hand, an extremely heavy economic loss was sustained in the transfer of ownership, as distinct from the political control, of property from German to Allied hands. It is not to be supposed that this economic weakening was primarily responsible for the ruin of the German financial structure. But it had some immediate, if not persistent, effect on the foreign exchanges (and so indirectly on public finance) and the Treasury's revenues were directly affected in a not inconsiderable degree by the consequent loss of income to the German citizenry. This is true whether the property had formerly belonged to the German state or to German private persons, individual or corporate. Contrary to well established international law, private property belonging to Germans, as contrasted with "Alsatians" for instance, was in some of the transferred areas confiscated, and an obligation was laid upon the German government to reimburse its nationals for these losses. All of this property, together with State property in the ceded territory, the Saar mines, practically the whole German mercantile marine, cables, railroad rolling stock, and a large amount of other goods was subtracted from the wealth of the present German population.[8] For this property no German received any *quid pro quo* whatever except at the expense of other German citizens. The income of the German population is therefore permanently diminished by the amount of the annual yield from this confiscated property. Since a large part of this annual yield was formerly imported into the present German territory the trade balance was disturbed to the extent of its loss and a corresponding pressure was exerted upon the exchange value of the German currency.[9]

The value of the capital goods surrendered by the Germans on the conclusion of the war has been variously estimated at from six to upwards of forty billion gold marks, the lower figure being that of the Reparations Commission and the upper that of the German Government.

[8] Except where German nationals formerly living and owning property in the ceded territories have remained there and have not been, and will not be, reimbursed from the German Treasury.

[9] The adverse effect of reparations and clearing costs on mark exchange was thus increased. Clearing costs were due to the balance between foreign pre-war private claims on Germany and German pre-war private claims on foreign countries. The impotent position of Germany led to immediate assessment of the claims against that country but to delays and diminutions in the counterclaims, which were subordinated to reparations. All current items are now, however, included in the general settlement reached under the Dawes and Young Plans.

The immense gap between the two estimates is due in part to different methods of valuation, in part to the omission of some categories in the Reparations Commission's appraisal, and in part to the fact that the property sequestrated was not as valuable to the new owners as it had been to the Germans. The loss to the Germans may fairly be computed at from 20 to 25 billion gold marks, of which the principal items were:[10]

	Billions of gold marks
Private property in the separated territories	10.0
State property in the separated territories	5.0
Merchant marine	3.5
Railroad material	1.4

This sum, it should be noted, was the value of capital goods only. It does not take into consideration the large current payments made on reparations account, or on account of costs of the armies of occupation or other headings, nor even the loss of capital involved in the forced annulment of Germany's claims upon her former Allies. The latter item amounted to 8.6 billion gold marks nominally but was of dubious real value. The great influence on the inflation process of *recurring* reparation payments will appear in the sequel but it does not concern us here. Of the capital items listed above some did not yield a cash return nor others a return which would pass over the present boundaries of Germany. While representing a diminution of German income, the failure of the yield on this property would not therefore affect the balance of international payments nor the exchange value of the German monetary unit, though it would make the payment, as distinct from the transfer, of reparations harder to bear. The loss of income from the remainder, moreover, was large, and had to be compensated by reduced imports or increased exports or both.

§ EXCHANGE RATES ONLY TEMPORARILY AFFECTED BY PROPERTY LOSSES

But though the cession of this latter type of property tended to bring about or accentuate the excess of international debits (imports) which appeared soon after the close of the war, it cannot be contended that this could have depressed the exchange value of the mark for more than a temporary period. The influence of a so-called unfavorable balance of payments upon the exchange and internal value of the currency concerned has been greatly exaggerated. Counting credit in various forms, and voluntary or involuntary gifts, no country can at any time have a

[10] cf. *Germany's Capacity to Pay*, H. G. Moulton and Constantine E. McGuire, Institute of Economics, McGraw-Hill Pub. Co., Inc., New York, 1923, p. 75.

favorable or unfavorable balance of international *payments* (there must be equilibrium) and an unfavorable balance of *trade* is rather more likely to be an effect than a cause of marked currency deprecia-tion.[11] It must be admitted, of course, that a present increase in the ratio of imports, or other international debits, to exports, or other inter-national credits, can occur and that it will lower the exchange value of the monetary unit of the country in question at least temporarily.[12] Given ordered domestic finances such a decline, however, normally con-tains its own corrective. That it might not have done so in Germany's case will later appear, but, if this was so, it was due to the uncon-ditional *recurring* obligations imposed upon the Germans rather than to the losses occasioned by the sequestration of income yielding property already in being when the Treaty of Versailles was signed.

In spite of the loss of German foreign income, merchandise imports into Germany did in fact greatly exceed exports from 1920 to the end of 1922, and this in the face of general conditions which clearly called for the opposite phenomenon. Such an excess of imports was possible only because: (1) foreign short-term credit was easily to be obtained in the immediate post-war period and, (2) currency was sold to foreigners as an investment. On the credit possibilities in the early post-war period it has been pointed out that:

"European markets seemed at first to display an illimitable power of purchasing goods at higher and higher prices.[13] . . . To practical men a German mark meant 23.82 cents. If for the time being the market quoted it at 6 or 4 or 3 cents, they attributed the fall to an adverse balance of trade. Once Germany's urgent needs for imports were satis-fied, surely, they argued, the mark would recover, perhaps not to its old parity (for loss of credit through defeat in war might prevent that), but at least to the 12 or 15 cents quoted after defeat had occurred and before the imports had begun. Rather than sell their marks at a ruinous

[11] An unfavorable balance of *trade* tends to occur, *e.g.*, whenever currency is sold abroad for investment purposes and the proceeds become available for the purchase of imports.

[12] In this case an involuntary credit is extended by foreign sellers. An un-favorable balance of payments may then, in one sense, perhaps, be said to be present.

[13] Author's note. The hunger after imports was very great. Evidence is conflict-ing as to whether the German people as a whole fully realized the inevitability of low standards of living. Great numbers of people shrank before the rise in prices but there were many who could and did spend their inflated incomes freely. So long as foreign private credit would support importers' purchases there was no check upon these expenditures. The cherishing of illusions was, however, by no means the peculiar property of the Germans at this time.

sacrifice, many of them held on. . . . Those traders and speculators who acquired holdings of the currencies and kept them in hope of a rise, instead of selling them in the market, delayed the process of adjustment. They were in effect *lending* to the country whose currency they held, and so helping to bridge the gap between exports and imports.

"The continuous fall in European currencies eventually frightened not only the American exporters but the banks which were financing them. . . .

"In January, 1920, the New York rediscount rate was raised to 6 per cent, and the patience of the American banks gave way. Advances to exporters on the security of European currencies were called in. The depreciation of these currencies, rapid as it had been, was accelerated to the point of panic. . . .

"This exchange panic marks a stage in the great post-war currency crisis. It was followed by a general recovery. . . .

"By cutting their losses the American exporters and the speculators had turned the greater part of their loans to distressed Europe into free gifts. They had also in the process relieved the exchange market of an incubus in the shape of a vast disappointed bull account. . . .

"The excess of imports, which had been swamping their [the central European countries] exchange markets, and was a transitory phenomenon, was not the true cause of the depreciation. So long as it continued it was merely a sign that the existing depreciation, as recorded in the market, was *insufficient*, and that equilibrium was not secured."[14]

§ CONTINUOUS UNFAVORABLE BALANCE OF CURRENT
INTERNATIONAL ITEMS IMPOSSIBLE

Excessive imports may possibly have initiated the early post-war decline in the exchange value of the mark but they could not have remained large, relative to exports, if the possibility of selling currency abroad had not still been open to the Germans.[15] This view is corroborated by the experience of 1923. By that date further sales of marks to foreigners for investment were impossible and, though the Germans were in dire need of imports, no excess over exports appeared. The reason for the elimination of the excess of imports in 1923 is obvious.

[14] See *Currency and Credit*, R. G. Hawtrey, Longmans, Green & Co., London, 1923, pp. 375 ff.

[15] The investment demand for German currency after 1920 did not come from unduly long extensions of commercial credits but rather from buyers intending to hold marks for an indefinite period.

Imports could by no hook or crook be purchased except from the proceeds of merchandise exports. This fact throws light on the whole question of the possibility of the destruction of the value of a currency through excessive international debits when such debits are not imposed from without as in the case of reparations.[16] Merchandise imports may at any time be ordered in excess of the current receipts of foreign exchange from exports or other credits and, when payment is required, the exchange value of the currency of the importing country may fall. If this fall does not of itself restore equilibrium by raising the price of imports and lowering the foreign exchange cost of exports (and it will later appear that it will sometimes fail to do so), and no method other than the export of merchandise is available as a means of providing payment for imports, the excess of imports will nevertheless be eliminated. Sellers will not indefinitely dispose of their goods without payment therefor. No positive minimum of imports is inevitable and the coat must be cut according to the cloth. If a country is poor it must adjust its imports to what it can in some way pay for and so must cut its own consumption of exportable goods to the point where the share of production exported is sufficient to cover any inadequacy in its international credits. Reference to Chart I will show that in 1923, when the Germans could no longer obtain foreign credits by the sale of marks, the export of manufactures made from imported raw materials increased substantially though the import of the raw materials used in the production of these goods declined. Accumulated stocks of raw materials may have been drawn on to some extent but it is more probable that domestic consumption of the exportable products was curtailed. In the construction of the chart the import and export in 1922 is taken as the standard (100) in each case.

Since imports for domestic consumption, imports, that is, over and above the amount for which payment is made by re-export in the same or different form, come into a country only because it is cheaper and more satisfactory to procure them by the exchange of domestic products than to produce them, or substitutes therefor, at home, they will tend to decline steadily whenever the price relationship with exports is seriously disturbed to the disadvantage of export prices. The matter is complicated by varying elasticities of demand and supply, on which something will later be said, but there can be no doubt that, so far as the power to adjust their international debits and credits lies in the hands of the nationals of any given country, the play of prices will prac-

[16] Reparations payments were suspended in 1923.

CHART I

IMPORT OF CERTAIN RAW MATERIALS OF GERMAN INDUSTRY AND EXPORT
OF PRODUCTS MANUFACTURED THEREFROM; 1922 AND 1923

(1922 = 100)

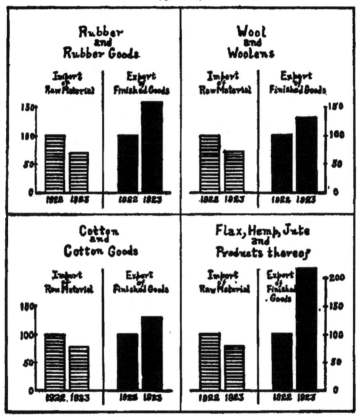

tically always prevent the occurrence of persistent pressure on exchange rates no matter what sudden alteration in wealth and income, even from extra-national sources, may have taken place.[17] And if, in very exceptional cases, this does not happen, the refusal of sellers to deliver goods for which there is no prospect of payment will effect the same result.

[17] cf. *Die geldtheoretische Seite des Stabilisierungsproblems*, Ludwig Mises, Schriften des Vereins für Sozialpolitik, Vol. 164, Part II, Verlag von Duncker und Humblot, München and Leipzig, 1923, p. 23.

§ SALES OF MARKS NOT UNFAVORABLE TO MARK EXCHANGE

An unfavorable balance of trade cannot therefore be an important causal factor in the *persistent* decline of the exchange value of a currency. Nor will the sale abroad of the money of any given country in itself provoke collapse. It is true that if imports are first obtained by means of the sale of currency which is later sold back to the issuing country for what it will bring on the exchange market, and this process is repeated again and again, a vicious circle may be set up leading to continuous exchange depreciation. But such a situation would develop only if the domestic purchasing power of the currency is steadily declining from causes other than the effect of exchange rate movements on prices. Sales of a currency are also purchases of that currency and, in themselves, do not depress its exchange value. Along with the domestic, they create an equivalent supply of foreign exchange. The significant thing for exchange rates is not the sale, *qua* sale, but the *terms* upon which the seller and buyer of a given money are ready to part with the currencies they respectively possess. Those terms will depend upon the present relative purchasing power of the currencies in question and on the judgment of the parties as to the future of each. The use of a currency for investment purposes tends rather to elevate than depress its exchange value inasmuch as the exchange transaction gives a supply of immediately available foreign exchange against a supply of the domestic exchange which will not come into the market immediately and the advent of which may be indefinitely postponed. It cannot be said that sales of currency are a material factor in preventing as great a fall in its exchange value as would otherwise occur, since, as a result of the sales, imports may be larger relative to exports than would be the case if no sales of currency took place. But the sale of marks for investment or speculative purposes, merely by virtue of being sales, did not depress the exchange value of the German monetary unit. They simply permitted a larger ratio of imports to exports, measured by value, than could have resulted from a similar status of the exchanges if no such sales had occurred.

§ EXCHANGE RATES DEPENDENT SOLELY UPON THE INTERNATIONAL
TRANSFER OF MONETARY CLAIMS

Neither the excess of imports temporarily occasioned by the loss of German income from foreign sources nor that made possible by the sale of marks abroad can therefore be held to have led to the persistent decline in the *exchange value* of the German monetary unit, nor, *a fortiori*, to its general depreciation. The cession of territory and resources had equally little bearing on the collapse of the currency. *Exchange rates are affected only by the movement of monetary claims across the border*. The motivating force must be monetary claims rather than the tangible property itself and the claims must carry across the border. The actual transfer of property of any kind across national boundaries does not influence exchange rates except as it establishes or extinguishes *monetary* claims. Practically all of the German capital appropriated by the victor powers was already outside the post-war boundaries of Germany, or was composed of movable goods which were taken *in corpore*, and so did not affect exchange. The only way in which mark exchange could be touched by either of these operations was through the loss of such claims to income on former German capital as accrued outside of, and would have been brought into, the present German territory if the capital from which it issued had remained under German ownership.[18] By reason of the expropriation of this property by the Allies there was a somewhat smaller volume of annually recurring international credits to German account to meet the more or less flexible international debits. But, in view of what has been said above with regard to the adjustment of international debits and credits to shifting exchange rates, it is clear that, whatever may be thought of the justice or economic sense of the sequestration, it would be an error to attribute even to this phase of the total capital transfer any substantial share in the fall of the exchange value of the mark. If the Germans had possessed control over their international debits, if their debits had been dependent upon the volition of commercial creditors, the fact that their accruing credits had been reduced would of necessity have been compensated by a reduction of counterclaims, for the simple reason that they would not have been willing, or if willing, would not have been able to contract debits beyond this amount. This is true regardless of what might have happened to their currency. The currency might have been ruined but it could not have been ruined by a loss of income from abroad or by an excess of imports. In fact, however, a dominant part of their actual debits, reparations claims, was *not* volitional. It was thrust upon them not by those who were giving them goods—no commercial creditor would have been so foolish—but by those who were giving them nothing at all. So far therefore as an excess of international debits was responsible for the destruction of the German currency it was the obliga-

[18] The loss of income which accrued on property in the separated territory and would have been left or consumed in that territory by its former German owners, had they still retained control, would have no bearing on exchange.

tion to make payments out of assets *in posse* rather than *in esse* which exerted any influence. It was not the payment, in reparations, of what they had, but the attempt to pay what they had not, which could and did have a decisive bearing on the German monetary system.

II. THE INFLUENCE OF REPARATIONS

§ REPARATIONS TO MAY 1921

The history of reparations[19] till the adoption of the Dawes Plan in 1924 is an almost incredible tale of stupid persecution.[20] The confusion of counsels and the vacillation in action which prevailed among the creditor Powers until the adoption of the Dawes Plan, the bickering and endless negotiation, the frustration of all attempts at compromise, were fatal to an orderly process of payments on the part of Germany even if payments in the amount demanded had, at the time, been practicable. The Allies began by demanding the impossible and they capriciously imposed sanctions when the impossible was not performed. Pending final determination of claims, the Versailles Treaty, effective January 10, 1920, required the Germans to deliver bonds as an instalment on their total debt to the value of 100 billion gold marks. Of this amount 20 billion were to mature on May 1, 1921. Prior to that date the

[19] For an excellent and remarkably dispassionate treatment of reparations *cf. History of Reparations*, Carl Bergmann, Ernest Benn, Ltd., London, 1927. This book is the chief source of the very abbreviated account of reparations here given.

[20] Though practically all of the various *administrations* in Germany up to the invasion of the Ruhr made sincere efforts to satisfy the claims of the victors, a measure of persecution may have been necessary to break down the overt or covert resistance of financially powerful Germans in private life. The defiance offered the Allies by men like Hugo Stinnes greatly increased the suspicion and hostility toward the Germans, as a people, and was a fateful error. But though persecution may have been necessary to the securing of such reparations as the Germans could pay, if they would, the stupid malice of certain Allied politicians was heartrending. Much of it was due to the still ardent passions of war, either in the breasts of the politicians themselves or in those of their constituents, but a great deal must be attributed to sheer ineptitude. For a time it seemed as if reparation demands were being used merely as a weapon to bring about the disintegration of the Reich. But, if this purpose was ever held, the double-edged character of the sword soon became apparent. For years thereafter the policy was simply one of vacillation. The Bourbons were of the same mind as ever but they had somewhat lost in influence. Liberals grew stronger as time went on but for long the issue hung in the balance. Either party might attain a superiority and temporarily dominate the situation but the final adoption of a policy of moderation was not attained till the "spirited" group had had their fling in the Ruhr.

Reparations Commission was to fix the total of Germany's obligations and, on the total so fixed, interest was to run at 5%. The Commission did not hand down its decision till April 27, 1921, when the debt was set at 132 billion gold marks.[21] Meanwhile Germany had been making large payments in kind, the value of which was estimated by the Commission at 2.6 billion gold marks and by the Germans at several times that amount, but these were declared to have been inadequate to meet the costs of the armies of occupation. Though, in addition to the enormous levy on existing wealth under the Armistice and Treaty, the Germans had now for nearly two years been making large deliveries out of current production, they were held not only to have failed to pay any reparations at all, but to be steadily incurring still greater capital obligations through the accumulation of unpaid interest charges.

§ INAUGURATION OF CASH REPARATIONS PAYMENTS

All this time cash reparations had been in abeyance. Several conferences had been held, to some of which German representatives had been summoned and to others not, but, aside from the determination of the distribution of the payments when received, and demands for a series of annuities graduated steeply to 6 billion gold marks yearly, nothing decisive was done until the London Conference of March 1921. The Germans proposed at this meeting that they should assume a capital liability of 50 billion gold marks. Their offer was scornfully rejected, the Allies proceeded to occupy Düsseldorf, Duisburg and Ruhrort, to set up a customs barrier between the occupied and unoccupied parts of Germany, to sequestrate customs receipts on the Western frontier, and to enact Reparation Recovery Acts under which a large part of the value of their imports from Germany were retained for reparations purposes. The Reparations Commission followed this up with new demands which the Germans felt it impossible to meet. They again offered, however, to undertake an obligation of a capital sum of 50 billion gold marks and to pay annuities upon it up to a total of 200 billion. Though this is a much larger sum than will ever be paid under the arrangement now in operation,[22] and was probably more than the Allies even then ever expected to receive, it was contumaciously spurned, on the ground, ap-

---

[21] This sum is almost half the estimated total wealth of Germany in 1913. The maximum payments under the Dawes Plan were about one-third of the interest on this sum and even these have now been recognized by the creditors to have been excessive.

[22] The total payments under the Young Plan amount to 121 billion gold marks and something over 10 billion had been paid up to the time it came into operation.

parently, that Germans bearing gifts were to be suspected beyond measure. On May 5, 1921, a schedule of payments, drawn up at London by the Supreme Council of the Allies, required the delivery of bonds to the value of the gold mark total of the debt as set by the Reparations Commission,[23] ordered annual payments of two billion gold marks plus 26% of German exports, and demanded the immediate delivery of one billion gold marks in cash.

Just at this point the German government had brought its tax revenues into some semblance of equivalence with outlays,[24] foreign exchange rates had shown no rising trend for more than a year, domestic prices had been steady, and the circulation of Reichsbank notes, while increasing, had not risen consistently or at a very rapid rate. Under threat of further sanctions the Germans paid in May (1921) 150 million gold marks in cash (foreign exchange). Drafts on the Treasury maturing within three months and guaranteed by the German banks were tendered, and accepted, for the remaining 850 millions immediately payable. The purchase of foreign bills with which to cover these drafts drove the exchange value of the mark steadily downward. At the end of August 400 million gold marks were still unpaid but a six-weeks covering credit was arranged in Holland and England. The repayment of this loan extended the pressure on mark exchange into October. The index of the monthly average of dollar exchange rates (number of paper marks to the dollar equivalent of one gold mark) rose from 14.8 in May to 62.6 in November, the index of wholesale prices (1913 = 1) from 13.1 to 34.1, and the ratio of the monthly increase in the floating debt to all other state revenue from 50% to 155%.

§ TEMPORARY RELIEF TOWARD END OF 1921

By the end of October the payments on this first billion gold marks of cash reparations had been completed and the next payment of 500 million did not fall due till January 1922. On the eighth of November mark exchange steadied and within a little more than a month had increased in value by 88%. Internal prices, however, did not fall correspondingly, or at all. The upward movement in foreign exchange rates from May to November had far outstripped the rise in prices and, in the succeeding months, prices, instead of responding to the fall in foreign exchange, made up most of the lost ground. The public finances, on the other hand, rapidly improved again and by the beginning of the

[23] In exchange for the 100 billion originally delivered.
[24] Revenues, apart from borrowing, then covered about 60% of expenditures including payments under the Treaty of Versailles. By the end of the year they covered only about 28%.

new calendar year the monthly increase in the floating debt had once more been reduced to approximately 50% of all other revenues.

§ LOAN NEGOTIATIONS AND THEIR FAILURE

Before the year 1921 was out the German government had notified the Reparations Commission that it would be unable to meet its obligations maturing in January and February 1922 and it requested a postponement. This led to a protracted series of negotiations, interrupted, in the middle of the Cannes Conference (January 1922), by the fall of the Briand government and the elevation of Poincaré to the French premiership. With this political change the liberal element in the Reparations Commission was submerged and the Allied attitude toward Germany became markedly stiffer. As a temporary arrangement Germany was required to pay in cash 31 million gold marks every ten days. Later in the year, a provisional schedule calling for cash payments at the rate of 60 million marks monthly, and payments in kind at the rate of approximately 120 million marks every month, was set up. Under this steady pressure mark exchange immediately began to give ground, though, at first, the decline was slow. Negotiations for a tolerable solution of the reparations difficulties were in constant progress among the more moderate groups on both sides and the hope of an international loan for the rehabilitation of the German finances kept confidence alive. The hope burned brightly when a Loan Committee appointed by the Reparations Commission met on May 24, 1922. Including in its membership J. P. Morgan, Sir Robert Kindersley, and other prominent international bankers, this committee set about canvassing the possibilities of an international loan to Germany in a sympathetic and constructive way. Much was expected of it. Mark exchange steadied yet once more, the rise in the domestic price level was temporarily checked, and under the tax program enacted a few months earlier revenues began to cover all government expenses other than reparations. If a loan could be floated to take care of reparations temporarily, or if a postponement of payments could be obtained, all might still be well.

The hope was frustrated by the adamantine attitude of Premier Poincaré who refused to abate one jot or tittle of the French claims and vehemently attacked the financiers for favoring a reduction. The Loan Committee was forced to report on June 10 that, without an alleviation of the burden and a permanent settlement of the whole question of reparations, it could not recommend the contemplated loan, to say nothing of disposing of it to foreign buyers. Like so many earlier attempts at a solution the loan negotiations thus fell dismally to the ground. With them perished the last hope of foreign aid in German financial reconstruction. The Reich was abandoned to its fate.

§ DEATH OF RATHENAU, OCCUPATION OF THE RUHR, AND
COMPLETE CURRENCY COLLAPSE

The news of the failure to secure a loan was scarcely cold before Dr. Rathenau, the German Minister of Foreign Affairs, was assassinated. The loss was quite irreparable. Rathenau had been the life of the administration. Devoted to a policy of reconciliation with the victor Powers, possessing the confidence of many of the Allied leaders, influential at home, and able in negotiation, he had been indispensable in establishing such a relationship between Germany and her opponents as might give some prospect of restoration of the national fortunes. His death turned pessimism into panic. Palsy fell on the Wirth government and from this time forward the tide of inflation flowed irresistibly on. From June to December, 1922, the exchange value of the mark fell from 1/3 to 1/100 of an American cent, domestic prices were multiplied more than twenty times, the recovery of government finance was turned into a rout, and paper marks poured from the presses in an undammed stream.

Cash reparations *actually paid* no longer played a dominating rôle in inflation though the then hopeless prospect of a relaxation of the Allied *demands*, and the general expectation of the imposition of further sanctions, were potent influences. On July 12, 1922, Germany applied for a complete lifting of all further obligations for that year and stated that the desperate position of the fisc would make it impossible to meet the Allied demands for a further period of two years or more. After weeks of bickering among the creditors, during which Germany was held to the schedule earlier laid down, matters reached an *impasse* at the end of August. The deadlock was finally broken when the Belgians, who were to receive the balance of the 1922 payments, agreed to accept six months' Treasury bills (payable in gold and guaranteed by the Reichsbank[25]) in lieu of immediate cash. The respite thus gained by the Germans was of no avail. The toboggan of currency depreciation was then travelling much too rapidly to be checked by any such puny means and, before the notes fell due, the occupation of the Ruhr[26] pushed it over the precipice. Except to take up the bills given to Belgium in the preceding summer, no cash reparations were paid in 1923 and though, on the invasion of the Ruhr, reparations in kind were suspended *toward*

[25] The Reichsbank held gold reserves much more than adequate to cover this obligation.
[26] The justification alleged for this action was that the Germans had voluntarily defaulted in making the full *timber* deliveries required of them.

the occupying Powers only, that action was generalized in August. After the collapse of the attempt to support mark exchange in the first four months of the invasion, and of a second similar, but much feebler, essay in July, the era of astronomic monetary magnitudes began. Prices, exchange rates, and the volume of circulating medium vied with one another in daily and hourly upward leaps. The Reichsbank was finally reduced to making apologies for its inability to provide for a weekly output of more than several billion (or trillion) of marks of the required denomination and to an expression of its hope that this situation would be quickly remedied by an improvement in the speed of the printing presses! The printing presses did their bit. By the end of inflation the daily output of currency was over 400,000,000,000,000,-000 marks. But, strange as it may seem, this did not effect the expected cure!

III. THE FISC

§ PUBLIC FINANCE IN THE IMMEDIATE POST-WAR PERIOD

Though the war, and the peace, dealt heavy blows to the German economy and though poverty was for some years inevitable, the losses in domestic income like those in territory, natural resources, and property, furnish no adequate explanation of the collapse of the internal value of the currency.[27] Not even state bankruptcy is, in itself, a sufficient cause. "The existence of 'budgetary equilibrium' is not necessary [to stability of the currency]. . . . An absolutely bankrupt State can have a perfectly good currency without a trace of inflation."[28] But this possibility can be realized only by the outright repudiation of state obligations. The consequences of such repudiation must always be weighed against the dangers involved in meeting the situation by the issue of fiat money. In the case of Germany, repudiation of recurring reparations obligations would have meant an early application of military sanctions by the victor Powers and complete loss of German sovereignty. Few would deny that to keep things going even temporarily, by inflation of the currency, was the lesser of the evil courses open to the German government and people.

State bankruptcy lay on the knees of the gods. To repair the ravages of war and to restore order in public finance it was urgently necessary that all remaining economic resources should be carefully husbanded and that the fisc should be replenished with revenues derived entirely

[27] The reparations demands might, however, have caused a fall in the *exchange value* of the mark regardless of its value in the domestic markets.

[28] See *An Economist's Protest*, Edwin Cannan, P. S. King & Son, Ltd., London, 1927, p. 393.

from taxation. But, along with peace, revolution was ushered into Germany and the energies of the people were wasted in internal conflict. The struggle for control of the new republic not only prevented remedial measures in public finance but enormously increased the existing difficulties. The continuation of the war blockade till after the signing of the Peace of Versailles, June 28, 1919, further augmented the troubles of the government, for though circuses were denied, the people had to be supplied with bread.[29]

In the course of the year 1919 the outstanding volume of discounted Treasury bills rose from 55 to 86 billion marks,[30] the index of the cost of dollar exchange from 1.97 to 11.94 (1913 = 1), and the index of wholesale prices from 2.45 to 8.03 (1913 = 1). The increase in the currency from 33 to 50 billion marks was comparatively slight, showing that, in spite of the disturbances, the public or commercial· banks were buying the discounted Treasury bills from the Reichsbank. This buying was especially marked after the internal political situation had somewhat cleared but the sale of government securities was perforce confined to short-term issues since the future was too obscure to permit the flotation of bonds.

§ TAX REFORMS OF 1919 AND 1920

The administration was far from dilatory and the reform of the finances was attacked with vigor at the earliest practicable moment. The old central government had always been without direct taxing powers[31] and the new did not for some time acquire any greater authority. The constitution, adopted at Weimar August 11, 1919, gave to the Reich the right of legislation over the revenues to be devoted, in whole or in part, to its own purposes but it was not until December 13, 1919, that a federal tax administration could be provided for.[32] Meanwhile, cus-

[29] In order to prevent Communistic disorder relief had to be given to the unemployed and subsidies provided for the import of such foodstuffs as could, at whatever price, be obtained. A large part of the gold reserve of the Reichsbank was devoted to the procuring of food imports.

[30] This increase was equivalent to about $2,000,000,000 according to the average of wholesale prices for the year.

[31] Except in a limited measure the taxing power had been reserved to the constituent States.

[32] Before the war the federal government had had but the rudiments of a fiscal administration. All taxes were handled by the fiscal organization in the several States. Direct taxes were, in principle, confined to the States while indirect taxes were left to the central government. In the later years of the war, however, an excess profits tax had been levied by the federal government in addition to new and increased indirect taxes. Such a tax might come under the German concept of indirect taxes.

toms duties had been put on a gold basis, an extraordinary single levy had been imposed on corporations, and a heavy tax laid on war profits. Before the year was out legislation establishing a turnover tax had been passed and a special capital levy, the Reichsnotopfer, or National Emergency Contribution, had been ordered.[33] Under the leadership of Finance Minister Erzberger the whole taxing system was revised in March 1920, control of taxation was largely transferred from the States to the federal government, and new impositions were laid on corporations and on the yield of capital. Few sources of revenue remained unexplored and the rates imposed were heavy. But the government was running a losing race with inflation. Its efforts to balance its budget were unsuccessful, the deficiency was made up by short-term loans necessitating constant new issues of currency, and the resulting depreciation depressed revenues still further. Classes of property easy to tax and capable in normal times of providing large revenues were falling rapidly in real value. This was true of all securities yielding a fixed monetary return and also of rentals. The latter were practically confiscated by inflation and by housing legislation felt to be socially indispensable. The depreciation of the currency led to a proper resistance to the taxation of such paper mark incomes as were wholly illusory[34] but the resentment against injustice was perverted to secure unwarranted exemptions. The resulting complexity of the tax structure, the administration of which was necessarily inefficient,[35] still further reduced the revenues. The greatest source of loss, however, lay in the fact that, between the period for which a tax was levied and the dates of assessment and collection, a decline in the value of the currency might wipe out all but a small portion of the purchasing power of the sum received.

§ POSITION OF THE FISC IN 1921

There is, however, every reason to believe that, apart from the recurring impositions of the Treaty of Versailles, a budgetary balance would have been achieved and inflation checked. Tax revenues in 1920 yielded the equivalent of 4090 millions of gold marks and in the fol-

[33] As passed, the latter tax, instead of being a single contribution as originally intended, was distributed over a considerable period.

[34] When prices were rapidly rising goods might be sold for more than they had cost (in monetary terms) but for less than the sum at which they could be replaced. If so an accounting profit was actually a real loss.

[35] The system and the personnel were new and had no precedents on which to build.

lowing year 5235 millions.[86] Expenditures in 1921, exclusive of the deficit of the state railways and payments under the Treaty of Versailles, were equal to 5738 million gold marks. The railway deficit was eliminated in the following year.[87] Leaving it out of account, the ratio of taxes to outlays for domestic purposes in 1921 was 91.2%, an achievement which compared very favorably with that of most of the victor nations. The expenditures under the treaty, however, were themselves approximately equal to all other expenditures combined, and therefore to the total yield from taxes. Unless the improvement in the finances should proceed steadily forward the handwriting on the wall was clear and startling.

§ FAILURE TO ACHIEVE A BALANCE IN THE BUDGET

The facts are that neither in gold mark values[88] nor in the purchasing power of paper marks did revenues continue to advance. The appended Chart II shows the matter clearly. By the middle of 1921 the tax reforms of 1919-1920 had produced their maximum effect but it was far short of the requirements of the Reich and a further twist of the screw of taxation was obviously necessary. But tax revision takes time. A greatly extended and intensified tax program was adopted in the spring of 1922 and tax revenues once again, for a month or so, approached the level of expenditures. But it was then too late. The approach to a balance had been achieved only through a partial moratorium on reparations and the threatening attitude of the principal creditors left no hope of a permanent alleviation on this score. Moreover the last bulwark against currency collapse was crumbling. The people at home began to lose all confidence in their money. Exchange rates, prices, and governmental expenses soared, but tax revenues, while increasing in paper mark totals, lagged hopelessly behind. Finally, in late 1923,

---

[86] cf. Germany's Economy, Currency and Finance, p. 96. Paper marks are converted according to the index of cost of living which is the most representative index for expenditures other than those arising under the Treaty of Versailles.

[87] It reappeared, however, as inflation advanced.

[88] Gold mark values are obtained by converting paper mark figures according to the index of wholesale prices. Government expenditures were partly determined by exchange rates (cash reparations), partly by wholesale prices (reparations in kind and other purchases of commodities), and partly by the cost of living (wages and salaries). An official investigation showed, however, that the gold value of expenditures of the several sorts, when measured by the appropriate index, corresponded closely, *at this period*, with the gold value of the total paper mark expenditures converted according to the index of wholesale prices. cf. Germany's Economy, Currency and Finance, p. 95.

CHART II

REVENUE OF THE REICH, 1920-1922, IN PAPER MARKS
AND IN GOLD MARKS CALCULATED ON THE BASIS
OF THE WHOLESALE PRICE INDEX

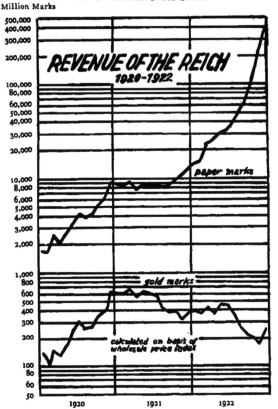

Million Marks

Reproduced from *Germany's Economic and Financial Situation*,
p. 27, with permission of the Statistische Reichsamt.

taxes covered only 1% to 2% of expenditures and many taxes did not yield the cost of collection.[39]

Table IV presents, in gold marks, the revenue and expenditures of the Reich from 1920 to 1923 and Chart III shows the ratio of taxes to total revenues (or expenditures) compared with the monthly average index of exchange rates. The general inverse correlation between the movement of foreign exchange and the proportion of expenditures covered by taxation is clear except in the first half of 1922 when the revised and extended tax program raised the ratio of taxes to outlays in spite of the fact that exchange rates (and prices and wages) were rising at a rapid rate.[40] The

[39] Adjustment of yields was attempted for the different taxes through:
  (1) The raising of rates, or adding of supplements, on existing taxes.
  (2) Levies in kind, usually commuted to an equivalent in money.
  (3) Changes of base from physical volume to current value.
  (4) Multiplication by a factor of depreciation.
  (5) The speeding up of payment.
  All proved inadequate. *cf. Besteuerung und Geldentwertung*, Arthur Cohen, Verlag von Duncker und Humblot, München and Leipzig, 1924, p. 9.

[40] The marked influence of exchange rate fluctuations on the condition of

TABLE IV

REVENUE AND EXPENDITURE OF THE REICH; 1920–1923[1]

(Millions of gold marks)

FISCAL YEAR	MONTH	REVENUE				EXPENDITURE						RATIO OF TAXES TO TOTAL REVENUE OR EXPENDITURES %
		TAXES	FLOATING DEBT	SUNDRIES	TOTAL	REPAYMENT OF FUNDED DEBT	INTEREST ON FLOATING DEBT	CONTRIBUTION TO REICHSBAHN	EXECUTION OF VERSAILLES TREATY	OTHER EXPENDITURES	TOTAL	
1920	April	57	270	9	336	11	—	—	—	—	336	17.0
	May	93	534	9	636	11	—	—	—	—	636	14.6
	June	163	1,048	9	1,220	11	—	—	—	—	1,220	13.4
	July	220	870	9	1,099	134	—	—	—	—	1,099	20.0
	Aug.	185	559	9	753	134	—	—	—	—	753	24.6
	Sept.	193	692	9	894	134	—	—	—	—	894	21.6
	Oct.	239	173	9	421	5	—	—	—	—	421	56.8
	Nov.	311	489	9	809	5	—	—	—	—	809	38.4
	Dec.	508	375	9	892	5	55	198	634	—	892	57.0
	Jan.	491	192	9	692	89	54	125	424	—	692	71.0
	Feb.	512	479	-9	1,000	89	67	143	701	—	1,000	51.2
	Mar.	525	411	9	945	89	74	255	527	—	945	55.6
Total		3,497	6,092	108	9,697	717	—	—	—	—	9,697	
1921	April	409	484	6	899	94	69	129	607	—	899	45.5
	May	475	311	7	793	94	86	122	491	—	793	59.9
	June	423	614	6	1,043	94	71	102	776	—	1,043	40.6
	July	380	385	6	771	98	62	54	557	—	771	49.3
	Aug.	303	714	6	1,023	98	65	53	807	—	1,023	29.6
	Sept.	264	410	6	680	98	49	109	424	—	680	38.8
	Oct.	279	334	6	619	19	37	47	516	—	619	45.1
	Nov.	238	293	6	537	19	40	68	410	—	537	44.3
	Dec.	274	698	6	978	19	39	74	846	—	978	28.0
	Jan.	288	287	6	581	57	34	20	470	—	581	49.6
	Feb.	274	203	6	483	57	34	39	353	—	483	56.7
	Mar.	317	206	6	529	57	31	30	411	—	529	59.9
Total		3,924	4,939	73	8,936	804	617	847	6,668	—	8,936	

TABLE IV—(Continued)

REVENUE AND EXPENDITURE OF THE REICH: 1920–1923[41]

(Millions of gold marks)

FISCAL YEAR	MONTH	REVENUE				EXPENDITURE						RATIO OF TAXES TO TOTAL REVENUE OR EXPENDITURES %
		TAXES	FLOATING DEBT	SUN-DRIES	TOTAL	REPAY-MENT OF FUNDED DEBT	INTEREST ON FLOATING DEBT	CONTRIBUTION TO REICHS-BAHN	EXECUTION OF VERSAILLES TREATY	OTHER EXPENDITURES	TOTAL	
1922	April	260	178	3	441	8	18	−19	320	114	441	59.0
	May	330	156	3	489	8	21	−11	302	169	489	67.5
	June	305	100	3	408	8	28	25	232	115	408	74.8
	July	266	129	3	398	7	20	3	205	163	398	66.8
	Aug.	228	171	3	402	7	12	59	139	185	402	56.7
	Sept.	146	552	3	701	7	31	143	118	402	701	20.8
	Oct.	127	388	3	518	1	11	145	125	236	518	24.5
	Nov.	127	290	3	420	1	11	77	170	161	420	30.2
	Dec.	119	588	3	710	1	18	171	168	352	710	16.8
	Jan.	140	290	3	433	1	15	57	223	137	433	32.3
	Feb.	80	355	3	438	1	12	137	100	188	438	18.3
	Mar.	127	756	3	886	1	24	250	190	421	886	14.3
Total		2,255	3,953	36	6,244	51	221	1,037	2,292	2,643	6,244	
1923	Apr.	205	431	—	636	—	28	182	97	329	636	32.2
	May	220	289	—	509	—	26	193	136	154	509	43.2
	June	93	863	—	956	—	50	298	126	482	956	9.7
	July	70	619	—	689	—	30	183	75	401	689	10.2
	Aug.	106	1,354	35	1,495	—	61	384	59	991	1,495	7.1
	Sept.	66	2,166	53	2,285	—	264	564	49	1,408	2,285	2.9
	Oct.	17	1,235	9	1,261	—	113	388	31	729	1,261	1.3
	Nov.	53	1,185	28	1,266	—	75	422	—	—	1,266	4.2
	Dec.	270	289	19	578	—	—	—	190	—	578	46.7
Total (9 months)		1,100	8,431	144	9,675	—	647	2,614	—	—	9,675	

[41] This table is an average of three sets of figures calculated on the cost of living index, wholesale price index, and dollar index, respectively. The original figures are given in millions and tenths of millions of gold marks. since they run to the first decimal place only, slight discrepancies occur between the totals and the sums of the individual items when the average of the three sets is taken. The decimal place has been omitted in the above table and minor corrections made in order to secure consistent totals. The balancing of the original tables leaves something to be desired and some small adjustments were necessary on this account

CHART III

PERCENTAGE RATIO OF TAXES TO TOTAL REVENUE, AND MONTHLY AVERAGE INDEX OF
DOLLAR EXCHANGE RATES (1913 = 1); APRIL 1920 TO NOVEMBER 1923

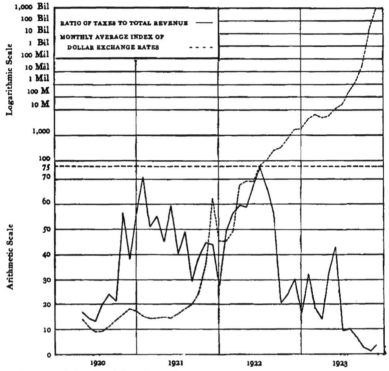

Exchange rate index plotted from figures in Table V.

relative improvement in the Treasury's position in April and May 1923
ensued upon a sharp drop in foreign exchange in February of that year
and upon the stability which obtained till the middle of April, though
this is largely obscured on the chart owing to the necessity of plotting
exchange rates, at this period, on a diminishing logarithmic, rather
than on an arithmetic, scale.

the German fisc will be apparent when it is noted that from April 1920 to May
1921 foreign exchange showed no upward tendency, that from June to November the dollar was five times multiplied in mark value, that from December
1921 to June 1922 a second period of relative stability in exchange intervened,
and that from July 1922 onward the upward march, or flight, of exchange
rates was practically continuous.

§ CAUSES OF BUDGETARY DEFICITS

The exchange value of the mark frequently fell much more rapidly than its internal purchasing power, or to put the other face on the matter, foreign exchange rose faster than wholesale prices and much faster than the cost of living. If the government had had only internal charges to meet, its expenditures, measured in gold according to the exchange rate, would not, in the early inflation years, have run much ahead of receipts. Receipts and expenditures would both have been in paper marks and the government's business would have been affected by the varying exchange value of the currency only so far as exchange rates reacted on prices but not on revenues.

The major difficulty up to mid-1922 arose from the fact that revenues were collected at one price level while a great part of government expenditures were made at a different and much higher level. Expenditures were of four types as follows:

(1) *interest on the public debt.* For any given amount of debt this was a fixed charge in marks the burden of which declined with every fall in the internal value of the currency. On this score the position of the government was constantly improving. The number of marks in circulation was increasing, mark prices and incomes were going up, some taxes were more easily obtained, yet mark payments on the old debt remained as they were.

(2) *expenditures on wages and salaries.* These varied roughly with the cost-of-living index. A considerable part of the taxes accrued from levies on income. "Earned" income varied in fairly close correspondence with the cost-of-living index so that, except for the shifts in distribution which accompanied inflation and made concealment and evasion easy, the tendency toward budgetary disequilibrium, so far as the share of income taxes in total tax revenues is concerned, was in some measure compensated by rising incomes.

(3) *expenditures for commodities.* This type of expenditure varied approximately with wholesale prices. After the reduction of railway subsidies it was of much significance only in the case of reparations in kind, of which the most important were coal deliveries. Since taxes on commodities varied with movements in wholesale prices, revenues grew, in this case also, in some measure of correspondence with increased expenditures.

(4) *cash reparations*. Payments under this head were fixed in terms of foreign exchange. The mark burden of these outlays consequently rose with every fall in the exchange value of the German currency. Whenever such a fall was disproportionate to the movement of internal prices and incomes there was no tendency whatever for any type of revenues (all of which accrued in paper marks) to respond to the increase in expenditures which the fall in mark exchange inevitably occasioned.

But whether the fall in the exchange value of the currency at any time was or was not greater than the decline in its domestic purchasing power, the result was merely to accentuate or mitigate the lag of revenues which was inherent in the depreciation itself. This is especially true of the period after the middle of 1922. For the year May 1921 to April 1922, a year of heavy cash payments on reparations account, the low relative value of the mark on the exchange markets was of great importance in determining the condition of the Treasury, but the mere fact of currency depreciation, regardless of the relation between the internal and external value of the monetary unit, was thereafter the sole significant factor. For the greater part of 1923 there was a steady rise in the *relative* value of the mark on the exchanges[42] but this was of slight consequence since the government was then making no cash reparations payments and the precipitous fall in the absolute value of the currency, both within and without the country, led, in any case, to exiguous revenues in comparison with the enormous increase in outlays.

In spite of decrees calling for the payment of taxes in anticipation of their due dates, of attempts to speed up their collection in other ways, and of tax rates which at the time they were imposed seemed intolerably severe, the actual receipts were ridiculously inadequate. According to the Act of December 23, 1922 the income of a married man with two children, such as was at that date equivalent to $1020, was subject to a tax the equivalent of $230 and, on the larger incomes, the ratio was much higher. But the levy and payment were both in paper marks. If this tax had been paid in full as early as the end of June 1923 (and some such interval must elapse to give time for assessment and collection) it would then have been worth slightly over $10, at the end of July about $1.50, at the end of August about 15c, at the end of September a fraction of a cent, while, at the end of October, it would have been in that twilight zone where infinitesimals fade into nothingness. With whatever pecuniary penalties delay in payment had been attended,

[42] *cf. infra*, Chart VI. The relative rise appears in the decline in the index of foreign exchange rates relative to that of wholesale prices.

and they were in appearance severe, the advantage of postponement could not but have outweighed them. This fact made collection difficult even though at the time the taxes became legally due they had already lost a great part of their sting. The only income taxes which bore heavily on the payer and brought in any considerable revenues to the government were those levied at the source. The result was that the wage worker, whose taxes were so levied, paid an ever increasing share of the total yield of income taxes.

Taxes on *commodities* tended to increase in paper mark totals as prices rose but, as the pace of depreciation waxed, even these were of little value by the time they accrued to the Treasury. The one gray spot on the otherwise immaculate blackness of the Treasury's position from mid-1922 to the end of inflation came as a result of the temporary stabilization of exchange rates and prices in the spring of 1923. This result, achieved through intervention by the Reichsbank on the exchange market, cost the bank heavily and, in the existing state of government finance, it was a gesture only. It temporarily raised the ratio of revenues to expenditures but the marked increase in the latter, consequent upon the policy of passive resistance, would have led to another reversal even if the support of the mark had been maintained for much longer than in fact proved possible. From May onward the ratio of the monthly increase in the floating debt to state revenue from all other sources grew higher and higher. In the last half-year of inflation, only an insignificant fraction of expenditures was covered other than by the discount of Treasury bills and the ensuing emission of Reichsbank notes. In practical effect the government had ceased to collect ordinary taxes[48] and was financing its activities all but solely through issues of fiat money.

§ INCREASE OF THE FLOATING DEBT

The upward march of the floating debt was never once interrupted from the end of the war till the currency reform in November 1923. Though this was not absolutely true of the issue of Reichsbank notes, owing to the fact that a larger or smaller proportion of the discounted bills was from time to time sold to the public by the Reichsbank, the connection between the two phenomena was close.

[48] Inflation was, of course, a concealed method of taxation. It has been stated, with apparent accuracy, that the German government would actually have been better off if it had given up ordinary tax collection altogether. Taxes, as a whole, cost more to collect than they brought in. The issues of fiat money would therefore have been smaller if the whole of the ordinary taxing machinery had been discarded.

TABLE V

DISCOUNTED TREASURY BILLS OUTSTANDING AND ISSUES OF REICHSBANK NOTES; 1919-1923

(Billions of marks)

END OF	1919		1920		1921		1922		1923	
	DISCOUNTED TREASURY BILLS OUTSTANDING	REICHSBANK NOTE ISSUES	DISCOUNTED TREASURY BILLS OUTSTANDING	REICHSBANK NOTE ISSUES	DISCOUNTED TREASURY BILLS OUTSTANDING	REICHSBANK NOTE ISSUES	DISCOUNTED TREASURY BILLS OUTSTANDING	REICHSBANK NOTE ISSUES	DISCOUNTED TREASURY BILLS OUTSTANDING	REICHSBANK NOTE ISSUES
Jan.	59	24	88	37	156	67	256	115	2,082	1,985
Feb.	62	24	89	41	162	67	263	120	3,588	3,513
Mar.	64	25	92	45	166	69	272	131	6,601	5,518
April	67	27	95	48	173	71	281	140	8,442	6,546
May	70	28	102	50	177	72	290	152	10,275	8,564
June	73	30	113	54	185	75	295	169	22,020	17,291
July	76	29	123	56	191	77	308	190	57,849	43,595
Aug.	78	28	129	58	203	80	332	238	1,196,295	663,200
Sept.	81	30	138	62	211	86	451	317	46,716,616	28,228,816
Oct.	83	31	141	64	218	92	604	469	6,907,511,103	2,496,822,900
Nov.	85	32	148	64	227	101	839	754	191,580,465,422**	400,267,640,300
Dec.	86	36	153	69	247	114	1,495	1,280		496,507,424,800

** As of November 15.

Sources of data: (1) *Germany's Economy, Currency and Finance*, p. 63. (2) *Zahlen zur Geldentwertung in Deutschland* 1914 *bis* 1923, p. 46.

Table V shows by months the total amount of discounted bills outstanding and the volume of Reichsbank note issues. The figures in the table are not, of course, to be interpreted as representing the difference between financing the state requirements partly by taxation, as in the earlier years, and wholly by fiat money, as in the later. They reflect this situation very obscurely and show, in the main, simply the depreciation of the currency. The hundreds of quintillions of marks, in November 1923, were actually of much less gold value than the comparatively insignificant totals of discounts and note issues in earlier years. The depreciation of the currency thus not only wiped out the pre-inflation federal debt but also was continually reducing the burden of the enormous current borrowings. If one were to take thousand-mark notes and pile them tightly together one on top of the other the sum of values would not equal the government's borrowing from the Reichsbank until the pillar was twenty-five billion times as high as the loftiest mountain on earth.[45] Yet, at the rate at which the mark was converted into the new stable-value currency (a trillion to one), the total discounted bills outstanding on November 15, 1923, were worth less than fifty million dollars.

§ INTERRELATIONS BETWEEN EXCHANGE RATES AND THE STATUS
OF THE FISC

The relation between foreign exchange rates and the status of the fisc may have been due to the fact that shifts in exchange rates affected the position of the Treasury, that the position of the Treasury affected exchange rates, or that these factors reacted upon one another. The last is the most likely. Vicious circles are germane to the whole process of inflation and the connection between exchange rates and the public finances in Germany is but one aspect of a phenomenon which occurred in many forms. Deficits in the state finances, increases in the volume of circulating medium, the rise of internal prices, and upward movements in exchange rates were all tied together and the order of their coming was by no means fixed. Any one of these factors in inflation might alter independently, exert its influence on any or all of the others, and be affected in turn by the changes which its own movement had initiated. Not only was the whole circle of changes then again set in motion and indefinitely repeated but from each of the changing factors a new set of impulses, either independently or as a resultant, was constantly being communicated to each of the others, and was from each again passed on with ever accelerated momentum. Once inflation was fully under

[45] The illustration is taken from *Germany Since the War*, Peter P. Reinhold, Institute of Politics Publications, Yale University Press, New Haven, 1928, p. 53.

way the process was an inverted spiral with the sweep always widening and the vertical distance between the coils growing greater with every revolution.

The ramifications of the process cannot well be presented in a single picture but it may be helpful to outline one full circle, remembering that any one of the factors might be causal, that the influence of a change in any of them was exerted on those which precede as well as on those which follow it in the list, and that the order in which they are set down merely reflects the random selection of a starting point. Such a circle, beginning with exchange rates, would be:

> Rising foreign exchange rates, rising domestic prices, increase of governmental expenses, larger budgetary deficit, increase both in the absolute volume and in the rate of acceleration of government discounting of Treasury bills, diminished public demand for such bills, increase in the absolute amount and in the rate of issue of Reichsbank notes, larger cash and credit volume of· circulating medium, further rise in exchange rates and prices, and so on in indefinite repetition.

The circle might at any time be short-circuited in any direction, but this would not diminish, but rather increase, the strength of the current throughout the line.

An opposite trend in any of the factors would, of course, act cumulatively toward deflation. Cases of this sort occurred but they were sooner or later checked by the failure, even at the best of times, of state revenues to cover expenditures (including reparations), and by the recurrent pressure on exchange rates issuing from attempts to meet elastic demands from the victor nations. The latter persistently took the position that whatever was paid or offered was but an inchoate essay at fulfilment of the·obligations due.

IV. SPECULATION

§ POWER OF SPECULATION TO DEPRESS EXCHANGE

Great has been the abuse heaped upon the exchange speculator as a destroyer of currencies. Most of this abuse is due to the conscious or unconscious search for a scapegoat and· is unwarranted by the facts. But though speculators who persistently operate against the trend of fundamental forces are certain to be eliminated, and so cannot long affect the market, it is not to be denied that bear speculation may depress the exchange value of a monetary unit, that the fall in the currency's exchange value may provoke retrogression in its domestic purchasing power and in the public finances of the country concerned, that new issues of notes may thus be induced, that the consequent further fall in exchanges may justify the speculation from the point of view of private profit and may lead to continued bearish operations which, in the manner just indicated, actually bring about the depreciation on which the operators count.[46]

§ THE VENUE OF SPECULATION

Speculation in the mark was rampant both on the bull and on the bear side of the market though the two movements did not by any means coincide. The post-war history of German inflation, so far as foreign exchange is concerned, shows several clearly marked major movements as follows:[47]

(1) The period of immediate post-war adjustment, November 1918 to February 1920, characterized by a steady fall in mark exchange.

(2) The period from March 1920 to May 1921, a year and a quarter of stability considered as a whole, though with an upward movement of the mark from March to May 1920, a downward movement from August to mid-November, and an upward movement from mid-November 1920 through January 1921.

(3) The period from June to late-November 1921, the months of heavy cash reparations payments, characterized by a rapid fall in mark exchange.

(4) The period from December 1921 to May 1922, a half-year of comparative stability again.

(5) The period from June 1922 to the end of inflation during which the trend was steadily downward.

In the immediate post-war period the speculative[48] dealing was predominantly on the bull side of mark exchange and, indeed, till late in 1922, the persistent foreign speculative buying of German currency was one of the most striking aspects of inflation. It is doubtful whether bear activities ever fully counteracted this steady buying. As a result, however, of the operation of forces much more fundamental than speculation, the mark sagged in 1919 at a steady and, for that time,

[46] cf. *Valuta*, Karl Diehl and Paul Mombert, Verlag G. Braun, Karlsruhe, 1925, p. 13.
[47] Prices and volume of circulating medium showed generally similar movements.
[48] "Speculative" is to be construed broadly to include the activities of commercial houses who took claims to future marks in exchange for goods.

rapid rate, and the speculators as a group took heavy losses. Those who had played the part of bears of course made money but the situation was reversed after March 1920 when, in the course of a little more than two months, the mark rose nearly 200% (100.13 to the dollar on March 4; 34.75 to the dollar on May 25). This was the heyday of the bull movement and as usual it was overdone. The exchange value of the mark had been carried beyond the point at which it would be sustained by basic factors and it slowly slid back toward the current equilibrium level. In the ensuing months speculation was not very active except for the so-called investment demand[49] but, with the beginning of cash reparations, the bears were presented with a near certainty of success. Knowing that the government must procure foreign exchange in large volume, and that it had no means of doing so except by further note issues, the "spot" purchase of foreign exchange or the sale of mark futures carried a rich promise of profits to the speculator. This situation continued from June to November 1921. Investment buying of marks was then on the decline and it is probable that speculative selling operated to produce the situation it anticipated. The farther bear speculation drove the mark down the worse became the situation of the fisc. The discounts of Treasury bills and emissions of Reichsbank notes consequently grew larger, with a reflex again on the exchanges, and so on in indefinite repetition. The only escape was to have mark exchange fall so far below the domestic purchasing power of the currency as to lead to purchases for present use or to speculation for a rise. If this should occur the spin of the circle would be checked and perhaps reversed. It actually *was* checked when relief from reparations payments was temporarily obtained in late 1921.[50]

§ THE FLIGHT FROM THE MARK

The greatest effect exerted by speculators in exchange is ordinarily supposed to have occurred after the middle of 1922 when the home population, having lost all confidence in the currency, rushed in a frenzy into the exchange markets and initiated the so-called export of capital. The export of capital and the flight from the mark, so far as the latter phrase means the exchange of the mark for foreign currency, have been generally used as synonymous expressions. In reality they have no connection with one another. The essence of an export of capital is the

[49] Purchases made with the intent of holding the currency indefinitely.
[50] cf. *Die Reichsbank*, Gert von Eynern, Verlag von Gustav Fischer, Jena, 1928, p. 74. Von Eynern thinks that the exports which had gone out in response to the low exchange value of the mark were primarily responsible for this improvement in the exchange situation.

transfer to residents of a foreign country of the ownership of immediate claims to goods (and later, when the claims are exercised, of the goods themselves), without any obligation on the capital importer to furnish similar immediate claims in return.[51] A foreign exchange transaction is not of this type but is a barter of immediate monetary claims to goods in one national market against immediate monetary claims to goods in another.[52] It is true that either or both of the bartered claims may have been obtained in exchange for deferred obligations in the other currency (a claim to future goods) or may later be used to purchase them. But there is nothing in the sale of a currency itself to show that this is occurring. There can, indeed, be no net export of *real* capital in the actual purchase and sale of exchange. All that happens is a swapping of claims on currencies, with the nationals of each country, after the transaction, owning the equivalent in *present* goods (or claims thereto) of their former possessions. This is true whether, for instance, a German sells for marks American exchange to another German, to an American, or to a foreigner not a citizen of the United States. Whatever the details, in no case would either country send out capital in the exchange transaction.[53]

§ MECHANISM OF CAPITAL EXPORT

Since an exchange transaction cannot of itself involve a net export of capital it follows that capital must be exported outside the exchange process. There is an inchoate export of capital as soon as immediate monetary claims to goods in one country are given to another in excess of the immediate claims received by the former from the latter.[54] This is not an exchange transaction. When, however, such immediate claims

[51] The *quid pro quo* is usually a claim to future goods (securities) though capital may of course be exported as a gift or as tribute.

[52] Other than sight bills of exchange would not strictly meet this definition but, though payment in this case is not immediate, it is deferred for a few months at most. As a *national* matter payment may, however, be deferred indefinitely whenever a fund of foreign exchange is acquired by the creditor country the constituent units of the fund constantly coming to maturity and as constantly being replaced by new units. There was some export of capital, in this sense, from Germany, but the amount involved does not appear to have been large. *cf. infra*, Chap. x.

[53] If the term "capital," which is ambiguous, be used to include immediate money claims both countries would, at most, export "capital" in equal measure, with no net change in the national position. But see *supra*, note 52.

[54] Such a transaction has been called an *inchoate* export of capital in order to avoid confusion in the use of the word "capital." "Capital" will henceforth be used in this discussion to mean real things rather than claims thereto. "Wealth" is probably a better word for the concept but it has no currency in the idiom of international finance.

are *sold* the exchange of the lending country will tend to be depressed. The actual export of capital is made in the form of commodities and, when an equivalent additional volume of commodity exports attends an undertaking to export claims to capital, exchange rates tend to be restored to their old position. Similarly, a *constructive* export of capital, without effect on exchange rates, takes place whenever the borrower (the seller of future obligations) takes the present foreign exchange proceeds of his borrowing and spends such exchange on tangibles left in the lending country. The only effect on exchange rates of an export of capital claims occurs, therefore, when the newly acquired rights of the borrower, in the form of the money of the lending country, are sold for what they will bring in his own money. The resulting temporary fall in the exchange value of the currency of the lending country is due not to the export of capital, as such, but to the fact that there is a momentary redundancy in the foreign holdings of rights to the lending country's money rather than of its commodities. The lending country's money therefore falls in exchange value against other currencies and it will pay to change it into goods. As soon as the cash holdings are expended for commodities, whether or not such commodities are imported into the buyer's country, the redundancy of the lender's currency on the exchange markets is reduced and exchange rates tend to recover.

§ EXPORT OF CAPITAL FROM GERMANY SLIGHT

Now the flight from the mark was not due to an impulse on the part of Germans to export capital, that is, an impulse to give to foreigners immediate claims on German goods in exchange for a postponed command over foreign commodities, but merely to a desire to swap present purchasing power in their own currency for anything which would retain its value. If capital had really been in process of exportation from Germany there would have been no trouble. It is just because there was almost no capital capable of export that mark exchange fell so rapidly. Insofar as German exchange was held by foreigners as an investment, and thus approached the category of securities,[55] it is much more nearly true to say that capital was being *imported* into Germany, either actually, in the shape of an excess of commodity imports which would otherwise not have been possible, or constructively, in the acquisition by sellers of marks of *present* property in foreign countries.[56] In exchange for the capital actually or constructively imported the Germans offered marks or mark claims which were, in effect, promises to

[55] Albeit of the character of wildcat mining stocks.
[56] The exporter of capital acquires rights to *future* not to *present* goods.

pay on demand, throughout an indefinite period, an undetermined but steadily diminishing amount of purchasing power over German goods—provided the withdrawal of those goods were permitted by the German authorities. So far as the marks were bought and held by foreigners till they became worthless this process was not even an *exchange* of capital, to say nothing of a net export. It is therefore all but quite erroneous to speak of the flight from the mark into foreign currencies as an export of capital.[57]

It has already been pointed out that the sale of marks, in itself, did not tend to depress mark exchange. When buyers were eager, as in 1920, the sale (which was also a purchase) of marks was attended by a rising value; when they were reluctant and sellers were eager, as in the second half of 1922, mark exchange fell. The crux of the matter is not that marks were being sold abroad but that they were being sold under the hammer without reservation of price. Assuming that the Germans would have had the same foreign obligations, whether or not marks had been sold abroad, the sales to "investment" buyers acted to sustain or improve the exchange value of the German currency precisely as if the Germans had been in the second stage of the export of real capital—the sending out of goods rather than of monetary claims against them—or had been borrowing in foreign countries through the issue of securities.

Marks could not be sold without being bought and when foreigners purchased marks, or claims to marks, they could do one of three things with them. (1) They could hold them either abroad or on deposit in Germany or they could lend or otherwise invest them in Germany. In this case the original support given the mark by their demand would be subject to no diminution. (2) They could later buy exportable goods with them. If these goods would not otherwise have been purchased the upward impetus to mark exchange arising from the original demand for the marks would be sustained. (3) They could sell the marks already purchased. In this case the original support given the mark by the investor's purchase might in part be cancelled.[58] But even here any decline in the value of the mark between the date of the original and the

[57] The scintilla of truth in the expression lies in the degree in which Germans bought foreign exchange with immediately cashed claims to marks and held a *fund* of it as an investment. But even this was compensated, many times over, by foreign holdings of marks.

[58] There would, however, be no effect on mark exchange if the marks were sold to another foreign investor who would otherwise not have been in the market.

later transaction would make the pressure on mark exchange much lighter than an equivalence with the support originally given.

§ SALES OF CURRENCY AS A BULLISH FACTOR ON MARK EXCHANGE

It is clear that, taking the whole period of post-war inflation into consideration and assuming that a fixed amount of foreign exchange was unconditionally required by the Germans, the sale of the currency was a bullish factor on its exchange value. This was specially true of the earlier years. In the final stages of inflation, moreover, it was not the sale of the currency (the so-called export of capital) which was of any significance in depressing its value but the fact that sellers were intensely eager and sales extremely hard to make. In the first place they were prohibited by the German government[59] but, more important perhaps, the lists of gullible foreign buyers had by this time been fairly well exhausted. There were few individuals ready to buy, with stable-value currencies, a monetary unit which was rushing to its doom. Clearly it was the attitude of the buyers and sellers of marks toward the wares of which they were making disposal and acquisition, and not the sales themselves, which was the fundamental influence in driving the value of the mark downward and, *per contra*, in raising to the sky the mark value of foreign exchange.[60]

From the beginning of 1923, at latest, practically the sole sources of foreign exchange were the proceeds of German commodity exports or of such property as foreigners bought in Germany. Exchange dealings involving the mark must have been confined largely to the Germans themselves since foreign sellers of goods to Germany were invoicing in stable currencies, German sellers were in large measure also follow-

---

[59] Exchange dealings were authorized only for mercantile transactions. The idea was that by diminishing the offers of marks the exchange rate would be sustained. It is an open question whether the policy did not defeat its own end since the passion to sell marks merely impelled their possessors to offer them clandestinely on ever cheaper terms in the competition to obtain buyers in a greatly narrowed market. The mark was, as it were, squeezed into a funnel.

[60] It should be noted that, while in the absence of a sufficient export of goods and of investment opportunities in Germany, buyers of marks as a group were almost sure to lose, no matter how apparently cheap the German currency on the exchange markets seemed to be, this was not necessarily true of individual buyers. It was a question of how quickly the marks could be turned into real values. This led to a scramble, with the devil taking the hindmost, but with the foremost emerging with considerable gains. The latter possibility was always a force on the bullish side of mark exchange. It was not sufficient, to keep exchange rates at anything like par with internal prices, since the chance of *large* gains had to be present, but it imposed some limit on the upward movement of foreign currencies.

ing this practice, there was no foreign investment demand for marks, and the supply of marks purchased by foreigners in previous years, and subject to sale, cut no appreciable figure at the value to which the mark had then fallen. Practically the sole market for marks thus lay with German exporters who had acquired foreign exchange and were ready to part with it at a price which would enable them to employ immediately, and at a profit, the mark proceeds of the sale of their exchange. The transaction thus resolved itself into a close calculation of the relative advantages of holding foreign exchange or of selling it against marks and buying goods at home. There was thus no tendency for exchange rates to rise far in advance of prices, and internal prices at this time did, in fact, advance even more rapidly than foreign exchange. (See *infra*, Chart VI.)[61] There is thus no reason to believe that the panic flight from the mark expressed itself primarily in the exchange markets. On the contrary the evidence runs in the opposite direction. The final cataclysm can therefore not be attributed to speculation on the exchange markets even when that term is extended to include German buying of foreign currencies as a safeguard against ruin and with the intention of holding the purchased moneys indefinitely. Purchases of foreign exchange were only one, and it would seem not the dominating, aspect of a general repudiation of the mark. The exchange market was closed to legal speculation and, even if exchange bootlegging had been successfully prevented, it is unlikely that the rates would have deviated very widely from those actually established. Arbitrage as between foreign exchange and commodities would have kept exchange rates in approximately the same relation to domestic prices as did in fact take place. Domestic prices were affected as directly as exchange rates by the flight from the mark and exchange speculation was no more active than speculation in commodities.

It is true that the first access of panic in mid-1922, when the final relapse of the currency began, affected exchange markets first of all and, in the manner already described, helped to realize the fears of the population with respect to the monetary unit. The fall in mark exchange which occurred at that time was certainly a factor in destroying whatever chance then existed of rehabilitation of the public finances just as the fall in 1921, attendant on cash reparations payments, had ruined an earlier favorable prospect. To this extent speculation may have been in some measure responsible for the ultimate collapse. But in view of the enormous sale of marks to eager foreign buyers, rather

[61] In the chart the relatively slower rise of exchange rates is shown by a ratio declining with respect to prices.

than by urgent German sellers, up to the middle of 1922, and of the peculiar situation in 1923, it seems probable that, over the whole period of inflation, speculation was a favorable rather than an adverse influence on the exchange value of the German currency unit and, inasmuch as the sales abroad removed some of the issues of mark notes from the only *milieu* in which they could affect prices, it is equally probable that speculation prevented as rapid a fall in the internal value of the mark as would otherwise have taken place.

V. BANKING

§ GENERAL INFLUENCE OF BANKING ON INFLATION

The basic though perhaps not originally causal factor in the complete syncope of the German financial structure was the constant and eventually overwhelming increase in the issue of Reichsbank notes. Whether or not the forces impelling such issues were capable of restraint is an open question. But when, in the fall of 1923, even a box of matches sold for more marks than were in existence in pre-war Germany, it is clear that, but for the flood of notes, the depreciation actually realized would have been impossible. Yet it was constantly and vehemently asserted in Germany that note issues were the result rather than the cause of the decline in the value of the mark. There is, moreover, some basis for this contention. Causes and effects here as elsewhere were confused and reciprocal. They were but another phase of the protean vicious circle. Note issues were a consequence of government deficits and government deficits depended largely on exchange rates and prices. Exchange rates and prices were thus an important causal factor in fixing the amount of notes in circulation at any given moment, yet at the same time they were affected in part, but in part only and to an indeterminate degree, by the past, present, and highly uncertain prospective volume of such note issues.

Whenever gold payments are suspended the gold value of a currency may depreciate gravely as a result of the operations of commercial banks even if such banks have no note issuing powers. The range of depreciation is ordinarily widened if the government is forced to resort to short-term borrowing but, if its obligations ultimately find their way into the investment portfolios of the public, the road to recovery is still open. State borrowing may indeed be carried on in excess of the absorptive capacity of the public, and without irreparable damage, provided the banking organization takes up an adequate volume of the government's floating obligations. Up to this point inflation can be confined to an expansion of bank *credit* on a relatively constant *monetary* base. Though such credit may be stretched far, the more or less stable proportion of money to credit instruments which is required by established business habits keeps *credit* expansion within at least measurable bounds. This is especially true where, as in Germany, the commercial banks are dependent for cash reserves on the note issues of the central institution.[62] But, when a government can no longer in any manner place its securities, and is forced to cover deficits by persistent direct issues of notes, the constant growth in the monetary base greases the ways for the launching of unlimited currency depreciation. The post-war inflationary experience of Great Britain, where the original value of the monetary unit was eventually restored, may be taken as partially representative of the first type of inflation, that of France, where a large floating debt was a constant menace until the reforms of 1926 resulted in the stabilization of the currency unit at about 1/5 of its original value, as typical of the second,[63] while Germany is the arch-exemplar of the third.

§ METHOD OF GERMAN NOTE ISSUES

The German government did not, it is true, issue its own notes in any considerable volume but operated through the Reichsbank. All government revenues in excess of tax and long-term loan receipts being obtained by the discount of Treasury bills it made little difference whether the government took the proceeds of such discounts in Reichsbank notes or in deposit credit. Reichsbank notes or their equivalent passed into the hands of the public as soon as the government settled its accounts either by payment in cash or by draft on the Reichsbank.

To the extent that the Reichsbank could dispose of Treasury bills to the commercial banks or to the general public it could withdraw its own issues from circulation and to the extent that the Treasury could sell its bills directly to the same buyers no new issues of paper money were involved. If the Reichsbank had ever been able to effect a per-

[62] *cf. Currency and Credit*, R. G. Hawtrey, Longmans, Green and Co., London, 1923, pp. 51, 52. Hawtrey points out that in countries like Germany, where deposit credit is not highly developed, the control of credit by the central bank is comparatively easy.

[63] From the end of the war onward the circulation of notes in France was a fairly constant quantity. It fluctuated between 35 and 40 billions of francs from the middle of 1919 to the end of 1924. In the latter year an increase began which carried it to 56 billion in 1926 and France was, for a time, in grave danger of treading in Germany's footsteps. Only at the eleventh hour was the process checked by the vigorous measures adopted by the Coalition Cabinet under Premier Poincaré.

manent reduction in its holdings of Treasury bills, or even to prevent their increase, the progress of inflation could have been stayed. But it will be remembered that, from the Armistice to the end of the period of inflation, the end-of-the-month figures of outstanding discounted Treasury bills show an absolutely uninterrupted increase although the holdings of such bills by the Reichsbank were, on several occasions, temporarily lowered. These reductions correspond roughly with improvements in the exchange value of the mark, though the cause and effect relationship is not indisputable.[64] Whatever the causal sequence may have been, the correlation is significant of what might have been accomplished if the reduction in Reichsbank holdings could have been made other than ephemeral. But of this the persistent growth in the total of Treasury discounts did not permit. Statistics on the amount of Treasury bills held by the Reichsbank, the proportion which the latter bore to the total Treasury bills discounted, and the ratio of Reichsbank note issues to its holdings of these bills are given in Table VI.

§ REICHSBANK HOLDINGS OF TREASURY BILLS

It will be noted that, from the beginning of 1922 onward, the rise in the Reichsbank holdings of Treasury bills was as uninterrupted as had been for several years the progress of total government discounts and that the increase in the Reichsbank's *share* of the growing total was almost as steady as the rise in the absolute figures. This means, of course, that the commercial banks and the public were then constantly reducing the relative volume of their purchases. The movement is especially marked after the middle of 1922 when, for several months, not only did the proportion of Treasury bills outside the Reichsbank show a declining trend but, in spite of the fact that there was a rapid increase in the total output of the bills, the absolute volume of non-

[64] Over the period of 60 months from January 1919 to December 1923 a reduction in the Reichsbank end-of-the-month holdings of bills was generally accompanied by an improvement in the exchange value of the mark and an increase in holdings was generally accompanied by a decline in that value. This inverse correlation fails to occur, however, in 19 of the 60 months. Assuming a lag of exchange rates behind holdings of Treasury bills of one month, there are only 17 points at which the movements of the two series are in the same direction. Considering only the period from February 1920 through December 1923 (47 months), the number of points where the two series do not move in opposite directions are as follows: with no lag, 16 points; with a lag of exchange of one month, 13 points; with a lag of exchange of 15 days, 11 points.

TABLE VI

REICHSBANK HOLDINGS OF TREASURY BILLS, RATIO OF SUCH HOLDINGS TO TOTAL
TREASURY BILL DISCOUNTS, AND RATIO OF REICHSBANK NOTE ISSUES
TO HOLDINGS OF TREASURY BILLS; 1919–1923

END OF MONTH	AMOUNT OF DISCOUNTED TREASURY BILLS HELD BY THE REICHSBANK (BILLIONS OF MARKS)	RATIO OF REICHSBANK HOLDINGS OF TREASURY BILLS TO TOTAL DISCOUNTS OF SUCH BILLS (%)	RATIO OF CIRCULATION OF REICHSBANK NOTES TO DISCOUNTED TREASURY BILLS HELD BY THE REICHSBANK (%)
1919 Jan.	26.8	45.7	88.1
Feb.	27.1	44.0	88.9
Mar.	29.9	46.9	85.3
April	31.3	46.6	85.0
May	28.5	40.5	98.9
June	33.1	45.1	90.6
July	30.4	39.9	96.4
Aug.	31.0	39.6	91.9
Sept.	33.6	41.7	88.7
Oct.	33.7	40.5	91.7
Nov.	33.8	39.7	94.4
Dec.	41.3	47.8	86.4
1920 Jan.	38.8	43.9	96.4
Feb.	38.1	42.8	107.6
Mar.	42.7	46.6	105.9
April	38.4	40.4	124.7
May	36.7	36.1	136.2
June	45.0	39.8	120.0
July	40.1	32.7	139.2
Aug.	40.9	31.6	142.8
Sept.	49.6	35.9	124.4
Oct.	48.6	34.6	130.9
Nov.	51.4	34.8	125.1
Dec.	57.6	37.7	119.4
1921 Jan.	50.6	32.5	131.6
Feb.	53.7	33.2	125.5
Mar.	64.5	38.8	107.6
April	58.8	34.0	120.4
May	63.0	35.7	114.0
June	79.6	43.0	94.6
July	80.0	41.9	96.7
Aug.	84.0	41.4	95.4
Sept.	98.4	46.7	87.8
Oct	98.7	45.3	92.7
Nov.	114.0	50.3	88.5
Dec.	132.3	53.5	85.9

TABLE VI—(*Continued*)

REICHSBANK HOLDINGS OF TREASURY BILLS, RATIO OF SUCH HOLDINGS TO TOTAL
TREASURY BILL DISCOUNTS, AND RATIO OF REICHSBANK NOTE ISSUES
TO HOLDINGS OF TREASURY BILLS; 1919-1923

END OF MONTH	AMOUNT OF DISCOUNTED TREASURY BILLS HELD BY THE REICHSBANK (BILLIONS OF MARKS)	RATIO OF REICHSBANK HOLDINGS OF TREASURY BILLS TO TOTAL DIS-COUNTS OF SUCH BILLS (%)	RATIO OF CIRCULATION OF REICHSBANK NOTES TO DISCOUNTED TREAS-URY BILLS HELD BY THE REICHSBANK (%)
1922 Jan.	126.2	49.3	91.4
Feb.	134.3	51.1	89.4
Mar.	146.5	53.8	89.2
April	155.6	55.4	90.2
May	167.8	58.0	90.5
June	186.1	63.0	90.9
July	207.9	67.5	91.3
Aug.	249.8	75.3	95.3
Sept.	349.8	77.5	90.6
Oct.	477.2	79.0	98.4
Nov.	672.2	80.1	112.2
Dec.	1,184.5	79.2	108.1
1923 Jan.	1,609.0	77.3	123.3
Feb.	2,947.4	82.1	119.2
Mar.	4,552.0	69.0	121.2
April	6,224.9	73.7	105.2
May	8,021.9	78.1	106.8
June	18,338.2	83.3	94.3
July	53,752.0	92.9	81.1
Aug.	987,218.8	82.5	67.2
Sept.	45,216,224.4	96.8	62.4
Oct.	6,578,650,938.8	95.2	38.0
Nov. 15	189,801,468,187.4	99.1	48.9

Sources of data: (1) *Germany's Economy, Currency and Finance*, p. 63.
(2) *Zahlen zur Geldentwertung in Deutschland* 1914 *bis* 1923, pp. 45-7.

Reichsbank holdings fell off. The situation up to September 1922 is depicted in Chart IV.

Even though the commercial banks could borrow from the central institution at low rates there was no profit in investing in Treasury bills and, as the currency depreciation proceeded, Treasury bills became quite obviously a very poor type of secondary reserve. They were still less desirable investments for the public at large who, unlike the commercial banks, could not easily hedge on their transactions by borrowing at low rates from the Reichsbank in monetary units which fell in value *pari passu* with their investments, and who therefore had to take an uncompensated loss with every decline in the value of the

CHART IV

TREASURY BILLS AND THEIR DISTRIBUTION; JANUARY 1920-SEPTEMBER 1922

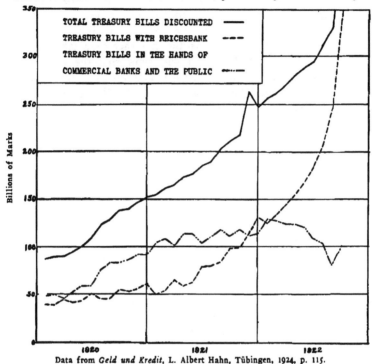

TOTAL TREASURY BILLS DISCOUNTED ———
TREASURY BILLS WITH REICHSBANK – – –
TREASURY BILLS IN THE HANDS OF
COMMERCIAL BANKS AND THE PUBLIC —··—

Data from *Geld und Kredit,* L. Albert Hahn, Tübingen, 1924, p. 115.

mark. The growing disinclination to invest in such "securities" forced the Reichsbank to absorb an ever increasing proportion of each new issue and, in order to keep any outside market at all, it was impelled to repurchase as large an amount of the old issues as might be offered to it. Its holdings thus increased at certain periods at a faster rate than the government borrowings. The volume of notes in circulation was, of course, correspondingly enlarged.

§ DISCOUNT OF COMMERCIAL BILLS AND POLICY OF REICHSBANK
TOWARD PRIVATE BORROWING

But Reichsbank note issues were not dependent on Treasury borrowing only. In pre-war days the non-cash cover of Reichsbank notes had consisted of commercial bills. Against the discount of such bills the bulk of the pre-war circulation had been issued. The provision permitting commercial bills as cover was retained in the war- and post-war period and the output of notes was thus conditioned by private as well as by government borrowing.[65] The percentage of Reichsbank note issues to the total of discounted Treasury bills in the portfolio of the bank was therefore frequently above 100% though the ratio was reduced by the share of both private and government discounts which were left on deposit in the central institution rather than taken in the form of notes. Reference to Table VI will show that the volume of note issues began to exceed the Reichsbank holdings of Treasury bills at the beginning of 1920. The use of commercial bills had almost entirely ceased during the war and was not widely resumed till the middle of 1922 so that, to that time, the cover for Reichsbank notes, other than that provided by Treasury bills, was either coin, bullion, Reichskassenscheine or Darlehnskassenscheine. None of the latter types of cover were of great quantitative significance in comparison with the Treasury bill. Inflation, till mid-1922, was therefore dominated by Treasury deficits.

The shrinkage of all types of bank deposits and the resulting scarcity of credit, which grew marked as inflation advanced,[66] impelled the Reichsbank, in the summer of 1922, to urge the readoption of the commercial bill as a credit instrument. A low discount rate was applied and, under the existing condition of continuous currency depreciation, the rediscounting of commercial bills became an obvious recourse for the private banks. The Reichsbank's portfolio of commercial bills consequently grew rapidly in spite of a gradual diminution in the bank's enthusiasm in the matter and of subsequent large but always inadequate increases in the rate. The figures for discounted commercial bills, for total discounted bills (commercial plus Treasury), and for note issues are given in Table VII.

[65] Notes might be issued against "cash" cover consisting of gold, German coin, Treasury notes (Reichskassenscheine), or Loan Bureau notes (Darlehnskassenscheine) or against non-cash cover consisting of Treasury bills (Reichsschatzwechsel) or commercial bills. In May 1921, (inauguration of cash reparations), the regulation requiring that at least one-third of the note circulation must be backed by "cash" cover was indefinitely suspended.

[66] No one was willing to leave sums on deposit only to have their value melt away. The commercial banks, moreover, did not follow the Reichsbank lead in keeping their interest rates low but stepped them up in some degree of correspondence with the presumptive loss of value between the date of borrowing and of repayment. Up to the end of 1921, however, bank deposits had fairly well kept pace with the depreciation of the currency. Dr. Alfred Lansburgh, writing in *Die Bank*, July 1922, attributes this to the deposit in German banks of actual mark currency reimported from abroad.

TABLE VII

REICHSBANK DISCOUNT OF COMMERCIAL BILLS, TOTAL BILLS DISCOUNTED, AND
NOTE ISSUES; 1922 AND 1923[67]

(Billions of Marks)

DATE END OF	COMMERCIAL BILLS DISCOUNTED AT REICHSBANK	TOTAL BILLS DISCOUNTED AT REICHSBANK	REICHSBANK NOTE ISSUES
1921 Dec.	1.1	133.4	113.6
1922 Mar.	2.2	148.7	130.7
June	4.8	190.9	169.2
Sept.	50.2	400.0	316.9
Dec.	422.2	1,607	1,280
1923 Jan.	697.2	2,306	1,985
Feb.	1,829	4,777	3,513
Mar.	2,372	6,924	5,518
April	2,986	9,211	6,546
May	4,015	12,037	8,564
June	6,914	25,252	17,291
July	18,314	72,066	43,595
Aug.	164,644	1,151,863	663,200
Sept.	3,660,094	48,876,319	28,228,816
Oct.	1,058,129,855	7,636,780,794	2,496,822,900
Nov.	347,301,037,776	444,175,368,026	400,267,640,300
Dec.	322,724,948,986	322,724,948,986	496,507,424,800

[67] The excess of the total of bills discounted over the issue of notes is presumably due either to private holding of Treasury bills or to deposit credits (in lieu of notes) with the Reichsbank.

Source of data: *Zahlen zur Geldentwertung in Deutschland* 1914 *bis* 1923, *passim.*

§ RATIO OF DISCOUNTS OF COMMERCIAL BILLS TO TOTAL NOTE ISSUES

From a negligible amount in June 1922 the Reichsbank discount of commercial bills thus rose to one-third of its total discounts in April 1923, that is, the commercial bills amounted to one-half as much as the Treasury bills. From then on a relative decline in the volume of commercial bills discounted set in and this tendency continued till just prior to the currency reform in November. After November 15 there was no further discounting of Treasury bills, the former government discounts were taken up,[68] and commercial bills occupied the whole stage.[69] Though discounts for the Treasury continued to be preeminent up to the end of inflation the credits put at the disposal of the com-

[68] Through an arrangement made by the government with the Reichsbank and the Rentenbank.

[69] The figures for December are convertible into rentenmarks at a trillion to one.

TABLE VIII

COMMERCIAL BILLS DISCOUNTED BY THE REICHSBANK AS A PERCENTAGE OF
TOTAL NOTE CIRCULATION; 1914-1923

(By years 1914-1919, by months 1920-1923)

DATE MONTHLY AVERAGE (END OF MONTH FIGURES)	PERCENTAGE OF COMMERCIAL BILLS DISCOUNTED TO TOTAL NOTE CIRCULATION[70]	DATE (END OF MONTH) 1920	PERCENTAGE OF COMMERCIAL BILLS DISCOUNTED TO TOTAL NOTE CIRCULATION[70]
1914	41.9	Jan.	1.0
1915	10.1	Feb.	1.6
1916	8.0	Mar.	3.1
1917	3.1	April	5.8
1918	1.2	May	9.0
1919	0.7	June	8.8
		July	8.6
		Aug.	7.6
		Sept.	7.2
		Oct.	6.8
		Nov.	5.5
		Dec.	3.7

DATE (END OF MONTH) 1921	PERCENTAGE OF COMMERCIAL BILLS DISCOUNTED TO TOTAL NOTE CIRCULATION[70]	DATE (END OF MONTH) 1922	PERCENTAGE OF COMMERCIAL BILLS DISCOUNTED TO TOTAL NOTE CIRCULATION[70]
Jan.	3.5	Jan.	1.3
Feb.	3.5	Feb.	1.4
Mar.	2.8	Mar.	1.5
April	2.5	April	1.6
May	2.2	May	2.1
June	1.9	June	2.6
July	1.3	July	4.0
Aug.	1.1	Aug.	8.6
Sept.	1.2	Sept.	15.1
Oct.	0.9	Oct.	20.9
Nov.	1.3	Nov.	32.1
Dec.	0.9	Dec.	32.6

DATE (END OF MONTH) 1923	PERCENTAGE OF COMMERCIAL BILLS DISCOUNTED TO TOTAL NOTE CIRCULATION[70]	DATE (END OF MONTH) 1923	PERCENTAGE OF COMMERCIAL BILLS DISCOUNTED TO TOTAL NOTE CIRCULATION[70]
Jan.	34.9	Aug.	24.6
Feb.	51.7	Sept.	13.0
Mar.	42.8	Oct.	42.2
April	45.4	Nov. 15	42.6
May	46.6	Nov. 30	86.8
June	39.9	Dec.	65.0
July	41.8		

[70] This total includes Reichsbank notes, Darlehnskassenscheine, Reichskassenscheine, and the notes of the four private banks with note issuing powers.

Source of data: *Zahlen zur Geldentwertung in Deutschland* 1914 *bis* 1923, *passim.*

mercial banks thus played a rôle of considerable importance. The ratio of Reichsbank discount of commercial bills to total note issues is given in Table VIII. Though, even in 1923, the ratio did not rise much above the status in 1914 it must be remembered that in the pre-war period the Reichsbank did comparatively little discounting for the government. The fillip given to inflation by the premium put on private borrowing from the Reichsbank cannot therefore be denied.[71] In this connection the relation between prices and exchange rates is worthy of notice. Up to 1923 domestic prices had risen much less than foreign exchange rates but in that year they no longer lagged behind. The conclusion is possibly warranted that the volume of notes issued as a result of Treasury operations only, huge as it was, had been short of the amount necessary to sustain the domestic price level on a basis of equality with the depreciation in the exchange value of the currency, but that, when Reichsbank credit was made easy to private banks and commercial borrowers, the total volume of means of payment was extended to any degree requisite to keep pace with the plunging value of the currency on the exchange markets.

The intensity of the stimulus toward borrowing from the Reichsbank may be gauged from a comparison of the sluggish rise in the discount rate at the central bank with the ever-accelerated pace of currency depreciation. From the early days of the war till the end of June 1922 the Reichsbank rate remained unchanged at 5%; it was raised to 6% in July, to 7% in August, 8% in September and 10% in November 1922, to 12% in January 1923, 18% in April, 30% in August and 90% in September. But these increases were as nothing when measured alongside the progressive lightening in the burden of a loan during the time for which it ran. Though, after September 1923, a bank or private individual had to pay at the rate of 900% per annum for a loan from the Reichsbank, this was no deterrent to borrowing. It would have been profitable to pay a so-called interest, in reality an insurance, charge, of thousands or even millions of per cents per annum, since the money in which the loan would be repaid was depreciating at a speed which would have left even rates like these far in the rear. With a 900% interest rate in September 1923 the Reichsbank was

[71] A good share of the borrowing was for the purpose of buying foreign exchange as an investment. cf. *Deutsche Währungs- und Kreditpolitik*, Rudolf Dalberg, Verlag von Reimar Hobbing, Berlin, 1926, p. 12. Foreign exchange could be used as collateral for further loans. Business concerns were therefore under no disability in acquiring accumulations of exchange. The privilege of borrowing on foreign exchange collateral was eventually withdrawn but exchange might then be used to buy stable-value German government loans which were, in turn, used as collateral for borrowings in marks.

practically giving money away and the same is true of the lower rates in the preceding months when the course of depreciation was not quite so headlong. The policy of the Reichsbank authorities in encouraging the discount of commercial bills that they might thus mitigate the scarcity of credit was but further evidence of the Alice-in-Wonderland determination of the directors of that institution to run ever faster in order to keep up with themselves. The scarcity of credit was due solely to currency depreciation and the cure prescribed was to increase the volume of means of payment! The Reichsbank could not refuse to discount Treasury bills[72] but the policy on commercial bills was a gratuitous mortification of an already fatal wound.

§ COMMERCIAL BANK DEPOSITS

Aside from accepting the opportunity to secure central bank credit which was thus thrust upon them, and of somewhat extending their own operations on the basis of this credit, the commercial banks played a subordinate part in the whole inflation process. Deposits in the commercial banks grew, of course, as paper money streamed forth from the Reichsbank, and the credits granted corresponded measurably with the upward surge of prices. But the commercial banks had no note issuing powers[78] and their own contribution to inflation was therefore necessarily confined to an expansion of loans the proceeds of which were left on deposit. No figures are available which make it possible to separate with any precision commercial deposits resulting from loans from those actually brought in by customers. Table IX, however, shows total bank deposits in comparison with total money in circulation and the ratio between them. Except in 1922, when rediscounting of commercial bills at the Reichsbank was being encouraged, the ratio, during inflation, was lower than in the pre-war period. The figure at the end of 1923 is affected by the fact that the currency reform had just then been gotten under way. Time deposits which had wellnigh vanished under the spell of depreciation were not yet being restored and the banks were extremely cautious about extensions of commercial

---

[72] In March 1922 the Reichsbankgesetz had been so amended as to make the institution "completely" independent of the government. The legislation was adopted under external political pressure and was a dead letter from the beginning.

[78] Besides the Reichsbank, the four *quasi-official* banks of Bavaria, Saxony, Würtemberg and Baden had the right to issue notes. (These banks are usually designated "the private banks of issue.") While their quota was from time to time, during the inflation years, extended, it was always insignificant in relation to Reichsbank issues and declined in comparative importance as inflation proceeded.

TABLE IX

BANK DEPOSITS AND MONEY IN CIRCULATION IN GERMANY; 1913 AND 1920–1924

(*Millions of Marks*)

END OF	1913	1920	1921	1922	1923	1924[74]
Deposits (demand and time) in seven large banks[75]	4,852	60,214	111,247	1,590,631	1,063,034,288[76]	3,572[77]
Deposits in all commercial banks[78]	9,642	83,891	154,989	2,216,067	1,481,019,370[76]	4,977[77]
Savings deposits	19,689	43,100	46,500	136,180	—	—
Total money in circulation	6,070[79]	81,388	122,500	1,295,231	2,274,000,000[76]	3,891
Ratio (per cent) of total *commercial* deposits to total money in circulation	158.8	103.1	126.5	171.1	65.1	127.9

[74] Gold marks.

[75] These are the deposits of the seven biggest Berlin banking institutions, namely: Deutsche Bank, Diskontogesellschaft (including the Schaffhausenscher Bankverein, absorbed in 1914), Dresdner Bank, Commerz-und-Privatbank, Mitteldeutsche Kreditbank, Bank für Handel und Industrie, and Nationalbank für Deutschland. In November 1921 the two last named institutions were amalgamated under the name Darmstädter und Nationalbank and the figures thereafter are for the six banks into which the original seven had by then evolved. In 1913 the deposits of these seven banks constituted about 50%, and in 1920, mainly as a result of amalgamations, 72% of all commercial deposits.

[76] 000,000 omitted.

[77] End of February 1925.

[78] Figures for total commercial deposits in 1913 refer to 160, and in 1920, to 105 commercial banks, the reduction in number being due to amalgamations. The figures for the total for all banks in 1921, 1922, 1923 and 1924 are estimates based on the relation of the deposits in the seven largest banks to the total deposits in 1920. Since this figure is merely an approximation the ratios in the bottom line are not precise.

[79] The figure for total monetary circulation has been changed from that quoted in the source so as to include gold as well as notes in circulation in 1913.

Source of data: *Memoranda on Currency* 1913-1921, 1913-1922, and 1913-1923, and *Memorandum on Currency and Central Banks* 1913-1925, League of Nations Publications, Geneva, 1922-1925, *passim*.

credit. The *ratio* of deposits had been further reduced by the incredibly rapid issue of bank notes in the last days of the old mark. The 1924 figure is given to show the gradual return to "normal" stable-standard conditions.

So far as *total* deposits go it would seem that operations of commercial banks had no inflationary effect except in 1922 and 1923 (up to the reform) and then only at the instigation of the Reichsbank.

This assertion is based on the facts that up to 1922 total deposits, as compared with 1913, had declined in importance relative to note issues and that the increase in the ratio in 1922, and till November 1923, was presumably due to the Reichsbank's encouragement of the rediscount of commercial bills. The index of deposits relative to total money in circulation, when expressed as a percentage of the 1913 ratio, was, for the end of the years 1920, 1921, 1922, 1923, respectively 65%, 80%, 108%, 41%. But a sizable part of the total deposits were time deposits which tended to disappear as the risk of depreciation grew. If therefore, instead of total deposits, demand deposits[80] of the type designated "Kreditoren," the deposits most affected by loans, are solely considered, a better picture of the action of the commercial banks in extending or reducing the scope of inflation will be obtained. Taking as a base the 1913 ratio of "Kreditoren" deposits to total money in circulation, the percentage figures for later years were as follows: 1920, 148%; 1921, 164%; 1922, 341%; 1923, 276%.[81] It would appear, therefore, that the commercial banks extended loans throughout the period of post-war inflation considerably in excess of a proportionate relationship with the increase in the monetary base and that the relative decline in total deposits was due to the shrinkage in the value, or the withdrawal from the banks, of time moneys at interest or to the general reluctance actually to *deposit* cash even if subject to demand draft. The increase in deposits issuing from *loans* was especially marked in 1922 and till stabilization in 1923, owing to the fact that rediscounting of commercial bills at the Reichsbank gave the private banks an enlarged base for extensions of credit. This increase was enough to carry upward the ratio figure for total *commercial* deposits. The growth in commercial bank loans took place in spite of the fact that the Reichsbank's rediscount of commercial bills was by no means confined to banks but was also done for approved business concerns and for individuals and at a rate far below what the commercial banks were charging. The explanation lies in the fact that only a certain group of business interests enjoyed the Reichsbank's favor and others were forced to go to the private banks. Nevertheless the commercial bills held by the Reichsbank at the end of 1922 formed nearly half of all

[80] Figures are available only on the basis of deposits payable within seven days. These are construed as demand deposits.

[81] Computed from data in the *Memorandum on Currency and Central Banks 1913-1924*, League of Nations Publications, Geneva, 1925, Vol. II, p. 269. The figure for 1923 is based on data in which no figures from the Deutsche Bank were included. It has been assumed that the movement in the Deutsche Bank paralleled that in the other institutions.

the commercial bills in circulation in Germany at that date. In view of
the fact that the central banking institution was supposed to accept
only bills of the first quality it may perhaps be assumed that the remaining moiety was ineligible.[82]

§ MONETARY RATHER THAN CREDIT ISSUES THE DOMINANT FACTOR

Though the increase in the ratio of loan-initiated deposits to total
money in circulation cannot be dismissed as a negligible factor in inflation the situation was nevertheless dominated throughout by monetary, as distinct from credit, expansion.[83] At times the swollen volume
of note issues pouring into the coffers of business concerns rendered
them in part independent of bank credit. This was markedly true in
the last war-year when note issues were rising faster than prices. The
ratio of "Kreditoren" deposits to total monetary circulation, as compared with the situation in 1913, was, at the end of the years 1914,
1915, 1916, 1917, 1918, respectively 103%, 125%, 109%, 101%,
and 83%. But whether or not deposits issuing from loans rose relatively to money in circulation they were basically dependent on the
money factor. The commercial banks had not in pre-war days based
their lending on anything other than Reichsbank notes and they never
altered that practice materially. The course of inflation, so far as the
volume of circulating medium may be taken as a criterion thereof, can
consequently be traced through note issues about as well as through
the total volume of means of payment. Since statistics on the latter are
available only at infrequent intervals, note issues alone will be used
in the later discussion as representative of the monetary supply.

§ NOTE ISSUES OTHER THAN THOSE OF THE REICHSBANK

The notes issued by the Reichsbank were always the principal but
not the sole element in the circulation. In the war and early post-war
days there were, in addition to coin, Reichsbank notes, and the notes
of the four other banks of issue, a considerable volume of Reichskassenscheine (Treasury notes) and Darlehnskassenscheine (Loan
Bureau notes). Gold and silver coin was withdrawn by the banks, or

---

[82] The *gold* value of the discounted commercial bills was never more than
half that of the pre-war Reichsbank holdings though the proportion of the
total of bills in circulation to the total supply of money was much above the pre-
war status. The gold value has little meaning, however, since, with the very
great increase in the rate of monetary turnover, the gold or goods value of the
total stock of both money and deposit credits shrank to a small fraction of the
pre-war figures.

[83] This is natural in other than Anglo-Saxon countries since the check and
deposit mechanism has there had a comparatively slight development.

otherwise disappeared from circulation, early in the war. The iron, zinc, copper, and aluminum token-coins, issued to take the place of silver in small transactions, vanished during the second half of 1922 when they became far more valuable as commodities than as money. A quantity of small emergency paper currency had been put out by various agencies during the war to take the place of coin. In the post-war inflation these issues were greatly extended to meet the recurring need for more currency when prices rose at so rapid a rate that the printing presses were unable to turn out the desired amount of Reichs-bank notes of the smaller denominations. In the second half of 1922 these casual issues were withdrawn but they were much more than re-placed by emissions under authority of the Minister of Finance who was empowered under stipulated conditions to grant, not only to municipalities but even to private firms, the right to issue notes. At the end of 1922 the total issue of such emergency currency is estimated to have been about 20 billions of marks as compared with the 1280 billions of Reichsbank notes outstanding at that date. During 1923 the output of this sanctioned emergency money increased tremendously and at the end of the year reached a total of about 7½ quintillion marks.[84] In the final weeks of inflation the federal railways also emitted their own emergency currency on such a gigantic scale as to amount, at the end of November 1923, to more than a quarter of the total issue of 400 quintillion marks of Reichsbank notes outstanding at that date. In the chaos then prevailing not only did these huge *authorized* issues of emergency money take place but "money" was put out, with no authority whatever, by any municipality, or private business under-taking, ready and able to obtain in this way costless purchasing power. How much of such "money" was spewed forth will never be known but for the occupied part of Germany it has been estimated at 180 quintillion marks,[84] or between a third and a half of the maximum figure of the Reichsbank issues. The total volume of mark emergency money of all types in circulation in the whole of Germany at the date of stabilization was thus about three-fourths as large as the issue of Reichsbank notes.

In Table X are given the amounts of the various types of *authorized* paper mark issues outstanding at several dates together with figures on the coin in circulation at the same dates.

Alongside the various forms of paper mark circulating medium a variety of so-called stable-value currencies had come into use. In April 1923 the government put out an issue of Treasury bills payable in

[84] cf. Germany's Economy, Currency and Finance, p. 67.

TABLE X

AUTHORIZED MONETARY CIRCULATION OTHER THAN STABLE-VALUE ISSUES OF 1923; 1913–1923

(Billions of Marks)

| DATE | PAPER MONEY—ORDINARY ISSUES | | | | | PAPER MONEY—EMERGENCY ISSUES | | TOTAL PAPER MONEY | TOTAL AUTHORIZED CURRENCY |
	COIN	REICHSBANK NOTES	TREASURY NOTES	LOAN BUREAU NOTES	NOTES OF THE FOUR OTHER BANKS OF ISSUE	STATE RAILWAY	OTHER ISSUES		
Average of 1913	3.70	2.12	0.11	—	0.14	—	—	2.37	6.07
End of 1914	2.84	5.05	0.23	0.45	0.13	—	—	5.86	8.70
" " 1915	1.69	6.92	0.33	0.97	0.14	—	—	8.36	10.05
" " 1916	0.88	8.06	0.35	2.87	0.16	—	—	11.44	12.32
" " 1917	0.21	11.47	0.35	6.27	0.16	—	—	18.25	18.46
" " 1918	0.17	22.19	0.36	10.11	0.28	—	—	32.94	33.11
" " 1919	0.11	35.69	0.33	13.78	0.26	—	—	50.06	50.17
" " 1920	0.24	68.81	0.32	12.03	0.23	—	—	81.39	81.63
" " 1921	0.47	113.64	0.20	8.32	0.33	—	—	122.49	122.96
" " 1922	—	1,280.10	0.21	13.45	1.47	—	15.46	1,310.69	1,310.69
Nov. 30 1923	—	400,267,640,300.00	—	—	70,686,050,000.00	114,800,000,000.00	3,400,000,000.00	518,538,326,350.00	518,538,326,350.00

Sources of data: (1) *Memorandum on Currency 1913-1923*, p. 105. (2) *Zahlen zur Geldentwertung in Deutschland 1914 bis 1923*, pp. 47, 48.

gold, and in August to October a long-term loan in terms of United States currency of the one, two, and five dollar denominations and intended for use as money, was put upon the market. This was followed by an emission of gold Treasury bonds on November 4. The latter was issued to serve as gold backing for emergency stable-value currency put out by local authorities.[85] All of the issues of stable-value currency in the last three months of inflation were intended to bridge the gap until the rentenmark could be introduced. They were much resorted to and, in the final weeks of the old standard, formed an important part of the total circulating medium. They had been preceded by nearly a year by gold and commodity loans raised by municipalities or business concerns whose obligations served some of the functions of money. The Roggenrentenbank, founded in Berlin in 1922, issued bonds payable in rye, and other organizations put out loans calling for repayment in coal, lignite, coke, potash, wood and kilowatt hours. In Hamburg, a gold currency issued by two of the banks of that city, against the deposit of foreign bills of exchange, functioned satisfactorily as money in the autumn of 1923.

§ REICHSBANK NOTES THE SOLE LEGAL TENDER

To the very end, however, the central government retained the paper mark as the sole paper legal tender. The reasons are understandable enough. Not to have done so would have been a repudiation of the currency on the part of the government itself, would no doubt have accelerated the already dizzy pace of depreciation, and would have left the administration without any assurance whatever of the wherewithal to carry on the business of the state.[86] Whatever the defects of the existing currency the authorities were unwilling to abandon the one horse they surely had while it could still keep them above the flood. Early in 1923, nevertheless, the quoting of prices in foreign currencies or in conventional gold units—a practice which had long been in use in foreign trade—became wellnigh universal in the business world. It proceeded geographically from the borders inward and, by trades, from manufacturing industry to wholesalers, to agriculture, and even-

[85] Scrip of this loan was printed and when deposited with the Reichskredit-gesellschaft served as cover for stable-value emergency currency. Several of the constituent States of the Reich followed the action of the central government in the issue of gold loans.

[86] It was far from likely that any sizable issue of securities denominated in gold could have been marketed by the federal government. The attempts to do so met with very indifferent success whenever payment in stable-value currencies was required though the sale was easy enough when payment in paper marks was permitted.

tually to retail commerce. After a prolonged struggle wages were put on a similar basis. The mark was thus no longer used as a unit of account even in transactions covering a relatively short period of time and, of all the functions of money, it still fulfilled only that of a medium of exchange. The pace of depreciation eventually became so rapid that even for this purpose it became intolerable. Foreign currencies began to circulate. The intensity of the desire for some form of money which would hold its value may be gauged from the fact that the government securities designed for use as money, to which reference has been made in the preceding pages, rose to a high paper-mark premium over the American dollars they were supposed to represent.[87] The rentenmark was long in gestation and, in the meantime, the supply of fixed-value currency was too limited to afford much relief especially as the hoarding of currency of this type made its rate of turnover very low. Though, at the end of October, the gold value of the total stable currencies which had been issued by governmental authority was almost as great as the gold value of the total Reichsbank note issues (124 and 144 million gold marks respectively)[88] both together were worth less than 5% of the pre-war circulation.[89] It is improbable that the stable-value currencies circulated more rapidly than at the normal pre-war rate while, on the other hand, the paper mark was moving around with astounding celerity. Though practically all prices were by then quoted in gold, or the equivalent, and, expressed in paper, were moving upward in more or less close correspondence with dollar exchange, the bulk of payments was still made with paper marks.

§ POSITION OF THE BANKS

In the whole bedlam into which banking and currency had fallen it has often been alleged that the banks, and especially the Reichsbank, were great losers in the national *Casino* which was Germany. It is

[87] At one time the premium was as much as 600%. This was possible, of course, only by reason of the restrictions on foreign exchange transactions.

[88] Converted at the dollar rate of October 31.

[89] The amount of foreign currency hoarded, or in use, in Germany at this time is unknown, but may have been as much as the equivalent of two to three billion gold marks. *cf. Währungszerfall und Währungsstabilisierung*, Paul Beusch, Verlag von Julius Springer, Berlin, 1928, p. 8. The rate of turnover of this foreign currency was, however, very slow and though its value was probably several times as great as that of the total mark issues it did not do nearly as much monetary work. The use of foreign currencies, however, was a factor of considerable importance in depressing the value of the mark by limiting its sphere of circulation. On the other hand, each currency was used to buy the other and this increase in the use of the mark may have operated to support its value.

true that the Reichsbank lent, at low real rates of interest, stupendous sums to the government, commercial banks, and business men, and that these sums were repaid in money the value of which had withered away during the course of the loan. But the loans cost the Reichsbank nothing but printing expenses. The interest return was sufficient to meet operating charges and leave something over for profits. These profits when realized were, it is true, worth next to nothing. Measured in stable values the Reichsbank therefore made but small profits in the inflation years but it suffered no real losses except in the decline of its gold reserve. This decline was not due to inflation, as such, but to special causes of which mention will later be made.

The commercial banks may at times have suffered under inflation but as it progressed they began to exact from borrowers such interest rates as would more than cover the anticipated (though perhaps not the realized) decline in the value of the currency during the period for which the loans were to run. Their liabilities as well as their assets were diminished by currency depreciation and their only real loss occurred when they assumed demand liabilities, immediately called, in exchange for assets which were due only after the expiration of a certain term. When the practice of rediscounting commercial bills at the Reichsbank was renewed, and new loanable funds were thus obtained by the commercial banks, the risk of loss was thrown on the central institution which shed it in turn upon the public. The commercial banks were able to extend their physical assets very considerably in the years of high inflation. In spite of governmental regulations against the acquisition of foreign currencies for investment purposes they also acquired stable-value assets abroad[90] and their prosperity is attested by the mushroom growth, at this time, of small competing institutions. Most of the latter did not long survive the return of stable monetary conditions but this is certainly no evidence that inflation was not a favoring influence. The paper profits realized by the commercial banks, like those of the Reichsbank, were of course highly contractile as the value of the mark marched toward zero, and the real profits or losses of any given institution were dependent upon the ability of its administration to grasp what was happening and to

[90] In 1921 those assets of the German banks which, in the United States, would be included under the heading "Due from other Banks," part of which were foreign assets in stable-value currencies, were 12% of liabilities; in 1922 they were 47%. On the other hand, bill holdings, mainly Treasury bills, fell from 60% of all liabilities in 1920 to 46% in 1921 and to 20% in 1922. In addition to deposits abroad the banks held a considerable volume of depreciation-proof securities. cf. Economic Review, Vol. VIII, No. 7, London, August 17, 1923, p. 136.

take appropriate action. On the whole, such ability was not conspic-
uously common, and the banks, as a group, did not emerge from inflation in as good condition as might reasonably have been expected. It
has indeed been suggested that the big industrial borrowers virtually
stole the banks[91] but, insofar as this occurred, the commercial bank
directorates largely recouped their losses at the expense of the Reichsbank while the Reichsbank losses were only scraps of paper. The real
transfer of property was from the hands of holders of currency, or of
fixed-interest investments, to those of the entrepreneurs.

VI. MILITARY SANCTIONS AND GERMAN RESISTANCE

§ OCCUPATIONS OF DÜSSELDORF AND OF THE RUHR

The occupation of Düsseldorf, Duisburg and Ruhrort in 1921 and of
the Ruhr district in 1923 were both attended by interference with German control of customs. The customs barrier between the Rhineland
and the remainder of Germany, set up in the former occupation, was
withdrawn on October 1, 1921, after the Germans had accepted the
Allied terms on reparations. The *occupation*, however, continued. In
the case of the Ruhr, not only was a new customs area created and
special import and export duties levied but exports from the district
were altogether prohibited except under special license for which a
stiff price (in foreign currency) was charged. Taxes other than duties
were also imposed in the interest of the occupying Powers and were
made payable on a stable-value basis and even in foreign currency.

Immediately upon the marching in of the French and Belgian troops
the Reich government had forbidden its employees, including railroad
workers, to cooperate with the invaders, and had urged the industrial
leaders of the district to offer every possible resistance to the "enemy."
Not only were reparations (in kind) to the occupying Powers suspended
but, at the instance of the central government, coal deliveries were
refused even after payment had been offered the producers. The district simply went on strike. To this resistance of the Germans the
French commanders replied with extreme measures of coercion. Many
civil functionaries and many of the railroad workers and their families
were expelled. Industrial leaders who did not prove amenable were
thrown into prison. Courts-martial were frequent, seizures and confis-
cations of cash and commodities were common, and blood flowed freely.

The economic life of the district was stricken as by paresis and
the idle German workers became a charge on the central government.
Though this, in itself, would have been an insupportable burden, the

[91] *cf. The Recovery of Germany*, J. W. Angell, Yale University Press, New
Haven, 1929, p. 43.

Cuno government, through the Reichsbank, put huge credits at the disposal of the Ruhr industrialists.[92] The occupying Powers obtained little or nothing on reparations but Germany was brought to the brink of destruction. It is impossible to censure the German decision to resist the invasion to the limit but the abandon with which mark credits and Reichsbank notes were flung about was nothing short of financial insanity.

VII. SUMMARY AND CONCLUSIONS

In the closing phase of inflation there was little external pressure on *exchange* rates since all cash reparations were suspended. The exigencies of government finance within the country were then of almost exclusive import. Whether, in a consideration of the causes operating *throughout* the course of inflation, major stress is, as in this last phase, to be laid upon revenues inadequate for obligations volitionally assumed, or upon inescapable demands imposed from without, is a thorny question. The foregoing discussion attempts to show that certain alleged causes of depreciation such as speculation, or the losses of territory, population, and resources under the Treaty of Versailles, had almost no real influence, and that but a very slight measure of responsibility can be laid at the door of the private banking organization. The crux of the matter was the state of the public finances. The sequel will indicate that, up to 1923, exchange rate movements tended to dominate the status of the fisc. Since exchange rate movements were chiefly conditioned by obligations imposed from without, the principal *immediate* causes of the collapse of the German currency are to be traced to the action of the Entente Allies rather than to that of Germany herself. These immediate causes were, however, not necessarily definitive. Depreciation, as measured by internal prices rather than exchange rates, is ultimately dependent solely on note issues.[93] The decision as to whether notes should be issued lay with the German administrations. The hard fact of external pressure was, in itself, enough to ruin the *exchange* value of the currency, though a more than Spartan

[92] This was done, allegedly, to enable the industrialists to produce for stock rather than permit the French to benefit by export duties on sales outside the district. In actual fact, credits were so freely disbursed that they were used for speculation in foreign exchange and other purposes alien to the presumed intent of the administration. The mark was thus attacked from both sides at the same time and the government was furnishing the ammunition. The Reichsbank even refrained from any careful scrutiny of credit demands from the unoccupied area in order to forestall protests alleging discrimination.

[93] cf. infra, Chaps. IV-VI.

tax policy might perhaps have preserved its *internal* value.[94] The several administrations, however, though at times resolute, were fundamentally weak, and the interests on whom taxation must fall if it was to be productive were powerful enough to delay, or defeat, the passage of legislation. The slightest delay was fatal. In large measure inflation was carried forward by its own momentum[95] and it seems probable that, even without the reckless financial policy pursued in 1923, the final result would have been changed but little. Complete collapse might have been delayed but it lay in the stars. Nothing could have stopped inflation but the coincident retraction of strong external pressure and the stiffening of internal resistance. For this, nothing but the collapse, itself, sufficed.

[94] At the Conference of Brussels, in December 1920, neutral experts declared, however, that the German tax burden was nowhere surpassed and had reached the limit of the people's capacity. *cf. Das Geldproblem in Mitteleuropa*, Elemer Hantos, Verlag von Gustav Fischer, Jena, 1925, p. 20. The direct tax burden was, as we have seen, greatly lightened with the progress of inflation. The smallest real incomes sometimes paid extremely heavy surtaxes by reason of their increase in nominal amount. But, except on those incomes where the levy and payment were made at the source, the real burden was slight by the time the tax was actually paid.

[95] Inertia was favored by the attitude of the courts. Until very late in the inflation period the Reichsgericht refused to recognize the fundamental change in the value of the monetary unit which was in progress but kept insisting that a mark was a mark. So long as this attitude was maintained, borrowing, even at high rates of interest, was likely to prove extremely profitable and the greater the borrowing the larger grew the issues of currency.

CHAPTER III

BUSINESS REGULATION UNDER INFLATION

§ INTRODUCTORY

THE stresses developed under inflation evoked a series of governmental measures, and a private code of business practice, markedly different from that prevailing under stable monetary conditions. The present chapter will briefly describe such measures and practice.

I. GOVERNMENTAL REGULATION OF BUSINESS

Like many another government the German administrations while pumping money into circulation with one hand kept attempting to curb the inevitable effects with the other. The efforts to combat the manifestations of inflation took the following forms:

(1) Regulation of internal prices
(2) Regulation of foreign trade
(3) Regulation of dealings in foreign exchange
(4) Regulation of foreign exchange by direct action.

1. *Regulation of Prices*

The course of internal prices will be treated in detail in ensuing chapters and it will be sufficient here to say that the pressure on the government to take steps toward mitigating hardships induced legislation designed to keep down the cost of foodstuffs, of certain other commodities, and of housing. The methods adopted were similar to those employed in many other countries in the war and post-war years. Some of the measures employed in Germany in the inflation period were simply a continuation or resurrection of the war-time price-control. In the case of foodstuffs the supplies were rationed, part of the cost of certain staples was borne by the government, and farmers were required to deliver a quota of their harvests at arbitrarily established prices. *Commodity* price control applied however to relatively few articles, was not continuous, and, when it was operative, had the effect of setting up price differentials in the same article rather than of exerting any general influence.[1] With house rents, on the other hand, legis-

---

[1] The general policy of control was abandoned at the end of 1921 and only

lation was extremely important. Tenants were protected from eviction so long as they paid rentals officially determined on the basis of pre-war charges. The amount collectible was occasionally raised as inflation proceeded but the increases always lagged far behind the existing depreciation of the currency and were quickly rendered nugatory by the further loss of value of the monetary unit. At all times after 1920 rentals were more or less nominal, and, in the period of hyper-inflation,[2] housing was obtained practically free of charge. Except for a possible reversion when financial order should be restored the property of the landlords was to all intents and purposes confiscated.[3] The regulation of rentals had wide repercussions. It reduced the cost of living and diminished the pressure for wage advances to compensate for the rise in commodity prices.[4] It was thus a factor in keeping those prices below what they would otherwise have been[5] and in widening the differential between the domestic price structure and that of the outside world. Domestic prices, converted at current rates of exchange, were always low relative to those in countries with stable currencies.

Other causes, primarily connected with the foreign exchange markets, were, however, somewhat more influential in establishing the spread between external and internal prices and in leading, as a consequence, to the regulation of foreign trade.

2. *Regulation of Foreign Trade*[6]

§ WAR-TIME CONTROL

Control of exports and imports had been established during the war, first, to ensure to Germany a full supply of domestically-produced essen-

---

sporadic action was taken thereafter. Illicit trading at prices markedly higher than the official quotations was always rife.

[2] It is, of course, not possible to draw a strict line between high- and hyper-inflation but the latter period may be considered to have begun its course about the middle of 1921.

[3] Legal title was, of course, not disturbed but for the time being the possession of residential real estate was rather more likely to be a liability than an asset.

[4] Rentals on new houses were not strictly controlled but the generally low rate of wages made it impossible for workers to pay the rent necessary to yield any reasonable return on the cost of building new dwellings. A marked shortage of housing was the inevitable result.

[5] The writer does not here wish to take any position on the general question of the causal relationship between wages and commodity prices. There can, however, be little doubt that wages were at least *proximately* determined at this time by the cost of living and, insofar as rent restriction lowered the worker's cost of living, it had its effect on wages.

[6] The following account is derived mainly from: (1) *Grundriss der Sozial-*

tials of war and to prevent their egress into enemy hands and, second, to limit the domestic consumption of non-essential imports so that the import of war-materials might be more easily financed. When mark exchange began to waver in 1917 attention was directed mainly toward the preservation of the exchange value of the German currency and the control was enlarged and intensified. The administration of foreign trade control was at first in the hands of the Ministry of the Interior but, in 1916, a Federal Commissar for Export and Import Permits was appointed. He was assisted by an advisory council of representatives from the German Trade Council, the German Board of Agriculture, the War Committee of German Industry, and from all of the government ministries which were, or might be, interested. The Commissar, however, had a rather free hand during the war when the issues involved were simple and subject to little dispute.

§ AIMS OF POST-WAR CONTROL

In 1919, control other than by normal trade regulations was abandoned, partly as a reaction against the rigors of war and partly because the enemy occupation of the Rhineland made it impossible to enforce the measures which had hitherto obtained. Goods streamed in through the "Hole in the West" opened up by the Allied occupation and the feeling grew strong that the rapid decline in mark exchange which took place at that time was to be solely attributed to this cause.[7] On the other hand, the fall in mark exchange, both absolutely and in relation to internal prices, led to a draining of Germany of all exportable goods and to marked scarcity of essential domestic products in the home markets. At the end of 1919 limited control measures were therefore again adopted and early in 1920 the Germans were able to obtain the cooperation of the authorities in the occupied districts in the reestablishment of an effective customs frontier.

The objects of foreign trade control in the post-war period were of course other than those principally aimed at during the war. The protection of mark exchange, and of the German economy in general, against

ökonomik, V Abteilung, II Teil, *Der Moderne Handel*, Julius Hirsch, Verlag von J. C. B. Mohr, Tübingen, 1925, pp. 166 ff. (2) *Die deutsche Aussenhandelskontrolle*, Ernst Grünfeld, Bonner Staatswissenschaftliche Untersuchungen, Kurt Schröder, Bonn and Leipzig, 1922, *passim*. (3) *Die deutsche Ausfuhrkontrolle nach dem Kriege*, Arnold Richard Schwarz, L. Bamberg, Greifswald, 1923, *passim*.

[7] Smuggling was widely prevalent and many companies sprang up in Holland offering insurance against seizure. After this "Hole in the West" had been closed in 1920 the premium went to 15% and business declined. It is improbable that there was any great amount of inward smuggling thereafter except during the periods of further occupation of German territory.

such consequences of exchange vagaries as could not otherwise be prevented was the dominant purpose. Import was much less thoroughly regimented than export though licenses were required, and quotas established, for all imports other than textile raw materials and certain foodstuffs. Luxury imports were strictly limited.

In the control of *exports* the following complex ends were sought:

(i) *Assurance for the home population of a sufficient supply of necessaries.* Foodstuff exports were unconditionally prohibited, a certain latitude was given in the case of raw materials, while manufactured goods were, in the main, freely exportable.

(ii) *Assurance of reasonable prices.* Since domestic prices consistently lagged far behind the upward surge of exchange rates there was a constant tendency for such German exporters as were basing their quotations on domestic market conditions to sell their goods at extremely low prices when measured in stable-value currencies. The foreign exchange proceeds of exports tended therefore to provide for but a very limited volume of imports. The terms of international trade thus moved strongly against the Germans. In order to prevent a "selling-out" of the country at bargain-counter rates exporters were forbidden to dispose of their goods below certain minimum prices officially established for every transaction. This procedure was initiated not only to prevent exploitation of the German economy but to forestall the adoption of anti-dumping duties by foreign countries whose manufacturers were setting up a violent protest against the admission of German goods at prices with which they could not hope to compete. In addition to the system of minimum prices the necessity of invoicing in foreign exchange was urgently presented to exporters.

(iii) *Assurance that the foreign exchange proceeds would be brought back to Germany.* In order to avoid the loss of purchasing power which was involved in holding mark balances there was a strong disposition on the part of exporters to leave abroad the foreign exchange proceeds of their exports rather than convert them into marks. The supplies of foreign exchange requisite for imports and reparations were thus not forthcoming and, to combat this situation, the permit to export was made conditional on the delivery to the authorities of a smaller or larger share of the foreign exchange proceeds according as the raw materials required for the manufacture of the commodity in question were or were not of foreign origin.

(iv) *The participation of the Reich in the gains on export trade.* Since the minimum prices on goods sold abroad were ordinarily much above those currently prevailing in the domestic markets exporters were in a highly advantageous position as compared with producers of goods for home consumption. There was no reason for permitting the price differential officially established to accrue to one favored class. Duties were therefore imposed on exports. The rates actually levied, averaging about 3% of the price, were much too low to bring about equality in the position of exporters and other producers but, in the later days of inflation, they provided about one-sixth of all the tax revenues of the Reich. This sizable proportion was due rather to the decline in other revenues than to the absolute importance of the tax on exports.

§ ADMINISTRATIVE MACHINERY AND PROCEDURE

While the desirability, and even necessity, of a renewal of strict control of foreign trade was generally recognized in 1920, industry was then in no mood to accept the yoke which had been imposed during the war. Rehabilitation of the whole economic life of the country had at first been attempted by organized industry along consciously planned, rather than *laissez-faire*, lines (Planwirtschaft), and foreign trade control was part of this program. When this effort broke down the business leaders were unwilling to surrender to the government the independence just retrieved from the restraints of the war and would support measures designed to regiment foreign trade only on condition that the regulations should be imposed by their own organizations. To establish quotas of export and import, to determine the right to such quotas, to fix "reasonable" prices, and to levy varying rates of duty was a task of such magnitude as, in any case, to require the cooperation of all the interests affected. In 1922 the daily dispatch of goods amounted to more than 70,000 individual consignments, each requiring separate attention from the foreign trade control organization. To ensure expert judgment, especially in the matter of price revision on so large and varied a volume of transactions, resort was perhaps necessarily had to the trade associations and, in an effort to prevent arbitrary decisions, the system of Boards of Foreign Trade Control (Aussenhandelsstellen) was set up.

Procedure was as follows: The basic policy was decided by the Federal administration and permits were issued through the Federal Commissar for Import and Export Permits (Reichskommissar für Ein- und Ausfuhrbewilligungen). This officer was assisted by 150 immediate subordinates (Reichsbevollmächtigte) each of whom had a separate branch of industry under his jurisdiction and consulted with an advisory council of representatives of the manufacturers, dealers, workers, and consumers of the commodities with which he was concerned. On this basis seventy Boards of Foreign Trade Control were gradually built up, many with numerous subsidiaries, in all, 170 different boards with 4000 to 5000 persons engaged. Each of these boards pursued a separate and arbitrary policy. The minimum prices set on exports were supposed to be established on the basis of quotations in world markets but the practical policy seems to have been to fix low supplements to the domestic price in cases where the producing industry was depressed and high supplements where business was active. The whole organization was most unwieldy; there was no real coordination and no fixed rules of procedure. Special price examination offices (Preisprüfungstellen) did not greatly improve the situation. The real power lay in the hands of the subordinates of the Commissar, the Reichsbevollmächtigten, who distributed the assigned quotas, determined prices, and were charged with the duty of securing the designated share of the foreign exchange proceeds of exports.

These Boards of Foreign Trade Control exerted a powerful but indeterminate influence on external trade. Records, if ever compiled in any comprehensive way, have disappeared, and whether the activities of the boards were beneficial, on the whole, or vicious, is a much disputed question to which no certain answer can be given.[8] The matter will receive further attention in Chapter VIII.

3. *Regulation of Dealings in Foreign Exchange*[9]

Regulation of dealings in foreign exchange was undertaken in a long series of legislative and administrative decrees which imposed restrictions on the purchase of foreign money, prohibited the sale abroad of German currency,[10] or the purchase of foreign currency at rates other than those officially fixed in Berlin,[11] and required exporters to turn over to the Reichsbank the foreign exchange proceeds of their sales. It was also forbidden to demand payment in foreign currency in any domestic transaction and sellers of goods on the domestic market were laid under obligation to accept German currency.

As early as September 1919 a law designed to prevent the "flight of capital" prescribed that payments to foreign countries should be made only through banks and, in October 1921, legislation was passed giving

[8] The story of each of the boards was projected but only one small volume ever appeared and the information which it gives is not highly illuminating.

[9] This section is largely a résumé of the account in *Germany's Economy, Currency and Finance*, p. 69.

[10] The authorities evidently attempted a distinction between the purchase of foreign currency and the sale of the German. It is submitted that the two things were identical.

[11] In 1923 a considerable difference between the Berlin rates and those of other foreign exchange centers developed. In this book the Berlin rates are used throughout with one exception. See *infra* Table XIII. Wherever differences prevailed the Berlin rate applied to most of the transactions.

to the Reichsbank partial control of the proceeds of exports. The principal exchange regulations date, however, from early 1922. In February of that year it was enacted that transactions in foreign exchange must be confined to a limited group of specially authorized banks and then only on notification to the Ministry of Finance. Later in the year the permission of the Ministry was made a *prerequisite*, but firms which could show a certificate from a Chamber of Commerce that, in the nature of their business, foreign exchange transactions were regularly conducted were exempt from the ordinance. The loophole to evasion thus given rendered the measure of little effect. In May 1923 bank loans on foreign currency were prohibited, and loans on foreign bills were subjected to registration, with the purpose of preventing any holder of foreign exchange from retaining it as an investment or using it as collateral to secure funds for current needs. If this practice were prevented it was thought that private holdings of foreign exchange would be forced on the market. The Reichsbank was given the right to claim foreign currency and precious metals. This legislation was supplemented in September 1923 by a decree appointing a special commissioner with the most absolute powers of requisition of foreign means of payment including securities.[12] Previous to this, in June and August 1922, the order that transactions in foreign exchange must be made only at the officially established rates was promulgated and it was also decreed that marks must not be sold directly or indirectly to persons living abroad nor in any way placed at their disposal. The number of dealers who might legally carry on transactions in exchange was progressively reduced throughout the inflation period and control was centered in the Reichsbank. Finally, by ordinances of September 17 and November 2, 1923, a general obligation was imposed on exporters to hand over the foreign exchange proceeds of their sales to the Reichsbank.[13]

---

[12] "He may demand any information, may examine into anyone's affairs, search anyone; summon anyone before him to make declarations, and require anyone to make solemn affirmation as to the correctness and completeness of his declarations. He may seize in favor of the Reich without any compensation all foreign payment media acquired illegitimately or retained contrary to his orders. He may withdraw from banks the right to transact or negotiate business in foreign currency or in outstanding debts calculated in foreign currency; he may also withdraw from firms their Chamber of Commerce certificate and from persons and corporations the permit to do business on the stock exchange. He may limit the number of foreign-bills banks and of firms in possession of the Chamber of Commerce certificate mentioned above; he is also empowered to issue regulations for the transfer to, and import from, foreign countries of objects of value." See *Germany's Economy, Currency and Finance*, p. 70.

[13] That is, such proceeds as were not used immediately for the purchase of

Some of this regulation was perverse and all of it was futile. Bootlegging in exchange was widely prevalent, other evasion of the law was not unduly difficult, and it is questionable whether the interference of the government did not partially induce the evils it was designed to prevent. There is at any rate no evidence that it mitigated them in the slightest degree.

4. Regulation of Exchange by Direct Action

Several direct attempts to influence exchange were made by the Reichsbank on behalf of the government. The first of these was undertaken in the summer of 1922 when, after the chilling report of the Reparations Commission's Loan Committee and the assassination of Dr. Rathenau, the bottom fell out of the exchange market. The task of supporting exchange was reluctantly assumed by the Reichsbank and only after strong pressure from the government. The Reichsbank president, Havenstein, regarded it as ill advised, the whole matter was handled irresolutely, and the results were negligible.

A spirited intervention, however, was undertaken in the early months of 1923 in support of the policy of passive resistance to Allied coercion. It has already been pointed out that the invasion of the Ruhr was the signal for a renewed and precipitous decline in mark exchange. On the date of entry, January 11, the exchange rate was 10,260 marks to the dollar. On the thirty-first of that month it was 49,000. The German government was convinced that unless the decline in exchange was checked, passive resistance, to which it felt itself driven, was hopeless. For exchange operations which were likely to prove expensive it had no resources of its own but through all the vicissitudes of the time the Reichsbank had managed to hold on to a gold stock of over a billion marks. Except for the episode in 1922 it had consistently refused to risk any considerable portion of this sum in support of mark exchange but it was now prevailed on to make a determined effort in this direction. Had the finances of the government been in order, and had the flood of paper mark issues been able to be checked, the attempt could hardly have failed. On January 31, 1923, the total issue of paper currency (practically all of which was Reichsbank notes) was almost exactly two trillion (2,000,000,000,000) marks. At the exchange rate of that day this sum was worth about 172 million gold marks. The Reichsbank's gold reserve in its own vaults was 954 million marks, enough to redeem the total paper circulation at the existing exchange rate more than five times over. Given no new issues of paper currency and no reissues

raw materials or were turned in to the Boards of Control of Foreign Trade. The latter sums were eventually turned over to the Reichsbank in any case.

of redeemed notes the withdrawal of the paper currency from circulation by purchase with gold could easily have been continued, if necessary, until there was no paper left. Since no cash reparations were then
being paid there would have been no unconditionally necessary drain
of gold abroad and the chance of exhaustion of a 100% gold currency
by ordinary international business transactions is nil. As a matter of
fact all similar experience has shown that it would merely have been
necessary to establish confidence that the exchange value of the mark
would not fall below the current rate. If this had been accomplished
it would not only have been possible to keep in circulation the existing volume of paper but the wellnigh inevitable slowing down of the
rate of monetary turnover would have required greatly increased issues
if an inconveniently rapid rise in the value of the mark was to be
obviated.[14]

The intervention of the Reichsbank did, in fact, not only keep the
mark from falling farther at this time but, within a fortnight, had
multiplied its exchange value two and a half times. This was done
without any net deduction from the bank's gold reserve since it soon
developed that the bank could sell more marks against gold or foreign
currencies than it was obliged to buy. Prices steadied with the rise in
exchange rates, the real value of tax revenues mounted, and the ratio of
tax receipts to total expenditures increased. But with the immense new
burdens involved in the policy of passive resistance the improvement
was relative only. The absolute magnitude of the deficits continued to
expand and the one essential to permanent success, the cessation of
further note issues, was lacking. For two months and a half the bank
kept up the unequal struggle and maintained stability in the exchange
value of the currency but it was impossible to continue indefinite redemption of notes when for every million marks taken out of the circulation by exchange operations hundreds of millions were, at the behest
of the government, thrown upon the domestic market.

On the eighteenth of April demands for foreign exchange had to be
rationed by the bank and the final collapse of the currency began. In
July one more attempt to stem the tide was made. It was, however, but
a feeble and futile gesture and was soon abandoned. The successful
stabilization and redemption finally effected through the rentenmark—
merely a new tenor of paper currency—shows what might have been
done with gold. The two situations differed in only one vital respect.
When the rentenmark was introduced, an abrupt end was made of the

[14] cf. for example, *The Austrian Crown*, J. van Walré de Bordes, P. S. King &
Son, Ltd., London, 1924, *passim*.

rediscounting of Treasury bills;[15] during the earlier attempt at stabilization, on the contrary, rediscounting had proceeded at an ever increasing
tempo. By the time the successful effort at the end of 1923 was made the
costly pursuit of passive resistance had been given up; provided further
depreciation was avoided expenditures were, in consequence, within the
range of the yield from taxes; the right hand which offended with constant new emissions of currency had been cut off, and the work of the
left was thus not without avail.

II. BUSINESS PRACTICE[16]

§ FORESTALLING, ENGROSSING, AND REGRATING

Even where not subject to artificial control the response of different
groups of prices to the stimulus of inflation was very unequal. In practically all the vicissitudes of prices, moreover, wages were relatively
slow to move. The creditor was a fellow sufferer with the worker and
this is true of short- as well as of long-term loans since interest rates,
even on short loans, were never raised sufficiently to prevent a nega-
tive return to the lender. The shifting of income from the wage and
lending groups to industrial and trading enterprisers called forth great
numbers of middlemen who sought to take advantage of the increase in
the spread between the prices received by producers and those paid by the
consuming population, a spread which grew larger the longer the goods
were kept in circulation.[17] Forestalling, engrossing, and regrating, the
familiar progeny of declining currencies, became wellnigh universal
As the tempo of depreciation increased these traits of traders developed
into a positive reluctance to sell. Buyers, on the other hand, were eager
to purchase anything at all which would maintain its value. The effect
on prices of this reversal of ordinary business psychology may be
imagined. The more rapid the rise in prices the greater became the intensity of demand.[18] Business boomed, unemployment vanished, sales
were all too easy. There was of course an enormous amount of buying
which, under other circumstances, would have been quite senseless.

[15] With the introduction of the rentenmark the Treasury was helped over a
short transition period till taxes could take care of expenditures—a result
achieved almost solely because stabilization proved successful—by means of a
loan in the new currency.

[16] The material of this section is mainly derived from *Grundriss der Sozialökonomik, Der Moderne Handel*, pp. 38 ff.

[17] The gain in paper marks was in many cases merely an accounting profit.
The real gain, if any, after goods had been replaced was not nearly as large.

[18] People were not only *ready* to buy but were ardently determined to spend
as rapidly as possible all the money they possessed. The circulation of the
money of course kept this lively demand constantly renewed.

People purchased not what they wanted to use but whatever they could get, and the function of prices in directing production into the lines most likely to satisfy consumers was almost completely abrogated. One could produce anything material and be sure of a market. Corporations could not wait to distribute dividends to their stockholders without the latter losing all but a negligible fraction of the company's earnings. Profits were therefore immediately invested in "improvements" with little regard to the future or even present usefulness of such investments except as they were not so grossly inefficient storers of value as money had become.

§ EFFECT OF INFLATION ON OVERHEAD COSTS

With any temporary halt in the course of depreciation, and still more with a reversal of the movement, the shock to business as it had developed was of course very severe. Not only did the sellers' immediately change to a buyers' market, but producing organizations were prone to shut down instantly. Overhead costs, *on the books*, had become but a negligible fraction of total expenses. In some respects this was a real and in others an illusory gain to the producing concern. The real weight of interest on bonds and similar charges all but vanished[19] but, so far as productive physical property was concerned, it was of course poor accounting to continue to regard its worth, as expressed in the old immensely more valuable monetary unit, as comparable with similar nominal values in the highly depreciated unit in which the product was being sold. But, whatever the real situation, the low ratio of overhead costs, as reckoned on the books, greatly diminished the normal hesitation over a shutdown. So long as the march of prices did not show a consistent upward trend industry was therefore subject to a malarial infection with alternate fevers of activity and chills of depression.

§ FORMS OF CAPITAL ACCUMULATION

The loss of substance to which the lender of money was subjected very quickly suppressed the inclination to lend or to save in the monetary form. Except for the ploughing-in of profits by business concerns the accumulation of capital goods practically ceased.[20] Before the introduction of stable-value loans denominated in rye, coal, etc., long-term capital was, it is true, acquired partly by the sale of stock but, for the most part, new note issues provided the principal substitute for the former

---

[19] As in all other such cases "creditors were seen running away from debtors and debtors pursuing them in triumph and paying them without mercy."

[20] More or less durable *consumers'* goods are here excluded from the concept of capital goods.

mode of saving. Long-term needs were met either out of profits or by repeated short-term bank borrowing.[21] Since the borrowing concern received the notes when first issued it obtained them when their purchasing
power was relatively high. A form of involuntary saving was thus imposed upon all existing holders of money whose consuming power was
presently diminished by the automatic reduction in the value of money
which attended the new issue of notes. This involuntary saving accrued
to the borrower free of cost. It became *national* saving, of course, only
when used for investment purposes.

So far as capital was raised by sales of stock it became customary to
issue, to German nationals, preference shares with multiple voting
powers. This action was one phase of a general attempt to prevent the
foreign acquisition of German property (commodities or securities) at
the external rather than the internal value of the mark. Securities were
selling at levels which were essentially part of the domestic price structure and, though low, were within hailing distance of the prices of
domestic commodities. But, with the exchange value of the mark greatly
below its domestic purchasing power, they could be bought with foreign
exchange at prices which bore almost no relation to their real value
measured in terms either of foreign or domestic commodities. There was
thus a strong tendency for industry to be gobbled up by foreign investors
and for control to pass out of the hands of the Germans. On the whole,
however, the shift of ownership was much less than might have been
expected.[22]

§ SHIFTING OF THE INCIDENCE OF INFLATION

The action taken to prevent the loss of control of industry was paralleled by the raising of prices on exports above those prevailing in
the domestic market. Not only were prices on exports fixed by official
action but the sellers asserted against the buyer, both domestic and
foreign, further rights to protect themselves against losses arising from
inflation. Instead of delivering at a stated date they reserved the right
to deliver when they would, or even not to deliver at all, and this was
done despite the terms of existing contracts to the contrary.[23] Sliding

[21] In a good many cases, however, new issues of stock were made solely for
the purpose of paying off bank loans. This tended to happen whenever the
banks became restive about the liquidity of their assets.

[22] This was true of almost all forms of property. Legislative obstruction to
transfers to foreigners was common though not overt. A law put into effect
by Prussia, for instance, precluded transfers of urban real estate without the
consent of the local authorities.

[23] The dissatisfaction thus caused frequently led to the refusal of foreign

scales of prices, measured according to a variety of indices, were also adopted, and attempts were made to put the risk of exchange and price fluctuations upon the buyer. This might be accomplished either by quoting in terms of foreign exchange, with payment in marks at the prevailing rate, or by requiring payment in foreign currencies. Prepayment was insisted upon sometimes before work was begun, but, in any case, before delivery. If payment in marks was accepted it became customary to demand the equivalent of the foreign exchange price on the day, or even hour, of the *arrival* of the remittance. After dealings in foreign exchange had been restricted and the supply rationed, the risk of loss, even *after* the arrival of the mark payment, was thrust on the buyer. Finally, payment in marks was refused altogether whenever this was permissible under the existing legislation and, in numerous cases, where it was not.

§ WAGE ADJUSTMENTS

A thoroughgoing change in business practice occurred in the adjustment of wages to rising cost of living.[24] In the early post-war years the development of a system of regulation of the relations between employer and employed had brought the great majority of workers within the scope of agreements set up by collective bargaining between the organizations of employer and employee. The Minister of Labor might at any time declare such agreements compulsory upon the whole industry to which they applied. The progressive depreciation of the currency required constant revision of the wage clauses of these agreements and led to elaboration of the machinery of adjustment along certain well-defined lines.

The sections of the agreements dealing exclusively with wages were gradually made subject to revision without affecting the operation of other sections and, as time went on, the validity of the wage sections was restricted to shorter and shorter periods, or made conditional on changes in the cost of living, or both. After the middle of 1922, however, wage questions, for the most part, were dealt with quite independently of the general agreement. By the end of 1922 wage conventions were seldom concluded for longer than six weeks[25] and by the middle of 1923 for more than a fortnight.

business men to buy German goods no matter how attractive the quoted price might be.

[24] cf. *The Workers Standard of Life in Countries With Depreciated Currency;* International Labor Office Studies and Reports, Series D (Wages and Hours), No. 15, Geneva, 1925, *passim.* The description here given follows this report closely.

[25] The average was much less than this.

The methods of revision of wage scales show a progressive tendency from a temporizing to a settled policy along two main lines: (a) maintenance of a basic wage supplemented by cost-of-living bonuses, adjusted, according to a variety of forms, to the rising level of prices; (b) complete revision of the wage scale. Owing to wide differences in prices between localities, a tendency which persisted owing to the fact that the effect of competition in ironing out such discrepancies always lagged behind the continuous alteration of monetary conditions, local supplements to general cost-of-living bonuses were of frequent occurrence in those agreements where a basic wage was maintained.

The basic wage plus cost-of-living bonus idea gradually evolved into proposals for a system of sliding wage scales calculated according to one of several available index numbers. But this method was not adopted anywhere without a struggle and, when adopted, it did not function without a great deal of friction. In the first place the choice of the basic wage was the subject of much controversy and, since the base chosen affected all future wages, the controversy was by no means pointless. Further than this many workers were at first reluctant to accept a schedule which changed only with changes in the cost of living since this condemned them, at best, to an unchanging real wage instead of giving them a share in any improvements in productive power which might take place.[26] As the tempo of inflation waxed, however, the workers' hesitation at accepting a sliding scale disappeared. The lag of wages then centered attention on preserving the existing real wage rather than going after advances. Employers, on the other hand, opposed sliding scales not only on the selfish grounds that they reduced their profits and increased their risks[27] but also because they tended, so it was said, to accelerate the course of depreciation. The latter possibility also rendered the governmental administrations antagonistic to the sliding-scale idea especially when efforts to stabilize the currency were being at all vigorously pursued. The employers, nevertheless, eventually agreed to pay wages based on dollar exchange rates. This proposal was rejected by the workers' representatives and a compromise was finally reached in mid-1923 under which basic wages were to be fixed

[26] In addition, the workers were apprehensive of a reduction in *money* wages should the index on which the wage was based show a declining tendency. As the wage would be based on the preceding month's index it might be lowered just as prices were starting on a renewed rise.

[27] Sliding scales based on the cost of living, for instance, might prove highly inconvenient in export industries if, in the vicissitudes of foreign exchange, a fall should take place unaccompanied by a similar and equal fall in the cost of living index.

at regular short intervals with due regard not only to the cost of living but to the general economic situation and the prosperity of the particular industry concerned. Within these intervals adjustments were to be made each week according to predetermined cost-of-living indices.

The wild pace of currency depreciation in the latter months of 1923 rendered even as flexible a standard as this far too rigid. It was necessary to adapt wage scales to the period when the wages would be spent rather than to that in which they were received. Enormous differences in wages arose from the fact that one group of workers would be on a new scale while others still had part of their old week to run. Resort to payment more than once a week was then widely had and the cost-of-living index number was projected into the future in order to estimate in advance the prices likely to prevail in the period immediately ahead and to make the appropriate adjustment of wages.[28]

The discussion of sliding scales was accompanied by proposals for the payment of stable-value wages. So far as the mark was to be used as the medium in which payment was to be effected there was almost no difference between the two concepts, though this was by no means generally recognized. Demands for stable or gold value wages were construed, perhaps correctly, as being demands for pre-war wages. So far as sliding scales were adopted there was a partial divorce of the function of the mark as a unit of account from its function as a medium of exchange. The adoption of stable-value wages would simply have been more or less officially to recognize this *de facto* situation. Business with foreign contacts had long been using foreign currencies as a unit of account, insurance companies had obtained legal sanction for keeping all their accounts on a gold basis, wholesale concerns were quite generally following the same practice, and though retail traders were prohibited from quoting *prices* in anything but paper marks[29] their *reckoning* was more and more done in terms of the dollar or other stable currency. The result was greatly to reduce the deviation of prices from the prevailing rates of exchange and to weaken the force of objections

[28] All this was not done, of course, without conflict. Strikes were frequent but, as inflation progressed, they tended to be of short duration. The employer became ready to grant an increase of wages rather than suffer an interruption of activity when he found that he could almost certainly pass on the greater wage bill in enhanced prices for his product, and the worker accepted the offer of higher money wages in the delusion, or at least the hope, that it would enable him to purchase more goods than he had hitherto been able to obtain.

[29] Retail shopkeepers were obliged to keep their premises open during customary business hours and persons selling necessaries of life were obliged to part with them against mark payments. See *Deutsche Allgemeine Zeitung*, Berlin, October 24, 1923.

to putting wages on a straight gold basis. The opposition of the government to such a method of payments declined with the introduction of the pre-rentenmark currencies denominated in gold, and gold-value wages became common in the last few weeks of inflation. While *calculated* in gold they were still paid in paper marks as indeed was the case long after the currency had been stabilized. The system was adopted locally and was gradually spreading over the whole country when the currency reform shifted the center of attention from methods of payment to the old controversy over the basic wage.

For almost the whole of the inflation period the workers were thus engaged in a constant struggle to increase wages in order merely to keep pace with the ever-renewed spurts in prices and, in spite of the elaborate machinery of adjustment which was developed, they were usually a lap or two behind.

§ BUSINESS CONSOLIDATIONS

The concentration of business and industry which had been such a marked feature of German economic life in the pre-war era, and had been accentuated by the readjustments occasioned by the transfer of territory to other political units,[30] was carried even further in the inflation period. Eventually it went to lengths which were little short of the bizarre. Vertical integration was stimulated by the need for eliminating unpredictable shifts in the cost of raw materials and even for giving assurance that supplies would be steadily forthcoming. Horizontal, as well as vertical, combination was prompted by the desirability of spreading the risk of fluctuations in selling prices over a wider range of commodities, by the very vicissitudes of status which inflation brought in its train (the prosperous industries bought up those which were in financial straits), and by sheer exploitation of the opportunity to borrow and buy, paying back the loan in money worth but a fraction of the value of that which had been borrowed.

The dominant personality in the whole movement was Hugo Stinnes, and his greatest concern, the Siemens-Schuckert-Rhein-Elbe-Union. In this group were gathered enormous shipping, mining, iron and steel, and electrical enterprises. Stinnes acquired, in addition, through the holding company Hugo Stinnes G.m.b.H., all sorts of undertakings both in Germany and abroad, and is said at one time to have controlled the

[30] The loss of Lorraine and of parts of Upper Silesia had torn integral parts of the iron and steel industry asunder. A regrouping of component firms in the remaining German territory was natural, and even essential, and this led to several important mergers.

employment of 600,000 workers.[31] At the height of his power he was possessed of a controlling share in sixty large enterprises, aside from the Siemens-Rhein-Elbe group which was itself made up of 47 separate units,[32] and is said to have had important interests in no less than 4500 different companies.

Another large combination was that of the Allgemeine Elektrizitäts Gesellschaft with the interests of Krupp and Otto Wolff. These combinations were paralleled by vertical and horizontal consolidations in most of the mining industries, in oil, automobiles, and numerous other branches of production.[33]

When the stimulus given by inflation had ceased with the coming of stabilization, the Stinnes and several other combinations collapsed. Still others dissolved quietly into their component parts. There was, under a stable monetary standard, no justification for such monstrosities as had been thrown together by Stinnes, and many of the other groups were built on sands almost as shifting. The real integration effected in some cases, however, has left a lasting impress on the composition of German industry.

[31] cf. Le Commerce et l'Industrie devant la dépréciation et la stabilisation monétaire, Gaston Giustiniani, Félix Alcan, Paris, 1927, p. 65.

[32] cf. Drei Verderber Deutschlands, Curt Geyer, J. H. W. Dietz Nachfolger, Berlin, 1924, p. 48.

[33] cf. Konzerne. . . . Ende 1926, Statistisches Reichsamt, Berlin, 1927, passim. In addition to the motivating forces listed above vertical combination was provoked in an effort to evade the turnover tax.

PART II

THEORY

CHAPTER IV

PRICE AND EXCHANGE RATE THEORY
AND THE FACTS IN GERMANY

§ ORTHODOX DOCTRINE

THE orthodox theory of the relation between changes in the volume of circulating medium, the general price level, and rates of exchange in a country on an inconvertible paper monetary standard may be stated in two propositions as follows:

(1) The relation is symmetrical. If the price level in other countries remains constant, the symmetry will be that of proportionality; if the price level in other countries alters, the proportionality between the volume of circulating medium and the domestic price level will be unaffected, but exchange rates will then be a function of two variables, that of the volume of circulating medium or domestic price level on the one hand, and that of the foreign price level on the other.

(2) The causal sequence runs from volume of circulating medium to prices to exchange rates.

This theory states tendencies only. It does not deny that in actual situations the symmetry which it asserts may be distorted. The relation between the volume of circulating medium and the price level is affected by changes in the velocity of monetary turnover, and by the total of transactions carried on with money, and the relation between domestic and foreign prices merely furnishes an approximate par of exchange from which the actual rates may at times deviate in considerable degree. But velocity of monetary turnover and the volume of transactions are comparatively stable factors and, though such changes as occur in them may be persistent, they are not likely to be large. Deviations of exchange rates from the norm, on the other hand, while frequently wide, carry their own corrective, and, whatever their temporary aberrations, continue to center about the purchasing power par established by current price levels in the countries involved. According to orthodox theory then, any departure from symmetry in the relation between money, prices, and exchange rates is likely to be inconsiderable or else an anomaly ever in process of elimination. Given the volume of circulating medium, or the general price level, or exchange rates, in a given country at two different and not very widely separated periods and the unknown items could be computed with substantial accuracy.[1] It is no more than an application of the rule of three.

Changes in the price level are asserted to have no effect upon the velocity of monetary turnover or upon the total of transactions nor do they condition the volume of circulating medium. They are, in fact, but the passive resultant of these three independently determined factors and themselves initiate nothing. The velocity of monetary turnover and the volume of transactions are likewise unaffected by the amount of money in circulation, and the amount of money, in turn, is unaffected by its rate of turnover or by the volume of transactions. The mobile causal factor is the volume of circulating medium; the mobile resultant is prices. As for exchange rates, these are but the price of one currency in terms of another. Since the only use for a paper currency is to make purchases in the country of origin, its value, in a *stable* foreign currency, will obviously vary in proportion to its purchasing power, that is to say, in inverse ratio to the domestic price level. If, however, the unit of measurement, the foreign currency, is unstable in goods value, the exchange rate of the two currencies against one another at any time will tend to express their current respective purchasing powers. In either case price levels are cause and exchange rates effect. Fluctuations in exchange rates may alter individual prices but they can have no effect upon the general price level.

The monetary experience of many countries in the war and post-war period has shown that the theory just laid down, if valid at all, is much too rigidly formulated.[2] Changes in the volume of circulating medium were frequently attended by changes in the price level and in exchange rates which, according to the theory, were by no means appropriate. Though the symmetry between price and exchange rate fluctuations was much closer than that between either of these and the volume of circulating medium there were cases in which it was far from ideal. Of the alleged chain of causation there was, in neither relationship, any

[1] For exchange rates the price level in other countries would also be required.
[2] It is doubtful whether any proponent would be as uncompromising in his exposition of the theory as is here suggested. Professor Irving Fisher, the stoutest champion of a strict construction of the quantity theory, admits that *in periods of transition* the postulates are not to be taken absolutely, and Professor Gustav Cassel, the most loyal adherent to a rigid purchasing power parity conception of exchange rates, recognizes circumstances under which deviations would occur. Other prominent advocates of the quantity theory, such as Professor E. W. Kemmerer, and of the doctrine of purchasing power parity, such as Professor A. C. Pigou, are much more liberal in their admissions.

obvious corroboration in the facts. The reaction, in some quarters, to these events, has been a more or less complete repudiation of the quantity theory, on which the supposed proportional relationship between volume of circulating medium and general prices rests, with an acceptance of the validity of the doctrine of purchasing power parity as an explanation of the relationship between prices and exchange rates, provided, however, that the causal sequence, prices to exchange rates, be not insisted upon. An attempt will presently be made to show that in neither of its phases is this reaction against classical doctrine fully justified. The topic will be dealt with under two general heads: (1) the relation of prices to the volume of circulating medium and (2) the relation of prices to exchange rates.

I. THE RELATION OF PRICES TO THE VOLUME OF CIRCULATING MEDIUM

§ VELOCITY OF CIRCULATION OF MONEY AS A FACTOR IN PRICES

It would be superfluous here to discuss the quantity theory as a general principle. Its adherents are by no means at one in their statement of what the theory is, and it has been noted that the version given above is, perhaps, extreme. The tendency to proportionality admits of great latitude in interpretation and some expositors of quantity theory doctrine are ready to abandon the notion of the complete passiveness of prices. When these concessions are made it is frequently difficult to distinguish a liberal quantity theorist from a moderate opponent. Both would at any rate agree that the "velocity of circulation" of money is the most important factor in the aberrations of prices from strict proportionality with changes in the volume of circulating medium. The most violent financial storms may sweep a country without greatly changing the output of commodities and, insofar as the volume of transactions carried on with money is conditioned by production, the range of variation of the volume of trade as a factor in the determination of the general price level is limited. It is true that volume of trade is but loosely tied to the total of production but possible downward changes in the volume of trade,[3] as of production, if a modern society is to survive at all, are of a low order of magnitude as compared with the fluctuations which may occur in the rate of turnover of money. Where currency depreciation is extreme and progressive at a rapid rate, moreover, the changes in the volume of production and in the

[3] It is the downward changes in trade which are alone significant in explanation of depreciation in the value of a currency relative to increases in its volume.

volume of trade are likely to move in opposite directions, production going down and trade per unit of production going up, under the influence of speculation. These counter movements tend to neutralize one another in their effect on prices. The failure of proportionate correspondence between the amount of money in circulation and the general price level must therefore be due, in the main, to shifts in the velocity of circulation of money.

Far from the comparative immobility which the quantity theory, in its rigid formulation, posits of monetary turnover, it has recently been asserted that the velocity of monetary circulation varies with the degree and rate of depreciation.[4] On quantity theory principles the total value of the circulating medium in any country, measured in a stable unit, would tend to remain constant regardless of volume.[5] But in many countries where post-war monetary depreciation was extreme, and specifically in Germany, the total gold value of the currency is supposed to have shown a tendency to *vary inversely* with its total volume. The inference from this is that velocity of circulation is indefinitely extensible and grows as inflation proceeds. On this view prices might rise indefinitely in something like the square of the rate of increase in the volume of circulating medium.

There is no doubt that great and rapid currency depreciation gives a tremendous shock to such long-established habits as are of significance in determining the rate of monetary turnover and that *inertia* is probably banished at an increasing rate according to the speed and scale of the depreciation. But while the assumption of stability in velocity of turnover is quite unwarranted it is equally wide of the mark to go to the other extreme and suppose that there are no limits on mobility at all. Even a casual investigation of German inflationary phenomena will show that while the gold value of the total circulation of inconvertible paper fell far during the course of inflation and, up to a certain point, dropped with accelerating speed as depreciation gathered momentum, it was nevertheless subject to check. The gold value of the total German note circulation, on the basis of purchasing power parities, is shown in Table XI and Chart V. That there was a limit on the decline in the total value of the currency is clearly shown by the figures of the table, and by the shape of the curve, in the final stage of inflation from the fall of 1922 till November 1923.

[4] cf. *Memorandum on Currency and Central Banks* 1913-1923, League of Nations Publications, Geneva, 1924, p. 19.
[5] Since, with the comparative stability of factors other than money, the value of a unit of the money would move in inverse proportion to changes in total volume.

TABLE XI

GOLD VALUE OF TOTAL CIRCULATION IN GERMANY ON THE BASIS OF
PURCHASING POWER PARITIES; 1918–1923

(*Millions of dollars*)[6]

DATE	1918	1919	1920	1921	1922	1923
Jan.	—	$6,247.56	$2,247.48	$2,213.27	$1,119.83	$161.90
Feb.	—	6,003.76	1,780.71	2,208.66	1,057.94	255.34
Mar.	—	6,345.18	1,943.19	2,215.35	871.06	433.87
April	—	6,382.43	2,322.17	2,152.33	814.06	417.35
May	—	6,466.55	2,507.54	2,157.80	894.00	300.29
June	$4,499.42	6,704.06	2,864.92	2,097.08	921.91	217.53
July	4,716.74	6,243.84	2,925.63	2,036.60	731.69	85.73
Aug.	4,555.28	4,983.39	2,744.11	1,563.46	480.43	105.72
Sept.	5,213.40	4,293.35	2,722.33	1,538.04	432.33	173.65
Oct.	5,490.34	3,880.41	2,646.36	1,367.42	290.81	101.06
Nov.	6,049.87	3,460.78	2,392.56	1,070.76	246.24	390.23
Dec.	6,502.02	3,321.45	2,416.19	1,180.44	323.81	680.68

[6] This table is computed by multiplying the total monetary circulation in Germany by the purchasing power par of the mark with the dollar (the dollar value of the mark as determined by the respective purchasing powers of the two currency units each in its own country).

Sources of data: For total circulation in Germany: *The Process of Inflation in France*, James Harvey Rogers, Columbia University Press, New York, 1929, p. 143. This estimate includes all forms of authorized currency but not illegal emergency issues. For purchasing power parity: (1) *European Currency and Finance*, pp. 534-5; (2) *Zahlen zur Geldentwertung in Deutschland* 1914 *bis* 1923, p. 18. Beginning with January 1923 purchasing power parity was calculated for the end of each month (rather than as a monthly average) from the end-of-the-month figures of German wholesale prices. From January to June of that year the official price index was quoted every ten days and from July to December weekly. Except for those months when a quotation happened to fall on the last day of the month, the end-of-the-month figure was approximated by interpolation between the last quotation for one month and the first for the succeeding month. To obtain the purchasing power parity for the end of October, however, the price quotation of October 30 was used. The daily rate of increase in prices was then growing so rapidly that this quotation seems more appropriate than the figure obtained by interpolation between the quotations of October 30 and November 6.

The total monetary circulation in Germany in 1913 was approximately six billion marks, the equivalent at that time of about $1,430,-000,000. Since gold is by no means a perfectly stable standard, and the goods value of gold fell between 1913 and 1920 by something more than half, a doubling of the gold value of the German paper money circulation might on this ground have been expected at this time. On the other hand the decline in German production and trade relative to 1913 would have had some tendency to lower the total gold value of

CHART V

GOLD VALUE OF TOTAL CIRCULATION IN GERMANY (MILLIONS OF DOLLARS) ON THE
BASIS OF PURCHASING POWER PARITIES; 1918-1923 (LOGARITHMIC
AND ARITHMETIC SCALES)

the paper currency.[7] Reference to Table XI will show that the gold value
of the German currency in early 1919 was, in fact, more than four
times as great as in the pre-war period.[8] As a result of the German occupation, during the war, of Belgian, French, Russian, and Roumanian
territory there had been a great increase in the area in which the mark
circulated and it was thus possible to put out notes without a corresponding depreciation of their value. Even after the conclusion of peace

[7] This is because mark prices would tend to be increased more than in proportion to the augmentation of the currency and rising mark prices would tend to
lower the value of the mark in terms of gold. The smaller territory in 1920
would also be of some import.

[8] In the pre-war period it was about 6000 millions of marks; in June 1919 it
was 6700 millions of dollars.

the volume of mark notes in German territory—and this was the only significant thing for German internal prices—was much less than the total issue. This is by no means the sole reason for the high total value of the mark circulation in 1919—the tendency toward a reduced rate of monetary turnover being more important—but it was nevertheless a factor of some weight. The gold value of the total circulation began to drop in July 1919 but for two or more years thereafter it must have been in some measure supported by the export of marks attendant upon foreign purchases of currency and the consequent withdrawal of such marks from the area in which they could have had any direct effect upon German prices. The rapid fall in the total value of the circulation which occurred between July 1919 and February 1920 was therefore clearly due to an increase in the velocity of monetary turnover.[9] There was a reversal of this tendency in March 1920 when the upward movement in foreign exchange rates and domestic prices was for the time being checked, and the gold value of the total circulation consequently rose. A renewed steady acceleration in the speed of monetary turnover set in in May 1921 as part of the phenomena initiated by the payment of cash reparations and, though a temporary halt occurred at the turn of the year 1921-1922 when the pressure of reparations was reduced, the total value of the circulation shrank rapidly till November 1922. At this point stubborn resistance to a further increase in the rate of monetary turnover developed and the figure for the gold value of the total circulation then attained took on something of the character of a norm. Abstraction having been made of the influence of factors in the monetary equation other than the volume of circulating medium and the rate of monetary turnover—and these other factors could have been of but slight relative importance—one may estimate, roughly, that the rate of monetary turnover at that time was some nine or ten times as great as that of the pre-war currency.[10] This figure is not meant to be precise, since the factors which have been ignored as of minor significance[11] would alter it somewhat on one side or the other,

---

[9] Changes in the volume of production, trade, credit, number of workers engaged in earning occupations, and the like, no doubt played some part. But they would in some degree tend to cancel one another and were in any case of minor relative importance.

[10] The total gold value of the currency in November 1922 was about 1/6 that of 1913. Since, in 1922, gold was worth about 2/3 its 1913 value the total value of the currency, measured in a stable standard, was thus about 1/9 of the pre-war value. In other words the rate of monetary turnover had been multiplied approximately nine times.

[11] Their calculation could at best be but very rough and it seemed advisable to omit them altogether.

but it gives some idea of the by no means indefinitely elastic limits of the rate of monetary turnover even when all circumstances are conspiring to make it as high as possible. It is true that in some months of 1923 the total value of the circulation fell to 1/2 or 1/3 of that of November 1922 but there was always a rebound. The absolute minimum in the total value of the circulation, and presumably, the absolute maximum in the rate of monetary turnover, was reached in July 1923 when the gold value of the circulation was only about 1/17 of what it had been under the stable monetary conditions of a decade earlier. Allowing for changes in the value of gold this gives a rate of monetary turnover about twenty-five times as great as in 1913.[12]

Table XII presents by months from June 1918 to December 1923 indices of wholesale prices, of the total volume of monetary circulation, and the resultant rough index of the rate of monetary turnover.[13]

§ LIMITS ON MOBILITY IN THE RATE OF MONETARY TURNOVER

The results depicted in Tables XI and XII and Chart V show a high degree of mobility in the speed at which money may circulate but they also suggest that there is a "ceiling" beyond which the rate of monetary turnover cannot be driven. One of the notable features of German inflationary experience was a recurring shortage of currency.[14] In view of the colossal issues of notes this has its amusing aspect but it was a real and serious difficulty nevertheless. At the prices which had become current when such a shortage of currency occurred it was impossible to transact business. There was not money enough to go round.

[12] In 1923 the calculation is affected by the fact that two types of money then in circulation to a large but unknown amount, viz. foreign currency and illegal emergency mark note issues, are not included in the computation. The failure to do so leads to an undervaluation of the total money supply and consequently to an overestimate of the rate of monetary turnover.

[13] All factors in the monetary equation except volume of money, its rate of turnover, and prices, are again excluded. Though the excluded factors, if measurable and included, would affect the rate of monetary turnover in varying degree *throughout* the period under review the greatest deviation from the figures of monetary turnover given in the table would probably be in the year 1923 when production was low. The figures given for monetary turnover in that year are probably higher than was actually the case, not only for the reason given in the preceding note but also because the height of prices, one of the two principal factors in determining the figure for monetary turnover here given, was occasioned in part by the low volume of production.

[14] A similar phenomenon has been noted in many other cases of currency depreciation. See, for example, *Foreign Banking Systems*, H. P. Willis and B. H. Beckhart, Ed., Chap. XIII, *The Banking System of Russia*, S. S. Katzenellenbaum, p. 905. Even in the relatively mild inflation of our own greenback period a recurring shortage of currency made its appearance.

TABLE XII

Relation of Index of Wholesale Prices to Index of Total Circulation and Resulting Rough Index of Rate of Monetary Turnover; 1918–1923

DATE	INDEX OF WHOLESALE PRICES 1913=1 (MONTHLY AVERAGE)	INDEX OF TOTAL MONETARY CIRCULATION 1913=1[b] (END OF MONTH)	ROUGH INDEX OF RATE OF MONETARY TURNOVER: INDEX OF PRICES / INDEX OF CIRCULATION	INDEX OF WHOLESALE PRICES 1913=1 (MONTHLY AVERAGE)	INDEX OF TOTAL MONETARY CIRCULATION 1913=1[b] (END OF MONTH)	ROUGH INDEX OF RATE OF MONETARY TURNOVER: INDEX OF PRICES / INDEX OF CIRCULATION
1918				**1920**		
Jan.				12.56	8.415	1.49
Feb.				16.85	8.971	1.88
Mar.				17.09	9.820	1.74
April				15.67	10.28	1.52
May				15.08	10.59	1.42
June	2.09	3.405	0.61	13.82	11.25	1.23
July	2.08	3.461	0.60	13.67	11.50	1.19
Aug.	2.35	3.702	0.63	14.50	11.93	1.22
Sept.	2.30	4.065	0.57	14.98	12.49	1.20
Oct.	2.34	4.399	0.53	14.66	12.75	1.15
Nov.	2.34	4.824	0.49	15.09	12.76	1.18
Dec.	2.45	5.454	0.45	14.40	13.45	1.07
1919				**1921**		
Jan.	2.62	5.690	0.46	14.39	12.98	1.11
Feb.	2.70	5.808	0.46	13.76	13.20	1.04
Mar.	2.74	6.135	0.45	13.38	13.25	1.01
April	2.86	6.346	0.45	13.26	13.38	0.99
May	2.97	6.576	0.45	13.08	13.47	0.97
June	3.08	7.035	0.44	13.66	13.99	0.98
July	3.39	6.903	0.49	14.28	14.28	1.00
Aug.	4.22	6.735	0.63	19.17	14.64	1.31
Sept.	4.93	6.968	0.71	20.67	15.64	1.32
Oct.	5.62	7.151	0.79	24.60	16.44	1.50
Nov.	6.78	7.482	0.91	34.16	18.00	1.90
Dec.	8.03	8.266	0.97	34.87	20.26	1.72

Table XII—(Continued)

Relation of Index of Wholesale Prices to Index of Total Circulation and Resulting Rough Index of Rate of Monetary Turnover; 1918–1923

DATE	INDEX OF WHOLESALE PRICES 1913=1 (MONTHLY AVERAGE)	INDEX OF TOTAL MONETARY CIRCULATION 1913=1[15] (END OF MONTH)	ROUGH INDEX OF RATE OF MONETARY TURNOVER = INDEX OF PRICES / INDEX OF CIRCULATION	INDEX OF WHOLESALE PRICES 1913=1[16] (MONTHLY AVERAGE)	INDEX OF TOTAL MONETARY CIRCULATION 1913=1[15] (END OF MONTH)	ROUGH INDEX OF RATE OF MONETARY TURNOVER = INDEX OF PRICES / INDEX OF CIRCULATION
1922				**1923**		
Jan.	36.65	20.50	1.79	4,626	332	13.94
Feb.	41.03	21.26	1.93	5,188	585	8.87
Mar.	54.33	23.15	2.35	4,835	916	5.28
April	63.55	24.84	2.56	5,988	1,090	5.49
May	64.58	26.78	2.41	10,713	1,426	7.51
June	70.30	29.78	2.36	29,223	2,867	10.19
July	100.59	33.48	3.00	183,510	7,231	25.38
Aug.	192.00	41.66	4.61	2,338,320	114,008	20.51
Sept.	287.00	54.79	5.24	66,361,885	4,720,487	12.79
Oct.	566.00	79.85	7.09	18,700,000,000	854,401,934	21.89
Nov.	1,154.00	126.77	9.10	1,380,150,000,000	245,107,084,000	5.63
Dec.	1,475.00	213.38	6.91	1,200,400,000,000	374,563,426,600	3.20

[15] The index of circulation is the same as that used in Table XI.

[16] Beginning with January 1923 the figures for the wholesale price index are determined in the manner described in the note to Table XI.

Source of other data: *Zahlen zur Geldentwertung in Deutschland 1914 bis 1923, passim.*

Messengers had to wait in queues for hours at the Reichsbank branches in order to obtain sufficient money to meet the indispensable requirements of depositors. The printing presses were belching forth an unceasing stream of notes and were constantly enlarging the proportion of the larger to those of the smaller denominations but they could not keep up with the rise in prices. The most acute shortages of currency occurred in the fall of 1922 and in the summer of 1923.[17] Reference to Table XII will show that these were the dates of the highest rates of monetary turnover. Prices were then rising precipitously and nobody imagined that they would cease to do so. There was thus the strongest sort of impulse to spend immediately and so to increase the rate of monetary turnover. But in 1922 the limit, for the time being, had been reached, and in 1923 something very close to the absolute maximum had been attained. Though the channels of trade were already choked with the mass of money that was being poured into them the volume of circulation was insufficient to meet requirements at the existing prices. But the money simply could not be made to move any faster. Unless more money were issued a fall in prices so sudden as completely to disrupt business was inevitable since the band of monetary elasticity had been stretched till it would stretch no more. More money *was* issued. The subsequent fall in the rate of monetary turnover has been construed as a temporary victory for the printing presses[18] but there is surely no reason to suppose that still further issues of money would operate to diminish the rate of its turnover. The fact that, in August, September and November 1923, prices did not rise as fast as the rate of increase in the volume of money in circulation[19] was certainly due to the circumstance that the "ceiling" in the rate of monetary turnover had been reached and that the height temporarily attained in July could not permanently be sustained.

§ NEW CONCEPT OF VELOCITY OF MONETARY TURNOVER

The phrase "velocity of circulation" is glibly employed in economic literature but the concept is vague. So far as velocity of circulation

[17] cf. (1) *Die Wirtschaftskurve*, Heft III, Frankfurter Societäts Druckerei, G.m.b.H., Frankfurt-am-Main, August 1922, p. 3. (2) *Berliner Tageblatt*, Berlin, February 3, 1923. (3) *Manchester Guardian Commercial*, Reconstruction Supplement, Article by Dr. Hjalmar Schacht on Discount Policy of the Reichsbank, Section XI, Manchester, December 7, 1922, p. 69. (4) *Economic Review*, Vol. VIII, No. 6, London, August 10, 1923, p. 115.

[18] The printing presses were, on this view, supposed to have turned notes out so fast that the notes did not have *time* to fall, in value per unit, proportionately to the increase in their total amount. The rate of depreciation of the currency *unit* in October renders this view somewhat ridiculous.

[19] See *infra*, Chart VI.

affects the price level, and this is the only sort of monetary velocity in which we are interested, none of the ordinarily accepted definitions seems apt. One such definition is "the ratio of money expended to the average money on hand."[20] This is unsatisfactory. With a given stock of money and a given population the average per capita amount of money on hand must be constant. But the amount expended may vary greatly and thus, according to this definition, affect velocity, though it may not exert any influence on prices. Suppose, for instance, that a group of men meet some Sunday evening to play poker. Each starts with an equal supply of poker chips of a fixed arbitrary value and, in the course of the evening, the men buy and sell these chips from one another as occasion requires. Coin is used for each transaction. When the evening's play is over each man is, let us suppose, in the position in which he started. The amount of money expended has been greater than would have been the case if the game had never been played, the average money on hand has not changed, and the velocity of circulation of money must therefore, on the definition given above, have been increased. But the arbitrary price of poker chips will certainly not have altered and it can scarcely be maintained that the prices of other commodities will be affected as a result of the evening's activities.

Whether the "person-turnover" or the "coin-transfer" method of calculating velocity of circulation is used makes no difference. The number of coins passing through each man's hands is increased as compared with what would have happened if they had all spent the evening quietly at home, while the average amount held, by the group certainly and possibly by each man in it, has not changed. Similarly, as a result of the play, the average number of times that money has changed hands in a given period has been increased.

It may be objected that the reason why prices do not change in the case here considered is that the volume of trading is augmented *pari passu* with the increase in the velocity of circulation. This is true, but the contention completely undermines the concept of velocity of circulation of money as an independent causal factor in prices, since velocity of monetary circulation, as that term is ordinarily defined, is then, at least in part, *dependent* upon the volume of trading and increases only *because* of the expansion in business transacted. Such a concept of velocity is of little value in the explanation of prices since the ratio of money expended to the average money on hand, or the number of times money changes hands, in a given period, may or may not be of any in-

[20] See *Purchasing Power of Money*, Irving Fisher, The Macmillan Co., New York, 1920, p. 352. It is not clear whether Fisher himself approves this definition.

fluence on prices. Further than this, as we shall later see, a change in prices, or price quotations, may *determine* velocity as above defined.

It is doubtful, therefore, whether the phrase "velocity of circulation" can properly be employed to denote the essential feature of monetary turnover which is not how many times the money supply is used in a given period but how large a proportion of it is in process of transfer at the time of maximum demand. There are peak loads in the requirement for money, and prices will be conditioned by the proportion of the total money in circulation which can be mobilized for the peak volume of transfers as well as by the proportion of total business done at the peak. Let us suppose that our group of poker-players on breaking up on Sunday night agree to come together next morning and resume their game. They do so and play all day with the same result as on the previous evening. If they had not been playing with the money they took into the game they would, let us assume, have used it once during the day in the purchase of commodities. Since the money fails to be so used, general prices, other things being equal, will *fall*. Commodities may be retained by their possessors and prices may thus be temporarily sustained. But, since production continues, goods will pile up and, when the card players' money eventually comes into the commodity market, the volume of goods will be expanded relatively to the money supply. In the absence of other changes they can be moved only at lower prices.

It is clear that the time when additional trading is carried on is a vital factor. If the same volume of trading is spread evenly over a given period prices will tend to be higher than with an uneven distribution of the volume of transactions. Suppose that, instead of playing cards, the group gathered together on Sunday night sell to one another commodities which would otherwise be sold on Monday. Suppose also that Sunday is a day of slack demand for money while on Monday the requirements are at their peak. On Monday there is the same amount of money available as would have been at hand in the absence of the Sunday activities but there are fewer commodities to be sold.[21] Prices will therefore tend to *rise*.[22]

The proportion of the total money supply offered at any given

[21] There may be the same absolute volume of commodities but there will be fewer commodities in the hands of people anxious to turn them into money.

[22] The poker-game illustration was originally chosen simply because the effect, if any, on prices was more clearly brought out. The volume of transactions, *whatever their character*, may change in any degree without affecting prices *provided the volume of trading at the peak is not altered*. On the other hand, the volume of transactions may show no change but prices will vary according as a larger or smaller share of the total occurs at the peak.

moment normally tends, of course, to accommodate itself to the business activity of the moment and thus to prevent incessant price fluctuations. The share of the total circulation actually in process of transfer varies greatly from hour to hour, day to day, and season to season. But the share in motion at the time of the peak requirement for money represents a maximum, established partly by physical factors, partly by legal or customary limitations on bank reserves, and partly by considerations of prudence on the part of individuals, and this maximum is the decisive factor in the determination of prices so far as monetary turnover is concerned. The self-interest of individuals and banks will lead to the proportion of means of payment in motion at the moment of peak demand being a maximum for the existing circumstances.

With a given volume of circulating medium prices cannot rise above the level which will absorb all of the means of payment capable of being mobilized at the instant of the peak volume of trading but though they *might* rise when the peak is passed they will normally not do so. In an economy where hard money is the sole circulating medium a large part of the total money supply will tend to be held out of use in inter-peak periods. In an economy where bank credit plays a large rôle, either in the form of bank notes or of deposits subject to check, it is the credit, in the main, which is held out of use when the demand for circulating medium is slack.[23] If the same proportion of the total available circulating medium were used at a moment of slack trading as at a preceding peak at which the maximum had been reached, if, in other words, the maximum became for the moment a norm, prices would rise. But unless the total volume of circulating medium were increased, or the previous maximum proportion in motion at a given moment were somehow raised, prices would fall with a crash when the next peak of monetary demand occurred. Under a monetary system in some measure conditioned by physical laws, such as is the gold standard, the circulating medium, even including credit, is not unlimited and the proportion of the total circulating medium which can be mobilized at a given moment does not change greatly. So far as money and monetary turnover determine prices the price level will therefore be set by the total volume of means of payment and by the proportion of this total which can be set in motion at the instant of greatest requirement for money. The price level so determined will tend to persist during off-peak periods.

---

[23] In the United States the larger adjustments take place through extensions or contractions of Federal Reserve credit while day-to-day variations are effected through a more or less active use of cash by individuals or business concerns and through fluctuations in the commercial banks' volume of loans and discounts.

§ VELOCITY OF MONETARY TURNOVER UNDER INCONVERTIBLE PAPER

With an inconvertible paper monetary standard the volume of circulating medium is quite unlimited and the indefinite rise in prices which this makes possible affects very greatly the proportion of the total volume of circulating medium that will at any moment be put in motion in the purchase of goods. The conditioning factor in this proportion is usually psychological though there is an absolute physical maximum. Several provisional psychological maxima may appear, dependent in each case upon law, custom, prudence, and the general social and economic conditions prevailing at the moment. No one of these several maxima is quite rigid. Each is clearly dependent on the will of individuals and on the strength of the forces leading to a decision to spend immediately or to refrain from so doing. As not all people will completely divest themselves of money, no matter what the strength of the impulse to do so may be, prices cannot rise to the level at which the total value of the transactions occurring at the moment of greatest trading would be equal to all the money in being at that time. The latter condition is, however, the absolute maximum of rate of monetary turnover.[24] Transfer of money takes time, especially if a considerable distance separates the prospective payer at the moment he receives funds from the payee to whom he will later turn them over, and this fact limits the amount of money that can be brought to bear at a given instant. This limit would never in actual circumstances be attained. But something very close to it happened in Germany. The desire to keep a certain amount of money in reserve was replaced by a passion for spending in order to avoid loss of purchasing power and, at the peak of monetary transfers, a very large share of the existing supply of money was in motion from one holder to another. The daily total German wage bill can hardly have been short of the equivalent of $10,000,000 to $12,000,000[25] and since practically all the workmen would *simultaneously* be in possession of their pay at the customary hour of payment, something like one-eighth (See Table XII) of the total money supply at certain times in the period of high inflation must have been required to cover merely this portion of the transactions occurring at that moment.

[24] The frequency with which the peaks are reached is, of course, of great significance. The maximum here indicated would perhaps be but momentary. If this level is maintained, and transactions so spaced as to reduce the volume of trading at the peaks and increase it in the troughs, prices might be driven still higher. On this point see *infra*, p. 112.

[25] This estimate makes allowance for the low money value of a given real wage at this time.

Yet such payments are ordinarily but a minor part of the total circulation of purchasing power.[26]

Not only was the proportion of the total volume of currency in motion at the time of maximum trading greatly increased during inflation but the trading peaks themselves were very much flattened. This was done by reducing the period between payments, particularly in the case of wages and salaries. When wage payments are shifted from a weekly to a daily basis the peak requirement for money for this purpose is cut to one-seventh of its former amount and this permits prices to rise much higher than would otherwise be possible.[27] Thus, though the reason for reducing the period between payments was to prevent a too serious loss of the purchasing power of the mark while it was being earned, the result was merely to cause a still more rapid rise in prices.

While, in the manner just described, the rate of monetary turnover in Germany was much increased, the symmetry between the volume of circulating medium, prices and exchange rates was reestablished in the final stages of inflation. The curve of monetary demand could at most be made flat,[28] the proportion of the total monetary supply in actual transfer could at most be 100%, and, as these limits were approached, the increase in prices *due to changes in the rate of monetary turnover* began to slacken and finally to disappear. Chart VI shows the indices of volume of circulating medium and of exchange rates in percentage relationship to that of prices, with October 1922 taken as a base = 100 in each case. There is no tendency for any of the indices to outstrip the others in this last year and a quarter of inflation. Inability to increase the rate of monetary turnover expressed itself in the shortage of cash. In the very final stages of inflation note issues rose more rapidly than did the index of wholesale prices, in other words, the whole immense upward movement in prices at that time was attributable solely to increases in the volume of circulating medium.

[26] *cf. Business Cycles: The Problem and Its Setting*, Wesley C. Mitchell, National Bureau of Economic Research, Inc., New York, 1927, p. 140. In the United States the payments of money incomes (of all sorts), *to individuals*, amounts to about 1/10 of the aggregate volume of payments. *op. cit.*, p. 149.

[27] Every flattening of the curve of monetary requirements has this effect. Prices under gold standard conditions, for instance, may, at certain periods of peak demand for money, be kept from falling not only by increasing the rate of monetary turnover but by shifting part of the transactions to off-peak periods.

[28] In practice, of course, this could never fully be achieved since it would involve an exactly equal volume of monetary transactions every minute of the day and night, week in and week out.

CHART VI

INDICES OF VOLUME OF CIRCULATING MEDIUM AND OF EXCHANGE RATES IN
PERCENTAGE RELATION TO THE INDEX OF WHOLESALE PRICES (OCTOBER
1922 = 100 IN EACH CASE); OCTOBER 1922-NOVEMBER 1923

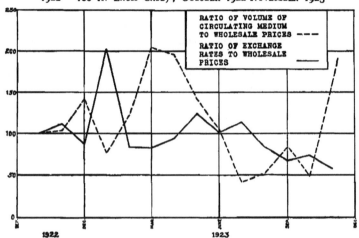

That there is a real even if vague limit to the possible increase in
the rate of monetary turnover may possibly be of comfort to some future
officer of government whose attempt to put a stop to depreciation is
temporarily frustrated by the failure of prices to respond to the cessation
of further issues of notes or to their reduction.[29] He has only to perse-
vere, in the firm conviction that, in the end, prices must cease to rise;
the rate of monetary turnover cannot expand indefinitely. If, indeed,
there were no limit, it might be impossible ever to stabilize a currency
where the psychological situation was unfavorable.

§ CAUSE AND EFFECT RELATIONSHIP BETWEEN VOLUME OF CIRCULATING MEDIUM AND PRICES

The relation of cause and effect in this matter, as in so many other of
the phenomena of inflation, is difficult to establish. There tends to be
interaction. A steady and rapid upward movement of prices impels
holders of money to get rid of it more quickly and this in turn acceler-
ates the upward swing of prices. This new rise in prices adds intensity
to the impulse to spend and so the spiral goes. On the other hand, if the
upward price movement is checked or reversed, the factors leading to
this result tend to be reinforced by the desire to hold money rather than

---

[29] This situation occurred in Czecho-Slovakia in 1920. *cf. La Déflation en
pratique*, Charles Rist, Marcel Giard, Paris, 1924, p. 87.

to spend it.[30] So long as the rate of turnover of money is subject to psychological forces it is extremely mobile whenever the value of money is itself in flux, and this mobility increases the range of price fluctuations in both directions.

In such situations it seems casuistical to insist that prices are passive, a mere resultant of changes in other factors. Not only does a rise in prices affect the *desire* to spend money but, on an upward movement, it *forces* the present expenditure of a larger share of the total circulating medium than if the price level had remained stable. With a given volume of currency and a given trade the rate of monetary turnover *must*, it is true, have increased not later than the occurrence of an increased level of prices. The proximate cause of the advance in prices may thus be said to be the change in the rate of monetary turnover. But a rise in price *quotations* (which are by no means the same thing as prices since prices issue only out of *realized* transactions) may practically compel an augmentation in that rate. Certain expenditures are necessary if life is to be preserved and will be made regardless of how large a proportion of the current monetary holdings of an individual they may require. These expenditures having been made at the high quoted prices the rate of turnover of money is *ipso facto* enlarged.[31] The sale of a portion of the available supply of commodities at prices which, at the old rate of turnover of money, it would have been impossible to obtain for the whole stock, thus so affects the rate of monetary turnover as to sustain the prices originally quoted and charged. Prices then more or less lift themselves by their own bootstraps and they stay high because they have gone up.

We may conclude that the rate of monetary turnover is determined, within certain bounds, solely by psychological attitudes and that these are affected by the course of prices. In the early stages of inflation there seems to be a tendency toward reduction in the share of the total currency supply which is in transfer at any given moment. This is no doubt due to the opportunity given to receivers of the enlarged flow of currency to withhold a larger share from circulation[32] and to a certain inertia in

[30] A quick drop in the rate of monetary turnover occurred in practically every case of stabilization effected in post-war depreciated currencies and required additional issues of notes to prevent the stabilization from turning into a sharp appreciation of the currency.

[31] The fact that rising prices may automatically increase the rate of monetary turnover, instead of vice versa, was pointed out to me by one of my students, Mr. A. J. Duncan.

[32] cf. *Russian Currency and Banking*, 1914-1924, S. S. Katzenellenbaum, P. S. King & Son, Ltd., London, 1925; p. 76. Katzenellenbaum notes a breaking point at which the tendency to hoard is suddenly changed to a tendency to spend.

price quotations. Balances in tills and in banks pile up until the wastefulness of this process, from the point of view of the individual, makes itself felt. This seems to have been the situation in Germany up to mid-1919.[88] Presently, approximately the old proportion of the total of circulating medium is again put into motion. Prices rise, but confidence in the currency is not yet so undermined as to lead to a concerted movement toward the immediate use of all accruing funds. Something like the original rate of monetary turnover then again establishes itself. This phase is represented by the situation in Germany after relative stability in exchange rates and prices had been reached in 1920. It lasted till the beginning of cash reparations payments in mid-1921.[88] But when the value of money continues to fall the desire to get rid of the money grows, and, once under way, proceeds at heightened speed so long as psychological factors are the dominating influence. Under conditions of rapid depreciation there is then small probability that the price level will vary in proportion to the volume of note issues until after the maximum rate of monetary turnover is reached. On the contrary, in the period immediately following the "break" in general confidence in the currency, the relation between changes in prices and in the volume of circulating medium is likely to approach more nearly a geometric than an arithmetic scale. This was the case in Germany from late 1921 till something approaching the maximum rate of turnover of money was reached in November 1922 and, in part, till the absolute "ceiling" was attained in July 1923.

While the cause and effect relationship of rate of monetary turnover and prices is one of interaction, and while prices therefore do not respond in nice symmetry with the volume of circulating medium, there can be no doubt that the ultimate causal sequence runs from volume of money to prices. This proposition was by no means generally conceded in Germany. The rise in German prices far beyond the measure of arithmetic proportionality with the increase in note issues gave rise to

cf. also *Monetary Reform*, J. M. Keynes, Harcourt, Brace and Company, New York, 1924, pp. 50 ff., where it is pointed out that the public is so accustomed to thinking of money as the ultimate standard that, when prices begin to rise, they believe that the rise must be temporary and hoard money by postponing purchases. Sooner or later, however, the second phase sets in and money, instead of being hoarded, is spent much more freely than would be the case under a stable standard.

[88] See Table XI. For an interesting discussion of changes in the total value of an inconvertible paper currency, based on the Revolutionary currency in the United States, cf. *Credit, Currency, and Banking; Considerations on the Currency and Banking System of the United States*, Albert Gallatin, Carey and Lea, Philadelphia, 1831, pp. 26 ff.

the belief that note issues had no effect on prices at all. Prices were supposed to be conditioned by exchange rates which fluctuated violently and apparently lawlessly. The conviction was therefore expressed, even by hitherto respectable figures in the field of finance, that note issues did not raise prices (which would go up anyway) but merely prevented a collapse of business. The same story is heard in every inflation, mild or extreme. Note issues, it is said, will take care of themselves. If they are not needed in business they will, it is alleged, be returned to the banks. Such sophistry takes no consideration of the fact that the "need" for notes is conditioned by the price level which the note issues themselves chiefly determine. The fact that the proportionate relationship between changes in the volume of circulating medium and in prices is frequently, or even normally, not preserved in periods of inflation, does not alter the fact that prices are fundamentally subordinate to the amount of currency in circulation. The connection may be slack but it is inevitable. Prices can never fail to be influenced by the volume of circulating medium though they may at the same time be influenced by other factors. Increases in the volume of circulating medium, on the other hand, at least in a régime of inconvertible paper, require an act of volition on the part of the issuing authorities[34] and being thus subject to arbitrary determination can be an effect of nothing but the will of the issuing instance. The authorities may be *im*pelled to issue notes as a result of any given price situation but since they cannot be *com*pelled to do so prices can in no true sense be held to be a cause of note issues. The chain of causation clearly runs the other way.

§ GENERAL CONCLUSIONS ON THE RELATIONSHIP BETWEEN
THE VOLUME OF CIRCULATING MEDIUM AND PRICES

While the facts are against the contention of rigid exponents of the quantity theory on both the main issues, that is, on the tendency toward proportionality between the volume of money and the general level of prices on the one hand, and on the passiveness of prices on the other, it is none the less true that the possible variations in any of the "other" factors involved in price determination are of minor importance beside the infinite expansibility of inconvertible paper currency issues. In the extreme stage of inflation prices therefore do tend to move in proportion to the volume of circulating medium. Under inconvertible paper monetary standards, moreover, the movement of prices can never be a true cause, even in part, of the volume of money in circulation and so, when

[34] The matter is somewhat complicated by the fact that a greater or smaller mass of the currency may have been exported and may at any time be brought back, but this does not seriously affect the proposition here laid down.

the rate of monetary turnover has reached its maximum, prices become a passive resultant of other causes. As currency depreciation proceeds from the great to the colossal the postulates of the quantity theory therefore come substantially closer to fulfilment. Prices not only then tend to move proportionately with the volume of circulating medium but have no longer any automatic tendency to affect other factors in the price equation.[35] The symmetry and sequence asserted in the quantity theory is at length practically attained.

II. THE RELATION OF PRICES TO EXCHANGE RATES

§ COMPARISON OF EUROPEAN INCONVERTIBLE PAPER CURRENCIES

Let us now turn our attention to the second phase of the alleged symmetry in monetary phenomena, that between the commodity price level and exchange rates. Investigation of price and exchange rate data in the period when inconvertible paper currencies were universal in Europe shows in most cases a rather close correspondence between actual exchange rates and the theoretical pars based on relative prices.[36]

Table XIII and Charts VII, VIII, IX present for twelve European countries, by months from 1919 to 1923, the percentage relationship between purchasing power pars and actual exchange rates against the dollar. The countries are ranged in order according to the average cost of foreign exchange relative to purchasing power pars.[37] At 100%, any

[35] This, indeed, is more truly the case under paper than under gold standards. Under the gold standard, rising prices (a falling value of gold) check gold mining operations and, by so diminishing the supply of money, put limitations upon their own advance. Of even greater significance is the tendency toward a greater use of gold in the arts as its value falls. How much monetary gold is melted down under these circumstances cannot be known, but it is, perhaps, a very considerable amount. Under paper standards there are no such automatic checks on the tendency of prices to vary directly (though for a considerable period not proportionately) with the volume of the *money material*.

[36] If in one country prices have risen to, let us say, three times their former level while in another they have not changed, the theoretical par of exchange is the old par (expressed in terms of the number of units of the now depreciated currency formerly exchangeable against one unit of the other) multiplied by 3. If in one country they have tripled and in another doubled, the theoretical par is the old par multiplied by 3/2. This ratio between the internal purchasing powers of two currency units gives their purchasing power par rate of exchange.

[37] The table shows nothing as to the *absolute* values of the several currencies nor as to such changes in absolute value as were continuously taking place. Whatever the absolute values, and however they might be changing, the ratio would be 100% so long as domestic prices and exchange rates moved in perfect correspondence.

TABLE XIII

PURCHASING POWER PARS OF TWELVE EUROPEAN INCONVERTIBLE PAPER CURRENCIES EXPRESSED AS PERCENTAGES OF THE EXCHANGE RATE OF EACH OF THE CURRENCIES AGAINST THE DOLLAR; 1919–1923[88]

	SWEDEN	SWITZER-LAND	SPAIN	NORWAY	NETHER-LANDS	CZECHO-SLOVAKIA	GREAT BRITAIN	DENMARK	BELGIUM	FRANCE	ITALY	GERMANY
1919												
Jan.	—	—	—	—	—	—	90.7	—	—	60.1	75.2	148.2
Feb.	—	—	—	—	—	—	89.6	—	—	59.7	73.8	155.2
Mar.	—	—	—	—	—	—	93.2	—	—	63.6	78.0	176.8
April	—	—	—	—	—	—	95.7	—	—	69.3	85.4	208.4
May	—	—	—	—	—	—	92.0	—	—	75.9	92.2	208.0
June	—	—	—	—	—	—	91.0	—	—	76.0	87.7	219.6
July	—	—	—	—	—	—	95.9	—	—	81.5	95.7	224.4
Aug.	—	—	—	—	—	—	98.4	—	—	94.1	104.1	229.6
Sept.	—	—	—	—	—	—	97.0	—	—	95.7	107.3	240.0
Oct.	—	—	—	—	—	—	93.0	—	—	91.7	107.7	241.0
Nov.	—	—	—	—	—	—	95.1	—	—	97.4	113.7	288.6
Dec.	—	—	—	—	—	—	103.1	—	—	110.1	123.4	315.2
1920												
Jan.	88.2	—	—	97.9	86.3	—	107.0	104.5	—	108.8	114.4	260.4
Feb.	93.8	—	—	105.2	88.4	—	109.1	—	—	121.7	145.7	311.4
Mar.	84.4	—	—	98.4	89.4	—	99.6	—	—	113.1	141.0	258.7
April	80.7	—	—	93.4	90.9	—	96.9	—	—	128.6	159.6	222.8
May	83.4	—	—	96.5	92.6	—	102.4	—	—	126.2	131.7	178.1
June	79.3	—	—	97.3	92.0	—	99.8	—	—	120.1	125.6	163.8
July	78.3	—	—	95.5	93.6	—	101.5	102.5	—	115.3	133.2	165.6
Aug.	80.5	—	—	99.2	98.0	—	104.2	107.7	—	123.8	145.8	180.5
Sept.	81.0	—	—	101.9	102.3	—	111.1	109.8	—	123.0	153.5	208.7
Oct.	80.2	—	—	98.0	97.1	—	104.8	102.6	—	124.2	156.9	231.1
Nov.	81.3	—	—	97.7	100.4	—	105.5	97.5	—	136.4	155.8	234.1
Dec.	80.1	—	—	86.4	99.8	—	102.6	86.4	—	134.1	151.0	216.1

TABLE XIII—(Continued)

PURCHASING POWER PARS OF TWELVE EUROPEAN INCONVERTIBLE PAPER CURRENCIES EXPRESSED AS PERCENTAGES OF THE EXCHANGE RATE OF EACH OF THE CURRENCIES AGAINST THE DOLLAR; 1919-1923[38]

	SWEDEN	SWITZER-LAND	SPAIN	NORWAY	NETHER-LANDS	CZECHO-SLOVAKIA	GREAT BRITAIN	DENMARK	BELGIUM	FRANCE	ITALY	GERMANY
1921												
Jan.	78.2	87.9	69.4	75.0	97.6	—	95.3	73.9	—	125.4	143.9	175.6
Feb.	75.4	82.1	69.8	75.6	95.5	—	93.4	79.8	—	114.2	137.8	168.4
Mar.	73.1	80.1	70.0	82.4	96.3	—	92.7	85.9	—	118.2	128.6	172.2
April	70.5	79.3	68.9	83.5	97.3	—	92.1	81.1	—	113.7	106.3	168.8
May	71.9	84.3	69.1	84.1	90.1	—	92.9	94.0	—	101.6	96.4	162.0
June	75.5	86.9	68.7	88.3	94.2	—	99.9	86.8	—	104.5	108.0	171.5
July	83.3	92.0	70.5	94.2	100.1	—	101.6	94.7	—	105.5	115.5	180.8
Aug.	85.3	92.0	72.8	97.8	102.3	—	104.5	92.3	104.8	106.7	116.9	147.9
Sept.	86.7	87.8	73.2	102.8	99.5	—	105.3	95.8	103.5	108.7	111.7	168.8
Oct.	85.4	81.6	72.0	105.0	101.0	—	109.5	99.3	103.3	114.2	115.1	201.5
Nov.	85.7	79.2	69.5	96.7	98.2	—	107.4	109.7	104.4	113.8	110.9	251.3
Dec.	81.4	78.3	70.7	91.4	93.9	—	104.4	102.1	97.1	105.6	102.3	181.1
1922												
Jan.	81.9	77.5	73.1	91.0	92.8	96.4	101.9	104.3	93.2	103.9	105.5	173.1
Feb.	80.9	81.2	81.5	89.9	91.3	101.5	101.5	103.8	92.1	101.8	98.6	170.8
Mar.	82.1	81.8	82.1	90.1	92.0	106.8	100.6	99.2	92.8	99.1	100.6	172.2
April	83.7	85.7	81.6	87.0	93.0	98.8	99.8	101.1	93.8	95.1	97.4	154.3
May	87.6	91.4	88.8	92.7	93.3	105.7	101.9	104.4	97.8	98.8	103.6	161.8
June	89.2	92.9	91.3	102.2	94.4	107.0	103.1	103.5	98.6	101.6	108.7	159.4
July	92.3	95.2	99.7	107.3	98.0	97.8	108.1	107.1	106.0	111.7	117.3	180.0
Aug.	91.2	95.3	105.8	106.5	102.8	78.1	111.2	107.1	110.1	113.4	116.2	190.0
Sept.	91.2	94.7	107.4	108.5	104.3	83.0	112.0	109.6	112.1	117.1	118.7	185.7
Oct.	91.6	97.8	112.6	104.7	102.5	89.7	110.3	116.3	112.5	119.7	118.5	200.0
Nov.	95.2	95.2	123.6	102.7	101.1	97.5	110.8	114.5	115.5	124.6	112.0	320.0
Dec.	95.1	93.1	125.8	100.5	101.6	102.8	108.4	111.4	112.0	114.9	103.2	250.0

TABLE XIII—(Continued)

PURCHASING POWER PARS OF TWELVE EUROPEAN INCONVERTIBLE PAPER CURRENCIES EXPRESSED AS PERCENTAGES OF THE EXCHANGE RATE OF EACH OF THE CURRENCIES AGAINST THE DOLLAR; 1919–1923[38]

	SWEDEN	SWITZER-LAND	SPAIN	NORWAY	NETHER-LANDS	CZECHO-SLOVAKIA	GREAT BRITAIN	DENMARK	BELGIUM	FRANCE	ITALY	GERMANY
1923												
Jan.	95.3	91.5	105.4	101.7	101.0	110.1	106.6	116.6	113.9	116.5	107.2	190.6
Feb.	95.5	91.8	105.9	101.1	102.4	105.1	105.1	114.5	117.9	116.8	107.9	167.3
Mar.	94.9	90.7	107.8	102.1	103.8	105.0	105.6	111.2	115.6	114.4	107.6	154.8
April	95.0	90.2	107.3	103.2	104.6	104.7	105.9	112.4	110.2	110.8	105.2	181.6
May	94.6	89.4	108.1	108.6	107.6	103.1	105.9	110.0	111.2	111.5	107.2	227.4
June	94.4	91.3	109.1	107.5	105.3	103.8	107.6	113.4	113.3	114.6	113.6	187.9
July	93.6	91.8	111.3	106.0	106.7	103.8	109.1	111.1	117.8	121.6	118.9	160.3
Aug.	93.3	91.8	115.8	106.9	107.9	108.2	108.9	105.3	120.4	124.1	118.3	111.7[39]
Sept.	95.6	95.8	117.1	109.5	108.7	108.4	110.0	112.4	117.5	119.6	117.6	—
Oct.	96.4	91.3	119.6	111.6	106.2	107.1	109.7	114.2	112.6	117.8	116.2	—
Nov.	96.9	91.7	118.8	115.0	105.1	109.7	108.2	114.5	116.5	119.9	117.7	—
Dec.	96.0	91.2	118.5	111.2	103.6	106.2	108.0	108.2	116.7	121.0	116.4	—
Monthly average 1919–1923	86.4	88.7	93.4	98.2	98.7	101.7	102.3	103.1	108.1	108.2	115.1	185.6

[38] Purchasing power parity for each currency is derived as follows: Bureau of Labor Statistics index number of wholesale prices in the United States multiplied by 1913 par of exchange and divided by foreign index of wholesale prices. The par of exchange, and the actual exchange rates necessary for the computation, were in every case used in the form of quotation: number of American cents per unit of the foreign currency. New York rates were used for all currencies.

[39] From September 1923 till the end of inflation German exchange rates were nominal only.

Source of data: *European Currency and Finance*, Serial 9, Volumes I and II, *passim*.

CHART VII

PURCHASING POWER PARS OF THE CURRENCIES OF SWEDEN, SWITZERLAND,
SPAIN, NORWAY, AND THE NETHERLANDS, EXPRESSED AS PERCENTAGES
OF DOLLAR EXCHANGE RATES; 1919-1923

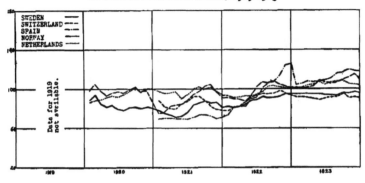

CHART VIII

PURCHASING POWER PARS OF THE CURRENCIES OF CZECHO-SLOVAKIA,
GREAT BRITAIN, AND DENMARK, EXPRESSED AS PERCENTAGES
OF DOLLAR EXCHANGE RATES; 1919-1923

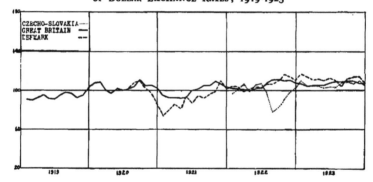

one of the currencies concerned would have the same value in exchange
against the dollar as in the purchase of goods in its domestic market;
at less than 100%, the exchange value would be high as compared with
domestic purchasing power; at more than 100%, the exchange value
would be relatively low. If we exclude Germany, the clustering around
the 100% figure is marked and aberrations were apparently self corrective. But Germany is in a class by itself. The internal value of the
mark in comparison with its exchange value was much higher than in
the case of any other currency, or, to put it from the other point of view,
its exchange value was much lower relative to domestic purchasing

CHART IX

PURCHASING POWER PARS OF THE CURRENCIES OF BELGIUM, FRANCE,
ITALY, AND GERMANY, EXPRESSED AS PERCENTAGES OF
DOLLAR EXCHANGE RATES; 1919-1923

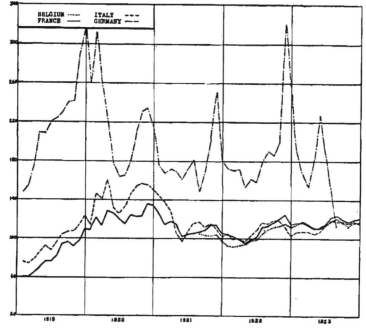

power. Nor is there any tendency toward the elimination of the discrepancy such as appears in the case of all the other currencies.[40]

Countries which were neutral during the war, Sweden, Switzerland,
Spain, Norway, and the Netherlands, show dollar exchange rates low
relative to internal price levels, that is to say the dollar was worth less
in each of these currencies than respective domestic purchasing powers
would seem to warrant. In the case of Sweden, Switzerland, and Spain the
difference was considerable while for Norway and the Netherlands it was
slight. In the next group come Czecho-Slovakia, a succession state, Great
Britain, the first of the great warring powers, and Denmark, another
neutral. With these three the adjustment was close but dollar exchange
cost on the average a trifle more than purchasing power par. With Belgium and France average dollar exchange rates were 8% higher than the

[40] In Russia and Poland similar phenomena may have occurred but the data
are inadequate to permit of assured conclusions.

theoretical par and in the case of Italy the percentage ran as high as 15. With Germany, however, dollar exchange cost consistently from 1 1/2 to 3 times the purchasing power par, the average agio was 85%, and fluctuations above this average, showing a relatively high cost of dollar exchange, were of much greater range than those below.

§ INTERPRETATION OF THE DATA

Not only is there a marked correlation between political status in respect to the war and the cost of dollar exchange relative to home prices but there is also a fairly close correspondence between *absolute* depreciation and *relatively* high cost of foreign exchange. Absolute depreciation in Spain and Norway was greater than in Great Britain but, aside from this, the order of arrangement according to the cost of foreign exchange relative to internal prices is also substantially the order of absolute currency depreciation.

Conceding, for the moment, the causal sequence from prices to exchange rates it would seem that current exchange rates were dominantly influenced by the current domestic purchasing power of the currencies concerned but that the following factors were also of importance:

(1) *Shift in international economic position.* Under gold-standard conditions an access of international liabilities, or a diminution of international assets, is normally accompanied by a relative fall in prices in the country affected and a consequent increase in the export-import ratio in adjustment to the changed situation. Under inconvertible paper currencies this adjustment tends to be accomplished through the foreign exchanges. Instead of the home exchange remaining stable while domestic prices fall, as happens under the gold standard, equilibrium in international transactions tends to be preserved by a falling exchange value of the currency while domestic prices remain stable or else rise less than in proportion to the increased cost of foreign exchange. The domestic purchasing power of the currency will then show a high ratio to its exchange value and this will encourage exports and retard imports. Those countries which during the war added to their international liabilities, or suffered a detraction from their international assets, will normally therefore appear in Table XIII with a ratio of the domestic to the foreign value of their currencies above those which improved their international economic position by the acquisition of securities, or other rights, giving them claims on future incomes which, in the postwar period, became current income. The neutral countries in general improved their international economic position during the war while the position of the warring countries, whether victors or vanquished, underwent a retrogression. Of the principal warring countries concerned

Great Britain probably suffered the least relative loss in this respect.[41] The relative improvement in the international economic position of the neutrals may explain the higher relative exchange values of their currencies. The acquisition of large gold reserves by the neutral nations in the course of the war was also of some significance since the sale of these reserves made it possible to sustain exchange rates for a considerable period above their "par" position. But these are, nevertheless, causes of the second order of magnitude and would not account for such great divergencies from purchasing power par as appear in the case of German exchange.

(2) *Probable future movements in exchange rates.* The possible rise in foreign exchange rates against an inconvertible paper currency (fall of the domestic exchange) is infinite, the possible fall (rise in domestic exchange) is ordinarily limited to the difference between the existing rate and the old gold par.[42] This fact is probably of some weight in depressing the current exchange value of currencies whose future is unfavorable or obscure (and so in raising the ratio of domestic to foreign value), though it would not be much of a bearish factor where, on other grounds, improvement was probable. The actual trend of foreign exchange, whether down or up, and the financial status of the paper issuing government is no doubt of great influence. Investment and speculative demand for a paper exchange at any given rate will be more or less keen according to its future prospects. The exchanges of France, Italy, and Belgium throughout and beyond the period of German inflation, and preeminently the exchange of Germany itself, would suffer from this cause; those of the neutral countries would benefit. The prospect of improvement in the exchange value of the latter currencies as a result of a favorable situation politically, including sound public finance, would no doubt have a bullish tendency sufficiently strong to outweigh any general bearish influence issuing out of the fact that the value of a paper currency can always fall farther than it can rise. The shift of the ratio, in the case of Spain, from below to considerably above the base line was no doubt due to the failure to realize the possibility of an early return to the gold standard and to the increasing uncertainty as to the future of the peseta. The high ratio of internal to external value of

[41] Excepting, of course, the United States, the currency of which is used as a measuring rod throughout. So far as the United States improved its relative international economic position during the war the dollar would tend to be high in terms of foreign currencies.

[42] If the import of gold is refused, as in Sweden during the war, the exchange rate against a gold currency may rise above the former gold par. This is a very unusual situation which did not apply in the post-war period.

the French and Italian currencies in 1920 is also perhaps solely attributable to this cause. Up to 1919 the franc and the lira had been pegged in New York. When the pegging was withdrawn both currencies rapidly declined in terms of the dollar. Uncertainty as to how far this movement would go would seem to have been the primary cause for the depression of their exchange relative to their domestic value.

(3) *Constant pressure on exchange rates arising from recurring fixed liabilities.* This was of preeminent importance in the case of Germany owing to reparation demands and is to be regarded as the chief factor in the relatively high ratio of the domestic to the exchange value of the mark through 1921 and 1922.

(4) *Panic.* The desire to exchange an inconvertible currency against foreign money, at any price whatever, in order to avoid persistent shrinkage in both its external and internal value may be the dominant element in depressing the exchange value of the currency concerned and so in raising the ratio of internal to external purchasing power. But this is nevertheless not as important a factor as is sometimes supposed. It depends on where the panic originates. If it originates at home the general fear is likely to express itself in rising internal prices[43] as well as in rising foreign exchange rates and the price increase may readily outstrip the movement of exchange. On the other hand, if it originates abroad, foreign exchange rates will almost certainly rise higher than the domestic price level. From January 1920 till January 1922, with one slight and one considerable exception, the ratio of internal to external purchasing power of the German mark, as shown by the monthly averages, followed the movement of exchange rates but from January 1922 onward no such tendency is apparent. Foreigners lost confidence in the mark sooner than did the Germans. When foreigners alone had lost confidence the mark price of foreign currencies rose (a fall in mark exchange) but internal prices were not greatly affected. Similarly, whenever foreign confidence was partially restored, the mark price of foreign currencies fell but internal prices remained relatively unchanged. The ratio of exchange rates to internal purchasing power was therefore dominated up to 1922 by the absolute movements in exchange. But when the Germans themselves lost confidence in their currency both prices and exchange rates were affected. Though exchange rates rose, prices frequently rose in greater degree, and the ratio of the domestic to the exchange value of the mark then declined. The flight from the mark thus did not tend to lower the exchange value of the German currency

[43] Unless the limit on the rate of monetary turnover has already been reached.

relative to its domestic purchasing power, a fact which has already been commented upon.

(5) *The absence of free commercial intercourse.* Control of imports and exports, especially the latter, may affect the relation between the exchange and the domestic value of a currency by inhibiting, in whole or in part, its use in foreign transactions. Unless this control is complete, however, as in Russia, the influence on the ratio is not likely to be great. In spite of respectable authority to the contrary the writer is of the opinion that it played no considerable part in the German ratio.

In addition to the factors just enumerated, special causes, affecting one country or another, may cause deviations of actual exchange rates from computed purchasing power pars. All such pars are measured from the relationship of prices and exchange rates in a prior year taken as a base.[44] The relationship in the base year may have been somewhat abnormal and, if so, apparent aberrations in later years may be due to this fact. Price indices, moreover, are merely approximations and vary in some measure according to their composition. The computation of the purchasing power par is thus subject to a margin of error. Further than this, changes in productive methods, or in the international demand for goods, may cause shifts in the price relationship between those commodities which in a given country are the object only of domestic trade and those which cross its borders. This would lead to shifts in exchange rates relative to internal prices. But all such factors sink in importance on a general view covering many countries. They could at most account for minor deviations. Operative, no doubt, to a greater or less extent in the case of all the currencies above listed they would, nevertheless, be unlikely to change very greatly the order in which those currencies appear even if they could be accurately estimated. They are of no significance whatever in the major distinction between the German currency and all the others. Properly to account for this requires an analysis of exchange markets in general and of the market for German exchange in the inflation period in particular. To this subject it seems best to devote a separate chapter.

[44] In practice, from a time when gold standards were mutually in operation. Purchasing power pars, moreover, as ordinarily computed, involve prices some of which are, in part, a *function* of exchange rates. Strictly interpreted then, prices of non-internationally traded commodities only should be included in the indices on which purchasing power pars are based. Even so purchasing power pars represent the theoretically *proper* (i.e. equilibrium) exchange rate only on the assumption that the sole change in conditions, as compared with the base year, has been in the monetary factor.

CHAPTER V

PRICE AND EXCHANGE RATE THEORY AND THE FACTS IN GERMANY (CONTINUED)

ANALYSIS OF FOREIGN EXCHANGE MARKETS

§ UNITY OF THE MARKET

THE market for the exchange of one money against another normally comprises at least two *loci*, one in each of the countries concerned. In each of these *loci* there will be buyers and sellers of both moneys. Since, however, the buyer of one currency on the exchange market is necessarily the seller of another it will be convenient to concentrate attention on a single currency. Let us take the German mark. The mark will be sold in Berlin by those who, for any reason, want pounds, dollars, or other currencies, and will be sold in London, New York, and other centers by those who, having marks, wish to dispose of them. The mark will, on the other hand, be bought in Berlin by those who, having foreign currencies, wish to dispose of them and will be bought in London, New York, and other centers by those who for any reason desire marks. Whether transactions occur in one *locus* or another is determined by trade practices and is a matter of almost complete indifference in establishing rates of exchange. A German exporter to the United States may draw a bill on the American buyer or he may ask the buyer to remit. In the one case, the German sells dollars in Berlin and, *ipso facto*, buys marks in that *locus* and, in the other, the American sells dollars and buys marks in New York. Either operation will increase the offer of dollars against marks. Similarly, an American exporter of goods to Germany may draw on the German buyer or he may request the buyer to take the initiative in paying. If the former practice is followed, marks are sold and dollars bought in New York and, if the latter, marks are sold and dollars bought in Berlin. Either operation will increase the offer of marks against dollars. Since a German export to the United States is an American import, and an American export to Germany is a German import, the illustrations just given cover the whole range of commercial transactions between the two countries. If one of the centers accumulates an undue share of bills on the buying or selling side of a given currency the matter is quickly taken care of by arbitrage operations. The "market" for exchange is thus unified and, though dealing is scattered among several or many centers, communication is now so rapid that substantially the same results occur as if the *loci*, instead of being separated by oceans, were on opposite sides of the same street.

The single schedule which results may be thought of as the demand for, and supply of, any given currency against other moneys, or as a reciprocal demand (or reciprocal supply) schedule of the various currencies against one another. The mark demand for foreign currencies and the supply of foreign currencies against marks may be alternatively described as the mark demand for foreign currencies and the foreign currency demand for marks or as the supply of marks against foreign currencies and the supply of foreign currencies against marks. For the moment it will be convenient to adopt the concept of reciprocal demand.

§ IRREGULAR CHARACTER OF FOREIGN EXCHANGE RECIPROCAL
DEMAND SCHEDULES

Reciprocal demand schedules for an inconvertible paper currency are by no means smoothly sloping curves. It is possible that a rising exchange value of a depreciated paper currency, instead of reducing the amount of that currency demanded by holders of foreign moneys, may increase it, and, instead of increasing the amount of the cheapening foreign currencies demanded by holders of the said currency, may reduce it. Similarly a falling exchange value, instead of augmenting the amount of that currency demanded in exchange for foreign moneys, may lead to a diminution, while, at the same time, the amount of foreign currencies demanded in exchange for the given money may be enlarged.[1] This phenomenon, which is common on all speculative markets, very much increases the range of paper currency exchange rate fluctuations. It is due to the fact that with paper exchanges there are no fixed pars. Under gold standards this negation of the usual operation of supply and demand can occur only within the very narrow limits of the gold points. With paper currencies, however, the stimulus of potential speculative gains, when

_____

[1] This may appear to be a confusion of the static with the dynamic. Under static conditions, it might be argued, reciprocal demand curves will never show "humps." Yet it is conceivable that, at any given moment, a prospective buyer would be ready to purchase more exchange at a higher than at a lower price. One might then resort to casuistry and contend that, if the price were different, the premises would be altered, or that the commodity offered (the foreign exchange) is not the same thing when its price is changed. In any case it is the dynamic situation which is of practical importance and there is no doubt of the fact that buyers frequently do purchase more at a higher than they would have taken at a lower price.

the paper currency exchange shows a rising inclination, or the fear of losses, when it falls, frequently leads away from rather than toward the establishment of an equilibrium. The equilibrating forces are not abolished; they are merely in temporary abeyance. When the movement of exchange rates has gone far from the "intrinsic" values of the respective currencies, as established by current relative purchasing power in their domestic markets, buying of the relatively depreciated currency will pick up and purchases of the relatively appreciated currency will decline. The "humps" in the reciprocal demand schedule will then be broken through and equilibrium will ultimately be established just as on the produce exchanges the vague but real value of commodities for consumption purposes imposes limits on price fluctuations.

There is, however, one aspect of the market for inconvertible currencies which has no parallel on the produce exchanges. With commodities other than exchange, a seller, having once disposed of his product, cannot sell again without first shifting to the buying side, or if "futures" are being dealt in, without incurring obligations to deliver which he must eventually cover by purchases. There is no prospect that he will be able indefinitely to make these purchases at continuously lower prices. But note issuing authorities can, if they are so minded, sell the domestic currency *ad infinitum*. It costs nothing to obtain;[2] it can be manufactured at will. Whether or not the authorities are selling the domestic exchange makes but slight difference if note issues are, in any case, steadily increasing, since holders or prospective holders of the currency can with some confidence count on obtaining future supplies at ever cheaper prices. They will therefore be disposed to sell freely for later delivery. The total amount of the domestic currency offered for foreign exchange may thus increase to any extent as the price of foreign currency rises. There is no limit on supply such as is imposed by nature in the case of produce and therefore not even a potential limit on the possible fall in price.[3] This risk is presumably in the mind of speculative sellers and prospective buyers of the inconvertible currency and will

[2] Except the price of paper, ink, and printing. This can always be reduced to a negligible proportion of the value of the note simply by raising the denomination. It costs no more to print a note for 100 million marks than for one of the 1 mark denomination. The commodity dealt in is here, of course, constantly changing in character.

[3] This fact has been commented upon by the late Professor Allyn A. Young in his preface to *The French Franc, 1914-1928*, Eleanor Lansing Dulles, The Macmillan Company, New York, 1929. Professor Young pointed out that the effects of speculation in inconvertible money are not necessarily short-lived nor do the ultimate determinants of the value of the money necessarily remain unaffected by the speculation.

keep them on the bear side of the market longer than would otherwise be the case. The exchange value of such a currency can therefore fall far below the current purchasing power par without provoking any considerable support. When panic develops the "bottom may drop out of the market."

§ ABSOLUTE AND CONDITIONAL DEMAND FOR EXCHANGE

The word "speculative" has been employed in the foregoing discussion in no disparaging way. It is used in the broadest sense to cover the activities of all individuals whose entry into the market is dependent on the rate of exchange. Reciprocal demand schedules are at any given time made up of two classes of buyers. The demand of one group is absolute and arises out of the need for foreign money with which to meet obligations already incurred. This class of buyers is in the market without reservation and must purchase regardless of price. The demand of the other group is conditional. They will buy only at certain rates. Many such buyers are not speculators in the narrow sense of that term since they may intend to use immediately in the purchase of goods, securities, or services, in the foreign country, such exchange as they may acquire. Or they may be residents of the country whose exchange they buy who are selling their more or less permanent holdings of foreign assets. All these are speculators merely in the etymological sense of the word, in that, before they are eliminated from the demand schedules by the act of purchase, they are *looking forward to new transactions on condition that they can buy exchange at a price which suits them*. On the other hand the absolute demand comes from those who are completing old rather than contemplating new transactions.

§ CONDITIONAL DEMAND THE EQUILIBRATING FACTOR

It will later appear that while the reciprocal absolute demand represents compulsory purchases of exchange it does not necessarily require the acquisition of fixed amounts of the currencies demanded. According as the monetary medium in which the contracts are expressed is or is not the same as that in which they must be paid, the amount of the respective currencies necessary to extinguish the respective absolute demands may vary, in either direction, with any given change in the rate. This matter will presently be discussed in greater detail. Since the variation may be in either direction according as existing contracts run in one currency or another it is clearly possible that the contracts may be such as to cause the variations to cancel out, and, for the sake of clearness, this will for the moment be assumed to be the case. The effect of alterations in exchange rates in at least ultimately inducing inverse shifts in the amounts of the currencies reciprocally demanded can then express itself. only through the conditional portion of the respective demands. If, at any moment, the absolute foreign currency demand for a given money be small relative to the absolute demand in that currency for foreign moneys, and if the conditional demand at existing prices is not equally weighted in the opposite direction, exchange rates must move adversely to the former currency. This movement of rates will persist until the conditional demand for the depreciating currency grows, and the conditional demand for the appreciating currency shrinks, to the point where the discrepancy in absolute demands is exactly compensated by a like discrepancy in the opposite direction in the volume of the respective currencies actually bought (and sold) in response to the conditional element in the reciprocal demand schedules.

§ DISTINCTION BETWEEN ABSOLUTE AND CONDITIONAL DEMAND UNIMPORTANT UNDER GOLD STANDARDS

The distinction between absolute and conditional demand is of no great importance under gold standards since, at the gold points, gold becomes a perfect substitute for foreign exchange as a means of meeting international obligations. At the gold points, therefore, the whole of the demand for the appreciating currency becomes conditional; there is no demand whatever for bills in this currency at any exchange rate in excess of the cost of transporting gold. *Within* the gold points, however, both absolute and conditional demands are present and important. Some exchange *must* be bought and some will be bought only if the price is "right." Any excess in the momentary absolute demand for foreign moneys as opposed to that for a given domestic currency will usually be fully neutralized by a contrary shift in the respective conditional demands somewhat before the gold point is reached. For, as that point is approached, new purchases of the depreciating (sales of the appreciating) exchange become numerous while potential buyers of the appreciating (sellers of the depreciating) currency tend to withdraw from the market.

The buyers of the depreciating (sellers of the appreciating) currency may be citizens of either country concerned. Residents of the country whose exchange is depreciating may sell property, such as securities held in the other country, to residents of the latter, and then buy their own exchange with the proceeds, or they may sell, in the same way, securities held at home. The initiative may, on the other hand, be taken by the buyer of such property. Short-term loans will also be made by holders of the appreciating currency who, in effect, transfer assets from the temporarily dear to the temporarily cheap currency in the confident expectation of transferring them back again at a later date and at a profit. Residents of the country of appreciating currency will tend to increase commodity purchases in the other or will buy exchange for later use in the purchase of commodities in that other country. On the other hand, residents of the country of depreciating currency will restrict their purchases abroad and will refrain from making purchases of the appreciating exchange which they *would* make if its cost in their own currency were lower.

The chance of loss of capital in purchasing foreign gold exchange at the lower gold point is nil since the purchased exchange can at any time be turned into gold and imported, with a net yield in the domestic currency equal to the amount expended on exchange. As the gold point is approached purchases of the depreciating exchange are thus wellnigh a "sure thing," since the sole substantial movement in its exchange value must be upward. This type of speculation seldom lacks takers. On the other hand, no one will purchase the appreciating currency in the expectation of making a speculative profit and any potential buyers of this exchange, whose requirements are not *absolute*, will postpone their purchases to a more favorable occasion.

Whatever the purpose animating buyers, conditional demand *on both sides of the market*, at any rate of exchange near either gold point, thus always operates in the equilibrating direction. So far as capital transactions (property rights of any sort whether it be title to real property or other claims to future income) are concerned, the adjustment, while prompt, is nevertheless likely to be but temporary, even if there is never a reverse transfer. The payment of the annual yield to the purchasers of the property rights, that is, in the main, to residents of the country of appreciating currency, will eventually increase the absolute demand for that currency. If the causes of its present appreciation are continuous and not merely seasonal, and if the purchases of property abroad do not continuously show an accretion in excess of the growing interest bill, final equilibrium must be attained through a shift in merchandise and current service transactions. The movement in exchange rates may be adequate to effect the necessary shift but, if not, gold must eventually flow toward the country of appreciating currency, and it must continue to do so until price levels in the two countries are so changed as to bring about the requisite alteration in the situation. The reciprocal *absolute* demand for exchange will then gradually change and bring equilibrium without greater shifts in the conditional demand than will normally be attained by exchange rate fluctuations within the limits of the gold points.

§ ABSOLUTE AND CONDITIONAL DEMAND UNDER PAPER STANDARDS

Where inconvertible paper currencies are involved the essentials are the same, with one important exception. Exchange rate fluctuations are then the sole reliance for equilibrating reciprocal demand. Since there is no substitute for exchange, such as is furnished by gold where gold standards prevail, absolute demand remains absolute regardless of exchange rate fluctuations, and conditional demand does not show as sure, smooth, or prompt an inverse response to changes in the exchange value of the currencies as under gold. With reasonably stable commodity prices, however, the range of exchange fluctuations will tend to be not much greater than the sum of the possible fluctuations under gold standards plus the percentage alteration in relative price levels which would bring permanent equilibrium were gold standards in operation. The conditional demand from individuals seeking bargains, whether in capital or consumers' goods, will lead to purchases of the depreciating exchange when it has fallen far enough to make such bargains obvious, while potential buyers of the appreciating exchange will prefer to keep their assets in the currency which is worth less on the exchange markets than in its purchasing power over goods in its own sphere of circulation. Even when prices are changing fairly fast, a sharp cleavage between the exchange value of currencies and their current purchasing power in the respective domestic markets will ordinarily soon set forces in operation which will reduce the differential. If the exchange value of a given currency remains long below its purchasing power in its domestic market the consequent increased foreign purchases in that market, and the reduction in foreign purchases by holders of the money in question, will presently alter the absolute demands in such a way as no longer to require a large compensating shift in the conditional portion of reciprocal demand.

Such is the usual course of events. It may happen, however, that a country on an inconvertible paper monetary basis must steadily purchase so large a volume of foreign exchange as to cause its absolute demand for foreign money at any given moment far to exceed the current absolute foreign money demand for its own currency while the conditional foreign demand is weak owing to the inability of the country to furnish a profitable use for such of its currency as might be purchased. Though its own conditional demand for foreign currencies be cut to the bone as exchange rates move adversely, yet, if the conditional foreign currency demand for that country's money does not grow in adequate measure, the discrepancy in absolute demand may remain without full compensation. Foreign exchange rates will then pursue their upward trend indefinitely.

§ IMPORTANCE OF ABSOLUTE DEMAND IN THE GERMAN
INFLATIONARY EXPERIENCE

From the middle of 1921 onward the German government was bound
to purchase large amounts of foreign exchange to meet cash reparations
payments. Unlike the ordinary absolute demand arising from past
commercial transactions which, while unaffected *in the present* by any
change in rates, is modified *in the future* as the exchange value of the
currency alters, this demand for foreign exchange was persistently
independent of exchange fluctuations. The absolute mark demand for
foreign currencies, so increased by the cash reparations burdens, was
far in excess of the current foreign currency demand for marks. In this
situation the exchange value of the mark was bound to fall (foreign
exchange rates rise) until the conditional reciprocal demand should
show an equal discrepancy in the opposite direction. But the means of
stimulating the conditional demand for German (supply of foreign)
exchange[4] other than from the sale of non-capital goods—means which
are of the utmost importance as quick resources and which are ordinarily
provided by the transfer of property or securities or the placing of temporary or permanent loans abroad—were all unavailable. The Reichsbank, it is true, had a not inconsiderable volume of gold which it could
have sold against foreign exchange. But to this it then clung tenaciously
as a last resource for which the need would be still greater when currency
reform should be undertaken. Properly enough deeming it useless to
throw its gold stocks on a market which would quickly swallow them
without showing any substantial improvement, it pursued a policy of
caution and refrained from any vigorous support of the exchange.[5]
Foreign loans were impossible owing to the threatening political situation. There were very few foreign securities, or other claims to foreign
property, held in the country, from the sale of which foreign exchange
could have been secured. The sale abroad of domestic securities of any
type was inhibited by the same lack of confidence as made new governmental borrowing impossible while foreign investment in real and other
forms of fixed property in Germany was not only subject to the prevailing
general distrust but was also practically precluded by rent limitation laws

[4] It will be more convenient here to take a fixed point of view, the German,
and speak of "the supply of foreign exchange" rather than of the "demand
for German exchange."

[5] When, in 1923, it was lured from this policy the results were such as to
provide a complete justification of its former refusal to use its gold reserve in
support of exchange. This justification was obtained in spite of the fact that
the chance of success in 1923 was considerably better than it would have been
in 1921, since, in 1923, cash reparations had been suspended.

and the possibility of confiscation.[6] Almost the whole burden of provision of the required supplies of foreign exchange was therefore thrust
on commercial, rather than on financial, transactions. A great part of
the existing transportable *capital* goods, however, such as the mercantile
marine, a considerable portion of the rolling-stock of the railroads, a
large number of farm animals, and equipment of various types had, as
we have seen, been delivered to the Allies under the terms of the Treaty
of Versailles, and, as a consequence, almost the sole means of procuring
foreign exchange was through the export of current commodity production or through sales of the currency for whatever price it would
bring.

Now a large and continuing exces f commodity exports cannot be
developed overnight. A transformation of the internal economic organization must first be achieved through a shifting of industry from production for the home market to lines which are capable of export. Of
necessity this is a matter of years. But the trouble was that the Allies
wanted reparations and they wanted them in a hurry. The supply of
immediately available exportable goods was insufficient to cover their
demands. Exchange rates being proximately determined by existing
reciprocal demand schedules, and by these alone, the possible future
supply of exportable goods was irrelevant except as it led to the present
purchase of German exchange for later use. The conditional demand
for German exchange was consequently dependent not upon the prospect of immediate and certain gains but upon a risky investment for an
indefinite term. Even if an adequate export surplus should develop,
progressive inflation would raise prices and reduce the value of any
mark exchange which might be bought at the moment and held for later
use. Before the conditional demand for marks would expand enough to
cover the difference in reciprocal absolute demand the exchange value
of the mark had therefore to fall to a discount on its current domestic
purchasing power sufficient to convince a large group of "investors" in
the German currency that the risk in this long-term investment was
worth the taking.

§ THE MARK DEMAND FOR FOREIGN EXCHANGE AS AFFECTED BY NOTE ISSUES

In order to meet its foreign obligations there was no course open to
the Reich administration but to secure (through the Reichsbank) the
necessary foreign exchange by selling marks. The Reichsbank, late in

---

[6] The fear of the Germans that control of properties would on a large scale
pass into the hands of foreigners (Überfremdung) and the measures adopted
to prevent this happening were unnecessary.

1921, denied that it was or had been selling marks abroad. This statement came in response to the charge that the Germans were deliberately depreciating their own currency. There is no doubt that the denial was honest. But though the Reichsbank was not selling marks abroad it was selling them at home. Where the sale was made did not at all affect the result. In purchasing foreign currencies on behalf of the government the bank was, *ipso facto*, selling German money, and it was, in addition, manufacturing the money which it sold. This enlarged supply of marks reduced their purchasing power at home and, while still further checking the growth of the conditional foreign currency demand for German money, prevented the decline in the private conditional mark demand for foreign exchange which would normally have attended the increase in the mark price of foreign moneys. The result was an exchange rate which bore a very remote relation to current relative purchasing powers of the mark and the foreign currencies against which it was exchanged.

§ DIFFERENCE BETWEEN CONDITIONAL AND ABSOLUTE DEMANDS AS EQUILIBRATING FORCES

However tardy may be the response of conditional demand to changes in exchange rates, the long-run *tendency* is always toward the establishment of equilibrium. So far as conditional demand is concerned a fluctuation in the rate is therefore essentially self-limiting. Such is, however, not the case with absolute demand. According to the tenor of the contracts for the payment of which exchange is necessary, movements in exchange rates may be self-limiting, self-inflammatory, or simply neutral.[7] Under one set of conditions a given exchange fluctuation, resulting from a disequilibrium in international debits and credits, will tend toward an immediate adjustment of existing claims and counter-claims and, quite apart from the influence of conditional demand, will itself operate to restore equilibrium. Under another set of conditions it will have just the opposite effect and will exaggerate rather than diminish the original disequilibrium. Under a third it will have no effect at all. A few examples will make this clear.

Let us suppose, first, that, with a rate of exchange at the old (and present) gold pars but with the United States on a gold and Germany on an inconvertible paper monetary standard, Germans trade with Americans in the following fashion:

---

[7] What is here said is a partial repetition of my former treatment of this matter in an article entitled "Self-limiting and Self-inflammatory Movements in Exchange Rates," *Quarterly Journal of Economics*, Vol. XLIII, February 1929, pp. 221-49. The editors of that journal have very kindly permitted me to reproduce parts of the article.

Case I (a)

Germans sell to Americans goods quoted in dollars to the amount of $1,000,000.

Americans sell to Germans goods quoted in marks to the amount of 4,200,000 marks.

The German exporters (or American importers, according as payment is made by draft or remittance) will have dollars for sale and will be in the market for marks and the American exporters (or German importers) will have marks for sale and will be in the market for dollars. Equilibrium will be reached at 4.2 marks to the dollar, that is to say, without any disturbance of the par rate.

Now, suppose that the American export of goods to Germany suddenly doubles in volume, on the same terms of the sale, while German sales to citizens of the United States remain the same. We then have:

Case I (b)

Germans sell to Americans goods quoted in dollars to the amount of $1,000,000.

Americans sell to Germans goods quoted in marks to the amount of 8,400,000 marks.

American exporters and/or German importers will now have 8,400,000 marks for sale against a dollar demand for these marks of only $1,000,-000. If no other buyers of marks come into the market[8] the mark must fall in value to 8.4 to the dollar. Such a rate will bring the accounts into equilibrium; the movement of exchange will be self-limiting. Expressed in terms of dollars the obligations of the German importers (the assets of the American exporters) will have shrunk in strict proportion to the decline in the dollar value of the mark (that is, to $1,000,-000, or one-half their amount before the decline in mark exchange) while the obligations of the American importers (the assets of the German exporters) remain the same. Expressed in terms of marks the obligations of American importers (the assets of German exporters) become twice as great while the obligations of German importers (the assets of American exporters) remain unchanged. Expressed in either currency, the assets of Americans, being claims to a fixed sum of marks, automatically diminish in relative value with a decline in the exchange

---

[8] Only passing attention will be paid in this treatment of absolute reciprocal demand to the influence of conditional purchases and sales of exchange. Where those conditional purchases are very tardy, as was the case with mark exchange in the inflation period, the effect is similar, though less exaggerated, than that which would occur if there were none at all.

value of the mark, and the assets of the Germans, being claims to a fixed sum of dollars, automatically increase in relative value from the same cause.

The liabilities of the Germans, while expressed in marks, are of course ultimately payable to the American exporters in dollars, and the liabilities of the Americans, while expressed in dollars, are ultimately payable to the German exporters in marks. But—and this is the significant point—the German liabilities are at any moment a fixed sum of marks but a variable amount of dollars and the American liabilities are a fixed sum of dollars but a variable amount of marks. When the American exporters bring the proceeds of their sales home they will obtain dollars in inverse proportion to the appreciation of dollar exchange; the German exporters, on the contrary, will obtain marks in direct proportion to that appreciation.

The upshot of the matter is that, when the transactions are completed and payment has been received by the exporters in their own currency, German exporters will have gained and American exporters will have lost through the exchange fluctuation while importers in both countries will be unaffected.[9] The Germans, taken as a whole, will get twice the physical volume of imports for a given volume of exports that they obtained before the decline in mark exchange, or, to put it in another way, they will have had half their liabilities wiped out. In the situation as outlined the Americans are mulcted as a result of having acquired their assets in marks and the Germans receive an undeserved windfall through having acquired theirs in dollars. Any individual buyer or seller could, of course, hedge on his transaction, but this would simply mean a shifting of the loss on exchange and not its elimination. It might however redistribute the national gains and losses. If, before the fall in exchange, Americans had sold mark futures to Germans, or Germans had sold dollar futures to Americans, the losses of the Americans and the gains of the Germans, taken as a whole, would be diminished; but if both had dealt in futures with their own nationals the national gain and loss would obviously be unaltered.

The situation just described would, of course, be reversed if mark

[9] Abstraction is made here, and throughout the discussion, of shifts in the internal purchasing power of either currency through inflationary or deflationary movements concurrent with the movements in exchange rates. To include them would not alter the essential conclusions but would unduly complicate their presentation. The matter in hand is a consideration of exchange fluctuations only. It is presumed that no one will deny that exchange rates may, at least temporarily, move far out of line with the internal purchasing power of the currencies concerned.

exchange should appreciate. If, for instance, Cases I (a) and I (b) should be reversed in time sequence, the Americans would gain at the expense of the Germans. Under the assumed conditions of sale a movement of the exchanges operates to diminish real obligations *pari passu* with an increase in their nominal amount and to increase real obligations *pari passu* with a diminution in their nominal amount.

The point should perhaps be noted that, in the case first assumed, neither the German importers nor exporters have any interest—any immediate interest at any rate—in preventing the fall in mark exchange. On the contrary, so far as contracts in being are concerned, the German exporters have much to gain by its fall while the importers will be indifferent since they have a fixed amount of marks to pay regardless of the fluctuations in exchange rates. American importers will also be indifferent, since they have to pay a fixed amount of dollars, but American exporters will have a very intense interest in preventing the fall in the exchange value of the mark. Under normal conditions they would, of course, refuse to sell their claims to marks at the sacrifice involved in Case I (b) and they would ordinarily find plenty of new purchasers—purchasers, that is, other than the original American importers—to take the marks off their hands. The presence of such buyers will prevent any considerable decline in mark exchange, but purchases of this type, as has been pointed out above, are by no means in every set of circumstances inevitable. In any case the effect of their presence or absence is entirely distinct from the effects of the exchange fluctuation on *absolute* reciprocal demand. Under the conditions of sale above assumed the movement in exchange rates itself, quite apart from any motivation to new purchases or sales, tends to be self-limiting. In the degree of its influence, which is strictly proportional to the magnitude of the movement, it will necessarily reinforce any other factors working in the direction of restraint on exchange deviations and will counteract those which may be working in the opposite way.

If now we turn to sales of goods in opposite terms we shall find that exchange movements, in and of themselves, far from being self-limiting, are then self-inflammatory. Let us suppose, instead of the situation described in Case I, that the matter stand as follows:

Case II (a)

Germans sell to Americans goods quoted in marks to the amount of 4,200,000 marks.

Americans sell to Germans goods quoted in dollars to the amount of $1,000,000.

Here, as in Case I (a), equilibrium would be reached at an exchange rate of 4.2 marks to the dollar. But if, on the same terms of sale, there be a doubling of German orders for goods in America while American orders for goods in Germany remain unchanged, the matter assumes an aspect very different from that of Case I (b). We should then have the following state of affairs:

Case II (b)

Germans sell to Americans goods quoted in marks to the amount of
4,200,000 marks.

Americans sell to Germans goods quoted in dollars to the amount of
$2,000,000.

Under these circumstances American exporters and/or German importers will have marks for sale[10] to such an amount as will, at the rate of exchange which becomes established, provide them with $2,000,-000. But the dollar demand for marks from American importers and/or German exporters amounts to only 4,200,000 marks. If no new buyers of marks come into the market, the price of marks must fall. Let us assume that, as in Case I (b), it falls to 8.4 marks to the dollar. Far from such a rate bringing the accounts into equilibrium it will merely make the disequilibrium so much the greater. At 8.4 marks to the dollar the mark claims on Americans will provide $500,000 only while Germans need $2,000,000 to meet the American claims on them. The mark will then fall farther. But every decline only makes the situation still worse unless new buyers of marks with dollars are eventually attracted by the bargain rates. If, to repeat, the mark were reasonably stable in domestic purchasing power, and if goods were freely available for export from Germany, such purchasers would certainly appear. But, in the absence of such conditions, a heavy fall in the exchange value of the mark may frighten away such purchasers as would otherwise be disposed to buy. The fall in the exchange value of the mark, instead of reducing the dollar value of American claims on Germans and increasing the mark value of German claims on Americans, as in Case I (b), will reduce the dollar value of German claims on Americans and increase the mark value of American claims on Germans. Under the former terms of sale the exchange movement resulted in a diminution of the real burden of the nominally larger claims and in an augmentation of the real burden of the nominally smaller until equilibrium was reached. But, under the present terms, the larger

[10] Though the goods are quoted in dollars American exporters will really have for sale marks to an indefinite amount corresponding to the number of marks for which their dollar claims on German importers will exchange.

(American) claims are augmented while the smaller (German) claims suffer a decline. The fall in mark exchange is thus self-inflammatory and cumulative, and, in the absence of new buyers of the mark, will have no bounds whatever until a large part of the American claims are extinguished by the bankruptcy of the German debtors.[11]

The American importers will now be the gainers and the German importers the losers, the exporters in both cases being unaffected. But how much the American importers will gain and how much the German importers will lose it is impossible to say since this depends on the extent of the exchange fluctuation. That fluctuation is quite indefinite and, indeed, theoretically infinite. The only thing that can check it is the operation of conditional demand.

The fall in the dollar value of the mark brings equilibrium in Case I while it increases the disequilibrium in Case II because, in Case I, the claims on both sides are expressed in a circulating medium other than that in which they are ultimately to be extinguished, while, in Case II, they are expressed in the same medium in which payment is to be made. In Case I the claims of Americans, having first grown relatively to those of the Germans as a result of the increased export of American goods, suffer a reduction proportionate to the decline in the exchange value of the unit in which they are expressed, a decline for which the growth of the American claims is itself responsible. The German claims, on the other hand, are proportionately increased. In Case II the German claims are proportionately reduced when the mark falls in exchange value and the American claims are increased. The original fall in the exchange value of the mark having been due to an excess of American claims the situation thus becomes worse and worse.

Continuing the comparison of Case II with Case I, it is the German importers, instead of the American exporters, who will now have a lively interest in preventing the fall in mark exchange (all other parties being indifferent or favorably disposed to that fall), and they will seek to secure dollars from new sellers of that currency. But there may be few or no individuals, other than the original exporters, who have, or can secure, claims against dollars. This was not far from being the actual case in Germany in the inflation period.

If we assume a change in the conditions of Case II with regard to the volume of purchases, such as would be involved if the German purchases declined instead of increasing, the course of the mark, under the same terms of sale of goods, would tend indefinitely upwards. This is how-

[11] They may avoid bankruptcy if marks in unlimited supply are furnished by the issuing authorities, provided *some* foreign buyers of marks enter the market. It would seem that this was, in fact, the case in Germany in the inflation period.

ever of little practical importance for the later consideration of actual phenomena since American importers were always in a position to secure marks by exporting gold, goods, property claims, or securities to Germany, though the necessity for doing so never arose owing to the fact that the Germans were constantly in arrears on reparations account and therefore always exigent buyers of foreign exchange. The conditional reciprocal demand would, in any case, have been promptly operative.

Though no one method of quoting prices is universal in foreign trade perhaps the more normal practice is that described in Case I.[12] This works well enough under stable exchanges but, when the exchanges become unstable, the sellers of goods in the country of the relatively appreciating currency quickly learn to quote in their own exchange in order to avoid losses. So far as the sellers in the country of relatively depreciating currency have been quoting, and continue to quote, prices in their own unit we then have the conditions of Case II. So far however as they have been quoting in the buyers' currency, or go over to that practice, we should have still another set of conditions under which existing contracts, on one side, are expressed in the monetary unit in which they are to be paid and, on the other, are not. These are the conditions set forth in:

Case III

Germans sell to Americans goods quoted in dollars.
Americans sell to Germans goods quoted in dollars.

Under this method of invoicing, a fall in mark exchange arising from an increase in the sale of American goods in Germany will increase the mark liabilities of the German buyers but will also increase the mark assets of the German sellers. The decline in the value of the mark will then, of itself, make the German position neither better nor worse. A downward movement of the mark will not, in the absence of new buyers of marks (sellers of dollars), be arrested or even retarded, but it will not, by its own fall, be accelerated. If the downward movement has been due to an increase in German purchases abroad the Germans will need more dollars to pay for this increase than are available from their sales of goods and, if these dollars cannot be obtained by increasing the offer of marks per dollar, mark exchange may, as in Case II, continue in an unchecked decline. But in order to

[12] cf. "Equilibrium in International Trade: The United States, 1919-26," J. W. Angell, *Quarterly Journal of Economics*, Vol. XLII, May, 1928, p. 397. It is doubtful, however, whether German foreign trade follows this practice as fully as does that of other nations.

check it the volume of new demand for marks (sale of dollars) will be the same after as before the decline occurred, while, under the conditions of Case II, it must needs be greater.[13]

It is unlikely that the demand for *goods* would expand quite so suddenly as has here been assumed. But an expansion, from whatever cause, in the requirements for foreign exchange would have, in the degree of its importance, the effects above described. Such an expansion in German demand for foreign exchange occurred with the lifting of the blockade and the release of the pent up demand for foreign goods in 1919, with the inception of cash reparations payments in the summer of 1921, and with the "flight from the mark" which reached large proportions in the middle of 1922. For a surprisingly long time after 1919 every downward movement in mark exchange tended eventually to be checked by purely gambling purchases (conditional demand) on the part of lambs who bought blindly. This support gradually weakened and practically disappeared during 1922 when it became obvious even to the most unsophisticated foreign buyer that a restoration of the German currency to anything like its former purchasing power was a possibility infinitely remote. When this mode of supply of foreign exchange vanished there were few ways in which it could be obtained, scant emergency resources of any kind, and therefore but a weak tendency for a fall in the mark to evoke sustaining forces.[14]

In general, it may be said of this phase of the exchange market that, when conditional demand responds promptly to a shift in rates, the influence of *absolute* demand, either in checking or in exaggerating the fluctuations in exchange according as the tenor of contracts in being runs in one currency or the other, is slight. A favorable or unfavorable balance of payments[15] is then of no great importance in effecting even temporary changes in the rate. A balance either way will be quickly compensated by a shift in that part of the volume of conditional recip-

[13] German exchange rate movements in the period of inflation were tested to determine whether the theory here advanced was corroborated by the facts. The degree of verification obtained was very considerable. See "Self-Limiting and Self-Inflammatory Movements in Exchange Rates," *op. cit.* pp. 245 ff.

[14] It would, of course, never be impossible to acquire by one means or another *some* foreign exchange. If none whatever had been available at any price a downward movement in mark exchange would probably have been interminable. The difficulty of procuring foreign exchange appears to have been sufficient to increase the range in fluctuations but it did not extend it *ad infinitum*.

[15] The phrase is used in the sense in which it alone has any meaning, viz. a decrease or increase in more or less involuntary short-term credits from foreigners.

rocal demand which is actually realized in purchases. But, when there is little conditional demand for the depreciating exchange, the rate may not only move adversely to that currency to an indefinite degree but, under certain types of invoicing, will automatically so alter absolute demand as to accelerate the fall rather than release forces to check it. There is reason to believe that this happened in the case of German exchange. The requirements for cash reparations payments were for a fixed amount of dollars, or their equivalent in other foreign exchange, and this was also true of a very large share of the payments for German imports. On the other hand a considerable share of German exports were invoiced in marks. Any decline in the exchange value of the mark therefore tended to induce a further fall.

§ EFFECT OF CHANGES IN THE VALUE OF THE MEASURING ROD

The effects on the exchange value of an inconvertible paper currency consequent upon recurring requirements for a fixed sum of foreign moneys are further influenced by an increase in the general purchasing power (fall in prices) of the currency in which the obligations must be paid. The volume of dollar exchange necessary to cover a given quantum of fixed obligations expressed in dollars would, of course, be unaffected by a fall in dollar prices but the supply of dollar exchange issuing from exports to the United States would tend to decline. The fixed demand for dollars having then grown in relative importance, the dollar would tend to rise more than in proportion to its increase in internal purchasing power, and this movement, in accordance with the principles just stated, might well prove cumulative. The effects would, of course, be reversed if the medium in which fixed obligations were payable should fall in domestic purchasing power. The facts are that the internal value of the dollar rose at a rapid rate from mid-1920 to the end of 1921 and that dollar exchange against the mark synchronously rose relatively to the respective domestic purchasing powers of the two currencies. But most of this rise occurred before cash reparations payments were initiated and, since the Germans had then but few fixed obligations in dollars, some other cause must have been principally operative. An alteration in reciprocal conditional demand leading to an enhanced desire for the appreciating currency, the dollar, was probably responsible. It is interesting to note that, under opposite circumstances, the increase in the internal purchasing power of the dollar resulted in a relative fall in its value in terms of another paper currency, the English pound. In the latter half of 1920 the exchange value of the dollar against pounds did not rise in anything like the degree of relative augmentation in purchasing power over goods at home. This is perhaps explained by the fact that the British had a fixed pound income on foreign investments while their outlay for a given quantum of imports varied not only with the exchange rate of the pound against foreign currencies but with prices prevailing in other parts of the world.

§ EXCHANGE AND THE PARADOX OF VALUE

One further possible result of rising foreign exchanges should be noted. A sharp rise in foreign exchange which is not paralleled by a corresponding upward movement of domestic prices will ordinarily lead to an increase in the physical volume of exports relative to imports, but the increased physical volume of exports, sold at the prevailingly low domestic prices may, at the new rate, fail to provide as much foreign exchange as formerly issued from a smaller export volume. Any absolute reduction in the volume of imports, on the other hand, may be insufficient to bring equilibrium in demand for and supply of foreign exchange at the new rate level. The inadequacy of the supply of foreign exchange at the old rate, which was responsible for the upward movement, may thus very possibly be exaggerated by the rise. The result is a further upward movement and a possible indefinite repetition of the phenomenon. If, for example, foreign exchange rates should double overnight, while no change had taken place in internal prices, it is most unlikely that the physical volume of exports of commodities could be suddenly doubled even at the bargain prices to foreigners which would then be in effect. But unless they are at least doubled they will fail to provide as large a supply of foreign exchange as did the original volume of exports. The entire burden of adjustment will then fall on exchange *demand*. If this, in large part, is incapable of reduction, as is the case with interest or tribute payments, there is no limit to the rise in exchange short of the point where new buyers of the depreciating currency appear in sufficient strength to check the movement.

It is only under unusual conditions that this case is of much practical importance. A rising exchange rate is almost certain to be accompanied by rising internal prices of all exportable goods of a standard type with a world market, and, somewhat more tardily, of other exportable goods. The considerably increased physical volume of export of these goods, which takes place owing to the fact that while there is a rise in internal prices toward the world level as determined by existing exchange rates, the rise falls short of complete correspondence with world prices, is almost certain to increase the supply of foreign exchange. Similarly, under ordinary conditions, the demand for foreign exchange will decline somewhat by reason of the high prices of imports measured in the domestic currency. The elasticity of demand for the country's exports is here of great importance but, while the total world demand for any given group of exportable goods may be highly inelastic, this is most improbable with regard to the exports from any one country, at least with respect to all commodities which are not solely produced in that land. The world demand for wheat, for example, may be very inelastic but let wheat be sold in any one country at a price which will permit it to be laid down in importing markets at a very slightly cheaper rate than that at which wheat can be obtained elsewhere and the whole world import demand will be directed toward that country. The elasticity of *total* demand for each of the exportable goods of any given country is therefore irrelevant and a rise in foreign exchange which makes the exports of the said country cheap to foreign buyers, and imports dear to domestic consumers, will ordinarily so affect the demand and supply relationship in the foreign exchange market as to prevent the occurrence of any cumulative tendency in the movement of exchange rates. But, if the domestic consumption of exportable goods is already small and there is, in consequence, little opportunity to increase the volume of exports, and if imports are already at a very low level, movements in exchange rates may, of their own momentum, easily become cumulative from this as well as from any of the other factors which have been described. It will later appear that, while the response of German exports and imports to changes in the relation of exchange rates to the internal purchasing power of the mark took place, it was not immediate, and it seems entirely probable, therefore, that foreign exchange continued to rise because it had already risen, not only as a result of the immediate but also of the later effects of the original movement.

§ RELATIONSHIP OF EXCHANGE RATES TO PRICE LEVELS
RECONSIDERED

Enough has been said to make it clear that, in certain circumstances, the tie between general price levels and exchange rates may be almost completely broken. Exchange rates at any given moment settle at the point which will equilibrate actual bids and offers. The fluctuations in the rate are unpredictable and frequently cumulative. They will be held in the neighborhood of purchasing power par only when conditional demand responds promptly to the stimulus which deviations from that par provide. In the German case conditional demand did not so respond and its failure to do so increased the strength of the forces operating through absolute demand. The respective weight of the several forces from time to time in operation it is impossible to determine. All the influences cited tended at one time or another to depress German exchange and, taken together, account for the unique character of the relationship of prices to exchange rates which appears in the case of the mark.

The price level was so far from dominating exchange rates that, on the face of the phenomena at least, it often seemed as if the causal sequence lay the other way. The actual sequence will be investigated statistically in the chapter to follow. It will be sufficient here to point out that some prices were directly affected by a fluctuation in the exchange value of the currency. This was true almost immediately of the prices of imported goods and, with a measure of retardation, of many exports as well.[16] To determine the effect on other prices it will be enough to consider the consequences of an upward movement in the foreign exchange. An increase in export and import prices as a result of rising foreign exchanges tends of itself to augment the rate of monetary turnover and so to permit other prices to rise. Rising prices of imports will first cause importers to reduce their monetary balances and will also encourage banks to lend larger amounts on the basis of a given stock of imported goods. Both phenomena will operate to increase the speed of monetary turnover. Similarly, on stocks of exportable goods, more money will be lent by banks. If the total lending power of the banks were strictly limited, a general rise in prices might not ensue, but otherwise it is almost certain. Importers and exporters distribute their increased funds in the course of their business operations and the increase in prices is thus transmitted to other goods. This raises the monetary value of the security back of all collateralled bank loans and leads to larger loans. The statistics of German inflation later to be examined leave no doubt whatever that, in the post-war inflation period, the chronological, if not the logical, sequence of events often ran from exchange rates to prices to volume of circulating medium.

A rigid control of money and credit might have kept domestic prices down. But, so long as reciprocal demand did not balance at purchasing power par, foreign exchange would not have remained low. If it be admitted that the demands of the Allies for immediate cash reparations could not be covered by the then available supply of exportable goods in Germany, and that borrowing abroad was impossible, exchange rates would have risen no matter what had been done with the domestic currency. If the Germans had been on a gold standard they would have been forced to abandon it through the complete exhaustion of their gold.

[16] Whether import or export prices will be first affected in cases of this sort depends on the nature of the trade. Standardized goods with a world market are the first to respond. If imports are predominantly goods of this character, and exports not, imports will show the effect of changing exchange rates before exports will and vice versa if the premises are the opposite.

If they had kept the issues of paper currency down, and with them domestic prices, they would have been denuded of all goods which could have been transported, and even then foreign exchange rates would not necessarily have fallen. On the contrary it is probable that Germany would have had in so exaggerated a form the phenomenon of two distinct price levels in foreign and domestic trade that complete industrial dislocation would have occurred. Though distinct internal and external price levels did develop the difference between them was constantly being diminished by rising prices in the domestic market. If such increase in domestic prices had been prevented it seems certain that the spread between the high prices on the foreign market, as measured in marks at the current exchange rate, and those prevailing at home, would have been greater than it was even though the absolute rise in foreign exchange had been somewhat curtailed.

It cannot be maintained that fluctuations in exchange rates ever absolutely dominate the internal price level of a country with a highly depreciated paper currency. But, on the other hand, it cannot be denied that they may occur in practically complete independence of the domestic value of the paper currency nor that a persistent tendency for foreign exchange to rule far higher than purchasing power par exerts a very strong upward pressure on domestic prices. The rate of monetary turnover will first be accelerated and, when this rate has reached its limit, the alternative to further note issues is a wellnigh intolerable spread between internal and external prices and consequent chaos in the whole price structure.

It should be noted, also, that equilibrium in foreign trade is more directly and readily reached under paper than under gold standards provided the movements in exchange rates under paper standards are not extreme. Where, on the other hand, the movements *are* extreme the achievement of equilibrium may very gravely be retarded.

§ REVISED THEORY OF RELATIONSHIP BETWEEN VOLUME OF
CIRCULATING MEDIUM, PRICES, AND EXCHANGE RATES

In summary it may be said that there is an essential if not always a close numerical relationship between the volume of circulating medium and prices, while between prices and exchange rates, the numerical relationship, though normally close, is not at all essential. If ineluctable and regularly recurring obligations in foreign currencies should exceed any possibility of acquiring those currencies, then the exchange value of the domestic currency would fall to zero regardless of its internal purchasing power. So far as causal sequence is concerned it may properly be held that though, under an inconvertible paper monetary system, note issues do in fact tend to be increased as a result of rising prices (in contrast with what happens under a gold standard where the gold supply tends to fall off), and though prices do not always respond to an expansion or contraction of the currency, it is none the less true that prices are fundamentally a resultant of the volume of circulating medium. The latter is, though with difficulty, subject to control. Exchange rates, on the contrary, are a resultant of a number of forces of which relative price levels are one. Usually this one force is dominant but at times it plays but a subordinate rôle. Exchange rates may in turn affect prices, regardless of the volume of note issues, through changing the rate of monetary turnover. It can scarcely be said therefore that the causal sequence runs any more strongly in one direction than in the other. Prices and exchange rates are in part determined independently of one another, in part react upon one other, and in part are self-determined. Fluctuations in either may be the cause of further immediate as well as future movements in the same index and may or may not affect the other. With a sufficiently great change in general prices exchange rates will move in correspondence. The converse is not necessarily true. In this sense alone are prices the controlling factor.

PART III

COURSE OF INFLATION
STATISTICALLY MEASURED

CHAPTER VI

PRICE AND EXCHANGE RATE THEORY AND THE FACTS IN GERMANY (CONCLUDED)

SEQUENCE OF CHANGES IN THE VOLUME OF CIRCULATING MEDIUM AND IN THE DOMESTIC AND FOREIGN VALUE OF THE MARK

§ CHRONOLOGICAL SEQUENCE AND CAUSAL RELATIONSHIP

THAT the price level in Germany in the period of inflation rose much more than in proportion to the increase in the volume of circulating medium and that internal prices failed to keep pace with the mark cost of foreign goods has already been indicated. In the present chapter the movements of the indices of volume of circulating medium, of internal, and of external prices will be examined in detail especially in their chronological sequence. Such sequence as may appear will perhaps furnish some presumptive evidence of causal relationships but it cannot be conclusive. It may always be pertinently argued that any variation in the external or internal value of the mark was due to anticipated, but not yet realized, changes in the volume of circulating medium. The real chain of causation would then be the reverse of what appears on the face of the phenomena. A distinction should also be made between actual and necessary causation. A rise in internal prices or exchange rates may *actually* have induced an increase in the volume of circulating medium though it would not *necessarily* do so. Further, what might otherwise have been temporary changes in one of the indices the variations of which were fundamentally, but not immediately, consequent upon one of the others, may have been made permanent by an independent change in that other. The real causal sequence would then again be obscured. The actual course of the phenomena, however, is itself interesting, and, with reservations, may be made the basis of some inferences as to logical causation.

§ THE MEASUREMENT OF INFLATION

In measuring the degree of inflation of an inconvertible paper currency it has become customary to use, along with indices of the volume of circulating medium and of internal prices, an index of exchange rates.[1] The two former indices proceed from an arbitrarily selected base year, usually the year prior to the inauguration of inconvertibility. The index of exchange rates, however, is quite generally based on the *current* price of the inconvertible paper in some other money. It is obvious that, since such an index has no fixed base whatever, it cannot properly, as a criterion of inflation, be compared with indices on a base fixed in a given year. From time to time the value of either or both of the currencies employed in the exchange comparison may rise or fall relative to their value in the year used as a base for the other indices and, if both change, the movement may be in the same or in opposite directions. If the changes were in the same direction, and of equal magnitude, the exchange relation between the currencies would tend to remain unaltered, if they were in the same direction, but of unequal magnitude, the exchange rate would tend to shift less than the alteration in the commodity value of the currency which showed the greater absolute movement, and, if they were in the opposite direction, the exchange rate would tend to shift more than the alteration in the commodity value of either. In none of these cases is the index of exchange rates directly comparable with that of prices or of the volume of circulating medium.

The difficulty noted in the foregoing paragraph has in this book been averted up to this point by comparing exchange rates not directly with prices but with purchasing power pars. In the computation of purchasing power pars price changes in both countries concerned are taken into consideration. But purchasing power pars are no more directly related to prices or volume of circulating medium in any given single country than are exchange rates. The very fact, indeed, that purchasing power pars are comparable with exchange rates precludes the possibility of their being directly compared with the other indices. Prices may be compared with volume of circulating medium, and purchasing power pars, which involve prices, may be compared with exchange rates, but a new index of *external* prices (a compound of exchange rates and foreign prices) is essential to a true comparison of volume of circulating medium with the domestic and external value of the currency unit.

The currency in which the exchange value of inconvertible paper is expressed is ordinarily based on gold. As compared with 1913 (the year usually selected as a base for measuring war and post-war paper money inflation), gold had, by 1920, fallen to less than half its 1913 value. It then rose rapidly till the beginning of 1922 when substantial

---

[1] The figures of volume of circulating medium and of exchange rates may be absolutes rather than indices. This does not affect the validity of anything hereafter said.

stability of value was attained at approximately two-thirds of its 1913 status. It is clear that exchange rates in this period can be employed as a measure of inflation comparable with the index of internal prices, or with that of volume of circulating medium, only if these fluctuations in the value of gold are taken into consideration. To do so, an index of prices in the gold currency, measured from the same base year as is used for the index of prices in the paper money, must be multiplied by the current exchange rate. Three comparable indices covering a given time period are then obtained: (1) the volume of circulating medium relative to the volume in the base year, (2) the number of paper currency units requisite to purchase in the domestic market the quantum of goods which in the base year could have been purchased in that market with a single currency unit, (3) the number of the domestic paper currency units requisite to purchase in foreign markets the quantum of goods which in the base year could have been purchased in those markets with a single such currency unit.

Table XIV and Charts X and XI show three such indices for the German currency, all based on the year 1913, and designated volume of circulating medium, internal prices, and external prices, respectively.[2] Chart X covers the years 1918 to 1923 as a whole; Chart XI shows the years 1919 to 1923 broken up into three periods. Chart X and the third section of Chart XI are on a logarithmic scale, the only practicable means of graphically presenting the immense magnitudes involved. The volume of circulating medium index includes only money, not credit, and represents the number of times the volume of money in circulation at any given date exceeded that of 1913. The internal price index is based on the German index of wholesale prices, as published by the government statistical bureau, and represents for any given date the paper mark equivalent of one 1913 gold mark in the purchase of commodities within Germany. The external price index is computed from the Bureau of Labor Statistics index number of wholesale prices in the United States and from the dollar exchange rate in Berlin and represents, for any given date, the paper mark equivalent of one 1913 gold mark in the purchase of American commodities. The latter are assumed to be typical of foreign commodities in general. An index of actual exchange rates,[3] and pre-armistice figures for all the indices, are given for comparative

[2] Table XIV shows only yearly averages from 1914 to 1918, but the monthly average has been plotted on Charts X and XII.

[3] The relationship between the exchange rate index and the index of external purchasing power does not alter when the American price level was stable. From early 1921 onward the two curves are substantially parallel since, after that date, the goods value of the dollar moved within narrow limits.

TABLE XIV

INDEX NUMBERS OF THE VOLUME OF CIRCULATING MEDIUM, OF INTERNAL AND EXTERNAL PRICES, AND OF EXCHANGE RATES: 1914–1923

DATE		VOLUME OF CIRCULATING MEDIUM (TOTAL VOLUME OF CIRCULATING MEDIUM RELATIVE TO 1913 TAKEN AS 1[4])	INTERNAL PRICES (PAPER MARK EQUIVALENT OF INTERNAL PURCHASING POWER OF ONE 1913 GOLD MARK[5])	EXTERNAL PRICES (PAPER MARK EQUIVALENT OF EXTERNAL PURCHASING POWER OF ONE 1913 GOLD MARK[6])	EXCHANGE RATE (PAPER MARK EQUIVALENT OF ONE CURRENT GOLD MARK[7])
1914 (Yearly Average)		1.16	1.05	1.00	1.02
1915		1.47	1.42	1.17	1.16
1916		1.72	1.53	1.67	1.32
1917		2.45	1.79	2.79	1.57
1918		3.75	2.17	2.80	1.43
		(End of Month)	(Monthly Average)	(Monthly Average)	(Monthly Average)
1919	Jan.	5.69	2.62	3.88	1.95
	Feb.	5.81	2.70	4.20	2.17
	Mar.	6.14	2.74	4.86	2.48
	April	6.35	2.86	5.96	3.00
	May	6.58	2.97	6.19	3.06
	June	7.04	3.08	6.77	3.34
	July	6.90	3.39	7.61	3.59
	Aug.	6.74	4.22	9.67	4.48
	Sept.	6.97	4.93	12.05	5.73
	Oct.	7.15	5.62	13.50	6.39
	Nov.	7.48	6.78	19.80	9.12
	Dec.	8.27	8.03	24.89	11.14
1920	Jan.	8.4	12.6	35.9	15.4
	Feb.	9.0	16.9	54.8	23.6
	Mar.	9.8	17.1	46.9	20.0
	April	10.3	15.7	34.7	14.2
	May	10.6	15.1	27.4	11.1
	June	11.3	13.8	22.6	9.3
	July	11.5	13.7	22.6	9.4
	Aug.	11.9	14.5	26.4	11.4
	Sept.	12.5	15.0	31.2	13.8
	Oct.	12.8	14.7	34.2	16.2
	Nov.	12.8	15.1	36.1	18.4
	Dec.	13.5	14.4	31.2	17.4

TABLE XIV—(Continued)

INDEX NUMBERS OF THE VOLUME OF CIRCULATING MEDIUM, OF INTERNAL AND EXTERNAL PRICES, AND OF EXCHANGE RATES; 1914-1923

DATE		VOLUME OF CIRCULATING MEDIUM (TOTAL VOLUME OF CIRCULATING MEDIUM RELATIVE TO 1913 TAKEN AS 1[4])	INTERNAL PRICES (PAPER MARK EQUIVALENT OF INTERNAL PURCHASING POWER OF ONE 1913 GOLD MARK[5])	EXTERNAL PRICES (PAPER MARK EQUIVALENT OF EXTERNAL PURCHASING POWER OF ONE 1913 GOLD MARK[6])	EXCHANGE RATE (PAPER MARK EQUIVALENT OF ONE CURRENT GOLD MARK[7])
1921	Jan.	13.0	14.4	26.3	15.5
	Feb.	13.2	13.8	23.4	14.6
	Mar.	13.3	13.4	23.2	14.9
	April	13.4	13.3	22.3	15.1
	May	13.5	13.1	21.5	14.8
	June	14.0	13.7	23.4	16.5
	July	14.3	14.3	25.8	18.3
	Aug.	14.6	19.2	28.4	20.1
	Sept.	15.6	20.7	35.4	25.0
	Oct.	16.4	24.6	50.7	35.8
	Nov.	18.0	34.2	88.1	62.6
	Dec.	20.3	34.9	63.9	45.7
1922	Jan.	20.5	36.7	63.2	45.7
	Feb.	21.3	41.0	70.0	49.5
	Mar.	23.2	54.3	96.3	67.7
	April	24.8	63.6	98.8	69.3
	May	26.8	64.6	102.0	69.1
	June	29.8	70.3	113.1	75.6
	July	33.5	100.6	182.0	117.5
	Aug.	41.7	192.0	419.0	270.3
	Sept.	54.8	287.0	535.3	349.2
	Oct.	79.9	566.0	1,168	757.7
	Nov.	126.8	1,154	2,661	1,711
	Dec.	213.4	1,475	2,824	1,808
1923	Jan.	331.9[8]	2,785	6,670	4,281
	Feb.	585.2	5,585	10,421	6,650
	Mar.	915.7	4,888	8,006	5,048
	April	1,090.0	5,212	9,246	5,826

TABLE XIV—(Continued)

INDEX NUMBERS OF THE VOLUME OF CIRCULATING MEDIUM, OF INTERNAL AND EXTERNAL PRICES, AND OF EXCHANGE RATES; 1914–1923

DATE	VOLUME OF CIRCULATING MEDIUM (TOTAL VOLUME OF CIRCULATING MEDIUM RELATIVE TO 1913 TAKEN AS 1[4])	INTERNAL PRICES (PAPER MARK EQUIVALENT OF INTERNAL PURCHASING POWER OF ONE 1913 GOLD MARK[5])	EXTERNAL PRICES (PAPER MARK EQUIVALENT OF EXTERNAL PURCHASING POWER OF ONE 1913 GOLD MARK[6])	EXCHANGE RATE (PAPER MARK EQUIVALENT OF ONE CURRENT GOLD MARK[7])
	(Selected Dates)	(Selected Dates)	(Selected Dates)	(Selected Dates)
1923 May 5	—	6,239	12,754	8,165
15	—	7,105	15,739	10,076
25	1,426[8]	9,034	20,204	12,935
June 5	—	12,393	22,853	14,888
15	—	17,496	39,380	25,655
25	2,867	24,618	41,775	27,215
July 3	—	33,828	57,398	38,113
10	—	48,644	66,906	44,426
17	—	57,478	78,205	51,929
24	—	79,462	148,519	98,618
31	7,231[1]	183,510	394,617	262,030
Aug. 7	—	483,461	1,179,786	786,000
14	—	663,880	1,073,215	715,000
21	—	1,246,598	1,966,310	1,310,000
28	114,008	1,695,109	2,289,025	1,525,000
Sept. 4	—	2,981,532	4,760,089	3,097,000
11	—	11,513,231	24,236,953	15,769,000
18	—	36,009,183	54,918,547	35,731,000
25	4,720,487	36,223,771	44,300,951	28,823,000
Oct. 2	—	84,500,000	116,704,000	76,227,000
9	—	307,400,000	437,636,000	285,850,000
16	—	1,092,800,000	1,495,260,000	976,656,000
23	—	14,600,000,000	20,423,059,000	13,339,686,000
30	854,402,000	18,700,000,000	23,705,336,000	15,483,564,000

TABLE XIV—(Continued)

INDEX NUMBERS OF THE VOLUME OF CIRCULATING MEDIUM, OF INTERNAL AND EXTERNAL PRICES, AND OF EXCHANGE RATES; 1914–1923

DATE	VOLUME OF CIRCULATING MEDIUM (TOTAL VOLUME OF CIRCULATING MEDIUM RELATIVE TO 1913 TAKEN AS 1[4])	INTERNAL PRICES (PAPER MARK EQUIVALENT OF INTERNAL PURCHASING POWER OF ONE 1913 GOLD MARK[6])	EXTERNAL PRICES (PAPER MARK EQUIVALENT OF EXTERNAL PURCHASING POWER OF ONE 1913 GOLD MARK[6])	EXCHANGE RATE (PAPER MARK EQUIVALENT OF ONE CURRENT GOLD MARK[7])
Nov. 6	—	129,000,000,000	152,100,000,000	100,000,000,000
13	—	265,600,000,000	304,200,000,000	200,000,000,000
20	—	1,413,400,000,000	1,521,000,000,000	1,000,000,000,000
27	245,107,000,000	1,422,900,000,000	1,521,000,000,000	1,000,000,000,000
Dec. 4	—	1,337,400,000,000	1,510,000,000,000	1,000,000,000,000
11	—	1,274,500,000,000	1,510,000,000,000	1,000,000,000,000
18	—	1,244,600,000,000	1,510,000,000,000	1,000,000,000,000
27	374,563,000,000	1,200,400,000,000	1,510,000,000,000	1,000,000,000,000

[4] Volume of circulating medium includes the following: Reichsbank notes, notes of the four other banks with issuing powers, Treasury notes, Loan Bureau notes, and coin. The base is the estimated average for 1913.

[5] This index is the general wholesale price index for Germany compiled by the Statistische Reichsamt.

[6] This index of external purchasing power is computed by multiplying the index of exchange rates (number of paper marks to dollar equivalent of one gold mark) by the index of wholesale prices in the United States (Bureau of Labor Statistics index number on a 1913 base).

[7] Exchange rates against the dollar, as quoted on the Berlin market, relative to 4.198 as 1 (par of gold exchange).

[8] For 1923 the index of the volume of circulating medium is computed from figures given in The Process of Inflation in France 1914-1927, James Harvey Rogers, New York, Columbia University Press, 1929, p. 143. In addition to the components given in note 4 these totals include authorized ordinary emergency money for all months of 1923, railroad paper mark emergency money for the months September-December, and, for the months October-December, the following types of stabilized currency converted into paper marks: Rentenmarks, gold loan notes, railroad stable-value emergency money, and gold loan stable-value emergency money. The value of the metal coins in circulation is lacking for the months October-December 1922, January-March 1923, and September-December 1923. On account of the great magnitude of total circulation, however, and the practical complete disappearance of coins, accuracy of the data is not impaired.

[9] These figures for volume of circulation may not always correspond exactly with the dates in the first column since they are all end-of-the-month figures; they have, however, been placed opposite the latest date in each month.

Source of data: Zahlen zur Geldentwertung in Deutschland 1914 bis 1923, passim.

CHART X

INDICES OF VOLUME OF CIRCULATING MEDIUM, OF INTERNAL AND EXTERNAL
PRICES, AND OF EXCHANGE RATES; 1918-1923

(1913 = 1)

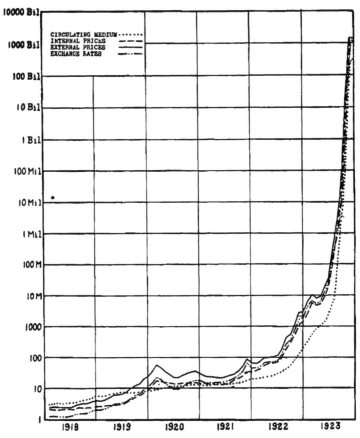

purposes. Attention will, however, be centered on the post-armistice
period when inflation worked out its effects without the disturbing factor
of controls instituted for war purposes.

§ COMPARISON OF INDICES

*Relationship Between Volume of Circulating Medium
and the Other Indices.*

The most prominent feature of the pre-armistice period is the height
of the index of the volume of circulating medium relative to either of

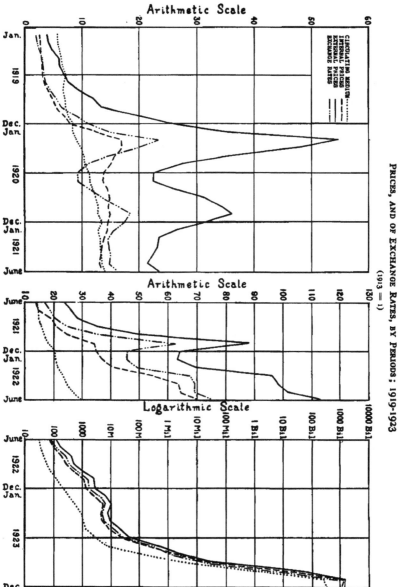

CHART XI

INDICES OF VOLUME OF CIRCULATING MEDIUM, OF INTERNAL AND EXTERNAL PRICES, AND OF EXCHANGE RATES, BY PERIODS; 1919–1923

(1913 = 1)

CHART XII

PRICE AND CIRCULATION INDICES IN THE WAR-PERIOD

(1913 = 1)

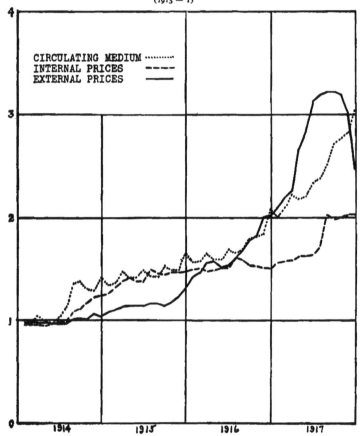

the others. (See Chart XII.) The causes of the failure of this increase
in the currency to stimulate corresponding price changes have already
been set forth. The temporary bulge during 1917 in the index of external
prices is of slight significance. The external purchasing power of the
mark was a more or less arbitrary thing in war-time Germany. Foreign
trade was greatly restricted by the enemy blockade and through the
control of exports and imports by the German Government. The latter
control proved at first not strict enough to prevent a disproportionate
rise in foreign exchange but the increase in the index of external prices
relative to the volume of circulating medium was soon brought to an

end by an extension of the restrictive measures.[10] It is interesting to note, however, that, from early 1916 onward, the external value of the German monetary unit was persistently less than its internal value (external prices were higher than internal). The contrary has been sometimes supposed to be the tendency in the early stages of inflation. The notion is based on a wrong interpretation not only of the German but of other monetary phenomena during the war and is due to the assumption that exchange rates serve as a measure of purchasing power comparable with the index of wholesale prices. The value of gold currencies in exchange for paper was, it is true, not very high in this period, but this was not surprising in view of the decline in the goods value of gold which was then everywhere taking place. Though the alteration in the dollar exchange rate was slight in relation to the rise in internal prices in Germany it was large in relation to the respective purchasing powers of the dollar and the mark.

Reference to Chart XI will show that, if the tendency to hoard was responsible for prices being low relative to the increase in the volume of money, a check in the tendency occurred as soon as the war was over. The index of external prices definitively took the lead in mid-1919 while the index of internal prices rose above that of the volume of circulating medium at the end of that year.[11] The volume of circulating medium again caught up with internal prices in mid-1921 but thereafter lagged far in the rear. The acceleration in the rate of monetary turnover increased prices relative to the volume of circulating medium, the rising prices gave a further fillip to the rate of monetary turnover, this again affected prices, and so on. The index of the volume of circulating medium consequently fell a great, *but eventually not increasing*, distance behind that of internal and external prices. The discrepancy between the curves was, indeed, somewhat enlarged during the middle months of 1923 though the then almost vertical character of their movement obscures the situation. This deviation was perhaps due rather to the rise in prices consequent upon the drop in production in the Ruhr than to any increase in the rate of monetary turnover. The "ceiling" to the ascent of that rate had probably then been reached.

Relationship Between the Indices of Internal and External Prices.

There was clearly a much greater sympathy, at any rate till 1923, between the movement of the indices of external and internal prices

[10] Dealings in foreign exchange, moreover, were centralized and the mark was supported, in certain foreign exchange markets, by the Reichsbank.

[11] A rise in the indices (which show the number of paper marks equivalent to one 1913 gold mark in internal and external markets respectively) means, of course, a fall in the purchasing power of the paper mark.

than between either of these and the volume of circulating medium. The spread between internal and external paper mark prices was greatest, for the post-war period, in the spring and fall of 1920, in the fall of 1921, and in the fall of 1922.[12] In all cases this was due to a relatively rapid rise in exchange rates. Objective and subjective factors were blended as causes but, on the whole, the objective seem to have been dominant. This is not to assert that subjective factors were not of the utmost importance in affecting both the external and internal purchasing power of the mark but that they were less influential than the objective in determining the *relationship* between these respective purchasing powers. This was the truer as inflation became extreme.

The 1920 *Peak of External Prices.*

The peak in external paper mark prices in the spring of 1920, the apex of an upward movement in both internal and external price curves, with the curve of external prices advancing at a more rapid rate, seems to have been due, first, to the shock to confidence arising from the loss of the war and the severe terms imposed by the Versailles Treaty and, second, to the rush of the German people for foreign commodities from which they had been so long excluded and access to which was not given till the lifting of the Allied blockade in June 1919. The then relative rise in external mark prices was thus due both to subjective and objective forces. The culminating point was reached when the world-wide post-war boom began to collapse and when, therefore, the German demand for foreign commodities, for purposes of industrial reconstruction as well as for direct consumption, began to fall off. The buying fever was suddenly checked in all parts of the world. Since the Germans had hitherto been buying foreign goods much in excess of foreign demand for German goods mark exchange tended to improve. Perhaps a not less important factor in the shift in the external value of the mark at this time was the failure of the Kapp rebellion to undermine the foundations of the new republic and the impression of political stability which this made on the outside world.[13] Here again psychological and objective forces were mixed and the change in the reciprocal demand for exchange was due partly to absolute and partly to speculative requirements.

The "wave" in the curve of external prices from the summer of 1920 to the spring of 1921, a movement unaccompanied by any substantial

---

[12] This latter movement does not show up so clearly on the chart as do the earlier movements owing to the fact that the third section of Chart XI is on a logarithmic and the first two sections on an arithmetic scale.

[13] The Kapp *Putsch* was an abortive attempt by reactionary elements to regain control of German affairs.

change in the internal purchasing power of the mark, was initiated by the following factors: (1) The fall in prices in the United States which began in June 1920. This increased the commodity value of the dollar and so tended to raise its price in marks which were, at that time, relatively stable in purchasing power over domestic goods. It should be noted that while the index of external prices in marks came back in 1921 to about the position held in mid-1920 this is by no means true of the index of exchange rates. This means that the mark would buy as much in American *goods* at the later, as at the earlier, date but would buy fewer *dollars*. (2) The breakdown of the Spa Conference in July 1920 and the sudden darkening in the political situation thus occasioned. (3) Reaction from the downward movement in foreign exchange which had occurred in the forepart of 1920. This downward movement had, in accordance with the principles laid down in the preceding chapter, carried farther than the long time demand and supply schedules would warrant.

The declining phase of the 1920-1921 "wave" coincided with the gradual allaying of apprehension over external political affairs. The downward movement in the curve, as the upward, was no doubt accelerated by the shift in speculative positions on the exchange market and by the self-stimulating impulse which any movement of exchange may develop.

The 1921 Peak of External Prices.

The 1921 peak in external paper mark prices is almost solely attributable to the inauguration of cash reparations payments. The rise in exchange rates, and so in the index of external prices, was no doubt enhanced by the psychological reaction to the Allied demands, but sheer objective forces would seem to have been dominant. From the middle of May till the end of November heavy purchases of foreign exchange for reparations purposes (at first dollars only, later other currencies also) were, as we have seen, necessary, and during all this time dollar exchange rose fast. The rise in internal prices in August, however, was still more rapid and the spread between the indices was temporarily somewhat reduced. The German announcement to the Reparations Commission, on December 14, 1921, that postponement in payments was essential caused an upward flutter in foreign exchange but the movement was slight and ephemeral and does not show in the monthly average figures. The removal of the objective pressure on the exchange value of the mark, consequent upon the lifting of the burden of payments, much more than compensated the additional weight of psychological forces on the bear side. An absolute fall in foreign exchange (rise of the mark) soon set in and the gap between the curves of external and internal purchasing power was greatly narrowed. In this whole incident of cash reparations objective forces were clearly of primary import. The decision on the Upper Silesia boundary question,[14] however, exerted some adverse effect on mark exchange through its influence on the psychology of buyers and sellers of marks.

The 1922 Peak of External Prices.

The widening of the gap between external and internal prices which occurred in the fall of 1922 was an aspect of that complete loss of confidence in the German currency which may be summed up in the phrase, "the flight from the mark." But though the spread between the curves temporarily increased it was not long before it narrowed again. This may have been entirely due to the speed with which the volume of circulating medium and internal prices were then adjusted to any advance which might take place in exchange rates. But internal prices could advance so fast only if buyers paid what was asked for commodities rather than use their money to purchase foreign exchange. The government, it is true, laid restrictions on the right to buy foreign currencies but it is doubtful whether these had much effect. It simply was not good business to buy foreign exchange at a very high premium. Commodities in the domestic market, being relatively low in price, were likely to rise farther than foreign exchange and it was therefore more profitable to use mark funds for the purchase of such commodities than for the purchase of foreign currencies. After the panic demand, mainly supported by the then slender resources of the old well-to-do classes, had exhausted its influence, the buying and selling of exchange was almost entirely in the hands of business men who alone had any free funds. Cash reparations no longer played an important rôle in the *absolute* demand for exchange while the *conditional* demand was dependent on the alternative use for funds in current business transactions in the domestic market. By 1923 the great bulk of exchange business involving marks was carried on in Berlin between German entrepreneurs. The exporters of commodities had foreign exchange for sale and the importers did the buying. Purchases of currency by foreigners for "investment" had practically ceased and there were relatively few capital transactions

[14] The Upper Silesia boundary question had been left by the Peace of Versailles for later settlement pending a plebiscite. Though the plebiscite as a whole went in favor of the Germans, the League of Nations, to which the matter had been referred, drew the line in accordance with the vote by localities. The result was to give to Poland by far the larger part of the industrial area of the district. The decision was handed down on October 12, 1921.

of any kind. As matters came on to a strict business basis, principally confined to trade in merchandise, conditional demand, responsive to rate deviations from the current purchasing power par, began to play the dominating rôle. Imported merchandise could not be sold in large volume when, as a result of a relative advance in exchange rates, its price rose far above the prevailing level for other commodities. Exports, on the other hand, were so stimulated as to force up export commodity prices in the domestic market. Both phenomena operated to keep exchange rates, and so external mark prices, from advancing at a faster rate than prices of domestic goods. In November 1922 the external purchasing power of the mark had been little more than one-third that of the internal. The spread was narrowed in the succeeding months though from February to April 1923 this was in large part due to the intervention of the Reichsbank in support of mark exchange. In May there was a reaction but the external value fell only to about one-half of the internal. A renewed coalescence brought the two curves to approximate equality in August. It should of course be remembered that the value of the mark, both in internal and external purchases, was depreciating at this time at a terrific rate. But the depreciation in exchange value proceeded much less rapidly than did that in domestic purchasing power. Absolute demand for foreign exchange was then occasioned only by commodity imports which tended to fall off when foreign exchange was high, practically all German exports were invoiced in foreign currencies and thus neutralized any automatic tendency for exchange rate movements to add fuel to the original fire, and conditional demand was in the hands of close calculators. The situation was thus markedly different from that of a year or two previous and the curve of external prices lost its *penchant* for outstripping both the other indices.

§ CHRONOLOGICAL SEQUENCE OF MOVEMENTS IN THE INDICES

Thus far, attention has been directed to the height of the several indices at different stages in the inflation period and to the relative amplitude of their variations. But amplitude and sequence are, of course, entirely distinct concepts. While it is obvious that, if, at a given date, any one of the three indices which start from a common base has advanced beyond either of the others, it must have risen at a more rapid rate, it does not follow that it rose sooner, or that, having reached a certain position, a further upward or downward variation has preceded corresponding changes in the other curves. Precedence of movement is concealed in the charts shown above both by irregularities in the curves in the earlier years and by the smoothing out which occurs when the enormous figures of the later period are plotted logarithmically. Some statistical technique is necessary to establish the sequence of variation. The remainder of this chapter will therefore deal with statistical measurements of the timing, rather than with the amplitude, of the variations in the several curves.

A careful investigation of mark exchange rates on New York, of German wholesale prices, and of the volume of circulating medium in Germany, for the period 1918 to 1923, has been made by Professor James Harvey Rogers in connection with his study of French inflation.[15] In this study the monthly deviations of each of the indices from its computed trend have been plotted and compared. While the curve of exchange rates and that of the index of external value of the mark are by no means the same thing, the time and direction of their movements will coincide whenever American prices remain stable at no matter what height. Substantial stability, following the war movement, was not attained in American prices until the spring of 1921 but, since the ratio of external to internal purchasing power of the mark consistently followed the movement of exchange rates until December of that year, Professor Rogers' results may be taken with confidence as applicable throughout to external mark prices as well as to exchange rates. A glance at Chart X will show the high degree of correlation in the movement of the two indices concerned.[16]

Professor Rogers' charts of the cycles of deviation from their respective trends of the curves of volume of circulating medium and of prices in one comparison, and of prices and exchange rates in another, are here reproduced as Charts XIII and XIV. His conclusions, based on statistical calculations as well as on the charts, and somewhat modified in wording, may be stated under the three following headings:

I. *Comparison between the movements of wholesale prices and the volume of circulating medium.*

There was a general tendency for movements in the volume of circulating medium to lag behind those in wholesale prices by approximately two months but this lag was greatly reduced during the middle months of 1921 and from the middle of 1922 onward. In the final months of inflation the lag disappeared altogether and was perhaps

[15] cf. *The Process of Inflation in France*, 1914-1927, Columbia University Press, New York, 1929, Chap. vii. Professor Rogers and the Columbia University Press have graciously permitted me to reproduce the charts from his book and to summarize briefly the results of his study.

[16] In order, however, to make assurance doubly sure, cycles of deviation from straight-line secular trends fitted to second logarithms were plotted both for exchange rates and for external prices and were found to correspond almost exactly.

CHART XIII

CYCLES IN THE MOVEMENTS OF INTERNAL PRICES AND IN THE VOLUME
OF CIRCULATING MEDIUM; 1918-1923

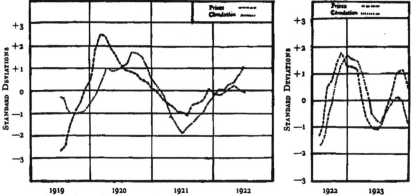

Reproduced from *The Process of Inflation in France* with the permission of J. L. Rogers and
Columbia University Press.

CHART XIV

CYCLES IN THE MOVEMENTS OF EXCHANGE RATES AND INTERNAL PRICES; 1918-1923

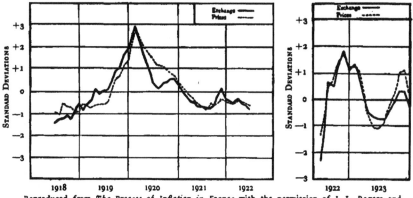

Reproduced from *The Process of Inflation in France* with the permission of J. L. Rogers and
Columbia University Press.

replaced by a converse lag of price movements behind those of circulation.
No positive assertion that the latter was the case may, however, be made.

II. *Comparison between the movements of exchange rates and wholesale prices.*

From June 1918 to July 1920 there was a tendency for movements in
wholesale prices to lag behind those in exchange rates by a month or a

little more, while from July 1920 to the end of the inflation period, November 1923, the movement of the two series was approximately simultaneous. There is a faint suggestion in the statistics, however, that exchange rate movements tended to lag behind those of prices by an interval of less than a month in the period August 1920 to June 1922.

III. *General interrelations of the phenomena.*

Adjustments were slow in the period of relatively moderate, but extremely rapid in the period of hyper-inflation. In the final stages all lags were largely or completely eliminated.

With these conclusions of Professor Rogers the present writer is in complete agreement.

§ INTERPRETATION OF THE SEQUENCE OF MOVEMENT

While there is conclusive evidence that the movements of internal prices at times preceded those in the volume of circulating medium there is no *absolute assurance* that the reverse situation ever occurred. Similarly there is conclusive evidence that exchange rate movements at times preceded those of prices without any *certainty* that the contrary was ever true. The approximate simultaneity of movement in all three curves which marked the final period of inflation may have been due entirely to a growing mobility in internal prices and in the volume of circulating medium. Any precedence that, up to this time, may have occurred in the movements of internal prices over those in the volume of circulating medium, and in the movements of exchange rates over those of internal prices, may then have continued but have been rendered statistically indiscernible by the rapidity with which adjustment was then taking place. It is certain that in the final months of inflation internal price quotations were made daily, or even more frequently, on the basis of the current exchange rate, and that notes were issued recklessly in response to business "needs." A real but very short lag would then completely disappear in figures based on monthly averages. But though this is a feasible explanation it is more probably true that the unproved suggestion, in the statistics, of a lag of the movements of internal prices behind those in the volume of circulating medium in the latter months of 1923, and in the movements of exchange rates behind those of internal prices in the period August 1920 to June 1922, was an actuality.

Precedence of Movements in the Volume of Circulating Medium over those in Prices in 1923 *and the Reduction of the Lag in* 1921 *and* 1922.

The implication in the statistics of the tendency for changes in the volume of circulating medium to take place in advance of those in prices in the final months of the inflation period supports the concept of a "ceiling" to the possibility of ascent in the rate of monetary turn-over. When that ceiling was reached, upward price movements were dependent on prior increases in the volume of means of payment. The reduction of the lag in the movements of the volume of circulating medium in the summer of 1921 and from the middle of 1922 onward was probably due to the weakening of resistance to new emissions of notes for private as well as for governmental purposes. The assertion here made is based on the assumption that the stimulus toward borrow-ing from the Reichsbank as the facilities for doing so increased, and as the discrepancy between the cost of loans and the benefits therefrom grew greater and greater, speeded the process of adjustment of the lagging volume of notes.

Precedence of Price Movements over those in Exchange Rates in the Period 1920 *to* 1922.

The year August 1920 to July 1921 was one of comparative stability in all the indices of German inflation. In times of this character such movements of internal prices as occur tend to dominate those of ex-change rates. There was, at this date, no persistent unconditional demand for foreign exchange on the part of the Germans, since cash reparations were not yet being paid, and speculative fishers were quiescent in waters which were not greatly troubled.[17] The potential independence of exchange rates was therefore not realized. A rise in German prices would tend to lower the ratio of exports to imports and to reduce the supply of foreign exchange relatively to demand while a fall in German prices would have the opposite effect. Exchange rates would thus move in dependence on prices. The relation between French prices and foreign exchange rates shows the same tendency in the period 1919-1922 the last three years of which were years of comparative monetary stability, while from 1923 to 1926, when both exchange rates and internal prices in France were rapidly rising, the precedence of the movement in exchange rates is clear. The latter period, one of disturbance, corresponds in general with the status of German monetary affairs from the end of the war to mid-1920, while the former period, one of stability, is analogous to the German situation of mid-1920 to mid-1921.

It is harder to explain the apparent continuation in the precedence of the movements of German internal prices over those of exchange rates up to June 1922. This was by no means a quiet period. It will be re-

---

[17] This does not mean that there was no speculation but that there was no rush from one side of the market to the other and no great increase in the number of buyers or sellers.

membered that both exchange rates and internal prices rose rapidly after the middle of 1921 and that, until December of that year, the advance of exchange rates far *outstripped* that of prices. But the figures intimate, nevertheless, that the movements of exchange rates did not *precede* those of prices at this time. It may well have been that the issues of marks, made for the purpose of purchasing the foreign exchange requisite for reparations,[18] reacted on prices, either directly or by antici- pation, almost immediately, and so brought about substantial *simul- taneity* in the movements of the price and exchange rate indices. But, if the apparent precedence of price movements was real, one can only suppose that, so far as reparations affected the situation, anticipations of their baneful influence on Reich finances and on note issues led to such an increase in the rate of monetary turnover as to raise prices sooner than the actual purchase of exchange exerted its influence upon the rates. It is, however, not impossible that the most valid explanation of all is simply that the seeming precedence of price movements in this period is an illusion arising from an imperfect price index.[19]

Sequence of Price and Exchange Rate Movements in 1923.

The approximate coincidence of fluctuations in exchange rates and in internal prices in the final year and a half of inflation may have been due not only to the already suggested progressive rapidity of adjust- ment of all the indices to one another but to the fact that subjective forces originating *within* a country in which all monetary phenomena are in a state of flux do not tend to act upon exchange rates in advance of their impact on prices but affect both simultaneously.[20]

§ SUMMARY OF SEQUENCES

In general it may be said that the proximate, *though not the ultimate*, chain of causation, up to August 1920 at least, and perhaps at other times, ran from exchange rates to prices to volume of circulating medium rather than in the reverse direction. The independent char- acter of exchange rate movements in certain circumstances is clearly indicated. The movements of exchange rates appear at times to have affected prices, first, by changing the rate of monetary turnover, and second, by leading, almost inevitably, to new issues of notes. The move- ments of prices also affected note issues. There was causal interaction

---

[18] The lag in circulation was greatly reduced during the latter part of 1921.

[19] The sharp rise in the price index for August 1921, due almost entirely to the great increase in one group, food grains and potatoes, presents an exaggerated picture of the change in the general price level at this time.

[20] See page 125.

among all three sets of phenomena. But, while internal price movements were ultimately, though very loosely, dependent on note issues (the tie being closer toward the climax of inflation), exchange rates maintained their potential independence to the end. There is, however, no clear case for the contention that changes in exchange rates were steadily an even proximate *determinant* of internal prices. If they had been, prices of imports would have shown changes consistently in advance of those in domestic commodities. The succeeding chapter will make clear that, if there was any such tendency, it was weak. On the other hand, there is next to no evidence that the movement in the prices of domestic commodities ever preceded that in the prices of imports. So far as domestic prices determined exchange rates, therefore, the influence exerted must have been merely toward the establishment of some sort of norm. The fluctuations of exchange rates about such a presumptive norm were entirely free and very wide.

So far as the theory set forth in the preceding chapters departs from orthodoxy it has, in the main, been inductively derived from the facts which the present chapter has developed. Those facts may not therefore be regarded as verification of the theory. It would seem that such verification may come, if at all, only should the peculiar features of the German situation be, at some later date, repeated.

CHAPTER VII

PRICE RELATIONSHIPS UNDER THE INFLUENCE OF INFLATION

§ TYPES OF PRICE SPREADS

THE fluctuating but persistently great discrepancy between the external and internal value of the mark established entirely distinct price levels for different phases of German business. Commodities directly affected by foreign prices and by the vicissitudes of exchange rates (imported commodities and, to a lesser degree, exports) tended to sell at higher prices corresponding to the small external purchasing power of the mark while the prices of other commodities were on a far lower level. The spread between the various classes of prices was even greater than that between the external and internal value of the mark since the internal value of the mark was dependent on the prices of a composite of goods which included relatively high-priced imports and exports as well as commodities wholly produced and consumed at home. The *general* internal price level was therefore considerably higher than that of commodities not entering in either direction into international trade, commodities which, for want of a better term, will be called domestic.

But price differences were by no means confined to goods directly affected by movements in exchange rates in contrast to those not so affected. They appeared also within the range of purely domestic commodities. In many cases this was due to governmental intervention and its consequences. It has already been noted that such intervention was of greatest importance in the realm of house rents. The rent-restriction legislation, working out its effects in a level of wages considerably below that which would otherwise have prevailed, ramified through prices in rough proportion to the share of labor in the production of the various commodities. Interference with the free play of competition thus exaggerated the disruptive influence of inflation, an influence which was in itself sufficient to provoke great deviations from any sort of symmetrical movement in the prices of different types of goods. Some idea of the range of price variations may be obtained from the tables and charts which appear below. In all cases relationships only are shown; the absolute movement of prices was too great for exposition or even comprehension.

§ THE DISPERSION OF PRICES

In order to determine the force of inflation as a price-dispersing agent an index of price dispersion was computed from the link relatives of a series of index numbers (on a 1914 base) of commodities so widely diverse in character as to form a fair cross section of the whole commodity price structure.[1] The results appear in Table XV.

A glance at the table will show that the degree of dispersion varied directly with instability in the general price level but that, in the later phases of an upward swing of prices, the scope of the dispersion tended to narrow. The index of dispersion begins with a period shortly following the first large upward price movement, which culminated in March 1920, and it shows a steady decline during the period of stability in the general level of prices which then ensued. The range of dispersion increases as the general level of prices starts a second upward march in July 1921 but toward the end of this rising movement the range of dispersion again diminishes. It falls farther as stability in general prices emerges once more in the months from November 1921 to February 1922. In the period March 1922 to February 1923, a time of steady rise in the general price level yet without a very rapid acceleration in the earlier months, the index of dispersion remains substantially constant till July-August 1922, rises with the acceleration in the upward movement of the general price index till December, and then declines. This decline is accentuated during the two and a half months of general price stability consequent upon the action of the Reichsbank in support of exchange in the spring of 1923. Finally, a new augmentation in the range of price dispersion initially accompanies the last upward sweep of general prices from May 1923 onward yet again it fails to maintain its pace and drops off in September and October when the general price level was soaring to unheard of heights.

It is clear that with the *initiation* of an upward movement in general prices a series of lags in individual prices developed, that these lags tended quickly to disappear when stability of general prices was reached

---

[1] The price data for these commodities were derived from unpublished official figures. Average figures for the period covered are available every fourth month in 1920, quarterly in 1921, bimonthly in 1922, and monthly in 1923. In some months price data for some of the commodities were missing but the number on which quotations are available was never less than 88. The maximum number was 100. The data apply to prices of the various commodities as they were ordinarily sold for final consumption.

TABLE XV

INDEX OF THE DISPERSION OF PRICES IN GERMANY; 1920-1923[2]

YEAR AND MONTH	INDEX OF DISPERSION	DESCRIPTION OF PERIOD
1920 May–Aug.	17.75	May 1920 to June 1921.
Sept.–Dec.	15.95	A period of general price stability.
1921 Jan.–Mar.	10.45	Range of variation of general wholesale price index
April–June	5.90	(1913 = 1): 15.09 to 13.08.[3]
July–Sept.	15.85	July to November.
Oct.–Dec.	12.10	Increase in general prices. Range of general wholesale price index: 14.28 to 34.16.
1922 Jan.–Feb.	9.05	Nov. to Feb. Stability. Range of wholesale index: 34.16 to 41.03.[3]
Mar.–April	12.80	
May–June	13.15	
July–Aug.	12.95	Mar. 1922 to Feb. 1923.
Sept.–Oct.	19.20	Rapid increase in general prices.
Nov.–Dec.	19.50	Range of wholesale index: 54.33 to 5,585.[3]
1923 Jan.	18.90	
Feb.	16.10	
Mar.	14.55	Comparative price stability.
April	9.90	Wholesale index: Feb., 5,585; Mar., 4,888; April, 5,212.[3]
May	11.20	
June	16.20	
July	29.70	Immense acceleration in general price level.
Aug.	34.80	Wholesale index: May, 8,170; Oct., 7,094,800.[3]
Sept.	30.90	
Oct.	21.90	

[2] The index is derived from a fractional part, .6745, of the standard deviation (measured by logarithms) of the link relatives of the separate price indices and represents the approximate percentage limits, measured from the geometric mean, within which 50% of the price relatives would fall if the distribution of logarithms of the price relatives were normal. For the method of calculation and a detailed discussion of this index the reader is referred to *The Behavior of Prices*, Frederick C. Mills, National Bureau of Economic Research, Inc., New York, 1927, pp. 256 ff.

[3] Statistisches Reichsamt index number of general wholesale prices.

on a new level, or when general prices fell, but that they were nevertheless progressively eliminated even though the general price level continued to rise. In both cases the formerly lagging commodities, once they had started to rise in price, gathered momentum. If the upward movement of other prices ceased or was reversed, the laggards continued to rise. This is, of course, to be expected. But, even though the upward movement of the former leaders showed no fatigue, the formerly lagging prices eventually rose at a still more rapid pace and the distance between the various commodities thus tended to close. This coalescence of prices in the later stages of inflation in general, and even in the later stages of each of the several phases, will be noted at several other points in the sequel.

§ PRICE CLASSIFICATION

Perhaps more significant phenomena than those which apply to prices in general may, however, be developed through a contrast of prices by groups or classes. Table XVI and Chart XV give the ratio (per cent) of the indices of various classes of prices to the index of wholesale prices in general.

Reference to Chart XV will show that the relative position of the several indices in January 1920 (the order in which they are named in Table XVI and Chart XV) was fairly well preserved throughout. The highest indices are those in which the relatively low external value of the mark was effective in raising prices, either because the foreign price must be paid or because it could be obtained for all, or at least the bulk, of the commodities included in the index in question. Such prices applied to all the items in the imported goods index, to most of those in the index of raw materials and in that of exported goods,[4] and to a considerable number of those in the index of finished goods. Even in the index of domestic goods some exportable articles appear.[5] The cost of living was, in the main, determined by the prices of domestically produced and consumed commodities, and, until the very end of inflation, wages were not greatly affected by the external value of the mark.

The prices of stock exchange securities were affected by the failure on the part of the public fully to realize that stocks and bonds were poles apart in the matter of the incidence of inflation, by the prevailing insecurity in the business world, and by the fact that there was much watering of the shares through new issues to stockholders at extremely low prices. A share of stock throughout the four years here under review was by no means a homogeneous thing but was usually declining in real worth, as measured by the physical assets behind it, and the index of stock prices is therefore scarcely comparable with the other indices given. It is none the less true that the prices of stocks were very much below a fair capitalization of the yields that might be expected over a long period of time. The reasons for this are, perhaps, not far

[4] The index taken to represent exported goods is that of machinery. A few types of machinery, however, would not be exported.

[5] The official index of domestic goods includes a group of commodities produced within the country but not necessarily wholly consumed there.

Table XVI

Index Numbers of Wholesale Prices of Imported Goods, of Industrial Raw Materials, of Exported Goods, Finished Goods, Domestic Goods; Retail Prices; Wages of Unskilled Workers, of Skilled Workers; Prices of Stock Exchange Securities; Housing Rentals; All Expressed as Percentages of the Index Number of General Wholesale Prices; 1920-1923

(1913 = 100 in all cases)

MONTHLY AVERAGE	WHOLESALE PRICES OF IMPORTED GOODS	WHOLESALE PRICES OF INDUSTRIAL RAW MATERIALS	WHOLESALE PRICES OF EXPORTED GOODS (MACHINERY)	WHOLESALE PRICES OF FINISHED GOODS	WHOLESALE PRICES OF DOMESTIC GOODS	RETAIL PRICES (COST OF LIVING EXCLUDING HOUSING)	WAGES OF UNSKILLED WORKERS	WAGES OF SKILLED WORKERS	PRICES OF STOCK EXCHANGE SECURITIES (SHARES)	HOUSING RENTALS
1920 Jan.	217.4	136.0	106.1	94.4	76.5	—	53.3	39.8	13.2	—
Feb.	241.1	139.8	—	—	71.8	62.7	39.8	29.7	11.9	9.9
Mar.	234.9	146.4	—	—	73.0	70.0	39.2	29.3	11.5	10.0
April	219.6	152.6	—	—	76.1	83.5	58.1	42.8	11.7	11.2
May	171.4	137.1	121.0	92.7	85.7	91.9	60.3	44.4	10.6	11.7
June	153.2	135.5	—	—	89.4	98.5	73.1	55.0	12.1	12.9
July	138.8	130.5	—	—	92.2	97.8	73.9	55.6	13.7	13.1
Aug.	140.7	122.8	—	—	91.9	88.3	69.7	52.4	14.1	12.6
Sept.	148.7	123.4	—	—	90.3	84.8	67.4	50.7	14.7	12.3
Oct.	158.8	139.9	108.1	98.0	88.3	91.5	68.9	51.8	16.7	12.8
Nov.	156.5	126.7	—	—	88.7	93.0	66.9	50.4	17.2	12.5
Dec.	140.5	124.6	—	—	91.9	101.0	70.1	52.8	19.0	13.3
1921 Jan.	126.7	121.1	—	—	94.6	102.9	79.2	59.1	19.3	13.6
Feb.	120.6	123.7	114.7	109.4	95.9	104.5	82.8	61.8	18.9	14.4
Mar.	120.7	125.9	—	—	95.8	106.6	85.2	63.5	19.8	14.8
April	117.6	128.7	—	—	96.5	106.4	86.0	64.1	20.7	15.3
May	116.4	127.4	121.9	119.3	96.8	107.1	87.2	65.0	21.2	15.5
June	116.8	133.5	—	—	96.6	107.0	83.5	62.2	21.9	15.3
July	120.5	123.9	—	—	95.9	109.9	79.8	59.5	23.6	14.6
Aug.	100.9	96.9	—	—	99.8	87.5	69.9	51.6	20.3	11.0
Sept.	127.9	104.3	89.1	89.8	94.4	83.7	64.8	47.9	23.8	10.2
Oct.	145.7	103.2	—	—	90.9	77.2	76.4	56.9	26.2	8.9
Nov.	165.7	105.9	65.3	67.8	86.9	65.9	55.0	41.0	27.4	6.5
Dec.	145.4	113.8	—	—	90.9	70.3	53.9	40.1	21.0	6.5

TABLE XVI—(Continued)

INDEX NUMBERS OF WHOLESALE PRICES OF IMPORTED GOODS, OF INDUSTRIAL RAW MATERIALS, OF EXPORTED GOODS, FINISHED GOODS, DOMESTIC GOODS; RETAIL PRICES; WAGES OF UNSKILLED WORKERS, OF SKILLED WORKERS; PRICES OF STOCK EXCHANGE SECURITIES; HOUSING RENTALS; ALL EXPRESSED AS PERCENTAGES OF THE INDEX NUMBER OF GENERAL WHOLESALE PRICES; 1920-1923

(1913 = 100 in all cases)

MONTHLY AVERAGE	WHOLESALE PRICES OF IMPORTED GOODS	WHOLESALE PRICES OF INDUSTRIAL RAW MATERIALS	WHOLESALE PRICES OF EXPORTED GOODS (MACHINERY)	WHOLESALE PRICES OF FINISHED GOODS	WHOLESALE PRICES OF DOMESTIC GOODS	RETAIL PRICES (COST OF LIVING EXCLUDING HOUSING)	WAGES OF UN-SKILLED WORKERS	WAGES OF SKILLED WORKERS	PRICES OF STOCK EXCHANGE SECURITIES (SHARES)	HOUSING RENTALS
1922 Jan.	138.5	107.9	84.4[6]	76.1[6]	92.3	69.2	55.4	41.2	20.3	6.4
Feb.	141.4	106.7	—	—	91.7	75.1	49.5	36.8	20.5	5.8
Mar.	137.4	102.1	77.5[6]	71.9[6]	92.5	68.0	37.4	27.8	18.1	4.6
April	129.1	107.9	—	—	94.2	69.4	47.0	34.3	16.0	4.5
May	133.4	117.7	97.9[6]	87.5[6]	93.3	75.7	59.5	43.3	13.5	4.6
June	134.8	116.6	—	—	93.0	75.9	65.7	48.2	11.7	4.5
July	137.7	111.5	62.4[6]	67.2[6]	92.5	69.2	56.6	41.6	8.9	3.4
Aug.	169.2	100.3	—	—	86.1	52.3	44.4	32.3	6.0	2.1
Sept.	150.2	118.2	78.5[6]	60.4[6]	90.0	60.4	56.2	41.0	4.4	1.5
Oct.	159.6	100.6	—	—	88.1	50.5	33.7	24.4	3.6	1.4
Nov.	185.5	118.8	97.1[6]	82.5[6]	82.6	50.2	28.9	20.9	4.4	1.0
Dec.	164.9	139.7	—	—	87.0	60.4	37.6	27.1	6.1	1.1
1923 Jan.	170.8	126.5	100.4[7]	101.5[7]	85.8	52.2	32.0	23.1	8.1	1.3
Feb.	157.5	142.7	120.0[7]	89.7[7]	88.5	61.5	33.3	24.0	8.1	1.0
Mar.	139.4	159.4	142.2[7]	109.3[7]	92.1	75.6	47.5	34.3	6.9	2.3
April	143.2	145.2	129.2[7]	105.2[7]	91.3	73.0	44.5	32.2	9.6	3.5
May	166.5	142.0	108.4[7]	93.4[7]	86.7	60.2	38.6	28.0	11.6	2.6
June	160.8	143.8	105.9[7]	78.2[7]	87.8	51.4	42.8	31.0	18.2	1.6
July	134.0	124.8	99.6[7]	72.4[7]	93.2	65.5	46.1	33.3	18.0	1.0
Aug.	140.4	156.6	146.8[7]	106.4[7]	91.9	81.0	84.7	61.2	13.2	0.5
Sept.	135.3	158.8	159.0[7]	123.4[7]	92.9	81.4	69.3	50.1	22.1	1.3
Oct.	130.5	143.7	159.6[7]	144.0[7]	93.9	67.1	109.9	80.3	24.1	0.8
Nov.	112.9	112.1	159.6[7]	194.9[7]	97.4	117.4	55.4	43.4	32.7	3.0
Dec.	127.1	122.1	131.2[7]	140.8[7]	94.6	123.8	62.6	55.0	21.3	17.3

[6] End of month. The mean of two successive monthly averages of the index number of general wholesale prices (the index used as a base for the calculation of all ratios in this table) has been used as an estimate of the end-of-the-month figure.

[7] Middle of month. The dates of the quotations of the general wholesale price index differ in some cases from those of the quotations of the index numbers of the prices of machinery and finished goods. In such instances interpolation has been made in the general wholesale price index to give an estimate for the corresponding date.

CHART XV

INDICES OF CLASSIFIED PRICES EXPRESSED AS PERCENTAGES OF THE INDEX
OF GENERAL WHOLESALE PRICES ; 1920-1923

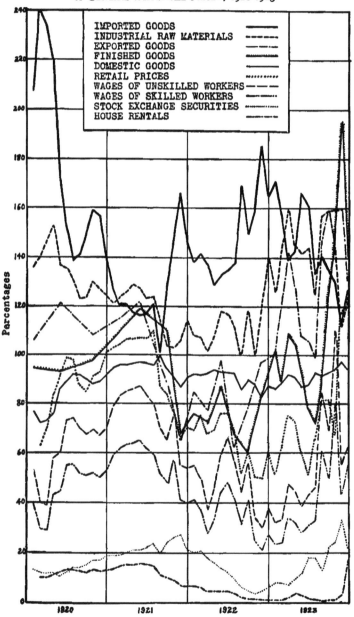

to seek. Though speculation was active the funds available for purchases of stock were relatively slim. The mounting commodity prices absorbed so large a proportion of the monetary supply that relatively little was left for the working of the financial markets, and the banks were not inclined to put credits at the disposal of stock speculators.[8] Further than this a purchase of company shares was a long-time investment. Measured in real values the companies were paying very small dividends. Their profits were frequently great but it did not do to hold them for distribution since they would lose much of their purchasing power in the interval between the date of earning and that of receipt by the stockholder. They were therefore ploughed back into the business. But, in a period when the rate of time preference was high, few people were ready to pay much for the possibility of indefinite future returns. The current high real rate of interest resulted in low capitalized values and the real rate, moreover, was confused with the enormous nominal rates imposed as insurance against depreciation. All these factors operated to depress the price of company shares to a remarkably low level.

The cost of housing (rentals) has been included in Table XVI and Chart XV in order to show the effectiveness of the rent-restriction laws. In comparing the wage and retail price (cost-of-living) curves it should be noted that the latter does not include housing. The total cost of living was therefore much less in advance of wages than the retail price curve suggests. The matter will be more fully treated later in this chapter.

In the immediately succeeding pages the relation between certain of those classes of prices the curves of which have just been presented will be examined in detail. The base on which the ratios are computed has, however, been shifted from the index of wholesale prices to that of the external value of the mark, since, in an examination of correlations, it seemed best to have a base which was not itself affected by changes in any one of the indices for which it was being used as a measuring rod. General wholesale prices would be influenced, in some measure, by a change in any one of the groups of classified commodity

[8] If the disposition to purchase stocks had been very strong, funds would no doubt have been diverted in large volume from the commodity to the stock markets. The Germans were under the impression that they were being so diverted, but the facts, as they appear in the relative price of stocks, would seem to put this impression in the category of illusions.

prices and the percentage relationship between the price index of the group in question and that of wholesale prices in general would therefore not accurately reflect the real alteration in the aforesaid group index. The external value of the mark, on the other hand, would be unaffected, at least directly, by a change in any internal price index.

The relationship between the several classes of prices will be treated by grouping them according to a principle of presumed intimacy of movement as follows: (1) prices of import, of export, and of domestic commodities, (2) prices of imported commodities, of industrial raw materials, and of finished goods, (3) wholesale and retail prices, (4) wages and the cost of living.

1. PRICES OF IMPORT, EXPORT, AND DOMESTIC COMMODITIES

§ GENERAL RELATIONSHIP BETWEEN SUCH PRICES

Table XVII and Chart XVI present for the period 1920 to 1923 the relations between the ratio indices of three groups of wholesale prices representative of import, export, and domestic commodities respectively.

The price index of each of the groups here shown is expressed as a percentage of the synchronous index of external mark prices. All indices are on a 1913 base. The curves thus show the number of paper marks which at any given date must have been paid for a given quantum of typical import, export, and domestic goods in percentage relationship to the number of paper marks which would have been required, at the date in question, to purchase a given quantum of foreign goods in general.[9] Data are not available for the construction of a complete index of exported goods and the index of prices of machinery has therefore been taken as typical of German exports. The two other indices have rather narrow bases, the index of imported goods including but sixteen items and that of domestic goods, eighteen. The domestic goods index, moreover, is comprised, in part, of commodities occasionally or even steadily exported. Raw materials of industry and foodstuffs dominate both the indices of import and domestic commodities. The figures are therefore at most *representative* of the relations between the groups of prices affected; no claim that they are precise criteria can be made. But whatever their defects, they are, it is submitted, the best to be had, and even if they will not show refinements

---

[9] The quantum taken, in all cases, was the amount purchasable in 1913 with one gold mark.

TABLE XVII

INDEX NUMBERS OF WHOLESALE PRICES OF IMPORTED GOODS, EXPORTED GOODS (MACHINERY), AND DOMESTIC GOODS, EXPRESSED AS PERCENTAGES OF THE INDEX OF EXTERNAL PRICES; 1920-1923

(Monthly averages)

DATE	IMPORTED GOODS	EXPORTED GOODS (MACHINERY)	DOMESTIC GOODS	DATE	IMPORTED GOODS	EXPORTED GOODS (MACHINERY)	DOMESTIC GOODS
1920 Jan.	76.1	37.1	26.8	1922 Jan.	80.3	49.5[11]	53.5
Feb.	74.1	—	22.1	Feb.	82.9	—	53.8
Mar.	85.6	—	26.6	Mar.	77.5	44.2[11]	52.2
April	99.2	—	34.4	April	83.0	—	60.6
May	94.3	66.6	47.2	May	84.5	67.8[11]	59.1
June	93.7	—	54.6	June	83.8	—	57.8
July	84.0	—	55.8	July	76.1	37.0[11]	51.1
Aug.	77.3	—	50.5	Aug.	77.5	—	39.5
Sept.	71.4	—	43.4	Sept.	80.5	55.6[11]	48.2
Oct.	68.1	46.3	37.8	Oct.	77.3	—	42.7
Nov.	65.4	—	37.1	Nov.	80.5	45.0[11]	35.8
Dec.	64.8	—	42.4	Dec.	86.1		45.4
1921 Jan.	69.3	—	51.8	1923[10] Jan.	75.2	48.5	43.0
Feb.	70.9	67.4	56.4	Feb.	109.4	74.5	66.9
Mar.	69.6	—	55.3	Mar.	83.9	85.6	55.5
April	70.0	—	57.4	April	83.9	82.0	57.2
May	70.8	74.1	58.9	May	75.0	48.9	39.2
June	68.2	—	56.4	June	79.1	47.1	37.5
July	66.7	—	53.1	July	92.1	79.8	69.8
Aug.	68.1	—	67.4	Aug.	77.6	100.3	58.7
Sept.	74.7	52.0	55.1	Sept.	100.0	105.8	59.8
Oct.	70.7	—	44.1	Oct.	102.0	114.1	67.3
Nov.	64.3	25.3	33.7	Nov.	74.2	103.8	63.2
Dec.	79.4	—	49.6	Dec.	104.5	109.3	79.0

[10] 1923 values for all the index numbers refer to the middle of each month.
[11] 1922 values for machinery are end-of-month figures.
Source of data: *Zahlen zur Geldentwertung in Deutschland* 1914 *bis* 1923, *passim.*

they are capable of giving a fair impression of the broad differences which prevailed between these several price groups.

§ IMPORT PRICES

It is at first blush surprising that the index of prices of imported goods does not more nearly approach 100% of the index of external prices in general. In the first half of 1920 it did come close to par but it then fell to a low of 65% in December of that year. Throughout

CHART XVI

INDICES OF IMPORT, EXPORT, AND DOMESTIC COMMODITY PRICES EXPRESSED AS
PERCENTAGES OF THE INDEX OF EXTERNAL PRICES; 1920-1923

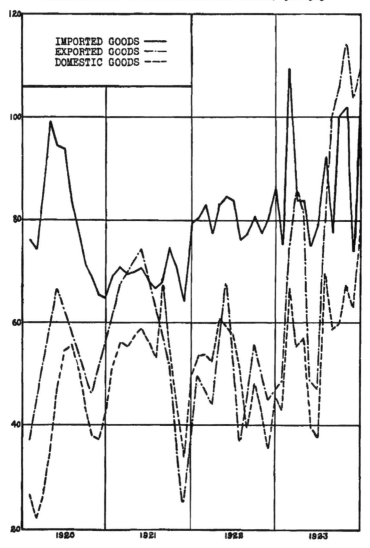

most of 1921 it fluctuated between 65% and 75% of par; it then reached a norm of about 80% which was maintained pretty steadily throughout 1922 and, with occasional great upward flurries, in 1923. The question arises as to why the mark prices of imported goods should have been rather consistently below a true correspondence with the purchasing power of the German currency over foreign goods in general. Several explanations suggest themselves:

(1) The prices of goods which are included in the index were not as high in foreign markets relative to their 1913 level as were foreign goods in general. The bulk of Germany's imports are foodstuffs and industrial raw materials. With the world-wide collapse of the post-war boom in 1920 the prices of these commodities quite generally fell farther than the prices of manufactured goods. This explains the sudden drop, in the summer of 1920, in the ratio of the prices of imported goods to the external value of the mark. Furthermore, Germany imports in part from countries which, in the period under consideration, were undergoing monetary experiences similar to her own. The exports of these countries (German imports) would perhaps tend to be low in price when measured in the gold currency of the United States here used as the base for computation.

(2) German import tariffs, measured in gold, tended to fall as a result of inflation. As early as 1919 customs duties were put on a gold basis by means of a surcharge roughly corresponding to the depreciation of the currency.[12] But there was, nevertheless, a lag of the surcharge rates behind the actual depreciation of the currency and this kept the prices of imports in the internal markets somewhat below a proportionate relationship with the fall in the external value of the mark.

(3) The handling of the goods after their purchase abroad, but before their inclusion in the German wholesale price index, was done at a cheaper rate relative to their cost in the country of export than had been the case in the base year 1913. This was but one aspect of the low domestic price level.

(4) The quality of the goods imported had probably declined. The index is thus defective inasmuch as it does not compare strictly identical commodities.

(5) In 1920 and 1921 a sizable portion of the imports were invoiced in marks. A rise in foreign exchange between the date of order and of

---

[12] Payment, however, was still made in paper marks. There is a real difference between putting an assessment on a gold basis and in making it payable in gold, or its value equivalent, on the day when payment is actually made. It was not until the days immediately prior to the stabilization of the currency that tax payments in general were required in the latter form.

payment would then have no effect on the cost to the importer. This may account for the low status of the ratio from the middle of 1920 till the close of 1921.

§ GENERAL RELATIONSHIP BETWEEN IMPORT, EXPORT, AND DOMESTIC COMMODITY PRICES

Contrasting the relationship between the curves it will be noted that an intermediate position of the index of exports is, in general, maintained.[13] This is in accord with theoretical expectation. When the value of a currency is relatively depressed on the exchange markets—presumptive evidence that the volume of imports is too high relative to that of exports—equilibrium tends to be attained through the establishment of the following price scheme. All domestic commodities, both those exported and those consumed at home, become low in price in comparison with the price of imports, but the prices of exportable goods become high relative to those of commodities which find their market solely within the country. The volume of exports is thus expanded both by the diminution in their home consumption and by the transfer of production from the relatively unprofitable non-exportable goods to lines capable of sale outside the country. The mechanism of this price adjustment under inconvertible paper conditions is entirely contained in the exchange rate movement itself. The price of imports is normally established in foreign markets and increases *pari passu* with a rise in the cost of foreign exchange.[14] The prices of commodities produced and consumed at home are directly affected neither by the prices prevailing in foreign markets nor by the exchange rate. The prices of exports are affected, on the demand side, by foreign monetary conditions and by exchange rates while, on the supply side, the domestic situation is determinative. They therefore tend to assume an intermediate position *below* those of commodities produced abroad but *above* those of commodities produced and consumed at home. It should perhaps be repeated that the prices here given for exports represent only the inland prices of exportable goods. Actual prices to foreigners were arbitrarily fixed above the domestic, but below the foreign, level by the Boards of Foreign Trade Control.[15] If the prices actually charged could be ascertained, they would no doubt lift the curve of export prices

---

[13] Some months in 1920 and 1921 form exceptions.

[14] With the possible exception of imports of which the sole or principal market is in the importing country.

[15] At least they were never consciously set above the foreign level on any goods the export of which was even partially free.

considerably above its present status although its intermediate position would almost certainly be maintained.

The ratio of exports to imports was, it seems, increased sufficiently to procure equilibrium in international debits and credits only through a huge price differential. The influence of cash reparations payments in leading to price movements essential to the relative expansion of exports in the measure required to cover the increased debits is, moreover, clearly evident. By the fore part of 1921 export prices had reached parity with those of imports. During the whole period of cash reparations payments (May 1921 to the end of 1922) they were far below. In 1923, when cash reparations had been suspended, the prices of exports again attained the level of imports and even went considerably beyond it.

Had not the Boards of Foreign Trade Control arbitrarily raised the prices charged to foreign buyers the relatively very low price of exportable goods in the domestic market in 1921 and 1922 would have required almost twice the quantum of exports to pay for a given volume of imports that was necessary before cash payments on reparations began. In other words, assuming a given volume of imports, exports would have had to have been doubled in volume before any foreign exchange whatever would have accrued to the Germans with which to meet their reparations obligations. Since a rapid doubling of exports is out of the question, the situation, if allowed to run uncontrolled, would have become persistently worse. At this stage a discrimination in the prices charged foreign buyers would seem to have been indispensable if the exhaustion of the country of all exportable goods, at prices which would have produced less foreign exchange than could be secured through a much smaller physical volume of export at controlled prices, was to be prevented. At other stages the control of foreign trade may have been nothing but a nuisance but at this time the evidence of its potential usefulness is clear.

While the prices of exportable goods were low to foreign buyers, their prices in domestic markets, to say nothing of the supplements obtained on actual exports, were high enough to put the producers of these goods in a peculiarly favorable position, especially when foreign exchange was rising. Costs were presumably no greater than those of producers of goods for domestic consumption and the price differential was, therefore, pure gain. The greatest gain accrued to exporters working up domestic materials. Both their labor and material costs were then paid at the low internal price level while their goods were sold at the high prices, *in marks*, which issued out of the relative depreciation of the German currency on the exchange markets. Exporters of goods made up of imported raw materials were not quite so well off but were nevertheless in a position to make large gains on the difference between their *labor* costs and their selling price. Importers, and the producers of domestically consumed commodities, shared about the same status of relative disadvantage. Importers obtained high prices for their commodities but had to pay correspondingly high prices to obtain them. Producers of domestically consumed commodities sold at relatively low prices but their costs were on the same level. The favored position was confined, in general, to exporters and was improved in proportion to the degree of independence of foreign raw materials in the manufacture of their products. The distribution of profits taken as a whole was therefore very uneven.

§ POINT-TO-POINT RELATIONSHIP OF IMPORT, EXPORT, AND
DOMESTIC PRICES

The shape of each of the three price curves shown in Chart XVI is, in general, similar, though that of imported goods fluctuates much less widely than the others. The latter is to be expected. If adjustment of import prices to current replacement costs had bee nimmediate and perfect, the curve of import prices would be a straight transverse parallel keeping a fixed relationship with the index of the external purchasing power of the mark, though, for reasons already stated, it might have been below the 100% line. The adjustment was, in fact, by no means immediate or perfect but there is nevertheless a tendency toward relative flatness in this curve. In the others the adjustment was less rapid and complete and the fluctuations are therefore wider. Since all German prices were rather consistently rising, and since foreign (gold) prices were substantially stable, the upward movements in the curves tend to occur when foreign (dollar) exchange rates fell, or when they rose less than general internal prices, while the downward movements normally come at times when foreign exchange rose in greater degree than such prices. The range of fluctuation in all the curves is affected by exchange movements in inverse proportion to the rapidity and closeness of correspondence of the several groups with the variations in exchange.

Though there was a lag of export and domestic commodity prices behind those of imports, in the sense that the prices of the former groups remained persistently lower than those of imports,[16] and though the greater range of fluctuation in export and domestic prices indicates a less immediate response to the changing external purchasing power of the mark, a *chronological* lag is nevertheless not obvious in the month-to-month fluctuations. In their broad movements, import and export

[16] An exception is to be made for exports in the final months of inflation.

prices show a substantial simultaneity, and though, in 1920, domestic commodity prices appear to follow those of the other indices at an interval of a month or two, there is no evidence of any such hesitation after that date. In so far as the movements in the curves are due to such fluctuations in the base as are solely attributable to a shift in exchange rates there would be simultaneity of movement in the curves when all commodity prices were inert. *But when they are due, as is frequently the case, to an upward movement of prices in greater or less degree than a concurrent change in foreign exchange in the same direction, a lag in the export, and, a fortiori, in the domestic price curves, might be expected. Fundamentally* the effect on domestic prices of changing import and export prices would seem to depend on a diminution in the supply of domestic goods arising from the shifting of industry to the production of goods for export. This would be a matter of months. Since any lag there may have been was certainly not as great as this, price adjustments must have been occasioned by a shift in demand rather than in supply. Demand appears to have been so quickly diverted to the relatively cheap goods that prices of all moved almost synchronously. The lesser range of fluctuation in the imported goods curve shows, however, that there was *some* lag in the others. Changes in the external purchasing power of the mark seem to have resulted in almost immediate, though not quite proportionate, changes in the prices of imported goods, while the movement of prices of other commodities was slightly less prompt.

The lag in the response of export and domestic commodity prices is evidenced by the relatively violent movement in the ratio curves of these prices. An extreme movement in one direction was generally followed by an equally extreme movement in the other. If the ratio indices of the prices of domestic or export commodities fell in any given month, owing to the fact that these prices had remained relatively unchanged while foreign exchange had risen, they ordinarily did not stay down for more than that single month. Either foreign exchange fell or domestic and export prices rose—the latter was usually the case— until practically the old relationship was restored. A flat curve means immediate adjustment to the external value of the mark, a curve of violent fluctuations and sharp peaks means a lag of less than a month, and a curve of violent fluctuations and rounded peaks a somewhat longer lag. The latter are conspicuous by their absence.

§ SEQUENCE OF MOVEMENT IN IMPORT, EXPORT, AND DOMESTIC PRICES

In order to test more thoroughly the sequence of movement in the prices of imported and domestic commodities[17] trend lines were fitted to the wholesale price index numbers of these classes of commodities, covering the months June 1918 to December 1923, and cycles of deviation from these trends were charted.[18] It was necessary to divide the series into two periods since the extreme rise in the indices in the final year and a half of inflation made it impracticable to fit any single curve to the whole series. The first period runs from June 1918 to June 1922 inclusive and the second from June 1922 to December 1923 inclusive. A compound-interest trend gives a fairly good fit for the former period while a compound-interest trend fitted to the logarithms of the original data was chosen for the second. Cycles were measured as percentage deviations from the trends; for the period June 1918 to June 1922 percentage deviations of the original items, and for the period June 1922 to December 1923 percentage deviations of the logarithms of the original items. These percentage deviations for each series were then expressed in terms of the respective standard deviations. The resulting Charts XVII and XVIII present the cycles for each series.

In order to calculate correlation coefficients the figures for the cycles[19] were multiplied together month by month, the products added, and the sum divided by the number of products.[20] The following coefficients of correlation were obtained:

CORRELATION OF CYCLES IN THE WHOLESALE PRICES OF DOMESTIC
AND OF IMPORTED GOODS

Period June 1918—*June* 1922

	Coefficient of Correlation	Probable error of r
With simultaneous items	$r = +.776$	$\pm .038$
With one month lag of prices of domestic goods[21]	$r = +.786$	$\pm .037$
With two months lag of prices of domestic goods	$r = +.723$	$\pm .047$
With one month lag of prices of *imported* goods	$r = +.681$	$\pm .052$

[17] The data on *export* commodities (machinery) are too meager to provide an adequate basis for a similar procedure for this group of prices.

[18] The use of the words "trends" and "cycles" may be questioned in view of the shortness of the periods involved. It seemed best, however, to avoid the awkward circumlocution which accurately descriptive expressions would necessitate.

[19] Percentage deviation (from the trend) expressed in terms of the standard deviation.

[20] This corresponds with the Pearsonian coefficient of correlation. These, and all the coefficients shown in this chapter, especially in the very short periods to which some of them apply, are of questionable value. The charts are probably better indicators of the movements since they give a picture of the *general* situation. One or two peculiar movements in the curves, on the other hand, may greatly alter the correlation coefficient.

[21] In this, and all succeeding comparisons of this sort, the curve indicated has been pushed one or more months to the left of that with which it is compared.

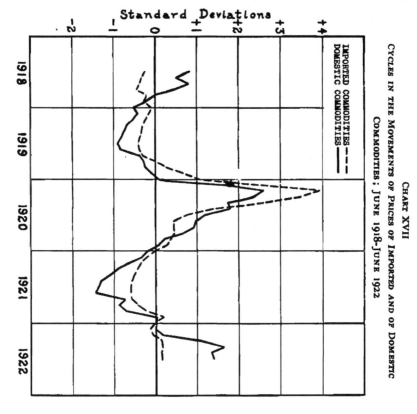

CHART XVII

CYCLES IN THE MOVEMENTS OF PRICES OF IMPORTED AND OF DOMESTIC COMMODITIES : JUNE 1918-JUNE 1922

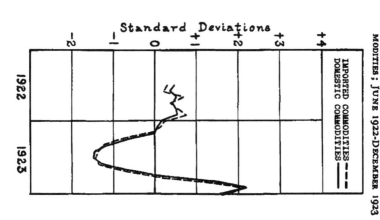

CHART XVIII

CYCLES IN THE MOVEMENTS OF PRICES OF IMPORTED AND OF DOMESTIC COMMODITIES : JUNE 1922-DECEMBER 1923

Period June 1922—December 1923   Coefficient of   Probable
                                          Correlation   error of *r*

With simultaneous items ....*r* = + .994 ± .002
With one month lag of prices of domestic goods ....*r* = + .831 ± .049
With one month lag of prices of *imported* goods...*r* = + .850 ± .044

For the period June 1918 to June 1922 the results are not very conclusive but they perhaps suggest a slight lag in domestic prices. It is
even possible that they indicate an alternation of cause and effect. If
exchange rates persistently dominated internal prices the movements
in the prices of imported goods might be expected to precede those of
domestic commodities. If, on the other hand, internal prices persistently
dominated exchange rates the movements in the prices of domestic commodities might be expected to precede those of imported goods. If either
of the two were persistently dominant a perfect lagging correlation
would thus be possible. If there was alternation, with exchange rates
generally dominant in sub-periods of disturbance and prices dominant
in sub-periods of quiescence, then, on the erroneous assumption that
either was dominant throughout, there would be a possibility, during any
given sub-period, of a *perfect* lagging correlation, and, in the succeeding sub-period, a possibility of *some* correlation provided the general
movement of the cycles was parallel. Over the whole period a considerable measure of correlation might consequently develop. The *trend*,
however, was chiefly determined by a cause acting on both curves,
viz. the extent of general inflation. The evidence of alternation is
therefore meager and it is not much greater in support of the assumption
that import prices were normally dominant. The most that can be said
is that there is still less reason to suppose that prices of domestic commodities took the lead.

In the period June 1922 to December 1923 it is clear that any lag in
either direction which may have been present up to mid-1922 was
greatly cut down or even completely eliminated. This is but another
phase of the tendency for all the phenomena of inflation to move simultaneously in the closing months of currency depreciation.

§ RESULTS OF THE SEQUENCE OF PRICE MOVEMENTS IN IMPORT,
        EXPORT, AND DOMESTIC COMMODITIES

Any tendency for the prices of domestic products to lag in time as well
as in degree must have placed the producers of those products in a still
less favorable position than was theirs by reason of the relatively low
status of domestic prices. Owing to rapid price adjustment the paper
profits of sellers of imported goods were no doubt large enough to yield

a real gain after their stock had been replaced, even though costs moved upward somewhat in advance of selling prices. It seems even more probable that prices on exports moved fast enough to give to the producers of exportable commodities, whose costs did not rise so rapidly, still larger profits than were inherent in the generally high relative prices of the commodities they were selling.[22] But producers of domestic commodities were not only forced to sell at relatively low prices but those prices changed but shortly in advance of costs. If the general movement of exchange rates and prices had been neither up nor down, if fluctuations had been about a level norm, producers of domestic commodities would have been in a relatively favorable position on downward fluctuations. In fact, however, they had but few compensations of this sort. The upward surge of prices was sometimes checked but, in no large measure, reversed. It is not, indeed, to be supposed that the producers of domestic commodities bore the brunt of inflation, which did not fall on the entrepreneurial class at all, but merely that they did not have the same opportunity for gain as did their confrères in other industrial or mercantile pursuits.

2. PRICES OF IMPORTED COMMODITIES, INDUSTRIAL RAW MATERIALS, AND FINISHED GOODS

§ GENERAL RELATIONSHIP BETWEEN SUCH PRICES

Table XVIII and Chart XIX show the relationship between the prices of imported goods, industrial raw materials, and finished goods, all expressed as percentages of external prices in marks. It will be seen that, until the final month of inflation, the prices of industrial raw materials ran consistently above those of finished goods. Reference to Chart XV will also show that prices of raw materials were generally higher even than those of typical exportable goods (machinery). The standardized quality of raw materials, and the nature of their market, make large price differentials, as between one country and another,[28] unlikely to occur under any currency system whatever. There is no sales resistance in custom, and little inertia of any kind, to be overcome. Raw materials have a world market and a world price in a sense which does not at all apply to finished goods. Nothing but rigid control of exports or imports can long keep their prices in any given market widely

---

[22] Such evidence as is available goes to show that there was a shorter, as well as a smaller, lag in export than in domestic commodity prices.

[28] Differentials, that is, apart from those due to costs of transport, tariffs, and similar causes.

TABLE XVIII

INDEX NUMBERS OF WHOLESALE PRICES OF IMPORTED GOODS, INDUSTRIAL RAW MATERIALS, AND FINISHED GOODS, EXPRESSED AS PERCENTAGES OF THE INDEX OF EXTERNAL PRICES; 1920–1923

(*Monthly averages*)

DATE		IM- PORTED GOODS	RAW MA- TERIALS	FINISHED GOODS	DATE		IM- PORTED GOODS	RAW MA- TERIALS	FINISHED GOODS
1920	Jan.	76.1	47.6	33.0	1922	Jan.	80.3	62.6	44.6[25]
	Feb.	74.1	43.0	—		Feb.	82.9	62.5	—
	Mar.	85.6	53.3	—		Mar.	77.5	57.6	41.0[25]
	April	99.2	68.9	—		April	83.0	69.4	—
	May	94.3	75.4	51.0		May	84.5	74.5	60.6[25]
	June	93.7	82.9	—		June	83.8	72.5	—
	July	84.0	78.9	—		July	76.1	61.6	39.8[25]
	Aug.	77.3	67.4	—		Aug.	77.5	45.9	—
	Sept.	71.4	59.2	—		Sept.	80.5	63.3	42.7[25]
	Oct.	68.1	55.7	42.0		Oct.	77.3	48.7	—
	Nov.	65.4	53.0	—		Nov.	80.5	51.5	38.3[25]
	Dec.	64.8	57.5	—		Dec.	86.1	73.0	—
1921	Jan.	69.3	66.3	—	1923[24]	Jan.	75.2	66.5	49.0
	Feb.	70.9	72.7	64.3		Feb.	109.4	106.5	55.7
	Mar.	69.6	72.6	—		Mar.	83.9	97.1	65.8
	April	70.0	76.5	—		April	83.9	90.5	66.7
	May	70.8	77.5	72.6		May	75.0	61.1	42.1
	June	68.2	72.1	—		June	79.1	66.8	34.7
	July	66.7	68.6	—		July	92.1	91.3	58.0
	Aug.	68.1	65.4	—		Aug.	77.6	103.9	82.4
	Sept.	74.7	60.9	52.4		Sept.	100.0	107.4	82.1
	Oct.	70.7	50.1	—		Oct.	102.0	105.0	103.0
	Nov.	64.3	41.1	26.3		Nov.	74.2	73.1	126.8
	Dec.	79.4	62.1	—		Dec.	104.5	103.4	117.2

[24] 1923 values for all the index numbers refer to the middle of the month.
[25] 1922 values for the finished goods index are end-of-month figures.
Source of data: *Zahlen zur Geldentwertung in Deutschland* 1914 *bis* 1923, *passim.*

divergent from their value abroad.[26] In spite of the restricted export of raw materials which prevailed in Germany the activity of the Boards of Foreign Trade Control in fixing raw material prices to foreign buyers at something approaching the world level was sufficient to lift raw material prices in the domestic market considerably above those obtaining for most other goods. The sale of these other goods was entirely de-

[26] "Their value" is to be construed as *their value to the exporter.* Special import duties of the exchange-dumping variety, duties which would tend to be borne by the foreign exporter, might keep their value in the levying country low *so far as the foreign exporter was concerned.*

CHART XIX

INDICES OF PRICES OF IMPORTED GOODS, INDUSTRIAL RAW MATERIALS, AND
FINISHED GOODS EXPRESSED AS PERCENTAGES OF THE INDEX
OF EXTERNAL PRICES; 1920-1923

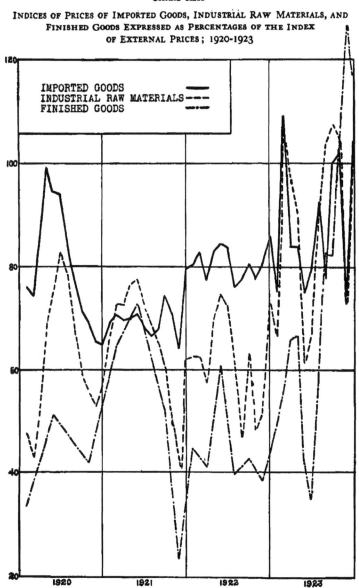

pendent on domestic demand or was conditioned by the fact that the quality of the goods, and therefore the advantage to a foreign buyer at the prices quoted, was by no means obvious. The prices of raw materials thus kept considerably closer to those of imported articles than did the prices of finished wares.

It should be noted, however, that the index of raw materials contains several imported commodities and that this accounts, in part, for the high position of this index relative to that of finished goods. The export of raw materials from post-war Germany was confined to a rather narrow range of commodities. The domestic producer of such materials may have secured a clear advantage over the producer of finished goods but the double gain of securing a high domestic price and a still larger price on export was realized in only a limited degree. Furthermore, the domestic prices of some important raw materials produced in Germany, such as coal and iron, were not substantially higher than those of finished goods, and coal was subject to a heavy tax. The relative gains obtained by the producers of raw materials were therefore not universal.

The general relationship between the prices of raw materials and finished goods on the one hand, and those of imports on the other, is much the same as that of export and domestic commodity prices relative to those of imports. The hunger for imports in 1920, the consequent low exchange value of the mark and high prices of imports, was succeeded by substantial equilibrium in early 1921. All the price indices then tended to coalesce. The equilibrium was disturbed by the break in exchange rates after May 1921 and was not again approached till the final stages of inflation. The raw materials index, so far as it was influenced by domestic commodities, was depressed in mid-1921 by the general *relative* lowering of domestic prices, and the finished goods index suffered a still greater relative decline. When the pressure of foreign obligations was removed in 1923 the tendency was again toward parity in all three curves. There is, however, a difference in the method by which parity was attained in the first half of 1921 and in the latter half of 1923. In the earlier period it was due to an absolute decline in the mark prices of imports (consequent upon a fall in foreign exchange) while other prices remained substantially stable. In the latter half of 1923 it occurred because the prices of imported goods, while rising at a tremendous rate, could not match the precipitous climb of the other indices. The relative immobility of certain prices in 1921 had completely disappeared in the later period. Price changes in 1923 might or might not conform to changes in external purchasing power but this was not due to any sluggishness in price movements.

Since the index of raw materials contains imported commodities, and the index of finished goods contains exported articles, the probability of being able to draw any significant inferences from such lags in the movements of the several curves as might develop from a correlation of cycles of deviation would seem to be too small to warrant the labor involved. Any tendency for the movements of prices of domestic commodities to lag behind those of imports and exports would conflict with a possible tendency for the movements of prices of finished goods to lag behind those of raw materials. Cycles of deviation for the indices of prices of raw materials and finished commodities have therefore not been worked out.

3. WHOLESALE AND RETAIL PRICES

§ GENERAL RELATIONSHIP BETWEEN WHOLESALE AND RETAIL PRICES

The relationship between wholesale and retail prices (each index expressed as a percentage of the index of external prices in marks) is shown in Table XIX and Chart XX.

The index of wholesale prices is the "all commodity" index while the cost of living (exclusive of housing) has been taken as the most appropriate index of retail prices. The most striking aspect of the curves is the tendency for the retail index to be above that of wholesale prices in the first half of 1921 and below it before and after that date.[27] This is in accordance with the well known relative inertia of retail prices. The absolute trend of wholesale prices was upward till January 1921; for the next six months it was, on the whole, slightly downward; from then on it was rapidly upward once more.[28] Retail prices lagged behind wholesale on all of these movements and so appear above those of wholesale in the fore part of 1921 when wholesale prices were falling. During 1922 and most of 1923 there is a rather close parallelism in the curves. They moved in similar fashion but at a distance from one another. This would seem to have been due to the fact that the principal element in the spread between retail and wholesale prices is the wage bill. The index of wages was consistently on a lower scale than commodity prices either at wholesale or retail.[29] The low rate of wages was consequent upon lower general productivity than in the base year, 1913, and upon housing legislation, as well as upon the normal lagging tendency of wages when prices are in flux. The prices of all domestically produced commodities were affected by low wages but those in which the

[27] In the final month of inflation, November 1923, the retail index rises above the wholesale. But stabilization had been effected on the 15th of this month.

[28] See *supra*, Table III.

[29] See *supra*, Table XVI and Chart XV.

TABLE XIX

INDEX NUMBERS OF GENERAL WHOLESALE AND RETAIL PRICES EXPRESSED AS
PERCENTAGES OF THE INDEX OF EXTERNAL PRICES; 1920–1923
(Monthly averages)

DATE	GENERAL WHOLESALE PRICES	RETAIL PRICES[30]	DATE	GENERAL WHOLESALE PRICES	RETAIL PRICES[30]
1920 Jan.	35.1	—	1922 Jan.	58.1	40.1
Feb.	30.8	19.3	Feb.	58.6	44.0
Mar.	36.5	25.5	Mar.	56.4	38.4
April	45.2	37.7	April	64.4	44.7
May	55.1	50.6	May	63.3	47.9
June	61.1	60.2	June	62.2	47.2
July	60.6	59.2	July	55.3	38.2
Aug.	54.9	48.5	Aug.	45.8	24.0
Sept.	48.1	40.7	Sept.	53.6	32.4
Oct.	43.0	39.2	Oct.	48.5	24.5
Nov.	41.8	38.9	Nov.	43.4	21.8
Dec.	46.2	46.6	Dec.	52.2	31.5
1921 Jan.	54.8	56.3	1923 Jan.	41.8	21.8
Feb.	59.0	61.5	Feb.	53.6	33.0
Mar.	57.8	61.5	Mar.	61.1	46.2
April	59.6	63.3	April	56.4	41.2
May	60.9	65.2	May	46.1	27.7
June	58.5	62.4	June	48.2	24.8
July	55.4	60.8	July	59.0	38.6
Aug.	67.6	59.1	Aug.	57.1	46.3
Sept.	58.5	48.9	Sept.	66.2	53.9
Oct.	48.5	37.5	Oct.	77.0	51.7
Nov.	38.8	25.6	Nov.	91.4	107.3
Dec.	54.6	38.4	Dec.	83.5	103.4

[30] Index number of cost of living excluding housing.
Source of data: *Zahlen zur Geldentwertung in Deutschland* 1914 *bis* 1923, *passim.*

labor element was relatively important were affected most. These were retail prices. The comparatively low position of retail prices in 1922 and 1923 was probably therefore not primarily due to a lag which would ultimately have tended to disappear had prices steadied, but to a difference in costs which would tend to be permanent so long as conditions affecting either the wholesale or retail index, or both indices in unequal degree, such as wages, remained unlike those prevailing in the base year. This conclusion is confirmed by the fact that in late 1923, when the ratio index of retail prices once more advanced beyond that of wholesale, wages had already shown a corresponding rise.

CHART XX

INDICES OF WHOLESALE AND RETAIL PRICES EXPRESSED AS PERCENTAGES
OF THE INDEX OF EXTERNAL PRICES ; 1920-1923

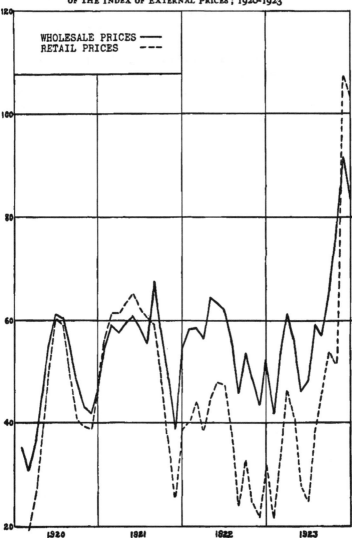

There is nothing in the charts to indicate that the *movement* of retail
prices, in the later years at any rate, was more sluggish than that of
wholesale. In order properly to trace various types of correlation it

would seem to be necessary, in general, to distinguish three separate types of lag. There is the lag in amplitude and there are two sorts of lags in timing, a lag for the whole duration of a trend in any one direction and a point-to-point lag. If wages should move more slowly than prices in general, and if wages play a more important part in retail than in wholesale prices, retail prices might be expected to show a trend lag, with respect to wholesale, as prices in general moved in any one direction. But the point-to-point movements within a trend might show no such lag in timing and they might even reverse it. If, for instance, increased monetary purchasing power is first directed toward consumers' goods, retail prices might, not improbably, show a point-to-point movement in advance of those at wholesale, though, as a result of other causes such as the lag in wages, their variations would appear on a chart from which trends had not been eliminated, persistently to the right of the wholesale price curve.

§ SEQUENCE OF MOVEMENTS IN WHOLESALE AND RETAIL PRICES

In Chart XXI the cycles of deviation of general wholesale and retail prices from their respective trends are given. The index of retail prices (cost of living exclusive of housing) is not quoted till February 1920. Yet, in order satisfactorily to measure trends, it was necessary to break up into three periods the four years covered by this index. The periods are: February 1920 through May 1921, May 1921 through June 1922, and June 1922 through December 1923. The series for wholesale prices was similarly divided. For the first period a compound-interest trend gave a fairly good fit for the wholesale price index while a straight line proved better for the retail. In the second period a compound-interest trend was again satisfactory for the wholesale index while a parabolic curve[31] gave the best results for the retail. In the third period a compound-interest trend was fitted to the logarithms of the original items of both indices. The calculation of the cyclical fluctuations and of the correlation coefficients was carried out in the manner already described in connection with the comparison of the prices of imported and domestic goods.

It is doubtful whether significant results can be obtained from periods so short as were necessary for the fitting of trend lines in these cases and the movement of the curves in the middle period, May 1921 through June 1922, is peculiar, a fact upon which more detailed comment will presently be made.

[31] A third-degree parabola.

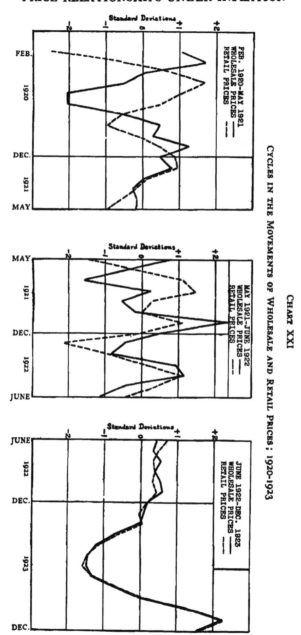

CHART XXI

CYCLES IN THE MOVEMENTS OF WHOLESALE AND RETAIL PRICES: 1920-1923

For the period February 1920 through May 1921 a lag of retail prices of about two months seems clear. The coefficients of correlation, with varying lags, are as follows:

CORRELATION OF CYCLES IN WHOLESALE AND RETAIL PRICES

Period February 1920—May 1921

	Coefficient of Correlation	Probable error of r
With simultaneous items	$r = -.369$	$\pm .146$
With one month lag of retail prices	$r = +.201$	$\pm .167$
With two months lag of retail prices	$r = +.621$	$\pm .111$
With three months lag of retail prices	$r = +.496$	$\pm .141$
With four months lag of retail prices	$r = +.065$	$\pm .194$

Period May 1921—June 1922

	Coefficient of Correlation	Probable error of r
With simultaneous items	$r = +.227$	$\pm .171$
With one month lag of retail prices	$r = -.175$	$\pm .181$
With two months lag of retail prices	$r = -.615$	$\pm .121$
With three months lag of retail prices	$r = -.156$	$\pm .198$
With four months lag of retail prices	$r = +.079$	$\pm .212$

There is no evidence here of any direct correlation at all in the movements of the two groups of prices in the second period. It seems improbable that, if there was a lag in the movement of retail prices up to May 1921, the tendency would be completely eliminated in the period May 1921 to June 1922 when the general simultaneity in the movements of all prices had not yet set in. For some reason wholesale and retail prices in this period simply did not move in any discernible relationship with one another. This is, however, not very surprising in view of the fact that the period covered, with monthly data only, is little more than a single year.

Period June 1922—December 1923

	Coefficient of Correlation	Probable error of r
With simultaneous items	$r = +.990$	$\pm .003$
With one month lag of retail prices	$r = +.842$	$\pm .046$
With two months lag of retail prices	$r = +.833$	$\pm .050$

Here, as in other cases at this stage of inflation, any lag that up to this time may have been present in retail prices tended to disappear or, at any rate, to be reduced to less than a single month's duration.

4. WAGES AND THE COST OF LIVING

§ GENERAL RELATIONSHIP BETWEEN WAGES AND COST OF LIVING

Finally, it seemed worth while to examine in detail the relationship between wages and the cost of living. Table XX and Chart XXII show

TABLE XX

INDEX NUMBERS OF WAGES OF SKILLED AND UNSKILLED WORKERS, AND OF COST OF LIVING, EXPRESSED AS PERCENTAGES OF THE INDEX OF EXTERNAL PRICES; 1920-1923

(*Monthly averages*)

DATE	WAGES OF SKILLED WORKERS	WAGES OF UN- SKILLED WORKERS	COST OF LIV- ING	DATE	WAGES OF SKILLED WORKERS	WAGES OF UN- SKILLED WORKERS	COST OF LIV- ING
1920 Jan.	13.9	18.7	—	1922 Jan.	23.9	32.1	32.3
Feb.	9.1	12.2	15.5	Feb.	21.6	29.0	35.0
Mar.	10.7	14.3	20.4	Mar.	15.7	21.1	30.1
April	19.3	26.2	30.0	April	22.1	30.3	34.8
May	24.5	33.2	40.2	May	27.7	37.6	37.3
June	33.6	44.7	47.9	June	30.0	40.8	36.7
July	33.6	44.7	47.1	July	23.0	31.3	29.6
Aug.	28.8	38.3	38.7	Aug.	14.8	20.4	18.5
Sept.	24.4	32.4	32.5	Sept.	22.0	30.2	24.9
Oct.	22.2	29.5	31.3	Oct.	11.8	16.3	18.9
Nov.	21.1	28.0	31.0	Nov.	9.1	12.5	16.8
Dec.	24.4	32.4	37.1	Dec.	14.2	19.6	24.3
1921 Jan.	32.3	43.3	44.8	1923 Jan.	9.7	13.3	16.8
Feb.	36.3	48.7	49.0	Feb.	12.9	17.8	25.4
Mar.	36.6	49.1	49.1	Mar.	21.0	29.0	35.6
April	38.1	51.1	50.5	April	18.2	25.1	31.9
May	39.5	53.0	52.1	May	12.9	17.8	21.5
June	36.3	48.7	49.9	June	14.9	20.6	19.0
July	32.9	44.2	48.4	July	19.6	27.2	29.7
Aug.	34.9	47.2	46.9	Aug.	35.0	48.4	35.5
Sept.	28.0	37.9	38.8	Sept.	33.2	45.9	41.4
Oct.	27.6	37.1	29.7	Oct.	61.9	84.7	39.7
Nov.	15.9	21.3	20.1	Nov.	39.7	50.6	82.7
Dec.	21.9	29.4	30.2	Dec.	46.0	52.3	82.6

Source of data: *Zahlen zur Geldentwertung in Deutschland* 1914 *bis* 1923, *passim.*

the ratio of wages of skilled and unskilled workers and of cost of living (including housing) to external prices in marks.

The similarity in the shape of the curves suggests that the response of the three indices to changes in the external purchasing power of the mark was about equal, and the curves also indicate that, in the first

CHART XXII

INDICES OF WAGES OF SKILLED AND UNSKILLED WORKERS, AND OF COST OF
LIVING, EXPRESSED AS PERCENTAGES OF THE INDEX
OF EXTERNAL PRICES; 1920-1923

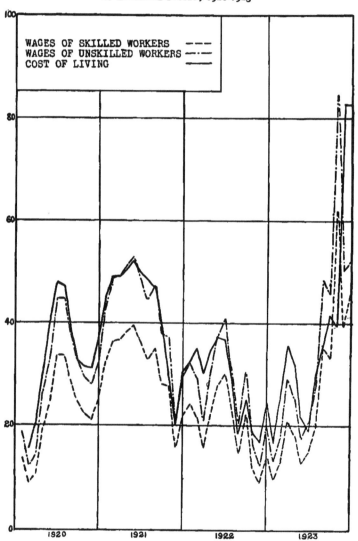

two years and a half of the period depicted, the response was rather, slow.[82] Exchange rate movements, in themselves, do not appear, during these two and a half years, greatly to have affected wages or the worker's cost of living. It should be noted that the composition of the cost-of-living index was changed in 1920, and thereafter includes a group of commodities which, in that year, could be obtained relatively cheaply. Wages were thus not as high relative to the 1913 list of commodities in the then cost-of-living index as Table XX and Chart XXII seem to indicate. There is, however, in the relationship between the curves of wages of unskilled labor and that of the revised cost of living, an interesting analogue to the operation of the old iron law of wages. Unskilled workers' wages in 1920 appear to have been down close to the minimum of subsistence and the amplitude lag between such wages and the reduced cost-of-living index was never thereafter great, however rapid the rate of currency depreciation might be. The adjustment of unskilled wages to the rising monetary cost of living from 1920 onward was necessarily quick and close. In the case of skilled workers, on the other hand, where there had been a margin of safety, a large reduction in real wages was persistently maintained; the margin of safety was wellnigh eliminated and the absolute level of real wages of skilled workers fell to a point not much above that of the unskilled group.

§ SEQUENCE OF MOVEMENTS IN WAGES AND THE COST OF LIVING

To test the response of wages to cost of living, or vice versa as the case might be, cyclical fluctuations in the deviations of the curves of wages of unskilled workers and of cost of living (including housing) from their respective trends were calculated. The data used were the simple index numbers of unskilled workers' wages and of cost of living and they were divided into the same three periods as those of wholesale and retail prices. Straight-line trends were fitted to the data of the first period, a compound-interest trend for wages and a parabolic trend for cost of living in the second, while compound-interest trends were fitted to logarithms of the original data in the third. Cyclical fluctuations and correlation coefficients were computed in the same manner as for the previous comparisons. The cycles of deviation are shown in Chart XXIII.

There is fairly clear evidence of a lag in the movements of wages of approximately one month in the period February 1920 to May 1921. The correlation coefficients are:

[82] The "waves" are rounded rather than choppy.

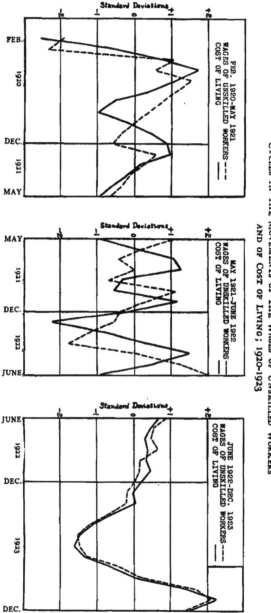

CHART XXIII

CYCLES IN THE MOVEMENTS OF THE WAGES OF UNSKILLED WORKERS
AND OF COST OF LIVING; 1920-1923

CORRELATION OF CYCLES IN WAGES AND THE COST OF LIVING

Period February 1920—May 1921	Coefficient of Correlation	Probable error of r
With simultaneous items	$r = +.627$	$\pm .102$
With one month lag of wages	$r = +.700$	$\pm .089$
With two months lag of wages	$r = +.144$	$\pm .177$
With one month lag of cost of living	$r = +.031$	$\pm .174$
With two months lag of cost of living	$r = -.471$	$\pm .140$

In the second period, May 1921 to June 1922, the curves of cycles of deviation are of roughly similar shape but examination of the charts suggests that wage movements preceded those of the cost of living in the second half of 1921 while in 1922 they appear to have succeeded them. Correlation coefficients for the whole period, however, are as follows:

Period May 1921—June 1922	Coefficient of Correlation	Probable error of r
With simultaneous items	$r = -.066$	$\pm .179$
With one month lag of wages	$r = +.359$	$\pm .163$
With two months lag of wages	$r = +.658$	$\pm .110$
With three months lag of wages	$r = +.035$	$\pm .203$
With one month lag of cost of living	$r = -.090$	$\pm .186$
With two months lag of cost of living	$r = -.205$	$\pm .187$

It is of course possible that, with increasing flexibility in all price phenomena, interaction between the movements of wages and those in the cost of living may have occurred, wages tending to affect the cost of living and the cost of living to affect wages. The causal sequence which consistently holds in the early stages of inflation is not necessarily, or even normally, maintained as currency depreciation becomes forseeable, and resistance in any of the phases of the price structure weakens. But, if there was this type of interaction between two forces, it would seem to make for approximate simultaneity in the month-to-month movements of the indices, such as developed in all the series from the middle of 1922 onward, rather than in an alternation of the dominant and recessive rôles. It seems unlikely, too, that wages should lag more in the second than in the first period, though the correlation coefficients carry this suggestion. The cycles of deviation of the indices of wages and cost of living in this second period must therefore be regarded as having been peculiar and not subject to any discernible law.

In the period June 1922 to December 1923, the high degree of simultaneous correlation, typical of all price phenomena in this final stage of currency collapse, appears. Correlation coefficients are:

Period June 1922—December 1923	Coefficient of Correlation	Probable error of r
With simultaneous items	$r = + .985$	$\pm .005$
With one month lag of wages	$r = + .777$	$\pm .063$

§ SOCIAL SIGNIFICANCE OF PRICE VARIATIONS

Certain classes of the population consistently secured a relatively large, and others a relatively small, share of the national income, not only because the prices in which they were concerned as producers were maintained at relatively high or relatively low levels compared with the prices in which they were concerned as consumers, but also because these prices were sensitive in varying degrees to a change in the general situation. The more sensitive the price the stronger was the general tendency toward the acquisition of undue gains, since the general movement of all prices was upward at an increasing rate of acceleration. The more ready the price response of any one group of goods or services, the greater, therefore, was the advantage to the sellers of commodities or services in that group. In some cases the persistent spread between different classes of prices was attended by a compensating spread in costs. This was true of sellers of imported wares. The relatively high selling prices of commodities at wholesale, as compared with retail prices, would also seem to have been related in some measure to corresponding differences in costs. In other cases the persistent spread in prices meant high profits. This was the case with producers of goods for export and with producers of commodities the prices of which were quick to respond to world prices. Unskilled workers steadily benefited at the expense of skilled and white-collar workers, while all workers were helped by the virtual confiscation, for the time being, of the property of urban landlords. On the other hand, workers, as a whole, were probably underpaid relatively to their pre-inflation position as modified by the change in general productivity and, if so, the employers obtained the benefit. The evidence for this lies in the fact that the index of wages (skilled and unskilled together) was steadily below that of a cost-of-living index composed of the cheapest means of subsistence.

The gains and losses from persistent spreads in prices were usually enlarged by such point-to-point lags as tended to occur, since the "normal" spread was more often increased than reduced by these lags. The progress of inflation, by increasing the flexibility of all prices, reduced the disadvantage of the sellers of those commodities which, in less disturbed conditions, tend to rise in price somewhat tardily. In the final months of inflation previously existing lags were, it appears in some cases, not only reduced but reversed, and the disadvantage under which the sellers of the lagging commodities or services had till then labored was turned into a temporary boon.

CHAPTER VIII

PRICE MOVEMENTS AND FOREIGN TRADE

§ STIMULUS TO EXPORTS AND RETARDATION OF IMPORTS

T HE persistently low relative value of the mark in the foreign exchange markets put a premium on exports and discouraged imports. The depreciation in the exchange value of the mark relative to its domestic purchasing power was, indeed, the measure of the motivation necessary to procure equilibrium in international debits and credits. It has been shown in the preceding chapter that the mark prices of German imports were high relative to the mark prices of practically all other commodities, and this of course tended to reduce the volume of imports. But the prices of German imports were lower than the general level of prices abroad. The domestic prices of German *exports* were therefore far beneath the foreign price level. Exports were, in consequence, greatly stimulated. The discrepancy between the German and foreign price levels is reflected in the relationship between the purchasing power par of the mark and actual exchange rates, and the strength of the stimulus to export, and of the retardation of import, is measured by the fluctuations in this relationship. It will be the object of this chapter to examine the response of exports and imports to this varying stimulus. Before proceeding to this examination however it will be necessary to take note of some complicating circumstances.

§ FOREIGN TRADE CONTROL

The situation under which exports sold at low and imports at high prices, measured in any currency whatever, though delightful to the heart of a protectionist, was very costly to the country. It meant that the Germans were paying a very heavy real price in terms of effort expended in producing exports for the comparatively small addition to their real incomes which an equivalent value of imports afforded. Though the full implications of the dissociation of internal and external price levels were not generally apprehended till the collapse of the currency was well under way the draining of the country of goods was obvious enough as early as 1919 and 1920.

The regulations in control of foreign trade, designed to prevent this drain, have been severely criticized by economists on the ground that they perpetuated the condition they were designed to combat. It is frequently alleged that, had exports been freely permitted, they would have so increased in volume, by reason of the low price in foreign currencies at which they could be bought, as to have readily provided the amount of foreign exchange necessary to meet the German requirements for external means of payment. The sale of goods at slaughter prices would then have ceased. The discrepancy between export and import prices would have been but a passing phase, the necessary mechanism for producing equilibrium.

This argument, normally valid, does not hold for Germany under post-war conditions. The Reparations Commission had fixed the total of German indebtedness on reparation account at 132,000,000,000 gold marks. Aside from the possibility of foreign borrowing or the sale of capital assets, both of which were practically precluded, Germany could not have secured the exchange requisite even for the service on this debt without developing an excess of commodity exports of nearly 7,000,000,000 gold marks. Even if it be assumed that the Allies never really hoped to receive sums of any such magnitude there would, nevertheless, have been no stopping short of this point so long as fair progress toward it was being made. The very fact of success would have prevented that reduction in the burdens which failure made imperative. Whatever might ultimately have been feasible there can be no question that an excess of commodity exports of 7,000,000,000 gold marks annually went far beyond any possibility of attainment at the time.[1] The utmost freedom of export could therefore not have prevented, as a persistent phenomenon, the depression of the exchange value of the mark below its internal purchasing power. It is quite possible, moreover, that with freedom of export, goods would have been sold at such prices as would yield less foreign exchange than a smaller volume sold under restrictions as to price. If this had been the case the exchange value of the mark would have sunk even farther below purchasing power par than it actually did. Whether or not a larger aggregate of foreign exchange would have issued from a non-interventionist policy there is no doubt that the physical volume of export would have been increased. Such increase would have gone into the insatiable maw of reparations and the German economy would have been exhausted of all transportable commodities. Control of exports probably reduced the volume of

---

[1] It should be noted that the *total* exports of Germany in the years in question did not amount to 7,000,000,000 gold marks and there was no excess of exports at all. The maximum reparations payment later made in any single year was 2,500,000,000 gold marks and part of this did not necessitate an international *transfer* of funds.

goods sent out to meet reparations claims but even the Reparations Commission apparently did not regard this as a deviation from the policy of fulfilment. It was perhaps, indeed, indispensable to German self-preservation.

Ideally conceived for the purpose of most effectively securing the largest excess of foreign exchange above the requirements of the domestic economy the system of foreign trade control would have centered round the following practices:

(a) *Limitation of imports to necessary foodstuffs and raw materials of industry.* In order to make this really effective in increasing the ratio of exports to imports a system of internal taxation practically confiscating incomes above a certain low minimum would have been necessary. Otherwise, domestic demand would simply have turned from imports to substitutes therefor produced at home, and would thus have reduced the total of goods available for export in approximately the same degree as imports were restricted. If such taxation had been put into effect import prohibitions might even have been superfluous.

(b) *Insistence that exporters should charge what the traffic, in competition with the outside world, would bear.* It seems strange that it should be necessary to *force* sellers to charge higher prices, but the fact is clear that, in the case of non-standardized commodities, the tendency toward equalization of prizes in different markets operates very slowly indeed, and that, when constant alterations in the exchange relation of one currency against another are in process, it scarcely operates at all or else is overwhelmed by the play of more potent forces. In some instances very low real prices will be paid by foreign buyers because of the fact that contracts have been made in the depreciating currency while payment is not effected until that currency has greatly sunk in value. But, more typically, sellers in the country where inflation is under way proceed more or less by rule of thumb and ask a price which merely covers their low and lagging costs of production plus the usual percentage profit. Instead of exploiting the market they permit the market to exploit them.

(c) *Heavy taxation of exports so that the difference between costs of production (including a normal profit) and the much higher selling price consequent upon the dislocation of the exchanges should enure to the state rather than to the producer who happens to be engaged in making exportable wares.* A still more thoroughgoing procedure would be for an organization in control of foreign trade, taking over the sale abroad of all exports, to pay to the exporters merely the domestic price of their commodities while using only part of the exchange proceeds of foreign sales to finance necessary imports. The sale of these imports at home could be made to yield sufficient sums to cover the prices paid to exporters for their wares.

The actual control of foreign trade instituted in Germany did not seek these aims at all purely. It has, indeed, often been asserted that the real object of the Germans in setting up the machinery of regulation was to obstruct, rather than further, the payment of reparations. This question it would be futile to discuss. The fact is that, whether the Germans wished to promote the policy of fulfilment or that of obstruction, it was in any case illogical to restrict the volume both of imports and exports. If the aim were to *build up an excess of foreign exchange for reparations purposes* it would have been appropriate to restrict non-essential imports and to encourage the sale of such a volume of potential exports as would give the maximum total return in foreign exchange. On the other hand, if the foreign trade regulations were designed to *prevent reparations payments*, imports should have been encouraged and exports restricted. The actual policy, whatever its motivation, was a compromise between conflicting purposes. Imports were curtailed, the consumption of the home population was reduced and larger payments to foreigners made possible, while, at the same time, exports were controlled to prevent those payments being so great as to reduce the German populace to destitution.

§ EFFECT OF PRICE-FIXING ACTIVITIES

There are no statistics reliable enough to permit conclusions as to the actual prices realized on the various types of export. It was comparatively easy for the Boards of Foreign Trade Control to establish export prices approximately at the world level for raw and semi-finished materials of standard type.[2] But experience goes to show that the play of competition would in any event have soon brought such prices to the producers if export had been free.[3] On the other hand, in the case of manufactured goods incapable of standardization, where competition is not nearly so effective, the Boards were not very successful in securing world prices. Such goods were persistently sold at far below their real competitive value. This would have occurred on a still more extravagant scale, however, if export had been free. Certain practices of the Boards of Control nevertheless wiped out much of the benefit which those Boards might here have conferred upon the German economy. Though they did succeed in setting some limits on the drain of goods at bargain prices,

[2] To a considerable degree the work of the Boards of Foreign Trade Control was facilitated, or rendered unnecessary, by the activities of cartels.

[3] cf. *Depreciated Exchange and International Trade*, United States Tariff Commission, Government Printing Office, Washington, 1922, *passim*.

yet, on the exports which actually took place, the national gain was small or non-existent. One of the most vicious of their practices was the discrimination between countries the currencies of which were not at all or not greatly depreciated and those where the exchange was, at the moment, in worse or in not much better plight than the mark. The assumption was that the nationals of countries with greatly depreciated currencies could not afford to pay as much as those where exchange stood high. This was, of course, wrong in theory and it resulted not only in the Germans making a present of part of the purchase price to buyers in countries the exchange of which was low but also depressed the price obtainable in other countries. It led, moreover, to a costly roundabout trade wherein the original buyers resold their cheaply purchased goods in the best markets available. A policy of this sort inevitably led to an increase in the proportion of sales at low prices to countries with highly depreciated currencies and to a decrease in the share of German exports directly taken, at higher prices, by the rest of the world.

Pressure was early brought to bear by the government and Reichsbank to have exports invoiced in foreign currencies but such action was not made imperative and was at times strongly opposed by the exporters on the ground that it made sales more difficult. If all foreign trade had been carried on in foreign currencies, *fluctuations* in the exchange value of the mark would, in themselves, have had no bearing on the national economy and certain losses which actually occurred would have been precluded. But this would not have prevented and, so far as it was in operation, did not prevent exports being sold at very low prices relative to what had to be paid for imported goods. Invoicing in foreign currencies obviated losses on exchange fluctuations *after the invoice was made* but had, of course, no effect on the tendency to quote low gold prices corresponding with the low internal cost of production in gold. On any sharp rise in foreign exchange not immediately accompanied by a proportionate rise in the internal price level it was possible to sell goods abroad at not only an apparent, but a real, profit to the enterpriser, though at a rate which was most disadvantageous to the national economy. The difference which then tended to develop between the foreign and domestic price of any given commodity might, on a sale being made, accrue either to the foreign buyer or to the domestic seller according to the price charged on export. Whether the buyer or seller secured the lion's share, or if the difference were split, one would expect a sizable increase in the physical volume of export. If the foreign buyer obtained the whole difference between foreign and domestic price he would be most eager to purchase, if the domestic seller could retain the bulk of it he would force his export sales, if both obtained a part both would be more than ready for the transaction. A fall in foreign exchange, on the other hand, would limit the gains of all parties to a German export or even make trade impossible.

The arbitrary fixing of export prices neutralized to some extent the effect of the spread between exchange rates and domestic purchasing power. Though the seller was even more eager the buyer's enthusiasm was somewhat checked. According to the measure of control exerted exchange rate movements were of less or greater significance to the buyer of German exports. If the execution of the control had been perfect, neither changes in exchange rates nor in German internal prices would have altered the price (in foreign exchange) which the foreign buyer must pay for German goods. There is no evidence, however, that the Boards of Foreign Trade Control, on goods which, as regards volume, were freely exportable, ever set prices at levels which would make sales difficult. Compromise was the general rule. The domestic prices were raised to foreign buyers, sometimes by 200% to 300%, but even so were kept substantially below the cost in foreign markets of similar commodities. Adjustments to fluctuating exchange rates were slow, and the foreign currency price of German exports therefore fell whenever the exchange value of the mark declined, in the same manner, if not in the same degree, as would have been the case if there had been no control at all. On the other hand, export prices were never reduced below those prevailing on the domestic market. They thus became higher, automatically, whenever the domestic purchasing power of the mark declined in comparison with its external value. In spite of the control, one might therefore expect a considerable measure of correlation between the volume of exports and the variations in the ratio of the internal to the external value of the mark. Since no attempt was made to control import prices the inverse correlation for the volume of imports should be even more marked, though this too would be affected by absolute restrictions on import and by other causes to which reference will later be made.

§ MEASURES OF THE RESPONSE OF IMPORTS AND EXPORTS TO THE PRICE SITUATION

It will be remembered that the ratio of the internal to the external value of the mark, which is the measure of the stimulus to exports and the drag on imports, is found in the percentage relationship between the purchasing power par of the mark and actual exchange rates. The volume of exports would be expected to show a direct correlation with the movement of this relationship and the volume of imports an inverse correlation.

Official statistics on the *values* of imports and exports are either not available at all in the period under review or they are thoroughly unreliable.[4] Fairly reliable figures by weight, however, are at hand. For some of the purposes at hand figures by weight are in any case preferable to those of value. The idea is to discover the response in the physical volume of exports and imports to changes in price. Figures of total values would but obscure the facts since, with a change in physical trade in strict inverse proportion to price variations, total values would remain constant and would, in every case, tend to vary less than prices. It would not do, however, to take the weight of exports or imports *as a whole* and contrast one period with another. Changes in the export or import of a few heavy commodities, particularly coal and iron ore, can revolutionize the statistics of total weight of trade without greatly affecting the value figures. The transfer to other flags of coal and iron ore deposits after the war, and reparations deliveries of coal (which do not appear in the official export figures and which were compensated from time to time by the import of foreign coal), shifted an enormous tonnage from the export to the import side. The same result followed the occupation of the Ruhr. There was naturally *some* effect on values, but a comparison of total weights would, nevertheless, wildly distort the value situation.[5] But if, instead of the *total* weight of exports and imports, the weights are taken by *classes of commodities*, this difficulty of comparison will largely disappear. Statistics of this type are available only from May 1921 onward and the examination here to be made can not begin earlier than that date.

§ TREND OF IMPORTS AND EXPORTS

The index of the ratio of the internal to the external value of the mark was far above 100% during the whole of the inflationary period.

[4] Thus in the introductions to *Statistik des deutschen Reichs* for 1920, 1921, and 1922, the value figures previously published in the *Monatliche Nachweise* are expressly repudiated. Even the figures by weight are at times inaccurate owing to: (1) the "Hole in the West" which was closed, however, in the spring of 1920, (2) the occupation of the Ruhr during 1923, (3) the prevalence of smuggling as the range of uncontrolled trade was narrowed, (4) the relative growth of "tourist's" purchases which escaped the attention of the inspectors.

[5] Thus, in 1913, coal alone formed almost 50% of the total weight of exports but only 5% of the value. In 1922 and 1923, on the other hand, exports of coal, aside from reparations, had become negligible, while, in some months of those years, imports of coal ran to more than 70% by weight of the total for all commodities. Between 1913 and 1922 the total weight of German exports sank by more than two-thirds, from 73.6 million tons to 21.9 million tons but of this decline the falling off in coal and coke exports accounted for 36.6 million tons. Excluding bar and other semi-manufactured iron products, the export of manufactured goods was only 14% less, by weight, in 1922 than in 1913.

Prior to the investigation of the correlation of exports and imports with *fluctuations* in this index it will therefore be worth while to observe their response to its general *status*. The fact that the internal value of the mark was consistently high (relatively low prices in the domestic market) would lead us to expect of imports a falling, and of exports a rising, *trend*.

In order to test this thesis, the movement, by weight, of each of the principal classes of German exports and imports not subject to special influences, as, for instance, coal, was plotted month by month as a percentage of the average export or import of the commodity in question over the whole period of post-war inflation for which statistics are available.[6] In the German schedule the groupings are such as, in some cases, to cover in the same classification a number of commodities some of which are imports and others exports. Thus raw cotton is grouped with cotton textiles, silk with silk textiles, copper with copper manufactures. In six cases, therefore, a given classification appears among both exports and imports. It is, however, by no means impossible to have an increased export of finished goods with a diminished import of the raw materials from which such finished goods are made, or vice versa. There is no necessary confusion in setting a given classification on both export and import sides. The comparison is not between exports and imports in any given month but between either of these in one month and in another.

Charts, drawn in the manner just described, furnished substantial corroboration of theoretical expectation. The results were:

Imports

The following classes of imports show a visible *downward* trend:

1A. Agricultural products
1C. Animals and animal products
2B. Ores, matrix, and ashes
2D. Mineral oils and certain other fossil raw materials
3. Prepared wax, solid acid fats, paraffin and similar candle materials, lighting material, wax products, soaps and other products of fats, oils, or wax
4C. Varnishes and lacquers
4E. Artificial fertilizers

[6] In all, forty-three out of a total of sixty-six classifications were included. There is no reason to believe that the excluded twenty-three would have shown movements widely divergent from those included. The great majority of them were omitted simply because they were unimportant.

Source of data: *Monatliche Nachweise über den auswärtigen Handel Deutschlands*, Statistisches Reichsamt, Berlin, monthly. The figures and letters designating the several classes are those of the original data.

5A. Silk, silk yarns, and products thereof

5B. Wool and other animal fibres, except horsehair, and products thereof

6A. Leather.

This group of commodities consists, in the main, of consumption goods or of raw materials of industry some of which are produced within

CHART XXIV

RELATIVE MONTHLY VOLUME OF IMPORT OF CERTAIN CLASSES OF COMMODITIES
WITH A DOWNWARD TREND; MAY 1921-DECEMBER 1923
(Average May 1921-December 1923 = 100)

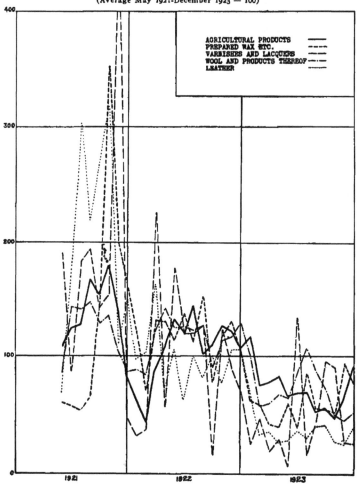

Germany as well as imported. Imports of such goods were readily susceptible to price changes. Consumption within Germany was either reduced absolutely or provided in larger measure by domestic producers or both. Chart XXIV showing the import of agricultural products, of prepared wax etc., of varnishes and lacquers, of wool and products thereof, and of leather, presents typical classifications in this group.

The following classes of imports show no visible trend, up or down:

1D. Products of industries associated with agriculture
1E. Food products not elsewhere specified
2A. Earths and stones
5C. Cotton, cotton yarns, and products thereof
17E. Tin, tin alloys, and products thereof
17F. Nickel, nickel alloys, and products thereof
17G. Copper, copper alloys, and products thereof.

CHART XXV

RELATIVE MONTHLY VOLUME OF IMPORT OF CERTAIN CLASSES OF COMMODITIES WITH
NO DECIDED TREND IN EITHER DIRECTION; MAY 1921-DECEMBER 1923
(Average May 1921-December 1923 = 100)

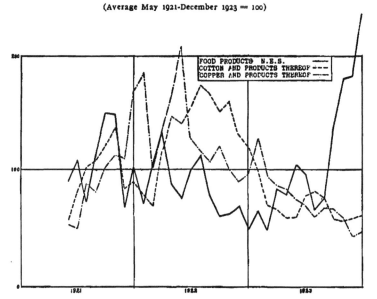

Many of these products are raw materials of industry not capable of being produced in Germany in any volume. A decline in such imports must have been accompanied by a falling off in exports of the finished products in the production of which these materials were used unless

CHART XXVI

RELATIVE MONTHLY VOLUME OF IMPORT OF CERTAIN CLASSES OF COMMODITIES
WITH AN UPWARD TREND; MAY 1921-DECEMBER 1923
(Average May 1921-December 1923 = 100)

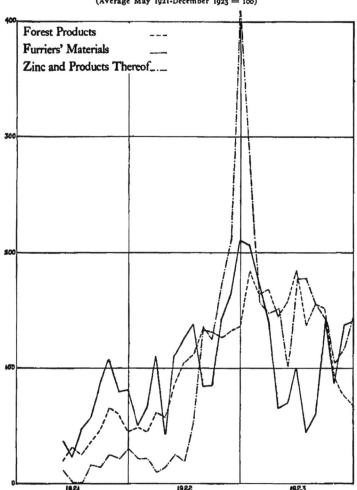

domestic consumption of the finished materials were cut still more
heavily. Domestic consumption *was* cut, but the stimulus to export
arising from the difference between the internal and external value of
the mark was, in the case of these raw materials, sufficient to balance
any general tendency toward a reduction of imports. Even though the

mark cost of import of the raw materials was relatively very high it could be reimbursed through the sale of exports manufactured from these raw materials at correspondingly high mark prices. The relatively low cost of fabrication tended to give an adequate impetus. The upward march of exports of finished goods involving the use of many of these materials, as well as of those involving the use of raw materials the import of which fell off, will appear in the discussion of export trends. Chart XXV showing imports of food products not elsewhere specified, of cotton and products thereof, and of copper and copper alloys, will give an idea of the movement in this group of commodities in which no trend in either direction appears.

Three classes of imports have an upward trend, viz.:

1B. Forest products
6c. Furs and furriers' materials
17D. Zinc, zinc alloys, and products thereof.

These also are raw materials of industry the import of which was affected by the possibility of export of the finished goods into which they enter. The increased import of furs (mainly skins) is reflected in an enlarged export of articles manufactured therefrom (see *infra*, this page) but, owing to the variety of their uses, it is impossible to say whether the same is true of forest products and zinc and its alloys or not. Chart XXVI depicts the trend of the classifications in this group.

Exports

The following classes of exports show a visible *upward* trend:

4A. Chemical elements, acids, salts and other chemical compounds
4E. Artificial fertilizers
4F. Explosives, ammunition, and combustibles
4G. Chemical and pharmaceutical products not elsewhere specified
5A. Silk, silk yarns, and products thereof
5B. Wool, wool yarns, and products thereof
5C. Cotton, cotton yarns, and products thereof
5J. Artificial flowers, umbrellas and parasols, shoes made of woven or felt materials
6c. Furs and furriers' materials
7A. Soft rubber goods
7B. Hard rubber and hard rubber goods
11. Paper, cardboard, and manufactures thereof
15. Glass and glass products
17G. Copper and copper manufactures
19B. Clocks
19c. & D. Clay instruments, toys.

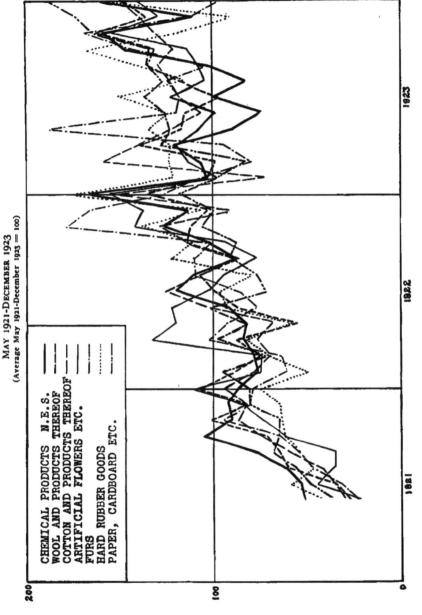

CHART XXV.I

RELATIVE MONTHLY VOLUME OF EXPORT OF CERTAIN CLASSES OF COMMODITIES WITH AN UPWARD TREND;

MAY 1921-DECEMBER 1923

(Average May 1921-December 1923 = 100)

CHEMICAL PRODUCTS N.E.S.
WOOL AND PRODUCTS THEREOF
COTTON AND PRODUCTS THEREOF
ARTIFICIAL FLOWERS ETC.
FURS
HARD RUBBER GOODS
PAPER, CARDBOARD ETC.

This group, with some notable exceptions, is comprised of commodi-- ties capable of some measure of standardization and not highly wrought. They are typically the semi-manufactured "raw material" of other industries. Buying of such commodities is on a basis of strict price comparison. Industries using these materials must purchase in the cheapest market or be put out of business by their competitors. Sales therefore respond readily to lowered prices; there is no cake of custom to be broken through. Though the domestic prices of these commodities were not nearly as far below world levels as was true of more highly wrought products, exports grew in volume while, as will presently appear, those of some finished commodities with a larger price differential remained stationary. Representative classifications in the group of exports with a rising trend are shown in Chart XXVII and include chemicals not elsewhere specified, wool and products thereof, cotton and products thereof, artificial flowers, etc., furs, hard rubber goods, and paper, cardboard, and manufactures thereof.

The following classes of exports show no visible trend, up or down:

4B. Dyes and dyestuffs
5H. Clothes, clothing accessories, and other sewn textile or felt products
6B. Leather goods
9. Brooms, brushes, screens
12. Books, pictures and paintings.
14. Pottery
17A. Iron and iron ores
17B. Aluminum and aluminum ores
18A. Machines
18B. Electro-technical products
18C. Vehicles
19A. Firearms.

For some of these commodities special reasons account for the failure of exports to expand. German dyes and dyestuffs, for instance, met the strongest sort of resistance in important foreign markets. High protective duties were thrown round competing concerns in other countries which, during the war, had been specially fostered by the governments concerned. Dyestuffs and explosives are to some extent symbiotic industries and, for military reasons, the outside world was not disposed to concede to the Germans the dominance in dyestuffs which had been characteristic of the pre-war period. As for iron and iron ores it has already been pointed out that under the changed political conditions and the loss of German resources the tendency was for home production to

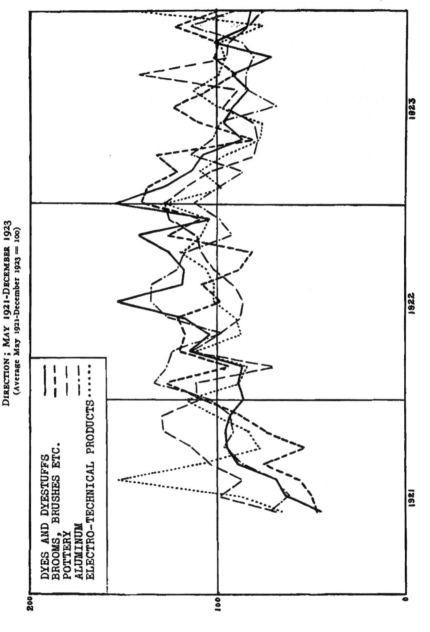

CHART XXVIII

RELATIVE MONTHLY VOLUME OF EXPORT OF CERTAIN CLASSES OF COMMODITIES WITH NO DECIDED TREND IN EITHER
DIRECTION; MAY 1921-DECEMBER 1923
(Average May 1921-December 1923 = 100)

DYES AND DYESTUFFS
BROOMS, BRUSHES ETC.
POTTERY
ALUMINUM
ELECTRO-TECHNICAL PRODUCTS

be inadequate to the supply of the domestic market. Many of the other groups comprise commodities incapable of accurate grading and stand-ardization. For such articles the taste and habits of the buyer play an important part and sales can therefore not be rapidly expanded even when prices are far below those prevailing in other countries for goods of no better quality. It is possible also that the swarm of "tourists" seeking bargains in Germany at this time bought up a great part of the supplies of articles of this sort and that these exports escaped inclusion in the official statistics. Chart XXVIII showing exports of dyes, of brooms, brushes, etc., of pottery, of aluminum, and of electro-technical products gives a picture of typical classifications of exports showing no trend in either direction.

Not a single class of exports shows any visible downward trend so far as weight is concerned. Statistics on vehicles are given by number as well as by weight, however, and the number of vehicles exported tended slightly downward.

In summary it may fairly be said that, as regards trends, there was a marked response on the part of both imports and exports to the relatively low external value of the mark. Ten classes of imports show a downward trend and, at most, one class of exports. On the other hand sixteen classes of exports show an upward trend and only three classes of imports. In these three, as also in the seven classes of imports which remained sub-stantially stable in volume, the explanation of the trend counter to, or at least not in the direction of, the reduction to be expected seems to lie in the expansion of exports in the manufacture of which these imports were necessary. There was thus a relative contraction of all imports. Of the twelve classes of exports in which, so far as the official statistics show, there was no growth, some were of a type in which "invisible" export would be prominent[7] so that the actual response on the part of exports was probably somewhat greater than appears on the face of the figures.

§ ELASTICITY OF DEMAND FOR IMPORTS AND EXPORTS

The marked decline in the volume of imports and the marked increase in the volume of exports, taken as a whole, disposes rather thoroughly of the contention that, unless a very long time is given for adjustment, inelasticity is a normal feature of the international trade of a country like Germany. The period covered was only of two and a half years' duration but a rather remarkable degree of elasticity appears. It might, of course, be alleged that the shift which actually occurred could not have been permanently maintained, but of this there is no evidence. The

---

[7] The term is here used to cover commodity exports taken out in the luggage of "tourists."

augmentation of the physical volume of exports relative to that of imports does not, it is true, imply a similar change in values. On the contrary, the causal factor in the shift, high prices of imports and low prices of exports, means that total values would inevitably alter less than volume. It is conceivable that total values might not alter at all or even that they might change in the direction opposite to that of the figures of physical volume. But this is very far from being probable. The prices of imports, measured in gold, were not changing very greatly at this time and those exports which grew in volume were principally commodities the mark prices of which were fairly quickly adjusted to something approaching equivalence with the gold price of similar commodities produced abroad. On other exports prices were at least partially adjusted by the Boards of Foreign Trade Control. The fact that the volume of exports rose in response to the low exchange value of the mark somewhat more readily than imports fell off shows, however, that such restrictions on exports as were imposed by these Boards did not seriously inhibit the influence of the discrepancy between domestic and foreign prices.

§ CORRELATION OF VOLUME OF IMPORTS AND EXPORTS WITH
FLUCTUATIONS IN PRICE MOVEMENTS

So much for the *trends* over the whole period of high inflation. Let us now look at the response of imports and exports to *fluctuations* in the ratio of the internal value of the mark to its external purchasing power. These fluctuations were large and frequent. If imports and exports were at all prompt in their response to *sudden* price changes they should show some point-to-point correlation with the price-ratio curve. It should be noted, however, that, whether or not they responded promptly, a lag of indeterminate length would tend to appear for both imports and exports. The actual passage of goods over the frontier takes place some time after the orders for those goods have been given and it is the orders, if anything, which would tend to correlate with the movement of prices. Most of the imports (largely foodstuffs and industrial raw materials) would probably be in existence at the time they were ordered and would be supplied out of the world stocks of these commodities. Insofar as this was true the delay in crossing the German borders would depend upon the time required for transport. While some of the exports could be supplied out of German stocks it would be necessary, in many cases, to wait for output. The period between the receipt of the order and the delivery of the goods would perhaps, therefore, average as long as in the case of imports. In both cases it would vary according to the nature of the commodity. Nor would the lag be constant with respect to all the increments of any one class of goods. With imports derived from diverse sources, widely separated geographically, some parts of the supply ordered at any given moment would arrive at German ports much earlier than others. Similarly, with exports, the time between order and delivery would be very different for different producers. This being so the actual imports and exports for any given month would include goods bought and sold at widely differing mark prices.

The actual receipt and delivery of goods at the German frontier in any given month would thus not accurately register the volume of orders in that or any preceding thirty-day period. But it may perhaps be assumed that the effect of suddenly and greatly altered prices should appear in the volume figures of both imports and exports within a month (or at most two months) of the price variation. This is long enough to permit the transfer from one country to another of goods already in being and it is probable that sales from stock would ordinarily dominate such *fluctuations* in imports and exports as were due to sudden price alterations. In any event the assumption of a longer period of lag would confuse rather than clarify the real situation. With the price curve fluctuating widely within short periods the longer the lag for which allowance is made the greater is the danger of having the sluggish effects of one price variation overwhelmed in the immediate effects of a counter movement. In the comparison of import and export fluctuations with the changes in the ratio of internal to external purchasing power of the mark a lag of one month, for both imports and exports, has therefore been assumed throughout. Where, however, a longer lag would give a better fit to the curves that fact has been indicated or will be obvious in the charts later to be presented.

It is clear that, when the movement in the ratio of internal to external purchasing power proceeded in the same direction for more than one month, such part of the total import or export of any given commodity as was tardy in its response would, in the later phase of such a movement, tend cumulatively to reinforce the statistical effects produced by such part as responded quickly, while, with every change of direction in the price ratio curve, it would tend to neutralize them. A greater measure of response to the broad swings in the ratio than to choppy fluctuations, however sharp the latter may be, is therefore to be expected.

It should also be noted that many imports and exports show a decided seasonal character and their month-to-month variations on this account might easily outweigh any putative response to price changes. In view of the highly unstable general situation and the short period for which figures were available it was not practicable, however, to take seasonal changes into account.

Innumerable other factors affect the monthly volume of all, or any single one, of the imports or exports. Such factors are : transport facilities, number of working days, strikes, stocks on hand, changes in style, weather, and what not, and all these may obscure such response to price changes as would otherwise be evident. But there was a more general cause, inherent in a change in the price ratio itself, which tended to prevent any *nice* converse movement in imports and exports when the ratio of internal to external purchasing power altered. It has already been pointed out that, where exportable goods are fabricated from imported raw materials, an expansion or contraction in foreign orders for such goods, consequent upon a relative rise or fall in the internal as compared with the external value of the currency, would lead to a synchronous expansion or contraction of the imported raw materials. The general tendency in the price situation toward opposite movements in imports and exports would, in consequence, not always hold for this group of products. Just as in the study of general trends exports showed a better response to the price situation than did imports, with the worst correlation among imports in the raw material group, so, in a study of month-to-month fluctuations, similar reactions may be expected.

In view of the many extraneous causes persistently operating it is not surprising to find that in no class either of imports or exports is there any exact month-by-month correlation with the internal-external purchasing power ratio curve. Correlation coefficients were computed (Pearson's method) for the classes of imports and exports which, on inspection, seemed to promise the best results, but the degree of correlation indicated was of no significance whatever.[8] It would be wrong to conclude, however, that there was no substantial and ready response to price variations, or that foreign trade was inelastic in its short-time movements. A much better test of the matter is furnished by noting the correlation of fluctuations in imports and exports with *major movements* in the ratio of internal to external purchasing power. In the period for which figures of imports and exports are available there are six such major movements (excluding the last, in November 1923, when *de facto* stabilization had been accomplished). The low points were in the summer of 1921, in the late spring and early summer of 1922, and in the spring of 1923. The high points were in the late fall of 1921, in the late fall and winter of 1922-1923, (this movement is of the saw-tooth type and sub-divisible into three sizable peaks and troughs) and in the summer of 1923.

Inspection of all the charts prepared gave a much better impression

---

[8] —.243 for the imports (Class 1D) and + .314 for the exports (Class 6B). Probable error ± .114 and ± .109 respectively.

of the real response to price changes than could possibly be obtained from ostensibly more precise statistical calculation. Though the import and export curves show every conceivable variety of fluctuation, and are far from any nice inverse and direct response even to the major movements in the price index, there can be no doubt whatever of the difference in the character of the correlation. Insofar as there is any correlation of classes of imports with the price ratio index it is inverse and insofar as there is any correlation of classes of exports it is direct.

Certain charts have been selected and are here reproduced in Charts XXIX and XXX to show the best, indifferent, and worst inverse and direct correlations for imports and exports respectively. In all cases the export or import curves are shown with a one month's lag relative to the price ratio curve.

The results of the examination of *all* the charted curves may be summarized as follows:

Imports

The classes of imports showing, on inspection only, some inverse correlation with the major movements of the price ratio index are:

1A. Agricultural products
1C. Animals and animal products
1D. Products of industries associated with agriculture
1E. Food products not elsewhere specified
4E. Artificial fertilizers
5A. Silk, silk yarns, and products thereof
5B. Wool and other animal fibers and products thereof
5C. Cotton, cotton yarns, and products thereof
17E. Tin and tin alloys
17G. Copper and copper alloys.

As is to be expected the correlations of consumers' goods are better than those of such raw materials of industry as are worked up into exportable products. With the exception of coal, which for special reasons given above was not studied, and iron ore, all of the ten most important German imports[9] fall within these classifications. Many other commodities just below the first ten also come within their scope. The only even moderately important class of imports, aside from iron ore, which shows no inverse correlation with the peaks and troughs of the price ratio curve is that of forest products. It is possible that the building which was undertaken to guard against loss of profits was partly responsible for this—or perhaps it was the increased use of paper necessitated by inflation!

[9] Arranged in order of value in 1913.

CHART XXIX

SELECTED CHARTS SHOWING THE BEST, INDIFFERENT, AND WORST INVERSE CORRELA-
TIONS OF THE RELATIVE MONTHLY VOLUME OF IMPORT OF CERTAIN
CLASSES OF COMMODITIES WITH THE PRICE RATIO
INDEX; MAY 1921-DECEMBER 1923

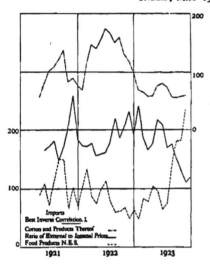

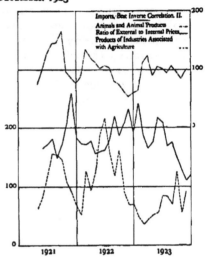

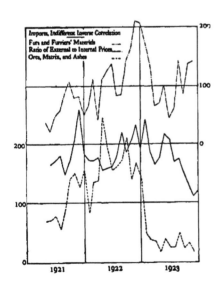

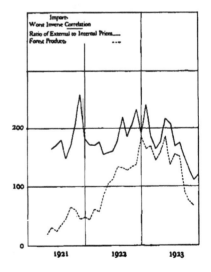

The fact that all of the more important classes of imports rose and fell in volume as their mark prices substantially declined or advanced in relation to the cost of domestic commodities, and that the fluctuations in volume of imports were, typically, at least as great as the fluctuations in relative prices, would go to show not only an immediate elasticity in the demand for all imports but an elasticity greater than unity. The total foreign exchange cost of the imports brought in when the prices to Germans were relatively high would therefore tend to be less than the total foreign exchange cost of the imports brought in when the prices to Germans were relatively low. So far as commodity trade on the import side was concerned there was thus a prompt calling of forces into play in correction of deviations of exchange rates from the internal purchasing power of the mark. Even those classes of imports which were necessary in the fabrication of customary exports responded to price changes in the same manner, though not to the same degree, as other imports, so that any expansion or contraction of exports fabricated therefrom, as the foreign exchange price of those exports fell or rose, must have been compensated by changes in domestic consumption rather than in total output.

Exports

The classes of exports showing, on inspection only, some direct correlation with the major movements of the price ratio index are:

5A.   Silk, silk yarns, and products thereof
5B.   Wool, wool yarns, and products thereof
5C.   Cotton, cotton yarns, and products thereof
5H.   Clothes, clothing accessories, etc.
6B.   Leather goods
7A.   Soft rubber goods
7B.   Hard rubber goods
9.   Brooms, brushes, etc.
12.   Books, pictures, and paintings
14.   Clay products
17A. Iron, iron alloys, and products thereof
17G. Copper, copper alloys, and products thereof
18A. Machinery
18B. Electro-technical products
18C. Vehicles
19B. Clocks.

The most important German exports not included in the above list are coal and dyestuffs. Coal, it will be remembered, was not included in the commodities studied, and dyestuffs were subject to special influences

CHART XXX

SELECTED CHARTS SHOWING THE BEST, INDIFFERENT, AND WORST DIRECT CORRELA-
TIONS OF THE RELATIVE MONTHLY VOLUME OF EXPORT OF CERTAIN
CLASSES OF COMMODITIES WITH THE PRICE RATIO
INDEX; MAY 1921-DECEMBER 1923

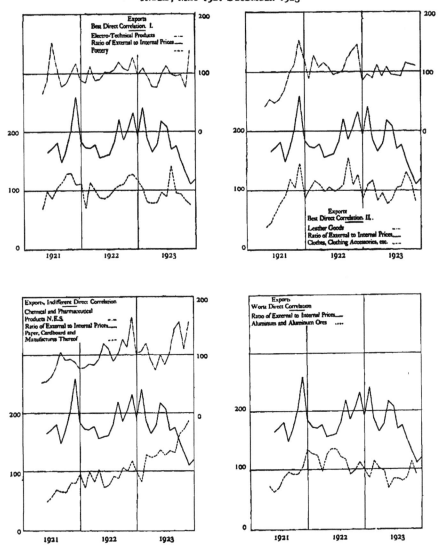

already commented upon. The response of exports as a whole to fluctuations in the price ratio curve was, therefore, prompt.

The *range* of the fluctuations in exports was, however, somewhat less pronounced than with imports. Imports were drawn from the whole world and available stocks were therefore greater than with exports, the source of which was restricted. The bulk of the adjustment was thus thrust upon imports. Exports were nevertheless by no means inelastic; there was nothing remotely approximating a fixed foreign demand for German goods taken as a whole, nor even for any fairly comprehensive category of them.

§ APPARENT ANOMALIES

There is a fairly general tendency for each of the import and export curves to reach its trough and peak respectively in response to the November 1922 rise in the purchasing power ratio index[10] though this rise is the middle of three culminating points in a general upward swing.[11] If the thesis that the effects of a long general movement in one direction would tend to be cumulative is correct it would seem that the greatest degree of correlation should occur at the final culminating point. At this point, January 1923, there is, in fact, almost no correlation. The explanation, so far as exports are concerned, is not far to seek. This final peak in the ratio index was the result of the rise in foreign exchange attendant upon the invasion of the Ruhr. The paralyzing effect of the occupation made increased exports impossible. The foreign demand was no doubt present but the supply was so reduced that domestic needs were preemptive. For imports the case is not so clear.

For some reason the response to the November 1921 peak in the purchasing power ratio occurred, in many cases, in January 1922, that is, with a two months', rather than a one month's, lag. A number of the curves do respond within a month, but the one month's lag is not nearly so universal as is true of the peak in November 1922.[11] The explanation probably lies in the shape of the respective peaks. The 1921 peak was the culmination of an upward movement of only three months' duration while that of November 1922 topped an upward swing which, with one break, covered seven months. The cumulative effect of many long as well as shorter lags would thus be present in the latter case within a month of the change in the direction of the purchasing power ratio but in the former case it would not appear so soon.

The high points in November 1921 and November 1922 are the most

[10] Typically with a one month lag.
[11] The statement is based on a study of all the curves charted. Most of these have not here been reproduced.

significant of all the fluctuations. At the low points of the price ratio curve, all of which were well above purchasing power parity, the advantage to foreigners in making purchases in Germany, and the difficulty to Germans in making purchases abroad, while much less than at the high points, was still great. The consequent, already noted, upward *trend* in exports and downward *trend* in imports tends to reduce the month-to-month correlation of export and import curves (from which the trend has not been eliminated[12]) with the downward movements in the purchasing power ratio index which, in themselves, would lead to fluctuations in the direction opposite to the trends. The degree of correlation with the low points of that curve is therefore likely to be less than with the high. The high points in 1923 are of less significance, for exports at any rate, than those in 1921 and 1922 owing to the disturbance to production all over Germany entailed by the decline in industrial activity in the Ruhr, a factor entirely distinct from the price fluctuations.

§ TABULATION OF CORRELATIONS

Taking the peaks in the price ratio curve in November 1921 and November 1922 and the low point between them, April 1922, as the dates at which the maximum response in imports and exports might reasonably be expected, the number of cases in which, within two months, there was a marked inverse movement of imports and a marked parallel movement of exports have been tabulated. It was by no means easy to decide whether the apparent correlation was or was not real, rather than accidental, and the results given in Table XXI may therefore be distorted by personal bias.[13] As detached an attitude as possible was taken but a critic disposed to question the whole notion of correlation between the phenomena under review would no doubt reach very different conclusions. The results, for whatever they may be worth, are as given in Table XXI on the next page.

Since, in addition to inappropriate movements, the failure of any curve to show the appropriate correlative movement *in a marked degree* was sufficient to lead to its omission from the tabulation, this evidence of a quick response of classes of imports and exports to changes in the price

[12] The period covered was so short and the factors affecting the volume of exports and imports varied so much from year to year that it seemed useless to attempt the elimination of trends.

[13] A given import or export classification might, for instance, show a marked fluctuation in apparent response to one of the major movements in the price ratio curve but a still greater fluctuation somewhere else. The decision as to whether the correlating fluctuation was or was not a true response was necessarily arbitrary and was based on the general character of the curve concerned.

ratio is by no means unconvincing. There were many neutral movements in the curves but almost none that were perverse.

TABLE XXI

RESPONSE OF IMPORTS AND EXPORTS, BY CLASSES, TO MAJOR MOVEMENTS
IN THE PRICE RATIO INDEX

PRICE RATIO INDEX	IMPORTS		EXPORTS	
	NUMBER OF CLASSES	NUMBER OF INVERSE CORRELATIONS	NUMBER OF CLASSES	NUMBER OF DIRECT CORRELATIONS
Peak of Nov. 1921	20	14	29	14
Trough of April 1922	20	11	29	10
Peak of Nov. 1922	20	8	29	24

§ THE MOVEMENT OF INDIVIDUAL IMPORTS AND EXPORTS

The total weight of imports or exports *in any given classification* might of course remain relatively constant, or might move in a manner inappropriate to a synchronous movement in the price ratio curve, owing to the fact that, while most of the commodities in the classification reacted appropriately, certain heavy articles took a perverse course. In order to test the results so far reached from an examination of commodities *by classes*, a more or less random selection of *individual* commodities was made and the monthly deviations of imports and exports of these individual commodities from their average for the period were charted. The upshot of this procedure was not very different from that attained where the commodities were taken by classes. Out of nineteen commodities predominantly imported[14] twelve show a downward trend throughout the period covered, six show no trend in either direction, and one shows an upward trend. Out of twenty-six commodities predominantly exported[15] sixteen show an upward trend and ten no trend in either direction. None shows a downward trend.

[14] These commodities were: wheat, raw cotton, raw tobacco, coffee, rubber, beef, pork, ham, bacon, fresh herring, salt herring, lard, oleomargarin, butter, eggs, egg-yolk, wool, silk, copper.
[15] These commodities were: silk lace goods, gimps, velvet and plush, cotton weaves, cotton gloves, stockings etc., women's and children's clothing, men's and boys' clothing, glazed cardboard etc., printing paper, note-books, books, sheet-music, maps, insulators, porcelain ornaments, sewing machines, printing presses, shoe machinery, dynamos, transformers etc., safety lamps etc., electric

In the matter of correlation of *fluctuations* in the movement of these individual imports and exports in response to broad movements of the price ratio curve ten of the nineteen import commodities and fourteen of the twenty-six export commodities show fair inverse and direct responses respectively, one month's lag being taken for both categories. The remaining commodities in each category fail to show the appropriate correlation though there is, of course, no case where there is any decided correlation of an inappropriate character (inverse for exports and direct for imports). Charts XXXI and XXXII depict typical good, indifferent, and poor correlations.

§ TRENDS VS. SHORT-TIME CORRELATIONS

While it is apparent from these results, and from those derived through the investigation of the movement of commodities by classes, that there was a real and quick response of foreign trade in both the import and export categories to *fluctuations* in the price ratio index, the correlation is far from being as decisive as is the general *trend* of imports and exports whether taken by classes or as individual commodities. Several explanations may be offered:

(1) A productive organization working close to capacity cannot immediately change the nature and direction of its output. Any immediate alteration in trade currents must therefore take place within the scope of existing and accruing stocks. So far as exports are concerned the available stocks set an outer limit on immediate *expansion* though contraction of export might occur in any degree. The persistently favorable prices at which German goods could be procured by foreigners during practically the whole of the inflation period tended gradually to shift German production into export lines and the trend of exports thus corresponds with theoretical expectation more closely than does the month-to-month movement. As regards imports, the consideration just advanced applies with much less force, since the stocks of German import goods held throughout the world were presumably adequate to take care of any fluctuation in German demand.

(2) An upward movement in exchange rates making imports more expensive might temporarily increase demand for those imports through the fear of a still further decline in the external purchasing power of the mark. Falling foreign exchange rates, on the other hand, may have encouraged waiting for a still more favorable situation. This may in part account for certain fluctuations in some classes of imports in the

light bulbs, telephone and telegraph apparatus, motor vehicles, musical instruments.

CHART XXXI

SELECTED CHARTS SHOWING THE BEST, INDIFFERENT, AND WORST INVERSE
CORRELATIONS OF THE RELATIVE MONTHLY VOLUME OF IMPORT OF
CERTAIN COMMODITIES WITH THE PRICE RATIO INDEX;
MAY 1921-DECEMBER 1923

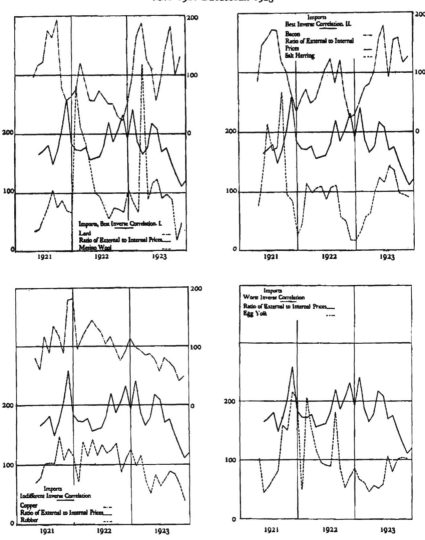

CHART XXXII

SELECTED CHARTS SHOWING THE BEST, INDIFFERENT, AND WORST DIRECT
CORRELATIONS OF THE RELATIVE MONTHLY VOLUME OF EXPORT OF
CERTAIN COMMODITIES WITH THE PRICE RATIO INDEX;
MAY 1921-DECEMBER 1923

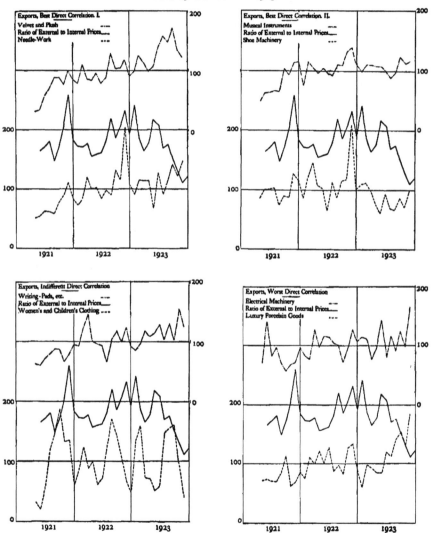

direction contrary to that which price considerations would indicate as probable. The response of buyers of German *exports* to changing prices (in their own currency) may, furthermore, have been at times inappropriate insofar as there was a tendency to wait for still better bargains when prices were falling or to snap up goods on a rising market.

(3) The practice of invoicing some exports in foreign currencies, at prices substantially determined by sales possibilities in foreign markets, tended to nullify the effect of exchange rate fluctuations.

(4) Quick action by any of the Boards of Foreign Trade Control in response to *movements* in exchange rates would keep such movements from exerting a marked effect though it might not obviate the general tendency of the low external value of the mark toward an increase of the ratio of exports to imports. Partly as a result of the action of these Boards, and partly because of inability of German producers greatly to increase export, the opportunity open to foreigners of buying cheaply in Germany as mark exchange declined was sometimes more apparent than real. Complaints on the part of buyers of German exports with respect to the slowness of delivery of goods and other unsatisfactory features of their purchases were frequent. The Boards did not hesitate to alter contracts, and foreign buyers were as often repelled by the inconvenience of buying in Germany as they were attracted by the quoted prices.

Any temporary inelasticity in the demand for German imports or exports might also have prevented a quick adjustment to price changes. It cannot positively be asserted that such inelasticity of demand was not present, but the steady growth of exports relative to imports is evidence to the contrary, and this evidence is confirmed, so far as exports are concerned, by the complaints of slow deliveries of which mention has already been made. It would seem therefore that, in a country with a diversified trade, the exports and imports of a wide variety of commodities will rather readily expand or contract with any sizable shift in the relationship between import and export prices.

PART IV

EFFECTS OF INFLATION ON THE GERMAN ECONOMY

CHAPTER IX

GENERAL EFFECTS OF INFLATION ON NATIONAL INCOME

§ DISTORTION OF REAL VALUES

THE most obvious effects of a depreciating currency are of course felt in the distribution, rather than in the production, of wealth and income. The practical nullification of contracts calling for future payment of fixed sums of money, such as occurred in Germany through the all but complete loss of value of the mark, transferred immense sums from creditor to debtor.[1] This involved not only fixed interest securities such as bonds, debentures, preferred stock, and mortgages, but also insurance contracts, savings bank deposits, and a variety of other obligations including house rents. The vicissitudes of prices, with unequal responses to the inflationary stimulus, likewise took from one man and gave to another, and the burden of ordinary taxes was shifted according as payment could or could not be postponed. In all this there was of course no justice but there was no national loss of substance. The misery which the collapse of the currency brought to countless thousands of people, the tragic drama of their sudden plunge from well-being to utter poverty, the terror of uncertainty, akin to walking the pirates' plank, which was the part of the whole population, all led to an erroneous conviction of national ruin. Inflation came to be regarded not as a blind god playing capriciously, though not destructively, with human fortunes but rather as a malevolent deity bent on smashing. The evils of inflation were plain; the counter-effects were somewhat obscure. Even those who had greatly benefited by depreciation were not always aware of their gains. The habit of thinking in monetary terms led to an enormous distortion of real values. In the earlier years of inflation real values were over-

---

[1] The mortgage indebtedness alone, in 1913, was about 40,000,000,000 marks, or about one-sixth of the total German wealth. In 1923 this was worth less than one American cent. After stabilization a small part of some of these debts was reestablished by legislation. cf. *Foreign Banking Systems*, H. Parker Willis and B. H. Beckhart, Editors, Chapter VIII, "The Banking System of Germany," Paul Quittner, Henry Holt and Company, New York, 1929, pp. 641 ff.

estimated; in the later stages, and after stabilization, they were greatly minimized in the minds of their possessors.

If one may hazard a generalization it may be said with some approach to accuracy that it was the middle-class, including skilled and salaried workers as well as those with sizable fortunes in fixed-interest securities, which bore the brunt of the loss from depreciation, that the great mass of unskilled workers did not long suffer any extreme derogation from their previous status, and that landowners (especially if the land was mortgaged),[2] the big industrialists, and merchants, materially improved their position.[3] The gains of the latter classes were concealed with the coming of stabilization when, in accordance with law, balance sheets were made out in gold units of account. In order to be safe, resources were at that time generally undervalued, and this reduction in the monetary value of assets was compensated on the liability side by a minimization of liabilities to stockholders. A much too pessimistic view of the capacity of properties to produce income resulted in a shrinkage in their capitalized value, much as if they had been viewed through the small end of a telescope, and this was as true of the securities which represented shares in the property as of the property itself.[4]

The ploughing-in of inflation profits had resulted in great extensions and improvements in industrial plants and while a good many of these "improvements" later proved useless there was nevertheless a marked

[2] The distinction should be made between landowners and landlords. *Urban* landlords were heavy losers by reason of the rent limitation laws, though they were partly compensated, in some cases, by the elimination of their mortgage indebtedness. *Rural* landlords, or landowners, were subject to no, or but slight, restrictions on the yield of their properties and they were, in most instances, able to lift, at a nominal real cost, a heavy mortgage burden. An urban landlord is, in the main, a building-lord. He may not own the land at all.

[3] The government, of course, also gained by getting rid of its debt. So far as the people in general are concerned this involves a shifting of the burden from those who would otherwise have had to pay taxes to meet the service of the debt to those who would be the recipients of interest.

[4] cf. *Germany's Industrial Revival*, Sir Philip Dawson, London, Williams and Norgate, Ltd., 1926, p. 106. Dawson says that the big banks and industrial concerns wrote down their assets in ratios of from 10 : 1 to 50 : 1. This gives an exaggerated picture, no doubt, since a number of concerns were later compelled to write off a considerable share of the assets they had counted upon at the time of stabilization. The general tendency, however, was certainly toward undervaluation. From January 1, 1924, onward, all accounts and statements of business concerns were required, by law, to be in gold marks. That corporation assets were very conservatively computed is shown by the fact that, in the course of the year 1926, stock prices more than doubled in value and thereafter maintained the level reached at the end of that year. This occurred despite the fact that, at no time since stabilization, has there been any undue optimism in Germany.

betterment in industrial equipment taken as a whole. Yet the prevailing undervaluation of assets by the class which had most benefited from inflation encouraged the belief that everybody had lost. This under-valuation was by no means a subterfuge. When stabilization of the currency was accomplished the expected crisis developed and the generally precarious position of German industry at that time justified a low valuation of productive assets. Presently, moreover, there developed a difficulty which was generally dubbed a shortage of "working capital." The phrase is ambiguous but the trouble was undoubtedly due to the shock to credit which had resulted from the robbing of creditors by inflation, and to the fear that the stabilization might be but temporary. The general lack of confidence forced the banking organization to restrict credits if stability in the currency was to be preserved and, though the rigid restriction of credits was abundantly justified, it had an immediately depressing effect. Business was bound to be bad for the time being and there was no knowing how long this situation might last. Productive assets were consequently estimated to be worth much less than actually proved to be the case. Business recovery was in fact surprisingly rapid and has, till recently, been well sustained.

Another factor leading to the writing down of capital values was the rate of interest which prevailed during and as a result of inflation, a rate which has remained rather high down to the present day. Since the capitalized value of a property varies inversely with the interest rate the wealth of the country was computed at not much more than half what the same physical assets would have been held to have been worth in the pre-war and pre-inflation period. It should be noted also that the reparations burdens which fell on industry tended to diminish the value of German properties, to their owners, by the capitalized value of the payments to be made. Those burdens would, however, have been at least as great had there been no inflation. Such losses in individual wealth and in national income as they involve cannot therefore be charged to the depreciation of the currency.

§ EXTENT OF UNDERCAPITALIZATION

The extent of undercapitalization due to the general pessimism current at the time the mark was stabilized is indicated by the fact that, in the five years 1924 to the end of 1928, the monetary wealth of the German people is estimated to have increased as never before in a similar period.[5]

---

[5] cf. "Die grossen Vermögen vor und nach dem Kriege," Rudolph Martin, *Westermanns Monatshefte*, 873, May 1929, p. 256. The prospect of the immediate continuation in the rate of increase of German real or nominal wealth has been shattered by the world-wide depression of 1930.

Real wealth has certainly not increased as rapidly as in some other quinquennia, since saving which, in its normal forms, was blasted by inflation has not yet fully recovered from the shock then suffered. It was not until 1927 that production reached the 1913 level while consumption has been relatively high since 1924. The growth in real wealth must therefore have been moderate. But improvement in the income from properties, the brightening of the economic prospect, and a gradual lowering of the rate of interest, have transformed capitalizations. The number of mark millionaires in Germany is said to have doubled in the period 1924 to 1928 and the prediction is made that, barring unforeseen catastrophes, this result will be repeated by 1933. If so, the pre-war figures will then have been surpassed.[5] These changes are certainly due rather to a revised appraisal of properties which had been grossly undervalued in 1923 than to such gains in real wealth as may have occurred.

National wealth is a slippery concept and rapid changes in the estimates thereof are rather more likely to be due to psychological aberrations than to objective factors. Objective factors, however, acting upon the distribution of *income*, may seriously affect estimates of *wealth*. After the stabilization of the currency German wages rose at a considerably faster rate than production and, insofar as this occurred, wages must have been paid at the expense of other forms of income. Yet interest rates were high and rents were rising. The brunt of the increase in wages must therefore have fallen on profits, and the consequent relatively small rate of profits in the early stabilization years kept the capitalized value of industrial properties—one of the principal components of wealth—at a comparatively low level.[6] After stabilization had been in effect for about two years, the *rate* of increase in wages slackened. The value of properties began then rapidly to rise. Though the improvement in wealth in recent years has been real, it has not, therefore, been as phenomenal as the estimates would, *prima facie*, indicate, and the difference, as compared with the inflation years, is not nearly as great as might be supposed. The real wealth which is only now beginning to show in

[6] The very fact that a generally low valuation was set on industrial properties when gold-value reckoning was again introduced in early 1924 probably enabled wage earners to secure an unusually large share of the national income. Competition would tend, for a time at any rate, to keep profits down to a fair return on invested capital rather than on reproduction cost. Properties built up during inflation were regarded as having cost almost nothing. This was, in a sense, true, since investment in capital was the only alternative to complete loss of substance. The result was to make it unnecessary to earn a return on plant and equipment and competition among employers tended to thrust the interest return, which must, under normal circumstances, have been paid to lenders of capital, into the lap of the laborer.

capitalizations was, to a very considerable extent, accumulated in the inflation period.

Income is a much more accurate criterion of welfare than is wealth and, since national real income is a function of national *production*, an attempt will presently be made to appraise the effect of inflation on German *production* during the years when currency depreciation was rampant.

§ EFFECTS OF THE WAR VS. THE EFFECTS OF INFLATION

The effects of inflation must be carefully distinguished from those of the war. The proper comparison is not between the production of the inflation period and that of 1913 but between the actual production in the post-war years and that which would have been attained had there been no inflation. Such a comparison is, of course, incapable of being directly made. But, by observing the course of production in Germany as inflation proceeded, and by comparing this production with that of countries similarly affected by the war yet relatively slightly touched by inflation, some approximation to the real results of currency depreciation may perhaps be attained.

§ BENEFICIAL AND ADVERSE POSSIBILITIES OF INFLATION

So far as inflation affects *national* income at all, it may prove beneficial or the reverse. On the side of benefit it would seem that the real income of a country might be increased in several ways through the adoption of a paper currency which later suffers extreme depreciation. These ways are:

(1) A costly metallic medium of exchange is dispensed with and replaced by one which costs almost nothing. The metal, of which part at any rate of the former circulating medium was composed, may then be exchanged for imported capital or consumers' goods which would otherwise not be available. This is as true of metallic reserves as of the money in the hands of the people since, once the metallic standard is abandoned, the reserves serve no purpose and, on rational grounds, should be sold. Reckoned in terms of recurring income this gain from the abandonment of a metallic currency is equal to the interest on the former metallic stock, or more accurately, perhaps, to the average yield which is obtained from capital goods of a value equal to that of the sold metallic stock.

(2) Sales abroad of the paper currency may be made for values in excess of those at which such sold currency is redeemed.

(3) Business activity tends to be stimulated, and unemployment reduced, by the depreciation of the currency and the consequent real or

nominal profits accruing to entrepreneurs. Further than this the general state of flux induced by currency depreciation makes adjustment to altered conditions easy and facilitates the reacquisition of markets temporarily lost.

(4) Wealth is transferred from passive to active holders without charge to the recipients[7] and without benefit of middlemen. Furthermore, many persons formerly living on the yield of fixed-interest investments are compelled to undertake productive work.

(5) Profits tend to be "ploughed in" by investment in plant as the best means of providing against losses from continuing currency depreciation. The accumulation of capital may thus be accelerated and future income increased.

Disregarding the injustices which redistribution of wealth through currency depreciation entails, the advantages alleged above may be compensated, in part, altogether, or even far outweighed, by the following considerations:

(1) Depreciation may become so extreme and incalculable as to check rather than stimulate business activity.

(2) A rise in foreign exchange rates relative to internal prices may lead to great national losses on foreign trade. Insofar as goods are sold abroad on terms corresponding to the general domestic price level they will yield a sum of foreign exchange which will procure a relatively small volume of imports. Since the sole purpose of exports, nationally considered, is to provide for imports, this is of course a very serious matter. The converse case, theoretically possible should foreign exchange rates rise less than in proportion to the internal price level, is practically excluded since most potential exports will then find no market abroad.

(3) The friction arising from maladjustment in the distribution of income may reduce productivity. This is an all-pervading factor but is most clearly seen in wage disputes.

(4) Unproductive employment may be increased. Currency depreciation in Germany, for instance, was attended by a great augmentation of speculative activities (using that term in its broadest sense to cover much retail trade) and by a rising ratio of clerical to manual workers. The former were increasingly required to take care of the vastly extended bookkeeping necessary to cope with the phenomena of inflation. The

---

[7] This is merely the principal argument for bank credit carried to its logical conclusion. The same phenomenon occurs in periods of a rapid increase in the world's gold supply. At such times "the prosperous phases of business cycles have been relatively long and intense." See *Business Cycles: The Problem and its Setting*, Wesley C. Mitchell, National Bureau of Economic Research, Inc., New York, 1928, p. 120.

necessity of calculation of the real meaning of price quotations absorbed a great portion of the effort of the increased number of clerical workers.[8] Wage payment adjustments also required the services of a big clerical staff and the mere task of reckoning in the stellar magnitudes of the day was responsible for much loss of time.

(5) When capital can be obtained by borrowing, not only without usance cost but without the necessity of repayment of anything but a fraction of the amount borrowed, production is abandoned in favor of mere business activity, and such production as is carried on is conducted by entrepreneurs of less average ability than where profits are possible only through skilful management. This loss is to be directly weighed against the productive advantage of a direct transfer of wealth from passive to active hands.

(6) Resort may sooner or later be had to foreign paper currencies for carrying on domestic transactions. This is, in effect, the granting of a loan without interest to the foreign country the currency of which is so employed.

(7) The disposition to save, in the current money at any rate, disappears. This may or may not be compensated by the tendency to save directly through the extension, out of profits, of the plant and equipment of industrial concerns, and by the purchase of durable goods on the part of the populace in general. Even if it is not so compensated the people may simply be producing (and consuming) more immediately consumable commodities in lieu of producing, in the present, less of such goods and a larger quantum of producers' goods. This is by no means a direct loss; it is merely a substitution.

(8) Commerce may be driven to barter which is, of course, an inconvenient and wasteful form of exchange.

§ SPECIAL CONSIDERATIONS IN THE GERMAN CASE

Some of these factors on the one side or on the other are, when separately considered, quite imponderable. All that can be done is to try to discover the net result of the conflicting groups of forces. Three special considerations applicable to German inflation should first, however, be noted:

(1) Germany was busy, and presumably productive, during the long period after mid-summer 1920 when industrial activity in almost every other country was at a low ebb. This result would seem to be ascribable directly to the currency situation in Germany. The matter is considered in detail in a later chapter. German export industry, moreover, was

---

[8] Nominally equal prices might really be very different according to the terms of payment demanded.

stimulated throughout almost the whole inflation period by the relatively low status of the mark on the foreign exchange markets.

(2) The invasion of the Ruhr in January 1923 was a heavy blow to German productivity and to per capita real income. The unoccupied part of Germany practically took over the support of the Ruhr population. This burden was concealed by the fact that resistance in the Ruhr was financed entirely by new issues of currency but it was just as real for all that. The new output of currency diminished the purchasing power of any given income and transferred to the citizens of the occupied Ruhr area the command over goods which would otherwise have remained in the unoccupied regions. But the same result would have occurred, in one form or another, had passive resistance been financed in other ways. Unless, therefore, the Ruhr occupation itself can be alleged to have been due to inflation it would be erroneous to attribute its results to that cause.

(3) The amount by which German income and consumption was diminished by reparations payments is not only not chargeable to inflation but was probably considerably diminished by reason of the collapse of the currency. Cash reparations and clearings payments, from the time of the armistice to the stabilization of the currency, amounted to 2365 million gold marks. This was not much more than the annual cash payment later made in a single standard Dawes Plan year. Had the Allies earlier cooperated with Germany in reconstruction measures, as they did under the Dawes Plan, there can be no doubt that Germany would, before 1924, have been able to make much larger cash payments than were actually realized. As a result of the collapse of the currency no cash payments were made (except to meet notes earlier given) from September 1922 till the inauguration of the Dawes Plan annuities in late 1924. It is not too much to say that inflation released the Germans from the necessity of making large payments which would otherwise have been abstracted from the German national economy.

§ GAINS AND LOSSES APPEAR IN PRODUCTION OR IN
INTERNATIONAL TRADE

All the *national* gains and losses of inflation may be summed up under the heads of production and international exchange. The net result will appear in the physical volume of national production *plus* imports *minus* exports. Unless currency depreciation led to a more intensive using up of preexisting capital goods than would otherwise have occurred, and aside from the slight influence of high business activity there is no reason why this should be assumed, any increase or decrease in the annual volume of physical production over what might have been expected under stable currency conditions will measure the effect of inflation on the purely domestic economy. This is true whether capital equipment was or was not replaced or increased. The production was so much; whether it was used for replacement or increase of capital, or for consumption purposes, involved a choice between present and future final consumption but did not change the total output of goods in the present. It merely changed the nature of the goods or of their use. The total national income depended, however, not only on production but also on the volume of imports obtained for a given real cost in exported means of payment. Any change in the terms of trade arising from inflation must be computed along with the alteration in domestic output in order to arrive at the net result on the German national economy. Only the roughest sort of approximation may be hoped for, but an attempt will be made to estimate (a) the volume of physical production within the country and (b) the gains and losses in foreign transactions in money and goods, insofar as both were affected by the state of the currency. It seems best to dispose of the international aspect of the matter first. The two immediately succeeding chapters will therefore deal with foreign sales and purchases of money and of goods and these will be followed by a chapter appraising the physical volume of domestic production.

CHAPTER X

GAINS FROM THE SALE OF MONEY ABROAD

I—SALES OF SPECIE

§ PRE-WAR STOCK OF SPECIE AND ITS DISPOSITION

AT THE beginning of the war the specie stock in Germany, including the reserves of the Reichsbank in German coin, is estimated to have had a face value of about 3.7 billion gold marks.[1] About one billion of this, being silver, was overvalued, but during the course of the war the value of silver so rose in terms of gold as to eliminate the necessity for correction on this score. In addition to its stock of German coin the Reichsbank held over 400 million marks in gold bullion or foreign coin.[2] We may therefore take the pre-inflation supply of precious metals in the monetary use to have been, in round numbers, 4 billion gold marks. Some of this was never completely withdrawn from use as money if the gold reserves held by the Reichsbank up to the period of stabilization can be considered as having served a monetary purpose. In the later stages of inflation, however, these reserves amounted to less than 500 million marks. All the rest of the original 4 billion disappeared from sight and sooner or later most of it must have found its way abroad in the purchase of commodities with which the German economy would otherwise have had to dispense. Even since stabilization the gold stock in Germany has been relatively small; the reimport of gold has not been equal to the exports during inflation. Gold is no longer in circulation and, in the first years of stabilization, the metallic reserves of the Reichsbank averaged only about 500 million marks. In recent years, however, this has been raised to about 2½ billion. The gain from dispensing with coin as money may therefore be set down as a capital sum of about 3,500,000,000 gold marks during the later years of inflation and at about 3 to 1½ billion thereafter. The annual yield on the saving of bullion, the amount by which the yearly income of the German people may be considered to have been directly increased by the abandonment of gold, would vary

---

[1] cf. Germany's Economy, Currency and Finance, p. 21.
[2] cf. Verwaltungsbericht der Reichsbank, 1914, Berlin, Reichsdruckerei, 1914, p. 7.

not only with the amounts involved but also with changing rates of interest. In the years immediately following the war, when capital was scarce and its marginal yield high, the annual gain could scarcely have been less than 200 to 250 million gold marks, no matter what had been the stability of the currency unit. In later years it did not amount to anything like this sum.

§ EFFECTS OF USE OF GOLD TO SUPPORT MARK EXCHANGE

There is the further consideration, however, that some of this specie was used by the Reichsbank to support the exchange value of the mark. The Reichsbank ultimately lost much of its hitherto carefully guarded gold reserve in these operations but one may not conclude that these losses were shared by the German economy taken as a whole. The sudden improvement in mark exchange resulting from the Reichsbank's intervention in February 1923 must, for instance, have had varying effects. There was no gain in it for the Reichsbank since it was giving gold or dollar exchange for its own obligations which had cost it nothing to create and which it was not compelled to redeem. The Bank, moreover, was raising against itself the value of these obligations and this might have been serious if they had ever been made exchangeable against hard money at the rate which was then being maintained.[3] Even if its action had been ultimately successful the most the Bank could have hoped for, in compensation for the increase in its obligations, was an augmentation in its supply of gold or foreign exchange as a result of having bought marks at a cheaper gold rate than that at which it later sold them. Such an increase could, however, have been secured directly, without any chance of loss, by the issue of new mark notes, and all the gold received would then have been a net gain instead of being, in large part, but a replacement of that previously expended.

So far as the German economy as a whole is concerned the rise in mark exchange occasioned by the Bank's action had nominal rather than real effects,[4] except insofar as:

[3] When the action in support of the mark was initiated in February the gold reserves of the Reichsbank were several times as valuable as the total volume of circulating medium converted into gold at prevailing exchange rates. But in April, just before the support was withdrawn, the value of the note issues then outstanding exceeded the value of the Reichsbank's gold reserve.

[4] There was, of course, a great shifting of purchasing power on this rise of exchange just as there had been in the prior fall. Investors in foreign exchange for use in future internal payments on mark obligations suffered heavy losses. But most of this was a Peter-and-Paul transaction between Germans themselves. There was no national gain or loss except as the purchasing power of Germans over foreign goods, or of foreigners over German goods, was affected.

(1) It augmented the real returns (the receipts in foreign exchange and the imports which that exchange would purchase) on all exports still being invoiced in marks. This gain would be at the expense of foreigners. On exports invoiced in foreign exchange the real return to the national economy (the imports for which such exports served as payment) would be unaffected. Since, even as late as 1923, a not inconsiderable portion of German exports were still invoiced in marks the gains realized by the use of gold to support exchange were perhaps sizable.

(2) It lowered the real cost of imports (the volume of exports which must be sent out in payment for imported goods) by reducing the return in marks to foreigners exporting to Germany. Since sellers to Germany, as a general rule, were not at this time accepting payment in marks the national gain to Germany on this score was probably negligible.

(3) It affected the dealers in exchange. Dealers who were long on foreign exchange would suffer; dealers who were long on marks would gain. If those dealers who were long on marks were mainly Germans, and those who were long on foreign exchange were for the most part foreigners, the German national economy would benefit. There is, however, no reason to believe that this was the case unless the German dealers got wind of the proposed action of the Reichsbank before their foreign competitors.

(4) It enabled "investment" holders of marks abroad to reconvert into foreign exchange at a rate much more favorable to them than would have been possible in the absence of intervention by the Reichsbank. This would be a national loss to Germany but was probably not done on any wide scale.

(5) It prevented the sale of German goods abroad at extremely low gold, or foreign exchange, prices.

In sum it may be surmised that the German economy as a whole gained slightly through this action of the Reichsbank. This gain is some counterweight to the loss on foreign trade which the usual relatively low value of the currency on the foreign exchange markets occasioned[5], but it is probably of insignificant comparative importance.

§ NET GAINS FROM SALE OF GOLD

Not only, then, was the Reichsbank's loss of specie a gain to the German economy insofar as it eventually was used for the import of goods which would not otherwise have been available but the manner in which part of that loss was sustained may well have furnished supplementary

[5] *cf. infra*, Chap. XI.

benefits. All such benefits were, however, but one phase of the effects of the deviation of exchange rates from internal prices, a matter to be more fully treated in the next chapter. It will here be the more conservative course to disregard them altogether and to put to the credit of inflation only the actual value of the precious metals released from the monetary use, that is to say, 3½ billion marks in the later inflation period and from 1½ to 3 billions thereafter.

The report, in 1924, of the Second Committee of Experts of the Reparation Commission—the McKenna Committee—put the sale of hard money at only 2½ billions, one billion during the war and 1½ billion from the cessation of the war to the end of 1923. These figures seem to apply only to gold and, if silver be included, the estimate would seem to be in substantial correspondence with that above given.

II—SALES OF PAPER CURRENCY OR CLAIMS THERETO

§ IMPORTANCE OF CURRENCY SALES

Of greater importance than the sale abroad of precious metals was the volume of paper marks, mark credits, and securities (bonds) calling for the payment of a fixed amount of German currency, which were disposed of to foreign buyers. The extent to which such sales proved possible was a surprise to everyone, including the Germans themselves, and the net national gain was the greater inasmuch as these marks cost the Germans nothing but the paper on which they were printed. On the other hand, the gold that was exported had originally been paid for with goods, though for internal monetary purposes it was no longer required and had therefore, *for the German domestic economy*, largely lost its value. The German gain on marks actually sent abroad and on sales to foreigners of mark balances in German banks, or other similar claims, was largely dependent on how long the "investment" was held. Marks or claims to marks bought before 1923 and held till stabilization were a pure gift to Germany of the amount of foreign exchange paid therefor. The stabilization rate of one trillion paper marks to one of gold was such as to make it useless to collect and transfer to Germany the notes that were held abroad, while foreign-owned balances within the country were then worth less than enough to pay the postage on a letter of inquiry as to their fate.

Since the gain to the German economy was dependent upon the *degree* of depreciation, and that depreciation became complete, the whole of the gold, goods, or foreign exchange proceeds of the sale abroad of unused and unredeemed German currency, or claims thereto, (such as deposits in German banks to the account of foreigners, mark credits in foreign countries, and securities payable in an unchanging sum of marks) is to be put to the credit of the post-war inflation no matter when the marks were acquired by foreign purchasers. There were also large gains to Germany on marks or mark claims repatriated at values far below those at which they had originally been purchased by foreign buyers.

§ ESTIMATES OF GOLD VALUE OF CURRENCY SALES

The most authoritative estimate of the total gains on sales of currency is to be found in the report of the McKenna Committee on the situation as of December 31, 1923. The report is by no means lucid, the estimates are not altogether consistent, and there are large gaps.[6] But it is, no doubt, as accurate as the facts permitted. The German surplus of imports during the war has been officially computed at approximately 15 billion gold marks.[7] Of this amount some 6 to 7 billions were met by the direct issue or sale to foreigners of paper currency.[8] Of the remaining 8 or 9 billion gold marks of this war-time excess of debits only 2 billion is accounted for in the *McKenna Report*, viz. 1 billion from the sale of gold and 1 billion from the sale of domestic securities. The balance of 6 to 7 billion was presumably covered by the sale of foreign securities owned by Germans, and by short-time foreign currency credits to Germans.[9] Such credits were subsequently paid off, directly or indirectly, with the proceeds of later sales of marks. These later sales will be covered in the estimates of the post-war period. Foreign securities were of course unaffected by the collapse of the mark. In computing the war sales of currency, never redeemed, both items in this 6 to 7 billion balance may therefore be omitted. Of the 1 billion gold marks' worth of domestic securities sold during the war a certain share was in bonds which eventually sank to complete worthlessness. It will therefore not be far wrong to take the *upper* estimate of 7 billion gold marks, arising

[6] See criticism in *The Reparation Plan*, H. G. Moulton, Institute of Economics, McGraw-Hill Book Company, New York, 1924, *passim*. The McKenna Report is printed as an appendix.

[7] See *Germany's Economic and Financial Situation*, p. 22.

[8] Since, in the course of the year 1919, the exchange value of the mark against the dollar fell from 12c to 2c, the loss to foreigners, and the gain to Germans, from these extra-national issues of marks, even if they were redeemed without much delay, must have been a very large percentage of the total value at the date of issue. Most of these marks had originally been put into circulation at a value of from 16 to 20c (American).

[9] See estimate of Dr. von Glasenapp, Vice-President of the Reichsbank, quoted in *Germany's Capacity to Pay*, H. G. Moulton and Constantine E. McGuire, Institute of Economics, McGraw-Hill Book Company, New York, 1923, p. 49.

from the direct issue or sale of currency abroad, as a conservative figure for the gains of the Germans from this source during the war period.[10]

For the post-war period the McKenna Committee estimated the *net* receipts from sales of marks or mark bank balances—the amount, that is, over and above any countervalues received for German currency returned to German ownership—at from 7.6 to 8.7 billion gold marks. Taking a round figure of 8 billion gold marks for the post-war period and adding to this the 7 billion acquired during the war, the total net receipts of the German economy from the sale of currency or its equivalent— receipts for which nothing but implied and unredeemed promises were ever given—reached 15 billion gold marks.

§ ALTERNATIVE METHOD OF ESTIMATE

This estimate may be checked by drawing up a balance sheet of German international transactions for the whole war and post-war period. The sale of marks and mark claims from the beginning of the war to the end of inflation was the principal means by which the Germans were able to secure a large value-excess of imports in the trade in commodities and, at the same time, in the post-war years, to make heavy payments under the Treaty of Versailles. If, therefore, to the adverse gold balance of trade in commodities from the beginning of the war to the end of inflation we add the cash payments on reparation and clearings account and such other debits as were involved, and subtract from this total such invisible credits, aside from sales of currency, as Germany acquired, we shall be able to obtain a rough notion of the net gain in gold arising from the sale of rights later rendered nugatory by the depreciation of the currency.

Several estimates of the German balance of payments in the period under review have been made. The material is gathered together in the Institute of Economics' book *Germany's Capacity to Pay* and the conclusions there reached, modified by the later findings of the McKenna Committee, are taken as the basis for the present computation. It should be understood that the results are necessarily far from precise. They are nothing more than reasonable guesses based on statistics which are of doubtful accuracy and in which *lacunae* are very frequent.

For the war-period the adverse trade balance covered by the sale of paper marks, or mark credits, by the export of German securities, or by short-term borrowing abroad, amounted to some 11 billion gold marks.[11]

---

[10] cf. *McKenna Committee Report*, Annex, Section II.

[11] This amount, with one billion from the sale of gold and three billion from the sale of foreign securities, covers the war excess of merchandise imports of 15 billion gold marks.

So much of the short-term borrowings from foreigners as were later paid off in real values must necessarily have been paid out of international credits accruing to Germany in post-war years. Inasmuch as German post-war credits, other than from sales of money, failed to cover current debits, the short-term obligations incurred during the war and later paid off, as well as the current excess of debits, must have been met directly or indirectly by renewed sales of marks or rights thereto. The same is true of any claims to marks acquired by foreigners during the war and used to make purchases in Germany in the post-war period. The domestic securities sold to foreigners during the war-period were to some extent, no doubt, stocks rather than bonds and therefore not subject to complete loss of value by the depreciation of the currency. If held to the present they represent still valid claims against Germany and so are not to be accounted as German gain. But, since the total of domestic securities of all kinds sold up to 1919 has been counted at only one billion gold marks, the adjustment on this account cannot be large. At the beginning of 1919 it can therefore be assumed that floating obligations to foreign countries covered a debt of 11 billion gold marks and that so far as these obligations were redeemed in later years the excess of debits must have been *pro tanto* greater than appears in the figures for current items. Sales of marks or mark claims in the post-war period must therefore have been large enough to take care of such redemption of the war obligations to foreigners as took place and, in addition, to cover the excess of debits on current items other than sales of currency.

After the Ruhr invasion Germany could no longer sell marks for investment purposes and was forced to give real values in exchange for foreign credits. The extent to which paper marks or mark credits were used to pay for current extra-national debts in the post-war period can therefore be estimated from the international accounts covering the years 1919-1922 inclusive. The accompanying Table XXII presents estimates for that period together with the floating debt carried over from the war and the estimated total yield from sales of unredeemed money and claims thereto.

The total net yield to Germany from sales of marks, mark balances, and securities payable in a fixed amount of marks thus appears, according to this method of computation, to have been between fifteen and sixteen billion gold marks as compared with the fifteen billion obtained by direct estimate. On the assumption that no great part of the marks and mark credits acquired by foreigners during the war were turned into real values in the post-war period (and this is certainly true of the largest item, the currency itself) these estimates also coincide reasonably

TABLE XXII

GERMANY'S BALANCE OF PAYMENTS, 1919-1922, TOGETHER WITH FLOATING
OBLIGATIONS TO FOREIGNERS OUTSTANDING AT THE BEGINNING
OF THE PERIOD

(Millions of gold marks)

CR.		DR.	
I. *Merchandise and Bullion* Net export of bullion and specie[12]	2,000	I. Floating obligations from the war-period (mainly paper marks or mark claims held abroad)	11,000
II. *Capital Items* Sales of foreign securities[13]	1,000	II. *Merchandise and Bullion*	
Sales of property including domestic share securities[14]	6,000	Excess import of commodities[18]	8,000
III. *Interest and Dividends* Yield on foreign investments[15]	600	III. *Other Items* Cash reparations, clearings, and similar payments[19]	2,365
IV. *Other Items* Net tourist expenditures[16]	600	Bank balances acquired abroad[20]	2,500
Net sundry credits (shipping and other transport receipts, remit- tances, commissions, foreign cur- rency expenditures of armies of occupation, etc.)[17]	1,000	Other property acquired abroad[21]	3,000
V. *Balance, paid for by unredeemed* *currency or its equivalent (mark* *bank balances, securities of fixed* *value in terms of marks) issued* *during or after the war*	15,665		
Totals	26,865		26,865

[12] During this period the Reichsbank's gold reserves fell by 1,258 million marks and net exports of specie on private account are assumed to have accounted for the remainder. In the figures on sales of specie given in the preceding section a total export over the whole war and post-war period of 3,500 million marks was given. The Reichsbank lost more than 500 million marks in 1923, leaving 3 billion to be accounted for prior to that time. The export during the war is computed by von Glasenapp at 1 billion so that, in the period 1919-1922, a total of 2 billion is indicated.

[13] *Wirtschaft und Statistik*, No. 2, 1923, p. 64.

[14] Computed from estimates in *Germany's Capacity to Pay*, pp. 89 ff., and modified by the figures given in the *McKenna Committee Report*. In the former book, urban real estate sales are put at 4 billion gold marks, rural real estate at 1 billion, and share securities at 3 billion. The securities may be assumed to have been half in stock certificates and half in fixed value securities. The value of the

well with the figures given by J. M. Keynes[22] and Kurt Singer[28] for the period from the end of the war till mid-1922. Keynes' figures are eight billion gold marks and Singer's ten. It will be remembered that war-

latter may be deducted from the total as being essentially a sale of marks, ultimately of no worth, and to be included in the category of sales of money. This leaves a total of 6,500 million. *The McKenna Report* indicates that this is an extreme overstatement. The amount has therefore been reduced to 6,000 million. If the McKenna estimate is nearer the truth the sums realized on sales of currency must have been much larger than is here indicated. It seemed best, however, to under- rather than over-state such sales.

[15] This is an arbitrarily estimated sum. The authors of *Germany's Capacity to Pay* think the amounts so received were negligible. On the other hand, similar receipts, during 1924 and 1925, have been officially estimated at 400 million gold marks for the two year period. (*Memorandum on the Balance of Payments and Foreign Trade Balances*, 1911-1925, League of Nations Publications, II, Economic and Financial, 1926, II, 51¹, Geneva, 1926). Germany had not by 1926 made any sizable new foreign investments and, while interest payments later resumed were in many cases not forthcoming in the immediate post-war period, some foreign property, later disposed of, was yielding a return in the earlier years. It would seem therefore that an annual average of 150 million gold marks receipts on this account is not an improbable estimate for 1919 to 1922.

[16] *Germany's Capacity to Pay*, p. 55.

[17] This figure is arbitrary. The authors of *Germany's Capacity to Pay* think that sundry net credits would not amount to more than 400 million.

[18] In *Germany's Capacity to Pay* the estimate (largely based on German official figures) is 11,000 million. *The McKenna Report* declares this to be much too large and computes the total of excess of merchandise debits and cash reparations at not more than 10,000 million. The figures on cash reparations are definitely ascertainable at 1,750 million gold marks. The figure of 8,000 million excess of merchandise imports would therefore seem to be approximately correct.

[19] Computed from *History of Reparations*, Carl Bergmann, *passim*. Nothing is here included except cash payments over German borders. It was officially reported in *Germany's Economic and Financial Situation*, that cash reparations payments in foreign currency up to the end of 1922 were 1750 million gold marks and clearings payments 615 million gold marks. Other cash payments there reported did not clearly require international transfers.

[20] This is a mean of the estimates of Sir Robert Horne, Mr. Reginald McKenna, and Professor J. M. Keynes. *cf. Germany's Capacity to Pay*, pp. 82-3.

[21] The total German holdings of property abroad at the end of 1923 have been estimated at from 5.7 to 7.8 billion gold marks. *cf. McKenna Committee Report*. Part of these were acquired before the war and part in 1923. The figures given in the present table are a guess at the amount acquired up to the end of 1922, including foreign bank notes held in Germany.

[22] Keynes' figure of eight billion is stated as a maximum. He is of the opinion that five billion is really more nearly correct. The difference is due to what he regards as an exaggerated excess of imports in the official trade figures for 1919. *cf.* Keynes' article in *Manchester Guardian Commercial*, Reconstruction Supplement, Section VIII, September 28, 1922, p. 480.

[28] Quoted in *Germany's Capacity to Pay*, p. 85.

time sales accounted for some 7 billion. These estimates would therefore give a total for the whole war and post-war period of fifteen to seventeen billion gold marks. All of the estimates are, to repeat, little more than more or less shrewd guesses. They perhaps indicate the general situation but must not be taken as precise.

It may be worth while again to note that, had not the value of the German currency unit sunk to a practical zero, these sales of currency and currency claims would have been merely postponed obligations.[24] As it was they were extinguished. The proceeds were a pure gift to the German economy attainable only by reason of the monetary collapse. They were, of course, of a very different order from the sales of hard money. The gains on the sales of hard money were in the nature of an economy; the gains on the sales of paper or bank deposits in marks were a swindle, unintended perhaps, but real, for all that. No sympathy, however, need be wasted on the majority of the victims. They were trying to get something for nothing; they received, instead, nothing for something.

The sale of vague promises thus proved immensely more profitable to the Germans than the sale of the precious metals. Germany increased her stock of consumable goods, as a result of both types of sale, by an amount equivalent to upwards of 20 billion gold marks, 3 to 4 billion on the sales of metal and 15 to 16 billion on the sales of paper. Even if the estimate of the latter, to be conservative, is reduced to, say, 12 billion, the total sum received from both types of sale is equal to some 4 billions of dollars. When it is considered that the annual income of the entire German nation in the most prosperous pre-war years was about 10 billion dollars the importance of this sum to the German economy will be appreciated.

[24] They might, of course, have been partly but not *fully* repudiated. This would have occurred if the mark had been stabilized at any substantial fraction of its original value.

CHAPTER XI

LOSSES ON FOREIGN TRADE IN MERCHANDISE AND CAPITAL GOODS

§ NATURE OF THE LOSSES

THE gains accruing to the German economy from the sale to foreigners of money which soon became moribund were in large measure cancelled by the losses on German exports of merchandise. The exporters themselves did not lose—on the contrary they were among the greatest winners from inflation—but, insofar as inflation led to exports being sold at gold prices greatly below those which would have prevailed under stable monetary conditions, the German economy as a whole bore the burden.[1] There was but slight compensation on the import side since the depreciation of the mark could not have greatly lowered the gold cost of imported goods. It is true that certain shippers of goods to Germany in the early post-war years invoiced in marks and took a loss with the decline in the gold value of the currency in the interval between the date of contraction and payment of the debt. Their loss was Germany's gain. But they were wary of repeating the error. Some shippers of goods from those countries with currencies declining even more rapidly than the German did, however, continue to invoice in marks in preference to using their own monetary unit. Whichever they used, the Germans were likely to gain. In the one case the Germans profited through the depreciation of their own, and, in the other, through the depreciation of the shipper's currency. These possibilities, however, were realized to a progressively smaller extent as invoicing of German imports in stable currencies became general. On the export side, then, losses were wellnigh certain no matter how the goods were invoiced—low prices were here the dominant factor—while, on the import side, a compensatory gain was fortuitous at best.

---

[1] The exporters did not lose because the prices of most of the things they bought (domestic commodities) were much below an equivalence with the prices of the things they sold. The German economy, on the other hand, was a loser since the prices of the things it bought (imports) were much above an equivalence with the prices of the things it sold (exports).

§ METHOD OF COMPUTATION AND THE STATISTICS INVOLVED

The net result of these gains and losses is not easy to determine. It has already been pointed out that the official figures on exports and imports, insofar as they are expressed in paper marks, are worthless. But, from May 1921 onward, there are official estimates of the gold cost of total imports and of the gold value of receipts for total exports, and these are much more reliable. There are also figures, from the beginning of 1920, of gold values, *at 1913 prices*, of the current physical volume of individual exports and imports. An index, moreover, on a 1913 base, of the presumptive prices of German imports and exports in the absence of inflation, can be computed with a fair approach to accuracy. Knowing the total value of imports and exports at 1913 gold prices, and having an index of presumptive gold prices on a 1913 base, multiplication will give the total gold values which would have been paid and received on the commodity imports and exports actually made, had a stable currency standard been in operation. Comparison with the gold values *in fact* paid and received will show the net result of inflation on the German economic situation so far as the foreign trade in merchandise is concerned.

Before proceeding to the requisite computation it will be worth while to examine more closely the statistics on which it will be based. In all cases they are derived from official reports of the Statistische Reichsamt. The figures on the total value of imports and exports at 1913 prices were computed, by that organization, by multiplying the actual physical volume (weights usually, but in a few cases, numbers) of the current separate import and export items by the 1913 average price per unit of volume of similar imports and exports. The *volume*, as contrasted with the price, statistics on foreign trade in the inflation years may be regarded as substantially accurate and, since the variety of goods in any one item of the import-export schedule is not great, no large error would arise through a change in the volume relationship of two or more commodities grouped in the schedule under a single heading.[2] There is, of course, no guarantee that the quality of the goods entering into any given schedule item of German international trade was identical, or even similar, in the pre- and in the post-war years. If the quality of both imports and exports in one of the periods was inferior to that in the other there would be an obvious error in multiplying the 1913 figures by any price index which assumed identical goods in the pre- and post-war periods. Even greater difficulties would arise if imports

[2] The number of separate headings is more than two thousand. These, however, are reduced by consolidation to something less than a thousand.

in general in the earlier years were inferior in quality and exports superior, or vice versa, or if, as was likely, there was, with innumerable variations, no definite trend in any direction. The best means of meeting the difficulty would seem to be to take the trade of 1924, 1925 and 1926, the first three years after the establishment of the currency on a gold basis, to compute for those years an index of export and import prices by dividing the actual gold total of imports and exports by the hypothetical total at 1913 prices, and to apply this index to the 1921, 1922 and 1923 trade. Price levels, measured in gold, were substantially stable throughout the six years involved[3] while the character of German import and export trade and the quality of the goods exchanged appears to have altered but slightly during that time. Any changes that might have occurred between 1913 and 1921 would then be irrelevant.

An example, using the index of gold prices in 1924 only, instead of an average of the years 1924-1926, will make the matter clear. In 1924 the actual value of German imports was 8,628,675,000 gold marks. The sum of the values, at 1913 prices, of the same physical volume of each of the separate import items would have been 6,769,010,000 gold marks. The 1924 import price index (1913 = 100) is therefore

$$\frac{8,628,675,000}{6,769,010,000} = 127.$$

It is immaterial whether the post-war quality of imports was better or worse than in 1913. Whatever may have been the situation in this respect the goods imported in 1924 were, on the average, 27% higher in gold price than the goods imported under the same names in 1913. On the assumption that the quality of individual imports was not greatly different in 1924 from that in the *immediately* preceding years,[4] the actual gold prices paid in 1924, when stabilization of the currency had been effected, would seem to give some indication of what must necessarily have been paid, in the period just prior to that date, if a gold currency had then been in operation. The fluctuation in world gold prices was, to repeat, not enough to have led to a substantial alteration in

---

[3] The average of the indices of wholesale prices in the United States for 1921-1923 was 150 while for 1924-1926 it was 153 (U.S. Bureau of Labor Statistics). Since, in this chapter, we are dealing with statistics and computations which cannot pretend to be precise it seems best not to attempt adjustment for this 2% difference but to assume that prices in the two periods were equal. Gold prices move in substantial correspondence the world over and prices in the United States would seem to be the best criterion of the world value of gold at this time.

[4] That is, from 1921 onward.

the gold prices of German imports during the period covered and so may safely be neglected.

Extending this method forward to 1926 and backward to 1921, for exports as well as imports, will no doubt lead to a greater margin of error in the matter of the quality of the goods entering German international trade (the assumption of unchanged quality during six years is clearly less warranted than during two) but on the other hand will tend to eliminate temporary aberrations, both in prices and quality, that may be present in the shorter period. It is to be justified, if at all, on this account. On the whole it seems improbable that any great error will be involved in assuming that the prices paid and received in 1924, 1925, and 1926 for German imports and exports of the composition and quality prevalent in the post-war period, are representative of the value of those goods in world markets in 1921, 1922, and 1923, or in supposing that they approximate the prices which would have been paid and received in the earlier period had Germany then been on the gold standard or its equivalent.

It is, indeed, not unlikely that this hypothesis of what would have occurred, if conditions had been other than they were, is quite as near the truth as are the statistics of what actually did occur. The official estimate of the gold value of the sums actually paid and received for German imports and exports in the inflation period is, in the case of exports, probably not very wide of the mark. But it is more dubious on the import side. For conversion, into gold, of the paper mark declarations of *imports* the Statistische Reichsamt has taken an arithmetic mean of: (1) the sum of the declared paper mark values of imports, converted into gold at the average dollar rate of the month preceding importation, and (2) the sum of the values of imports, at world market prices, at the time of the arrival of the goods.[5] It was felt that the former of the two totals from which the average is derived was too low because, though German imports are usually paid for about a month in advance of the arrival of the goods, the interval is often longer. Furthermore, part of the imports was paid for in gold marks. In either

[5] From March 1, 1921, onward, declared values (subject to revision by the Trade Statistics Council) have been used for all imports and exports. Previous to that date uniform official values were used for most imports. As late as September 1922 the calculations of world market prices were made *directly* on only 37 items in the tariff classification though these represented 40% in declared value of all the imports; by December 1922 this had been extended to 324 items and 77% of all imports, and by March 1923 to 598 items and 91% of all imports. For the remainder, declared values were multiplied by the coefficient already established for the items directly computed.

case, whenever the depreciation of the mark was continuous, a larger gold value would actually have been paid than would appear from the conversion of the paper mark declarations at the average exchange rate prevailing in the month prior to their entry into Germany. On the other hand, the latter of the two totals was regarded as being too high because part of the imports was paid for in paper marks. The gold cost of these imports was reduced whenever the exchange value of the mark fell in the interval between the date when the contract was made and when payment took place. In addition to this, part of the imports came from countries themselves having depreciated currency and selling their exports at prices below world levels.

It is, of course, a matter of doubt as to how far the averaging of an estimate of the gold value of imports at the date of arrival with the declared paper values converted into gold can be trusted to give a close approximation to the actual gold cost of imports. It is probable that the result for 1923 is substantially correct but, for the earlier years, it is to be gravely questioned. Some modification in these years will be suggested in the ensuing pages.

The estimates of the gold values actually received for *exports* rest on a much firmer foundation. Some 60% to 70%, by value, of the exports were invoiced and declared in stable foreign currencies and were thus easily and accurately converted into gold. For the remainder, conversion to gold was made at the average dollar exchange rate of the month of export.[6] Since prices were finally established by the Boards of Foreign Trade Control only when the goods were on the point of leaving the country this would seem to give a reasonably accurate picture of the gold values actually received.

§ THE PERIOD MAY 1921 TO DECEMBER 1923

In computing such profit and loss on German foreign trade as may be attributed to inflation, account will first be taken of the period May 1921 to December 1923, for which fairly detailed figures are available, and the investigation will then be pushed backward to cover the earlier years. The total gold value of German imports and exports in the period May 1921 to December 1923, *if they had been sold at* 1913 *prices,* is as follows:

[6] For a more detailed explanation see *Memorandum on International Trade and Balances of Payments* 1912-1926, League of Nations Publications, II, Economic and Financial, 1927, II, 68[I], Geneva, 1927. Figures throughout are for "Special Trade," from which transit trade and similar transactions are excluded, and represent values at the frontier (c.i.f. for imports and f.o.b. for exports) exclusive of duties.

German Imports and Exports 1921-1923, at 1913 Prices
(Thousands of gold marks)[7]

		IMPORTS	EXPORTS
1921	(May-Dec.)	3,821,400	2,975,800
1922	(full year)	6,301,147	6,187,794
1923	(full year)	4,808,174	5,338,110
		14,930,721	14,501,704

[7] *Memorandum on International Trade and Balances of Payments, 1912-1926,*
League of Nations Publications, II, Economic and Financial, 1927, II, 68II, p. 361.
The import figures for May-December 1921 are obtained by taking a proportion-
ate share of the amount reported for the full year 1921.

Gold prices in 1921-1923 were very different from those in 1913 but
were, it will be recalled, much the same as in 1924-1926. The actual
gold value of German imports and exports in 1924, 1925, and 1926,
and the value of the same physical volume of corresponding items at
1913 prices, are given as numerator and denominator respectively in
the figures in the subjoined table together with the resulting indices of
import and export prices on a 1913 base. These indices will presently
be used in application to the 1921-1923 trade.

VALUE OF GERMAN IMPORTS AND EXPORTS, 1924–1926
WITH AN INDEX OF PRICES (1913 = 100)

YEAR	IMPORTS *Thousands of Gold Marks*	INDEX OF IMPORT PRICES (1913 = 100)	EXPORTS *Thousands of Gold Marks*	INDEX OF EXPORT PRICES (1913 = 100)
1924 (actual)[8] 1924 (at 1913 prices)	8,628,675 6,769,010	127	6,649,922 5,133,943	130
1925 (actual)[8] 1925 (at 1913 prices)	11,743,952 8,997,790	131	8,930,474 6,595,830	135
1926 (actual)[8] 1926 (at 1913 prices)	9,652,487 7,966,473	121	9,965,392 7,371,991	135
Average index of prices		126.33		133.33

[8] The published statistics have been corrected to eliminate errors in declaration
and valuation as follows:

	1924	1925	1926
Imports reduced by	5%	5%	3%
Exports increased by	1.5%	1.5%	1.5%

This correction carries out an official suggestion of the Statistische Reichsamt in

Taking the average price index for imports and exports respectively in the years 1924-1926 as appropriate to 1921-1923, the *potential* gold values of imports and exports of the earlier period—the amounts, that is, which would presumably have been paid and received had stable monetary conditions prevailed—together with actual outlay and income on imports and exports, as estimated by the Statistische Reichsamt, are presented herewith.

AMOUNTS POTENTIALLY AND ACTUALLY PAID AND RECEIVED ON GERMAN IMPORTS
AND EXPORTS, MAY 1921 TO DECEMBER 1923
(Thousands of gold marks)

	IMPORTS		EXPORTS	
YEAR	POTENTIAL EXPENDITURES[9] $(1913 \text{ VAL-UES} \times \frac{126.33}{100})$	ACTUAL EXPENDITURES[10]	POTENTIAL RECEIPTS[9] $(1913 \text{ VAL-UES} \times \frac{133.33}{100})$	ACTUAL RECEIPTS[10]
1921 (May-Dec.)	4,827,575	4,014,900	3,967,634	2,401,300
1922 (full year)	7,960,239	6,200,400	8,250,186	3,970,000
1923 (full year)	6,074,166	6,149,729	7,117,302	6,102,318
Total (May 1921 to Dec. 1923)	18,861,980	16,365,029	19,335,122	12,473,618

[9] On the assumption that a gold standard had been in operation.

[10] *Memorandum on International Trade and Balances of Payments* 1912-1926, p. 361.

On this accounting the German economy obtained its imports during the period under discussion for 2,496,951,000 gold marks less than if stable monetary standards had been in operation but sold its exports for 6,861,504,000 less, a net loss of 4,364,553,000 gold marks.[11]

Part of the gain on imports was due to the fact that currency depreciation existed in countries other than Germany and cannot therefore be

its report to the League of Nations' statistical office. *cf.* for this and other data in this table *Memorandum on International Trade and Balances of Payments 1912-1926*, pp. 360, 361.

[11] It might, at first blush, be supposed that the computed gain on imports had already been accounted for in the estimates of sales of marks. This is not so, however, since the statistics of imports and exports, on which the estimate of sales of marks was based, purport to give the gold values *actually* paid and received. The present computation is based on *potential* payments and receipts. The Germans gained both by securing some imports at low gold prices and by paying in depreciating currency.

put to the credit of the inflation of the *mark*. It would have been obtained if Germany had been on the gold standard. It is doubtful, however, if this gain bulks very large. Germany's imports were predominantly standardized commodities, foodstuffs in crude condition and industrial raw materials. It has already been noted that the gold prices of such goods in all countries, whatever the monetary standard, rapidly attain approximate equality except for minor variations covering costs of transport, tariffs, and similar charges. It is therefore probable that the considerable gain on imports, which the *figures* show, is due to an understatement of the gold value of the actual amounts paid, especially in 1921 and 1922. For 1923, the index of *actual* import prices, on the basis of the estimates of actual payments converted into gold, is 127.90, a figure very closely corresponding to the computed average index of *potential* prices of 126.33. This goes to show that in 1923 the Germans were not obtaining their imports at less than world market prices. It is rather doubtful that they ever did buy them at much below world prices, though the estimated totals of actual import costs for 1921 and 1922, measured in gold, give price indices of 105.06 and 98.40 respectively, figures far short of the then current prices of German imports in world markets. It may have been that by 1923 it was no longer possible for Germans to buy from abroad goods invoiced in paper marks whereas, up to that time, they had been able to do so on a substantial scale and so had secured their imports cheaply as the value of the mark fell. But the fact that it was not until 1923 that most of the imports were directly included in the computation of gold costs suggests that the discrepancy really lies in the official figures. To allow for this, and to exclude gains on imports which would have accrued under any monetary standard in Germany, gains, that is, which were due to currency depreciation in other countries, it seems best to cut in half the computed gain on imports and make it 1,248,475,000 gold marks. This will increase the net loss on foreign trade in the period May 1921 to December 1923 to 5,613,028,000 gold marks.

The index of actually realized *export* prices works out for 1921 at 80.69, for 1922 at 64.16, and for 1923 at 114.32 (1913 = 100 in all cases). These figures compare with the index of *potential* prices of 133.33. There is no reason to believe that they are not substantially accurate. In 1922, therefore, the Germans sold their exports at prices less than half, on the average, of those which they would presumably have obtained under a stable monetary standard, in 1921 at less than two-thirds, and in 1923 at a discount of some 14%. The much more favorable result in 1923 is probably due to the high degree of mobility of paper mark prices attained by that date and to the rapid adjustment of prices and exchange rates to one another. Whatever may have been the influence of the control of prices of exports in preventing a still greater sacrifice of German goods in the earlier years than did, in fact, occur, it is clear that the control did not succeed in forestalling an immense shift in the terms on which the Germans exchanged their products for those of the outside world.

§ THE PERIOD PRIOR TO MAY 1921

Up to this point the calculation of gains and losses can be made with some confidence. But prior to May 1921 the statistical fogs hang heavy. There are no figures, on which any reliance whatever may be placed, for the period preceding 1920. The years of the war, however, can be excluded from consideration. Except for a few months in the summer of 1917 the exchange value of the mark did not deviate very widely from its internal purchasing power during the whole course of the conflict and it was about as frequently above as below the par relationship. There were thus, at this time, no substantial gains or losses in the exchange of merchandise exports for imports, at least none that can be attributed to inflation.[12] We are therefore reduced to arbitrary guessing for the single year 1919 only. For 1920, however, the statistics of actual values paid and received are available only in paper marks[13] and are to some extent subject to those defects in that method of reporting which a year or two later became so glaring. For the first four months of 1921 there is official authority for interpolating pro rata to the figures for the remainder of that year. This interpolation, having been made along the lines so far laid down, shows a net loss for January-April 1921 of 579,999,000 gold marks. Adding this to the net loss already established gives a total from January 1921 to December 1923 of 6,193,027,000 gold marks.

Turning now to the year 1920, we find that reported imports and exports, at 1913 values, were approximately equal at 3,928,700,000 and 3,709,300,000 gold marks respectively.[14] 1920 was a year of marked vicissitudes in the gold price level. Starting with an index of 233 (1913 = 100) in January, wholesale prices in the United States rose to 247 in May and then declined to 179 in December. This fluctuation in the value of gold, however, would not necessarily, or even probably, affect in any considerable degree the *relation* between the gold values of

[12] The price-level index in Germany during the war was never much higher than in the United States and was frequently lower. There was thus practically no war-time inflation in the sense of a paper currency of less value than gold.

[13] But gold values, at 1913 prices, are given.

[14] *Statistik des deutschen Reichs*, Vol. 317, Verlag von Reimar Hobbing, Berlin, 1925, p. 5.

imports and exports. After a number of unsatisfactory experiments with other methods it has consequently seemed best to assume that the values of German imports and exports in 1920, if they had been bought and sold at world prices in gold, would have been in substantial equilibrium just as the values at 1913 prices were.[15] But the *actual* reported totals, in paper marks, were 99,077,000,000 and 69,421,200,000 respectively.[16] The mark fluctuated during this year, *without any trend in either direction*, from 1.69 American cents in January to 1.05 cents in February, to 2.56 cents in June, to 1.32 in November and to 1.37 in December. Whatever the deviation of the paper mark valuations of the Statistische Reichsamt from actual prices, the errors would therefore tend to cancel out. The *appreciation* of the currency in the early part of the year would have an effect on the valuations which would neutralize the effect of the *depreciation* from July to November. Since the *potential* gold values of imports and exports in this year were equal, the difference between the reported paper mark cost of imports and the paper mark receipts from exports, when converted to gold, may consequently be taken as a fair measure of the net loss for 1920.

The average exchange rate of the paper mark against the dollar in 1920 was 1/15.01 of the gold mark par.[17] Converting the net excess of imports, 29,655,800,000 paper marks, at this rate, gives a deficiency on foreign trade of 1,975,736,000 gold marks as compared with the potential equilibrium under a stable standard. Adding this to the total, from 1921 to 1923, of 6,193,027,000 gold marks brings the net loss from 1920 to 1923 to 8,168,763,000 gold marks.

§ THE YEAR 1919

There remains to be considered the year 1919 for which not even tolerable data are at hand. In the course of this year the number of paper marks exchangeable against a dollar was multiplied six times

[15] From their peak in May the prices of raw materials, in the United States, had fallen by 35.5% in December; manufactured commodities had fallen by 34.3%. German imports are mainly raw materials while exports are manufactured commodities and there might therefore be a slight tendency for the potential gold total of imports to fall in a slightly greater degree than that of exports. Since, at 1913 prices, the total of imports was slightly greater than that of exports, a rather close approximation to equilibrium in import and export potential values may therefore be assumed. The changes in gold prices in 1920 are immaterial to the computation here made unless they affected imports and exports in different degrees.

[16] *Statistisches Jahrbuch*, 1921-1922, p. 144.

[17] This is an average of monthly averages. cf. *Zahlen zur Geldentwertung*, p. 6.

while prices in Germany a little more than tripled.[18] Even at the beginning of the year the exchange value of the mark had been rather low relative to its domestic purchasing power. The war-time control of foreign trade was rapidly relaxed, and there was thus no bar to the sale of exports at gold or foreign exchange prices very greatly less than those prevailing in the outside world. Contemporary observations leave no doubt that Germany was then one immense bargain counter. But on the other hand the stock of goods was very low and production was small. Four and a half years of war had depleted the country and recovery was slow. On the whole it is improbable that the net loss was greater than the annual average of the succeeding years and certainly was not less than half as much, that is to say, it was between one and two billion gold marks.[19] Counting it in at the higher, and more likely, figure, we may estimate the total depredations of inflation upon German foreign trade in merchandise, in the five year period 1919-1923, at roughly 10,000,000,000 gold marks.

§ THE MARGIN OF ERROR IN THE ESTIMATE

This estimate of losses more probably errs on the side of moderation than otherwise. On one or two scores it may, indeed, seem exaggerated. Until the spring of 1920 the Germans did not have control of their customs frontier in the Rhineland and they lost it on two occasions thereafter.[20] The collection of statistics, even of physical quantities, at these times was difficult and incomplete. The *lacunae* in the statistics, however, are probably much greater on the import than on the export side and since, on imports, the depreciation of the currency tended to yield the German economy gains rather than losses, the total net losses on foreign trade indicated by the official figures may for this reason be somewhat too large. But, on the other hand, there must have been a very sizable undiscovered export of German goods, bought at very low gold or foreign exchange prices, in the luggage of "tourists." There is every probability that the national loss on these transactions at least balances the defect in the statistics on the other side of the account.

Export duties, however, have not yet been taken into consideration. The valuations which have here been used, for both imports and exports,

[18] The exchange value of the mark fell from 12.21 to 2.1 cents: the German wholesale price index rose from 245 to 803.
[19] Total exports were reported at 1.76 billion gold marks. Under stable monetary conditions they would, in all likelihood, have brought at least twice as much.
[20] In the occupation of Düsseldorf, Duisburg and Ruhrort in March 1921 and in the occupation of the Ruhr in 1923.

are valuations free of duty. Whatever may have been the ultimate incidence of German import duties (and there is no reason to believe it was not upon the Germans), the foreign exchange cost of imports would not include the duties levied. The import valuations used in the foregoing computations are therefore appropriate to the purpose in hand. But with exports the matter is not so clear. Export duties may have been paid, at least in part, by foreigners,[21] and the foreign exchange receipts would, in consequence, cover not only the f.o.b. valuations but something on duties as well. The German losses on foreign trade would then be somewhat less than have been indicated. But the value of all export duties paid, from their inception in May 1920 to the close of the inflation period, was less than 450 million gold marks.[22] Even if it be assumed that this was paid *in toto* by foreigners it does not bulk very large in the account—and may well be included in the general margin of error.

It may therefore be concluded that the figure of 10,000,000,000 gold marks does not seriously, if at all, overstate the loss to the German economy in the exchange of commodity exports for imports during the inflation régime.[23]

§ THE MONTH-TO-MONTH SITUATION IN 1922 AND 1923

The available statistics make it possible to present the month-to-month situation during 1922 and 1923.[24] Table XXIII shows by months the actual payments for imports and receipts on exports, the payments and receipts which would have attended the identical trade under stable money conditions, the potential payments for imports and receipts on exports expressed as a percentage of the actual payments and receipts, and the actual return on German foreign trade expressed as a per-

[21] The question of incidence is not involved. The actual cash outlay for export duties may have been made by the foreign buyer either directly or through an agreement to reimburse the seller. This may or may not have resulted in lower prices, at the point of production, than if no duty had been levied.

[22] Converted according to the wholesale price index in Germany. If converted according to exchange rates it would be much less than this. *cf. Germany's Economy, Currency and Finance*, p. 33.

[23] Certain German business houses set up branches abroad and handled their exports through these branches. The price obtained by the branch on the sale of German goods may have been considerably greater than the price officially reported in German export statistics. To the extent that this occurred the loss to the German economy would, of course, be lessened.

[24] With the exception of the half-year April to September 1923 which had to be taken as a unit.

TABLE XXIII

ACTUAL AND POTENTIAL PAYMENTS ON IMPORTS, ACTUAL AND POTENTIAL RECEIPTS ON
EXPORTS, POTENTIAL PAYMENTS AND RECEIPTS AS A PERCENTAGE OF ACTUAL, AND
THE ACTUAL RETURN ON FOREIGN TRADE AS A PERCENTAGE OF THE
POTENTIAL RETURN; 1922 AND 1923
(All value figures in thousands of gold marks)

DATE	IMPORTS			EXPORTS			RATIO OF ACTUAL FOREIGN TRADE RETURN TO POTENTIAL RETURN (%)
	ACTUAL PAYMENTS	POTENTIAL PAYMENTS	POTENTIAL PAYMENTS AS A PERCENTAGE OF ACTUAL PAYMENTS	ACTUAL RECEIPTS	POTENTIAL RECEIPTS	POTENTIAL RECEIPTS AS A PERCENTAGE OF ACTUAL RECEIPTS	
1922							
Jan.	330,400	531,344	160.82	325,400	630,905	193.89	82.9
Feb.	359,600	471,337	131.07	297,900	560,386	188.11	69.7
Mar.	563,200	733,978	130.32	324,000	680,355	209.99	62.1
Apr.	508,000	733,220	144.33	327,000	631,909	193.24	74.7
May	565,200	788,678	139.54	416,200	676,799	162.61	85.8
June	564,600	749,516	132.75	427,900	679,043	158.69	83.7
July	684,800	843,885	123.23	336,300	650,780	193.51	63.7
Aug.	545,100	754,696	138.45	254,800	647,561	254.14	54.5
Sept.	421,800	683,446	162.03	290,900	703,317	241.77	67.0
Oct.	531,700	693,315	130.40	291,400	759,021	260.47	50.1
Nov.	536,200	725,690	135.34	255,200	723,805	283.62	47.7
Dec.	589,800	613,031	103.94	423,000	904,999	213.95	48.6
1923							
Jan.	563,061	617,374	109.65	310,315	634,784	204.56	53.6
Feb.	445,461	484,349	108.73	359,515	603,718	167.93	64.7
Mar.	502,361	476,770	94.91	434,715	621,585	142.99	66.4
Apr.-Sept.	3,201,792	3,126,794	97.66	3,341,883	3,339,516	99.93	97.7
Oct.	434,883	455,040	104.64	565,195	654,917	115.87	90.3
Nov.	432,836	433,312	100.11	513,675	608,518	118.46	84.5
Dec.	489,160	484,854	99.12	559,848	653,717	116.77	84.9

Sources of data: *Memorandum on Balance of Payments and Foreign Trade Balances
1910-1923*, p. 120; *ibid.* 1911-1925, p. 140.

Potential values were obtained by multiplying values of imports and exports based
on 1913 average prices by an index of potential prices calculated on the basis of values
in 1924, 1925, and 1926. See *supra,* p. 265.

Values of imports, at 1913 prices, from January to September 1922, inclusive, were
obtained from *Wirtschaft und Statistik,* 1922, p. 663. The values of imports for the
remainder of 1922, and those of exports throughout that year, have been computed
from official foreign trade figures for 1913 quoted in *Statistik des Deutschen Reichs* and
from figures of physical volume of the separate export and import groups for each
month of 1922 in *Monatliche Nachweise über den auswärtigen Handel Deutschlands.*
The quantity of exports and imports for each group (according to the German classification) was multiplied by the average value per unit of that group in 1913. All
groups were then added together to give the total value for each month. These totals
were corrected by reference to the yearly total as quoted in *Statistik des Deutschen
Reichs,* Vol. 317, p. 5.

Values of imports and exports, at 1913 prices, for each month of 1923 were obtained
from *Statistik des Deutschen Reichs,* Vol. 317, p. 6.

centage of the return which would have accrued under stable monetary conditions.[25]

Chart XXXIII correlates the movements in the ratio of actual to potential return on foreign trade with the movements in the ratio of the internal to the external value of the mark. The inverse correlation is clear. When, as a result of a rise in foreign exchange relative to domestic prices, the internal value of the currency rose in comparison with its external value, the loss on foreign trade increased. The relatively low prices in the domestic market then resulted in a sacrifice of German exportable commodities. When, on the other hand, the ratio of the internal to the external value of the mark fell, the returns on foreign trade became much more favorable to the Germans. The relatively slight loss in 1923 was due to the advance in domestic prices being more rapid than that in exchange rates.

§ RESULTS OF FOREIGN TRADE IN CAPITAL GOODS

There remains to be considered the gains or losses on capital, rather than current merchandise, account, such as were involved in the sale of property or property rights other than those in the paper currency itself. It has already been noted that there is a very great discrepancy in the estimates of authorities as to the extent of such sales and, consequently, as to the proceeds in stable currencies. Though there were substantial agreement on this score, as there is not, it would be impossible to gauge with even a remote approximation to accuracy the national gain or loss to Germany for the simple reason that there is no criterion by which the real value of such property may be measured. Such value will emerge only in the indefinite future when the returns on the purchases of such property by foreigners in the inflation period are actually realized. The *annual* return will be dependent, among other things, on future legisla-

[25] This is the ratio of the percentage of potential to actual payments on imports to the percentage of potential to actual receipts on exports. The figures for January 1922, for instance, show that the Germans were receiving 160.82 gold marks' worth of imports for every 100 gold marks' worth that they would have received under gold standard conditions and were giving 193.89 gold marks' worth of exports for every 100 gold marks' worth that they would have given had their currency been gold. Considering exports as the payment for imports, this means that they were receiving 82.9% of the imports they would have secured in exchange for a given quantum of exports, if they had had a gold currency.

tion affecting taxation, and on the progressive relaxation of rent restriction and other housing laws. Some of the property bought by foreigners

CHART XXXIII

CORRELATION OF MOVEMENTS IN THE RATIO OF ACTUAL TO POTENTIAL RETURN
ON FOREIGN TRADE WITH THE MOVEMENTS IN THE PRICE
RATIO INDEX; 1922 AND 1923

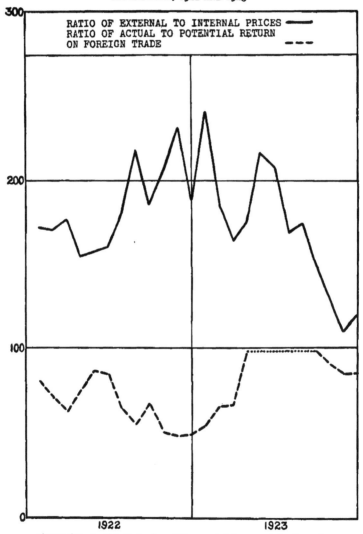

RATIO OF EXTERNAL TO INTERNAL PRICES ——
RATIO OF ACTUAL TO POTENTIAL RETURN
ON FOREIGN TRADE   – – –

Figures from April to September, 1923, prorated from total for 6 months.

was soon resold to Germans. On such transactions the net gain or loss
to the German economy might be accurately enough computed, in terms
of gold, provided adequate statistics were available. But on the property
held by foreigners up to the present time this would not be possible in
any case.

Some limits may, however, be denoted. The total sum, in gold, realized
by Germans on such sales has been estimated in the preceding chapter
at 6,000 million gold marks. In the face of a much lower figure given by
the McKenna Committee the estimate was deliberately put at a rather
high level in order to forestall exaggeration of the amount obtained
from the sale of marks. While some of the investments were poor the
yield of many of the properties has been increasing as the housing laws
have been modified and as the gold dividends on the shares of business concerns have been advanced. But it is doubtful whether, as late
as the early part of 1926 at any rate, it would be justifiable to assume that the value of these properties, taken as a whole, was greater
than the amount originally set down as the receipts from their sale
abroad. This conclusion is based on the figures for the German balance of payments since the war published by the Statistische Reichsamt.[26] It is there estimated that the net interest, dividend, and rental
payments of Germany to foreign countries in the first half of 1926 were
80 million gold marks. But the payments on long-term loans floated
since 1924 were 85 million. All other payments must therefore have been
5 million gold marks less than the receipts from German investment
abroad. That investment was estimated by the McKenna Committee to be,
at the end of 1923, about 6,750 million gold marks. But of this amount
some 1,600 had apparently been sold between 1923 and the beginning
of 1926,[27] leaving a little more than 5,000 million at the later date.
Since this investment yielded the Germans somewhat more interest than
all foreign investments in Germany made prior to 1924 gave to the
outside world, the real value of the latter, as late as 1926, cannot be
put at more than 5,000 million gold marks. Whether the Germans did
or did not lose substantially on the sale of properties is, however, a
matter of no consequence in the consideration of the net results of their
foreign transactions. If the proceeds of the sales of property, as given
in Table XXII, are overestimated, and the Germans lost considerably on
such sales, they must have obtained a *pro tanto* increase on sales of
currency over what has here been indicated. The net position is the same
in either event.

[26] *Vierteljahrshefte zur Konjunkturforschung*, 1926, Ergänzungsheft 2, Reimar
Hobbing, Berlin, 1926, pp. 5 *ff*.
[27] *ibid.*, p. 5.

§ NET RESULT OF ALL FOREIGN TRANSACTIONS

It is possible now to sum up the net results of inflation in the field of foreign transactions. Sales of money yielded a net *gain* of from 15 to 20 billion gold marks. On current merchandise transactions a *loss* of something like 10 billion gold marks was sustained as compared with the presumptive result under a stable monetary standard. On capital transactions no gain or loss is evident. The balance to the credit of inflation is therefore from 5 to 10 billion gold marks. Of this amount more than 3 billion was due to the sale of gold. Not all of this saving has been permanent. The economy in the use of gold was initiated by inflation but the gold standard as now maintained, without the presence of gold in hand to hand circulation and therefore with a smaller total gold supply, could have been established without currency depreciation. It is therefore questionable whether the whole gain on the sale of gold should be put to the credit of the paper currency system. If allowance be made for this, and if a middle figure be taken for total sales of money, the net gain on all foreign transactions which is directly attributable to inflation may be set in the neighborhood of from 4 to 5 billion gold marks.

It should be noted that much of the eventual *gains* from the sale of paper currency was obtained on issues made during the war when gold prices were high but that most of the *losses* on trade occurred after 1920 when gold prices had fallen. This means, if the present value of gold is used as a criterion, that the real gains as here estimated are somewhat overstated. The conclusions reached, however, can lay no claim to such precision as would make it other than absurd to attempt to introduce the refinement of allowing for the shifting value of gold. In dealing with paper mark figures, in which the unit of value is changing crazily, the relative stability of gold can be put in the class of absolutes and the actual gold estimate of gains and losses, if it is at all reliable, will furnish a sufficiently accurate notion of the real effect of inflation on the German economy.

CHAPTER XII

BUSINESS ACTIVITY AND PRODUCTION

§ PHYSICAL VOLUME DATA ALONE VALID

FROM data in monetary form it is clearly impossible to reach any valid general conclusions concerning the effect of inflation on German wealth and incomes. It is often alleged, for instance, that the wage earner suffered not only in being paid a sum which corresponded to the purchasing power of the currency at an earlier date but that he lost perhaps half of the real value of his pay, *at the date of receipt*, by reason of the necessity for spreading his expenditures over the period between pay days. The employer, on the other hand, is said to have been injured inasmuch as he had to provide for his pay roll in advance of the actual date of payment and, to do this, had to give countervalues which were greater than the purchasing power of the wages at the date they were actually paid. It is clear, however, that any change in the value of the currency unit (aside from such ulterior affects as it may have had on the physical volume of production) must have brought to *someone* real gains exactly compensating any losses which it entailed on others. However much distribution may be altered, the total *real* wealth and income of a people is not directly affected one iota by a fluctuation in the value of monetary counters. The *monetary* value of the wealth may change, however, not only in terms of the depreciating currency (a change inevitable in the very connotation of depreciation) but also in terms of gold or other stable money. But while the monetary value of wealth and income, expressed in the local currency, rises, its monetary value, expressed in gold, is more likely to show a fall. The latter will normally be the case when conversion into gold or foreign currency values is made at prevailing rates of exchange since those rates usually put a valuation on the depreciated currency far below that which it possesses in the country of origin. But, even when the computation in stable currency values is made according to the domestic wholesale price or cost-of-living index, the wealth of the country may seem to be declining when this is not in fact the case, because, in the prevailing uncertainty, all property tends to be capitalized at far below its earning-power value. This tendency came clearly to light in Germany in the extraordinarily low prices of stock exchange share securities throughout the whole period of inflation. Monetary data, therefore, offer a quite illusory criterion of the actual wealth and income.

The sum total of existing real *wealth* can be even indirectly affected by inflation only through production[1] (and use) and the same is of course true of consumable income. A reasonably good impression of the real national gain or loss arising from the depreciation of the currency may therefore be obtained from a study of business activity and production in the years when inconvertible paper money held sway.

I. BUSINESS ACTIVITY

§ COMPANY FORMATIONS, BUSINESS FAILURES, EMPLOYMENT

That business in Germany was booming during most of the inflation period is a universally admitted fact. This was especially true of the year 1922 when business activity was declared to be more lively than had ever before been experienced. Evidence of the "boom" may be drawn from statistics on company formations, on business failures, and on employment.

The rate of formation of new business units is reflected in the figures on new incorporations. The number of joint-stock and limited-liability companies at the end of 1913, 1919, 1922, and 1923 is shown in Table XXIV.

This table somewhat exaggerates the degree of activity, inasmuch as many private undertakings were being converted into joint-stock or limited-liability companies, but it leaves no doubt of the general eagerness to engage in business.

Conversely, bankruptcies were greatly reduced through the depreciation of the currency. Indeed, as the rate of depreciation became accelerated, it was next to impossible for a business concern to fail. Obligations in marks tended constantly to diminish and, in addition, it was ultimately so hard to obtain credit that there was no basis for bankruptcy left. Figures on business failures are shown in Table XXV, below.

Perhaps the best index of business activity, however, is furnished by the state of employment. Partly as a result of other causes and partly as a result of inflation, there had been large accessions to the working classes, accessions which much more than balance, in numbers at any

---

[1] It is true that the ownership of this wealth might change from German to foreign hands owing to the pressure on its original possessors arising from the consequences of a depreciating currency. Such changes in ownership have been treated in Chapter XI.

TABLE XXIV

NUMBER OF GERMAN JOINT-STOCK AND LIMITED-LIABILITY COMPANIES IN 1913, 1919, 1922, AND 1923

INDUSTRY	STATUS END OF 1913		STATUS END OF 1919[2]		STATUS END OF 1922[3]		STATUS END OF OCT. 1923[4]	
	NUMBER OF		NUMBER OF		NUMBER OF		NUMBER OF	
	JOINT STOCK COM-PANIES	LIMITED LIABILITY COM-PANIES	JOINT STOCK COM-PANIES	LIMITED LIABILITY COM-PANIES	JOINT STOCK COM-PANIES	LIMITED LIABILITY COM-PANIES	JOINT STOCK COM-PANIES	LIMITED LIABILITY COM-PANIES
Agriculture and forestry	4	115	2	185	18	325	36	401
Stock-breeding and fishing	21	59	25	73	32	113	40	119
Mining and smelting	223	475	216	661	288	951	369	1,031
Mining and smelting, mixed undertakings	38	3	40	14	50	20	57	23
Mineral industry (stones and earths)	366	2,050	332	2,078	545	2,880	737	3,310
Metal working	172	1,105	163	1,273	402	2,505	670	3,123
Machinery, instruments, and apparatus	618	2,834	684	3,587	1,306	6,429	1,952	7,641
Chemical industry	172	932	164	1,282	327	2,042	557	2,371
Industry of oils, fats, etc.	157	419	158	563	239	937	355	1,081
Textile industry	382	642	333	700	581	1,324	842	1,773
Paper industry	107	374	103	403	164	601	264	702
Leather and rubber industry	66	269	71	335	155	587	237	768
Wood and carvable materials	67	769	63	974	273	1,943	542	2,576
Foodstuffs, etc.	951	2,082	842	2,319	1,109	3,282	1,549	3,811
Clothing industry	20	288	27	309	162	893	355	1,337
Cleaning industry	5	97	2	90	4	116	9	132
Building trade	72	1,038	52	1,038	152	1,718	267	2,035
Printing, photographic, and allied trades	127	1,068	130	1,920	271	3,123	407	3,554
Commercial trading	835	9,409	872	11,420	2,084	23,850	4,145	30,874
Insurance	143	25	161	57	293	199	462	260
Traffic, transport, and communication	500	825	460	958	518	1,647	605	1,982
Hotels, restaurants, etc.	68	719	55	650	91	818	110	907
Musical, theatrical, and similar undertakings	61	331	50	370	57	526	71	594
Other companies	311	862	340	1,411	369	2,105	397	2,336
Total	5,486	26,790	5,345	33,670	9,490	58,934	15,035	72,741

[2] Figures for 1919 do not include the then ceded territories but do include Upper Silesia.

[3] The ceded parts of Upper Silesia are excluded.

[4] From January to October, 1923, increases only have been included.

TABLE XXV

NUMBER OF BANKRUPTCIES IN GERMANY

(*Monthly average*, 1913, 1919–1923; *number per month January* 1922–*December* 1923)

YEAR	MONTHLY AVERAGE NUMBER OF BANKRUPTCIES	MONTH OF 1922	NUMBER OF BANKRUPTCIES	MONTH OF 1923	NUMBER OF BANKRUPTCIES
1913	815	Jan.	140	Jan.	24
1919	83	Feb.	123	Feb.	17
1920	109	Mar.	151	Mar.	30
1921	257	April	107	April	45
1922	84	May	95	May	32
1923	22	June	91	June	35
		July	81	July	18
		Aug.	59	Aug.	13
		Sept.	45	Sept.	9
		Oct.	43	Oct.	15
		Nov.	34	Nov.	8
		Dec.	39	Dec.	17

Source of data: *Monthly Bulletin of Statistics*, 1923, 1924, League of Nations Publications, Geneva, 1923, 1924, *passim*.

rate, the loss of workers through war casualties.[5] But from the beginning of rapid depreciation of the mark in mid-1921 practically up to the time of the Ruhr invasion there was a progressive absorption of the unemployed till, in the autumn of 1922, there were only some 10,000 to 15,000 persons in the whole Reich in receipt of out-of-work relief. The figures of those in receipt of relief are not to be taken as accurately stating the absolute number of individuals out of work, but they are, nevertheless, a reliable index of the general movement of employment. The situation was better than it had ever been since the beginning of industrialization. Unemployment increased somewhat in the final months of 1922 and very greatly in early 1923 following the dislocation of industry consequent upon the occupation of the Ruhr. But within a few months the effects of even such a shock as this were largely dissipated by the persistent inflationary winds and unemployment, in the unoccupied area, again diminished from April to August 1923. Any

[5] It is estimated, somewhat loosely perhaps, that the number of persons in earning occupations in 1922 was three millions higher than would have been the case had there been no war and no inflation. *cf. Mythology of Reparations*, Robert Crozier Long, London, Duckworth, 1928, p. 108. The estimate is not Long's own but he does not give his source. Furthermore, as a result of the marked decline in the birth rate in the war years the average age of the population had risen and the number of workers per thousand of the total population had increased by a substantial amount.

tendency inflation may ultimately have had in curtailing business activity would seem therefore to have been postponed to within two or three months of currency stabilization. Figures on unemployment, by quarters, are given in Table XXVI.

TABLE XXVI

PERCENTAGE OF TRADE UNION WORKERS UNEMPLOYED; 1913, 1920–1923

END OF	1913[6]	1920	1921	1922	1923
First Quarter	2.3	1.9	3.7	1.1	5.6
Second Quarter	2.7	4.0	3.0	0.6	4.1
Third Quarter	2.7	4.5	1.4	0.8	9.9
Fourth Quarter	4.8	4.1	1.6	2.8	28.2

[6] 1913 was itself a year of great activity in which new high records were set in many branches of German industry.

Source of data: *Vierteljahrshefte zur Statistik des deutschen Reichs, passim.*

In a less tangible but equally convincing way the activity of business during the inflation years is attested by the practically unveiled opposition of the most influential business men of the time, Hugo Stinnes in particular, to proposals for currency reform. The business men were not, it is true, *perfectly* satisfied with the existing situation. But they were fairly content and insisted only upon the necessity of longer hours and more intense effort (*for their workers*) and not at all upon the need for monetary stabilization. The urge toward spending the depreciating money which affected the whole population made sales delightfully easy, and lagging costs made profits high. Why should so pleasant a status be disturbed?

The facts on new incorporations, bankruptcies, employment, and the attitude of business men place beyond doubt the assertion that business activity was intense during most of the inflationary period. The real question is, was it productive?

II. PRODUCTION

§ FAVORABLE AND UNFAVORABLE FACTORS

So much has been written about the "apparent" prosperity of boom periods in general, and of inflationary booms in particular, and the business world is so impressed with the inevitability of depression in sequence to industrial activity, that the benefits of so-called booms, which may simply mean capacity production, are persistently minimized. A high degree of industrial activity may even become a subject of dread. The prosperity of such a period is, however, by no means merely apparent. German factory chimneys were not smoking because their owners liked to burn coal. The factories were producing goods, and production means real income however that income may be shared. It is true that product, as distinct from activity, was impaired by some causes with which inflation had nothing to do, and by some for which it was responsible, but this impairment has ordinarily been exaggerated. Furthermore, it was in part compensated by forces acting in the other direction. The several forces acting on one side or the other are noted in the succeeding paragraphs.

The factors tending to increase the total output of German industry in the post-war inflation period were:

(1) All but complete abolition of the standing army and of the navy.

(2) Employment of women in industry on a large scale. Such employment was perhaps less widespread than in the war-period but much more so than in the period prior to 1914.

(3) Elimination of the idle rich through loss of the value of fixed-interest incomes and the forced "descent" of this group into the ranks of workers.

(4) Decline in unemployment.

All of these factors operated to enhance aggregate production, through an increase in the number of workers engaged in earning occupations, but only the last three were in any measure due to inflation.

On the other hand, the productivity *per worker*, and therefore of the economy as a whole, tended to be reduced by:

(1) Losses of real (as distinguished from monetary) capital during and immediately after the war. This was especially marked in agriculture, where the soil and animal equipment had been exhausted, and in transportation, but it was also true of manufacturing industry.

(2) The decline in the vitality of the population as a result of the privations of war, particularly underfeeding.

(3) The "dilution" of the working population by the admission of unskilled or otherwise incapable workers. Complaints are numerous in the economic literature of the time that the *tempo* of industry was being greatly retarded by the forced employment of war wounded, the lack of properly trained workers, and the admission of those with no training at all.[7]

(4) The increase of parasitic occupations, largely speculative in character. This phenomenon may best be noted in the excessive aug-

[7] The loss of capable workers killed or completely incapacitated in the war also gravely affected the average efficiency of the working class as compared with pre-war standards.

mentation in the number of business concerns and in the growth of trading as contrasted with industrial activities.[8]

(5) The rising ratio of ancillary to primarily productive workers. This was particularly prominent in governmental activity. Between 1918 and 1923 the list of Reich officials increased by 242%, that of the States by 61%, and of the municipalities by 27%.[9] At the latter date the total of governmental employees (which includes railroad workers) was about 4½ million out of perhaps 30 million earners in the whole country. As inflation proceeded clerical forces were perforce greatly augmented, especially in banking and similar occupations. But the number of clerical workers in industrial life, though absolutely much increased, still remained a relatively small fraction of the whole.

Of these factors tending to diminish productivity, inflation played some part in the last three[10] and the primary rôle in the last two.

It is impossible to gauge exactly the net effect of all these forces on the aggregate output of German industry or clearly to distinguish the influence of inflation. But it is probable that the total number of formerly voluntarily unemployed persons forced to work by the vicissitudes of the time was at least as great as the increase in the number of individuals unproductively engaged, and this, together with the larger productivity resulting from the practical elimination of unemployment (except at the very end of the period studied), should be set to the credit of inflation so far as its effect on the national income is concerned.

Total and per capita productivity in physical terms may be measured for the inflation period with as much accuracy, perhaps, as is ever present in such calculations. But to distinguish, with any precision, between such evil effects of the war as would have been present under any monetary system whatever and those which may have been due to an unstable currency is extremely difficult. A still more serious confusion arises from the occupation of the Ruhr. It will later appear that the German output in the year 1923 suffered an extraordinary decline. Part of this was certainly due to the paralyzing effect of the invasion, not only upon the industries in the Ruhr but upon all German economic life. The Ruhr is the heart of the German industrial system and the whole system felt acute distress when the action of the heart was crippled. Raw materials for the rest of German industry were suddenly cut off and a

[8] See *supra*, Table XXIV.

[9] *Economic Review*, Vol. VIII, No. 16, London, October 19, 1923, quoting *Deutsche Allgemeine Zeitung*.

[10] A marked feature of the inflation was the reduction of the difference between the wages of skilled and unskilled workers. The consequent lack of stimulus toward the acquisition of technical skill had its natural effect in diminishing the supply of well trained employees.

reduction in activity was inevitable. But whether the invasion was directly responsible for all, or even the greater part, of the decline is a question to which no assured answer can be given. Until late 1922 currency depreciation had been more or less orderly, and the pace, while rapid, had not been beyond possibility of prevision. The change in its character in the fall of 1922 may have turned it from a capricious but, in some respects, benign influence into a ravening and purely destructive force. Even a tentative judgment on the respective influences of the invasion and of the collapse of the currency must be reserved until the figures for production have been examined.

§ MEASURES OF PRODUCTION

Productivity may be measured forthright or by indirection. In the immediately succeeding sections direct estimates of production will be set forth. Following this, the volume of transport, as an index of general production, will be presented. Since production and total consumption (including in the latter term the net additions to, and replacement of, capital goods) are practically equal, figures on direct consumption and on the output (and consumption) of capital goods will then be offered. Finally, the aggregate real income of the German laboring population will be examined. All the direct and indirect indices of production will then be drawn upon to furnish a composite picture of the output of German economy. The effects of inflation will be developed through a running comparison with the presumptive output under a stable monetary standard.

1. DIRECT ESTIMATES OF PRODUCTION

§ GENERAL INDICES

Indices of the physical volume of agricultural and industrial production have been calculated for Germany, and six other countries, by M. Jean Dessirier and have been published in the *Bulletin de la Statistique Générale de la France*.[11] The year taken as a base was 1913 and the figures were weighted, for the agricultural index, according to the relative values of the several crops, and for the industrial index, according to the relative number of workers engaged in the several industries in each of the countries in the base year. M. Dessirier gives two sets of figures, the one covering the actual production and the other adjusted to meet changes in population.[12] The latter only will be reproduced at

[11] Vol. XVIII, section 1, October-December 1928, pp. 65-110. A uniform method of calculation and analogous indices already published by official agencies were used as far as possible.

[12] Changes in population *issuing out of transfers of territory* are also taken into consideration in the former of the two sets of figures.

this point as it is alone significant for the purpose in hand. This index shows production on the basis of a constant population or, alternatively, production per capita of the total population. Post-war figures take into account territorial changes. For purposes of convenient comparison, only the data for Germany, France, England, Belgium, Italy, West Europe, and the United States[13] are here given, and these merely for the years 1920-1927. This period covers the inflation years in Germany and the four years following stabilization of the currency. A judgment on the effects of inflation in the sphere of domestic production is afforded through the contrast between Germany and those countries where currency depreciation was mild or non-existent in the years under review.

§ THE INDEX OF AGRICULTURAL OUTPUT

The figures on agricultural production are given in Table XXVII.

TABLE XXVII

INDEX OF PHYSICAL VOLUME OF PRODUCTION OF AGRICULTURAL PRODUCTS; 1920–1927

(*Per capita of the total population.* 1913 = 100)[14]

YEAR	GERMANY	FRANCE	ENGLAND	BELGIUM	ITALY	WEST EUROPE	UNITED STATES
1920	62	83	89	78	73	73	112
1921	63	81	84	81	78	74	91
1922	69	92	91	91	72	77	100
1923	69	89	88	90	97	86	98
1924	71	104	92	89	85	86	95
1925	81	101	97	93	99	94	97
1926	67	79	91	91	94	80	98
1927	77	102	91	87	81	86	92

[14] *Bulletin de la Statistique Générale de la France, loc. cit.* The crops used for Germany were wheat, rye, barley, oats, potatoes, wine, hops, tobacco, hay. Figures from *Statistisches Jahrbuch.* For 1927 the index is calculated from the provisional results published by the International Institute of Agriculture at Rome.

So far as trust is to be reposed in the figures[15] the table shows that German agriculture has yielded persistently lower returns relative to the

[13] Russia is omitted owing to the extreme economic disturbances in that country, quite apart from those attributable to inflation. West Europe includes Germany, France, Belgium, and Italy. Figures for West Europe are weighted according to the population of the different countries included in the index.

[15] There was some concealment by German farmers of their yields for the purpose of avoiding their full obligation on the required delivery of part of their crop at fixed (low) prices. The consequent understatement of yields in the official statistics has been alleged (not very responsibly) to have amounted to as much as 20%. This is improbable, but it might well have been as great as 10%.

situation in 1913 than that of any other of the countries for which statistics are here presented. But this is clearly due to the effects of the war rather than to those of inflation. Except for the bad season of 1926 (due to weather conditions and reflected in the statistics of all the European countries), improvement in Germany since 1919 has been steady and was about as great throughout the inflation years as during the years of stabilization. The fact is that the German soil, which is in general of rather poor quality and requires constant fertilization if yields are to be maintained, deteriorated to a greater degree during the war than did that of any other of the countries engaged. The neglect which it suffered was inevitable. The pressure for food supplies led to as intensive cultivation as was in the circumstances possible while no adequate replenishment of the soil elements was made owing, in part, to the fact that some important fertilizers were simply not then to be had on any terms. The restoration to pre-war productivity is a matter of many years. Agriculture was further ineffective in the early post-war years because of a shortage of draught animals and the sequestration of farm equipment by the victors. The low status of the German per capita production since 1920, relative to that of 1913, may also be due in some measure to superior productivity in the separated territories as compared with the average of the lands within the present confines of the Reich, and to influx of population from the separated territories.

So far as inflation of the currency is concerned, there is every reason to believe that it stimulated rather than depressed agricultural yields. The wiping out of the burden of mortgages which attended the decline in the value of the mark was a boon to the farmer and the price structure during the period of monetary depreciation was not unfavorable to him. The throes of currency collapse in late 1923, which affected industrial production considerably, took place within too short a period to have any influence on agricultural output. The crops had already been planted and their yield was independent of the movement of prices. The farmers, moreover, were in a strategic position both then and in earlier years. Producing, for the most part, the most essential products, consumption of which could not be interrupted except at the cost of life itself, they were able to provide for their own needs and to protect themselves against exploitation even in the face of semi-confiscatory governmental action. The great difficulties of the German farmer began only after the mark had been stabilized and they had nothing to do with money, *qua* money. In the agricultural branch of production the national economy suffered no losses which can be laid at the door of abuse of the currency.

§ THE INDEX OF INDUSTRIAL OUTPUT

Turning now to industrial production, the situation was as appears in Table XXVIII.

TABLE XXVIII

INDEX OF PHYSICAL VOLUME OF INDUSTRIAL PRODUCTION: 1920-1927[16]

(Per capita of the total population. 1913 = 100)

YEAR	GERMANY[17]	FRANCE	ENGLAND	BELGIUM	ITALY	WEST EUROPE	UNITED STATES
1920	61	66	88	91	74	68	114
1921	77	58	61	55	66	68	86
1922	86	83	76	73	76	82	112
1923	54	93	80	84	85	72	131
1924	77	114	84	93	96	90	120
1925	90	112	81	84	120	101	130
1926	86	127	63[18]	110	116	104	134
1927	111	111	86	111	104	109	130

[16] *Bulletin de la Statistique Générale de la France, loc. cit.*

[17] The index here given is checked by reference to the post-inflation indices of the Institut für Konjunkturforschung and of the Reparations Commission, both of which are computed by methods quite different from that here used but nevertheless give like results.

[18] The decline in the English index in this year was mainly due to the coal strike.

This index, for most countries, is perhaps not as authentic as is that of agricultural output. In the case of Germany it is composed of the separate indices for mining (coal, lignite, iron ore, potash), metallurgy (pig iron and steel), mechanical industries (according to the consumption of steel), textile industries (according to the consumption of cotton and of wool), and building (for 1926 and 1927 only). This is a fair selection of basic industries but is not comprehensive enough to give assurance of its precision as a criterion of total industrial output. There is, however, no reason to doubt its representative character, and whether or not it gives a true picture of total industrial activity in the several countries relative to the 1913 situation in each, or relative to one another at any given date, it should reflect with some accuracy the changes from year to year. It more probably does so by reason of the shortness of the period covered since, in the eight years of its duration, no very sweeping alteration in the production and use of the index materials in their relation to total industrial activity did, in fact, take place.

§ CONTRAST BETWEEN THE SITUATION IN GERMANY IN 1921 AND 1922
AND IN THE OUTSIDE WORLD

The most striking feature of Table XXVIII is the contrast between the movement of the German index in the inflation years and those of all the other countries at the same time. In every other listed country production fell off very materially in 1921[19] and in most cases had not fully recovered by the end of 1922. Germany not only did not share in the general slump in 1921 but raised its production by 23% in that year and by an additional 12% in 1922. Since Germany, and one or two other countries with depreciating currencies,[20] were alone unaffected adversely by the deflation crisis which ran round the world after the collapse of gold prices in mid-1920, the presumption is certainly in favor of conceding to depreciation the credit for the sustention and increase of industrial activity in the Reich at this period. There is no reason to believe that, had the German price movement paralleled the downward trend in other countries, production in Germany would not have been subject to the decline which took place in the outside world. In all the other countries for which statistics are above given the fall in prices, regardless of the nature of their currency, was sharp. In Germany prices fell slightly in the latter part of 1920 and in the spring of 1921 but, by May of the latter year, the upward movement of prices was resumed and industrial activity rose coincidently. Not only was production stimulated by increasing domestic demand (measured in monetary terms) but the low exchange value of the mark relative to its internal purchasing power gave Germany a large share of such international business as was to be obtained. That it was the fall in the value of the mark which enabled Germany to escape the depression which at this time afflicted practically the whole outside world is further evidenced by the facts that in France and Italy, where post-war deflation was moderate, the decline in 1921 production was slight (12% and 11% respectively) as compared with that in countries like England and the United States (31% and 25% respectively) where deflation was severe, and that, in 1922, coincidently with a renewed rise in prices in the former countries, production advanced beyond the 1920 level, whereas, in England and the United States, where deflation had been as definitive as it was severe, production still remained below the 1920 standard.[21] Further than this, the index for 1926 production in France, the highest up to that time ever attained in that country, applies to the year of greatest depreciation of the currency, and the same is true of Italy in 1925 and 1926.

[19] The maintenance of the same figure for West Europe in 1921 as in 1920 is due solely to the increase in Germany's production which was sufficient to balance the decline in the three other countries (France, Italy, and Belgium).

[20] Poland, for instance.

[21] For *Belgium* there are no satisfactory general price level statistics prior to August 1921 so that the 1921 fall in prices cannot be precisely determined. Belgium has therefore, of necessity been omitted from the comparison.

§ STABILIZATION CRISES IN GERMANY

Germany suffered from business depression in 1924,[22] after currency stabilization had been effected, but this was slight as compared with that which occurred in England and the United States in 1921, or even with that in France and Italy. The latter countries went through the experience twice, once in 1921, when a measure of deflation occurred, and again in 1927, after their currencies had been put on a *de facto* gold basis.[23] It would thus seem that Germany accomplished the actual process of transition from the war to a stable post-war monetary structure at a lower real cost in actual production than did any of the other countries here considered. The reason for this is doubtless that there was at no time in Germany any substantial *deflation* and no expectation of continuously falling prices. It is the prospective appreciation of a *continuing* unit of account which is most crippling to business. The transition to the stable-value rentenmark in Germany was a shift to an entirely new monetary unit and, far from involving any fall in prices in the old paper mark, was accompanied by a rapid increase in such prices. Paper marks continued to circulate for more than a year alongside of the rentenmark and were for a considerable time the principal of the two media of exchange, though they were no longer the unit of account. After November 20, 1923, they were exchangeable into the new currency at a trillion to one but between the fourteenth of November, the day before the introduction of the rentenmark, and the twentieth, only six days later, when the official rate of conversion was established, the exchange value of the old mark against the new currency fell from 300 billion to one trillion. From the twelfth to the fourteenth of November it had already fallen from 150 to 300 billion. In the final week of a free value for the old paper mark, during the period when the new currency was in process of introduction, the old unit thus lost five-sixths of the very exiguous value it had possessed at the beginning of the week in question. The transition to the stable standard therefore involved an immense access of inflation rather than, as in some countries,

[22] Relative, that is, to 1922. The year 1923 for Germany forms no proper basis of comparison in the determination of the effects of stable and unstable money since production in that year was gravely affected by non-monetary causes.

[23] It is, of course, impossible accurately to impute the degree of depression due to falling prices as distinct from other causes. Under perfectly stable monetary conditions business cycles would perhaps recur much as they now do and price changes may be effects rather than causes of cycles. We do not know what production would have been if monetary conditions had been other than they were. Comparison with other countries where monetary conditions were different affords some, but by no means an infallible, criterion,

a severe lowering of prices. Business contracts made only a week before
stabilization (or even within that week), which called for the payment
at any later date of a fixed amount of paper marks, could be fulfilled
at a very low real cost.[24] There were, in consequence, no such difficulties
to business men (who are predominantly debtors) as are inherent in the
appreciation of a monetary standard which continues to be legal tender
and in which all accounts are expressed.[25] After November 20, 1923,
German business had to get along without any inflation stimulant but it
was not subjected to the burden of contracts payable in a more valuable
money than that current at the time the contracts were made. There
were difficulties in adjustment to the new monetary standard but they
were not exacerbated by those twin evils of deflation, the increase in the
weight of debts, and the difficulty of adjusting comparatively fixed
costs to steadily declining prices.

The difficulties actually incurred appeared in two separate depressions.
The first ran from the introduction of the rentenmark, November 15,
1923, to March 1924, a period of uncertainty, doubt, and hesitation due
to the shift to an entirely new monetary unit, to apprehension as to the
permanent nature of the currency reform, and to the rigid control of
credit necessary to ensure its success.[26] This depression, though sharp,
was short; the immediate transition was achieved at a relatively slight
cost in national productivity. A second, more lasting, depression broke
forth at the end of 1925 and carried through most of 1926. Whether or
not this depression is to be regarded as a phase of the process of currency
stabilization, or merely as one of the downs in the vicissitudes of business under any monetary standard, is an open question. The 1926 depression was apparently due to credit difficulties and these in turn were

[24] The bulk of contracts made at this time were actually drawn, of course, in
stable-value terms. But, even so, business men were subject to no disability; they
simply failed to receive undue gains.

[25] Gold prices in Germany fell by something over 10% in 1924 but the limits on
the decline were always clearly discernible.

[26] In practically all cases of transition from a situation in which the currency
is rapidly falling in value to one in which it is stable or appreciating, the rate
of monetary turnover is greatly retarded. Unless large new additions to the
volume of circulating medium are made there will develop a shortage of
"liquid capital," that is, money, and prices will tend to fall. But caution in
issue is necessary if a renewal of depreciation is to be prevented, and this is as
true of credit as of money. Confidence must be restored at whatever cost, but
confidence develops but slowly. The circulation in Germany was greatly expanded after stabilization had been effected. The process was somewhat too
greatly accelerated at first and success was ultimately achieved only after the
relative excess of circulating medium had been reduced through a sharp restriction of bank credit.

occasioned by the failure of domestic saving to recuperate other than haltingly from the terrific shock to which it had been subjected in the inflation years. One is perhaps justified, therefore, in attributing this second depression to the aftermath of currency depreciation.

§ BALANCE OF GAINS AND LOSSES IN DOMESTIC PRODUCTION

Disregarding for the time being the year 1923, which was dominated by the dislocation of industry attendant upon the events in the Ruhr as well as by the phenomena of extreme inflation, and going back to 1922, a year of high industrial activity, for a criterion of what the Germany of 1924 might have been expected to accomplish if it had not been in the throes of the birth of the new monetary system, we find that actual industrial production in 1924 was about 10% below par. This loss may properly be traced and assigned to the abuse of the currency in the previous years. Similarly, taking 1925, a good year, as a criterion of what might have been expected in 1926 if the German economy had not been plagued by the legacies of inflation, industrial production may be computed to have been adversely affected in the latter year by from 4% to 5%.[27] Both of these estimates may seem somewhat small in view of the general upward trend in production which makes one year's output too low a standard for the next. But since industry was still depressed in 1924 by non-monetary evils attendant on the Ruhr occupation, and since the depression in 1926 is probably not, *in full measure*, attributable to the prior abuse of the currency, the percentages given would seem not to understate the degree of industrial slump really due to adjustment to a stable currency and so to be attributed to the monetary disturbances to which that adjustment was an inevitable sequel.

These losses are small compared with the gains assignable to inflation in the upward swing of German production in 1921 and 1922. It has already been pointed out that the war left the productive equipment of Germany in a condition probably worse than that of any other country engaged[28] and that the situation was aggravated by the delivery, in accordance with the armistice agreement, of a large amount of the best railroad rolling stock, of machines, stationary engines, tools and imple-

[27] There is no evidence that agricultural yields in 1924 or 1926 were adversely affected by monetary phenomena.

[28] The authors of *Germany's Capacity to Pay*, quoting M. Tardieu, set the losses due to depreciation of plant and equipment at 43 billion gold marks. The total wealth of all kinds in Germany in 1913 has been estimated to have been approximately 300 billion gold marks but this includes land at 70 billion and foreign investments at 20 billion. See *Deutschlands Volkswohlstand* 1888-1913, Karl Helfferich, Verlag von George Stilke, Berlin, 1914, p. 113.

ments of all sorts. On the human side the loss in man power in the war and the decline in efficiency arising from a long period of under-nourishment of the civilian population was equally great. The relatively low index of production in 1920, 61 on a base of 100 in 1913, was clearly due to these factors rather than to such depreciation of the currency as occurred in that year. Production was bound to be low what-ever the monetary situation might be. There is no reason, indeed, to believe that inflation was not as effective in speeding up production in 1920 as it seems to have been in 1921 and 1922. Whether or not this is so, the impact of inflation on German domestic production, aside from 1923, seems, on the basis of the statistics so far examined, to have been beneficial rather than the reverse. So far as 1923 is concerned the falling off in German output was unquestionably due in large measure to the occupation of the Ruhr. It is quite possible that, though the pro-duction of the Ruhr district and of unoccupied Germany would have declined in any case, it fell farther because of the uncertainties attendant upon chaotic currency conditions, but it is arguable, on the other hand, that manipulation of the currency was the only thing which kept the Ruhr industries going at all.[29] Evidence later adduced will go to show that, even in 1923, inflation was not a retarding influence except for a very short period.

The conclusions expressed in the preceding paragraphs are tentative only. Formed on the basis of an index of general productivity which is subject to a wide margin of error they should be checked by reference to alternative indices. To some such indices attention will now be directed.

§ PRODUCTION OF BASIC MATERIALS

In the general index of industrial production the output of coal, iron ore, pig iron, and steel plays an important part. A substantial measure of correlation between the figures for these basic materials and the general index is, therefore, to be expected. Since however the statistics in the mining and metallurgical industries are more accurate than for other branches of production it may be worth while to present them separately. Table XXIX gives the output, and index numbers of produc-tion, of these four materials in the inflation and in the two post-inflation years, and contrasts it with the average of the five pre-war years. The index of general industrial production has been added for comparative purposes.

[29] The enormous paper mark credits granted by the government to the Ruhr industrialists would have been practically impossible under stable monetary conditions.

TABLE XXIX

PRODUCTION OF COAL AND LIGNITE, IRON ORE, PIG IRON AND FERRO-ALLOYS, AND
STEEL IN GERMANY;[30] AVERAGE OF 1909–1913, ANNUALLY 1920–1925
(*Absolute figures in thousands of metric tons*)

| | | | | | INDEX NUMBERS | | | | |
YEAR	COAL AND LIGNITE[31]	IRON ORE	PIG IRON AND FERRO-ALLOYS	STEEL	COAL AND LIG- NITE	IRON ORE	PIG IRON AND FERRO- ALLOYS	STEEL	GENERAL INDUSTRIAL PRODUCTION 1913 = 100
1909–1913	137,735	6,418	9,240	12,236[32]	100	100	100	100	100[32]
1920	156,218[33]	6,299	6,016	7,798	113	98	65	64	62
1921	163,547[33]	5,824	7,462	9,265	119	91	81	76	78
1922	160,423[33]	5,928	9,190	11,314	116	92	99	92	89
1923	88,500	5,188	4,936	6,305	64	81	53	52	56
1924	146,459	4,457	7,812	9,835	106	69	85	80	80
1925	163,790	5,923	10,177	12,194	119	92	110	100	94

[30] Post-war territories; Saar not included.

[31] Lignite is expressed in terms of coal according to thermal efficiency (9 units of lignite = 2 of coal).

[32] 1913 only; 1909-1913 average not available. 1913 was an exceptionally good year. Index of general production is the Dessirier unweighted index.

[33] The relatively large output of coal was called forth by the deliveries on reparation account.

Source of data: *Documents of the International Economic Conference*, League of Nations Publications, C.E.I. 17, Geneva, 1927.

It will be noted that from the end of the war to 1923 there was a fairly steady all round increase (except in the case of iron ore where the output remained substantially stable), and that, in all cases, 1922 production compares well with that of the pre-bellum production. The 1923 output of these materials was affected by the invasion of the Ruhr far more adversely than German production in general, seriously as the whole German economy was hit by that event. The occupied districts produce approximately 85% of the German pit coal and 75% of the total output of coal and lignite, between 75% and 80% of the production of pig iron, and about 85% of that of raw steel. The decline in the Reich production of these basic materials in 1923 is therefore almost solely attributable to the occupation. Inflation played a minor, if any, rôle in the matter.

§ PER CAPITA PRODUCTIVITY IN SPECIFIC INDUSTRIES

So far, the figures given have been of output in general or of output in those branches of production which may be regarded as typical of industry as a whole. Other types of industry for which comparable figures are available do not in themselves provide good indices of general productivity since they may be advancing or declining relative to total production. Thus, while statistics for cotton, artificial silk, and other similar products are available, they will not here be introduced. The cotton industry, since the war, has almost everywhere shown a tendency toward stagnation in districts where it has been long established. The artificial silk industry, on the other hand, is growing much more rapidly than production as a whole. But, though total production in any branch of industry which does not produce the raw material for a wide variety of manufactures is, when taken alone, of no value as an index of production in general, something can be learned from the output per worker per hour. The only data of this sort, relative to manufactured goods, that have come to light are provided in scattered investigations made by the *Frankfurter Zeitung.* The results are too fragmentary to furnish a reliable index of output of finished goods but, with relatively few exceptions, they show an upward trend in per capita per hour output in a variety of industries and a performance, in the later inflation years (figures for 1923 not available), considerably better than in the pre-war period.[84] Hours of labor were reduced in many industries in the post-war period and this tended, on the whole, to lower total production, a fact which should be kept in mind when comparing 1913 figures of other than hourly output with those of the period 1920-1923. The general impression obtained from a study of the *Frankfurter Zeitung's* figures on finished goods industries is that, in these lines, production was at a higher level relative to the pre-war period than was the case in the basic industries and that it advanced more rapidly during the régime of inflated currency.

Thus, though the index of general production is largely made up from total output in the basic industries and does not show production *per worker*[85] and, though the number of workers engaged in some of the basic industries rose relatively to production,[86] it would seem fair to assume that the increase in man-hour output in the finishing industries counteracted any tendency toward lower performance in the raw material group, and that total production per head continued, without doubt, to rise till

[84] cf. *Die Wirtschaftskurve* (the quarterly statistical publication of the *Frankfurter Zeitung*), Frankfurter Societäts-Druckerei G.m.b.H., Frankfurt-am-Main, *passim.*

[85] It merely shows production per head of the total population.

[86] This is shown both directly and by statistics on output per man-hour. The

1923. The bulk of the basic products produced were consumed at home.[37] Total production must therefore have moved in some correspondence with the output of industrial raw materials. If, in the raw material industries in any year, the number of workers engaged was larger relatively to total output (1913 being taken as a standard) than the ratio between the production of raw materials in the year in question and the production in 1913, the finishing industries must have been as much above the average current man-hour productivity as the raw material industries were below it.

2. INDIRECT ESTIMATES OF PRODUCTION. TRANSPORT

§ FREIGHT TONNAGE AS AN INDEX OF PRODUCTION

Perhaps the best indirect criterion of productivity is furnished by an index of the physical volume of freight transported. The chief defect in an index of this sort is the fact that an alteration in the relative tonnage of a few commodities of small value per unit of weight, such as coal, iron ore, stone, clays and the like, may make a difference in the

following figures of production in the Dortmund mines are probably typical of coal mining in general:

DORTMUND MINES. INDEX OF OUTPUT PER MAN-HOUR

Date	1919	1920	1921	1922
Jan.	89.2	91.8	82.4	85.5
Feb.	88.1	94.0	84.2	86.6
Mar.	90.2	84.4	84.0	87.5
April	76.6	83.6	85.3	86.8
May	91.7	85.8	86.1	85.8
June	94.7	86.1	87.1	86.8
July	96.4	83.6	85.4	85.8
Aug.	95.9	82.9	85.1	85.8
Sept.	94.6	82.9	85.1	84.1
Oct.	94.1	82.2	84.7	83.6
Nov.	99.5	82.9	84.4	83.0
Dec.	89.7	82.7	84.8	—

Hours worked were 8½ in 1913, 8 for the first three months of 1919, 7½ in April 1919, and 7 thereafter, so that the output per shift and per year, for a given number of workers, was considerably less than these figures would indicate. *Enquête sur la production*, Bureau International du Travail, Rapport Général, Vol. II, Berger-Levrault, Paris, 1923.

[37] Take for example, steel. The figures for 1913 and 1922, in million tons, are:

YEAR	PRODUC-TION	IMPORT	EXPORT	DOMESTIC CONSUMPTION
1913 (Pre-war territory)	18.9	0.24	5.3	13.84
1922 (Post-war territory)	11.7	1.80	1.7	11.8

index quite disproportionate to the real significance of the change so far as total value productivity is concerned. The transfer from Germany to France and to Poland of territory where heavy industry was prominent led to a great diminution in the weight of freight carried in Germany. The difficulty here involved is in part obviated by taking for the base year, 1913, only the present German territory. But, even so, complications arise from the fact that the traffic between two former German districts which are now politically segregated, one in Germany and one outside, would not be likely to take place on the same proportionate scale after as before the separation. This being so, the composition of German freight traffic might easily change from a greater weight of less valuable goods to a lesser weight of more valuable goods without any alteration in the total value output of German industry or even of the value of transported goods. Weighting according to value, however, being impracticable in the chaotic price situation during the period under review, it seemed best to take as the index of total freight transported, and so of production, a simple average of the indices (on a 1913 base) of the volume of traffic in *each* of the separate commodities listed in the German State Railroad's freight-classification. The influence of any alteration in the volume of freight in a heavy commodity, such as coal, which might materially affect the actual weight of freight moved and so exaggerate the change in productivity, is thus minimized and is brought into reasonable conformity with the real change in the output of economic values. While the index of transportation presented in the ensuing pages is an index of weights the method of construction is therefore such that it should offer a fair criterion of the total relative value of the transported goods.

The volume of freight carried, even so computed, and its value, too, may of course have varied independently of the volume and value of production as a whole. An increase in the territorial specialization of industry, for instance, would augment the volume of transport per unit of output and, on the other hand, developments might occur which would diminish freight transport relative to production. The troubles encountered when a shortage of fuel developed in Germany,[38] for instance, were in part solved by the expansion of lignite production and the conversion of this lignite into electric power at the mines. This process considerably reduced the volume of freight transport which would have been essential to an equal production of finished goods had coal been used in the old way. Changes of this sort cannot, however, be computed with any precision, and the index of transport must be taken as

[38] This shortage was largely occasioned by reparations deliveries.

TABLE XXX

INDEX OF COMBINED RAILROAD TRAFFIC AND TRAFFIC ON INLAND WATERWAYS IN
GERMANY; 1920–1924[39]

(1913 = 100)

	1920	1921	1922	1923	1924
1.[40] Horn, claw, hide, offal, etc., and bones	49.22	58.49	77.36	51.88	63.34
2. Raw cotton, cotton waste, etc.	34.90	54.70	54.97	41.37	51.78
3. Beer	43.27	49.85	39.45	28.01	41.89
4. Lead	46.52	60.06	71.66	40.22	57.78
5. Bark, tanning woods, and other tanning materials	85.65	60.57	69.36	43.97	75.55
6. (a) Brown coal	118.05	125.78	162.27	118.58	102.38
(b) Brown coal briquettes, brown coal coke	105.20	129.54	131.92	112.21	128.56
8. and 10. Chemicals, drugs, and fertilizers	68.75	68.46	82.63	56.69	66.06
9. Roofing materials, including tar paper and roofing felt	78.34	98.78	107.33	43.49	75.86
11. (a) Crude iron of all kinds	42.41	41.47	51.14	27.40	29.22
(b) Blooms and crude blocks of iron and steel	48.53	48.90	57.11	26.55	27.81
(c) Iron and steel scrap and waste	117.27	116.65	125.87	71.96	70.78
12. Iron and steel in bars, molds, plates, sheets	65.45	72.95	73.89	42.91	70.18
13. Iron rails, rail clamps, spikes and other such materials	40.16	50.47	55.05	39.96	58.72
14. Iron railroad-ties	34.53	62.22	47.60	31.50	50.91
15. Iron axles and trusses, wheels, etc.	92.21	103.92	98.35	75.00	129.66
16. Iron boilers, reservoirs, machines, etc.	93.19	83.89	95.09	61.15	66.10
17. Iron tubes and props	43.36	49.75	60.56	28.87	59.92
18. Iron and steel wire	59.81	59.80	80.95	44.05	67.42
19. (a) Iron and steel wares not otherwise specified	80.49	76.27	86.35	58.12	65.66
(b) Other metallic goods	83.44	75.36	132.22	65.57	85.15
20. Iron ore, exclusive of sulphur pyrites	41.66	34.11	51.86	26.19	42.57
22. Ores of lead, cobalt, nickel, zinc, copper, etc.	52.74	50.59	73.92	32.53	47.85
24. Fish and crustaceans	106.69	107.21	68.84	62.65	81.17
25. Flax, jute, oakum, tow	64.39	70.31	61.26	49.43	66.67
26. Meat, including bacon	321.47	180.35	130.01	152.92	167.90
27. Yarns	39.79	54.03	70.96	43.01	70.48
28. (a) Wheat	31.86	80.31	63.69	42.13	52.37
(b) Rye	54.58	67.52	83.03	113.37	81.22
(c) Oats	48.05	33.28	34.74	35.24	45.62
(d) Barley	12.90	23.95	18.01	26.63	38.49
(e) Millet, buckwheat, and legumes	153.66	92.09	48.58	42.55	51.01
(f) Corn	36.70	244.07	128.53	42.13	42.15
(g) Malt	16.25	41.66	40.86	30.96	48.56
(h) Linseed and other oil-bearing seeds	35.03	44.26	38.58	28.90	40.61
29. Glass and glass wares	61.55	60.36	79.46	50.67	61.79

TABLE XXX—(*Continued*)

INDEX OF COMBINED RAILROAD TRAFFIC AND TRAFFIC ON INLAND WATERWAYS IN
GERMANY: 1920–1924[89]

(1913 = 100)

		1920	1921	1922	1923	1924
30.	Hides, skins, leather, and furs	53.40	66.25	68.78	49.91	70.57
31.	Wood of all kinds	105.47	92.01	95.51	79.59	76.26
32.	Wood- and straw-pulp, etc.	73.10	77.23	93.30	75.10	80.08
33.	Hops	101.16	59.47	69.26	47.60	77.98
34.	Jute	31.92	62.84	81.47	70.77	92.03
35.	Coffee, cocoa, and tea	66.10	96.33	89.54	52.65	79.19
37.	Potatoes	194.87	143.43	157.66	133.93	111.83
40.	Rags	55.47	52.94	66.31	50.47	62.67
41.	Flour, mill products, bran	50.11	59.87	52.01	42.60	53.91
42.	Fruit, vegetables, plants, etc.	111.24	78.72	71.08	43.58	94.93
43.	Oils, fats, and tallow	102.44	104.33	95.04	81.63	87.36
44.	Oil-cake, cocoa-cake, etc.	22.51	32.74	32.71	22.12	29.06
45.	Paper, cardboard, and paper products	71.28	70.16	96.21	73.74	84.70
46.	Petroleum and other mineral oils	58.49	63.58	68.09	41.96	62.88
47.	Rice, flour, and rice bran	66.97	109.84	82.52	56.62	50.66
49.	Beets, sugar and feed-beets, chicory root	49.62	50.92	67.39	56.59	65.41
50.	Beet-syrup and molasses	86.36	103.87	109.09	88.25	78.93
51.	Saltpeter and acid salts	59.84	66.97	94.25	54.96	70.94
52.	Salt	166.83	98.29	165.11	98.58	109.10
54.	Sulphuric acid	61.27	68.81	60.92	36.41	47.19
55.	Soda of all kinds	60.10	61.85	85.33	60.59	73.77
56.	Brandy, spirits, and vinegar	58.48	88.29	93.19	69.25	73.81
57.	Starch, starch-sugar, etc.	39.85	42.70	48.80	40.57	47.73
60.	(a) Bituminous coal	63.31	59.88	61.94	32.46	51.12
	(b) Bituminous coal briquettes	87.30	94.98	92.80	20.65	40.70
	(c) Bituminous coal coke	89.64	95.80	89.03	32.55	40.41
61.	Raw tobacco, tobacco ribs	111.06	110.87	103.35	73.17	99.84
62.	Tar, pitch, asphalt, resin, etc.	61.96	66.84	61.28	35.75	47.61
63. and 48.	Clay, stone, and porcelain wares, clay and cement pipes and tubes	41.67	50.98	60.85	39.19	50.60
64.	Peat, peat straw, fire-wood	355.23	252.78	351.60	238.51	128.52
65.	Wine	123.97	112.79	86.85	47.35	101.53
66.	Wool	54.46	75.81	92.17	63.84	68.48
67.	Zinc, zinc-ash, and zinc scrap	55.48	58.55	48.64	36.54	47.48
68.	(a) Raw sugar	33.09	38.76	43.65	40.25	48.85
	(b) Refined sugar	46.59	61.62	58.44	53.56	71.49
7, 21, 36, 53, 58 and 59.	Cement, earth, gravel, marl, loam, clay, burnt chalk, slates, cut stone, marble, slabs and other marble products, building stone, crushed stone, etc.	43.53	54.26	65.56	45.71	52.38
23, 28(i), 39, 70(a), 70(b) and 71.	Dye-woods, seeds not otherwise specified, bone black, hay, straw, etc.	95.86	88.97	81.43	56.03	67.70

TABLE XXX—(*Continued*)

INDEX OF COMBINED RAILROAD TRAFFIC AND TRAFFIC ON INLAND WATERWAYS IN
GERMANY; 1920–1924[39]

(1913 = 100)

		1920	1921	1922	1923	1924
72.	Horses, asses, mules, including foals	129.88	99.30	71.74	35.65	60.41
73.	Steers, oxen, cows, beef cattle, including heifers and calves	47.90	71.53	72.25	46.29	69.96
74.	Sheep, including lambs	85.67	87.11	63.68	37.07	72.41
75.	Swine, including shoats	28.04	42.24	44.08	34.30	51.59
76.	Poultry	10.50	15.11	8.70	3.73	27.39
69.	Miscellaneous freight	44.01	108.87	115.07	72.61	76.55
	Index of total traffic[41]	74.23	77.60	80.63	55.21	67.58

[39] Figures for the base year, 1913, and all other years refer to the present German territory. The method of calculating the combined index of traffic (tons of freight) on railroads and inland waterways was as follows:

(1) Coalescence of freight categories was effected wherever necessary in order to make the commodity groups consistent for the two kinds of traffic and throughout the period covered.

(2) The 1913 figures were corrected for changes in territory. To do this, the "Lokalverkehr" (traffic within a given freight district) and "Auslandsverkehr" (traffic of a given freight district with foreign countries) for those districts separated from Germany after the war were subtracted from the total traffic in 1913. Traffic between the now separated districts and the rest of Germany has been included in the figures for 1913. It was then German domestic, it would now be German foreign, trade. The boundaries of the 1913 freight districts in the separated territories do not correspond exactly with the new political boundaries. The error involved in the overlapping one way or the other is unavoidable but is not large.

(3) Index numbers were calculated by commodity categories (79 in all) for both railroad and inland waterway traffic, with 1913, present territory, figures taken as a base.

(4) The ratio of the volume of each category of traffic in 1913 to total traffic in that year was then calculated for both types of transport.

(5) The index numbers resulting from step (3) were then multiplied by the ratios obtained in step (4) and added. The resulting index numbers of traffic on railroad and inland waterways are those given in the above table.

(6) The arithmetic mean of these 79 index numbers has been taken as the final index of total traffic on railroads and inland waterways combined.

[40] The numbers given are those in the official statistics where the goods are classified alphabetically in German.

[41] Average of all the items. Railroad traffic runs from 80 to 90% of the total in each year.

Sources of data: *Statistik der Güterbewegung auf deutschen Eisenbahnen,* 1913, 1920–1923, Vols. 80, 87–90, Statistisches Reichsamt; "Die Güterbewegung auf deutschen Eisenbahnen im Jahre 1924," *Statistik des deutschen Reichs,* Vol. 325, Statistisches Reichsamt; "Verkehr der deutschen Binnenwasserstrassen im Jahre 1913, 1920–1924," *Statistik des deutschen Reichs,* Vols. 274, 300, 306, 308, 313, 322, Statistisches Reichsamt, *passim.*

representative of total production with whatever reservations on this or other accounts may be necessary.

§ RAILROAD AND WATERWAYS TRAFFIC

Table XXX, above, gives index numbers, for the years 1920 to 1924 (base 1913 = 100), of the combined traffic on railroads and inland waterways for the 79 different categories of freight which can be separately distinguished, throughout the period, in the statistics covering these two methods of transportation. The 79 categories include all the freight transported either by railroad or inland waterways.

The average of the indices, the general index number at the bottom of the table, is probably fairly representative of the total production measured by value. A well recognized effect on the composition of German industry of the losses of territory in Alsace-Lorraine, Posen, West Prussia, and Upper Silesia is the transition to more highly wrought products, so that the gross weight of freight carried, if taken without correction, would provide a much less satisfactory index of production. There can be little doubt that the corrected index here offered gives a truer picture of the actual value of the output of German industry than do the relative total weights of goods carried in the pre- and post-war years.[42] The difference between the crude and corrected indices for traffic in general, one representing total traffic by gross weight, and the other traffic according to the method above described, is shown in Table XXXI.

TABLE XXXI

COMPARATIVE INDICES OF TRAFFIC ON GERMAN RAILROADS AND INLAND WATERWAYS
1913, 1920–1924
(*Present territory*)

YEAR	TONS CARRIED	CRUDE INDEX 1913 = 100	CORRECTED INDEX (ELIMINATING EXCESSIVE INFLUENCE OF CHANGES IN THE TRANSPORT OF COMMODITIES OF LOW VALUE PER UNIT OF WEIGHT) (1913 = 100)
1913	572,661,999	100.00	100.00
1920	380,444,337	66.43	74.23
1921	395,623,830	69.09	77.60
1922	432,509,192	75.53	80.63
1923	280,531,363	48.99	55.21
1924	342,221,347	59.76	67.58

[42] The transport of coal, for instance, which in 1913 formed 27% of the total railroad traffic, shows an index number in the later years consistently much below that for all commodities. The effect on the *value* of freight transported is, however, slight.

§ COMPARISON OF TRANSPORT AND GENERAL PRODUCTION INDICES

Let now the index of production, as evidenced by the corrected index of transport of commodities, be compared with the directly calculated indices of agricultural and industrial output. See Table XXXII.

TABLE XXXII

INDEX NUMBER OF COMBINED TRAFFIC ON GERMAN RAILROADS AND INLAND
WATERWAYS COMPARED WITH INDEX NUMBERS OF PRODUCTION;[43] 1920-1924
1913 = 100[44]

	1920	1921	1922	1923	1924
(1) Total traffic on railroads and inland waterways	74.23	77.60	80.63	55.21	67.58
(2) Industrial production	62	78	89	56	80
(3) Agricultural production	63	64	71	72	74

[43] As computed by M. Dessirier in the *Bulletin de la Statistique Générale de la France*. The production indices here given are indices of total volume of production unweighted for changes in population except those due to a transfer of territory. Such unweighted figures are more comparable with the freight indices than are the weighted statistics.

[44] Base figures refer to the present territory of Germany in both cases.

The three indices show a by no means bad correspondence with one another. Industrial production and traffic are in close relationship in 1921 and 1923 and the traffic index is intermediate between those of industrial and agricultural production in 1921 and 1922.[45] In 1920, however, the traffic index is considerably higher and, in 1924, considerably lower than either of the other two. The deviations in 1920 and 1924 may be due either to defects in the indices or to actual shifts between the volume of production and the volume of freight carried. On the whole it is probable that the transport index is more reliable in 1920 than are the direct indices of production[46] while, in 1924, it seems likely that total production revived rather more rapidly than did the volume of freight carried.

Taking the year 1920 as the first after 1913 in which war phenomena were not a dominating factor, and assuming that each of the three indices represents conditions in which, at that date, some considerable degree of adjustment to the new situation had been effected, it will be worth while to compare the relative movements in, rather than the status of, the several indices through the years 1920-1924. Such movements are shown in Table XXXIII which gives link relatives of the three indices

[45] This would, of course, be generally expected.
[46] The statistics on which the production indices are based are not to be greatly trusted in 1920.

TABLE XXXIII

LINK RELATIVES OF THE INDICES OF COMBINED TRAFFIC ON RAILROADS AND
WATERWAYS, OF INDUSTRIAL, AND OF AGRICULTURAL PRODUCTION

INDEX	1921	1922	1923	1924
(1) Total traffic	105	104	69	122
(2) Industrial production	126	114	63	143
(3) Agricultural production	102	111	101	103

here under review.[47] It will be noted that the correlation of movement
in the three indices is close and that the index of the movement of
traffic conforms with theoretical expectation in being intermediate between that of the two direct indices of production except in 1922 when
all three indices show much the same relationship to the 1921 figures.
The absolute agricultural production index grew steadily, if slowly,
from 1921 to 1924 and its growth presumably affected in proportionate
degree the index of transport. If all the indices here employed are to
qualify as really good criteria of total production, the fluctuations in the
index of transport ought, in consequence, to follow, with less marked
variations, the year to year changes in the index of industrial output. A
glance at Table XXXIII will show that this is in fact the case and it
can therefore be assumed with *some* degree of assurance that the figures
arrived at give a reasonably good indication of the actual value of
German production in the inflation years. The index of transport cor-
roborates the directly derived figures on production about as fully as
could well be expected.

3. INDIRECT ESTIMATES OF PRODUCTION. CONSUMPTION

§ STATISTICS ON CONSUMPTION INADEQUATE

A comprehensive index of national consumption, with allowances
made for foreign commercial and financial transactions and for the
growth or decline in capital equipment, would be as good a criterion
of production as direct statistics on the output of goods.[48] Consumption
of currently produced goods, including capital equipment, must be equal
to production plus import minus export. Though, in the inflation years,
the Germans gave a large amount of commodity exports per unit of
imports, the decline in consumption relative to production[49] (both being

[47] The index for each year is set down as a percentage of that of the preceding
year.
[48] The general index of production cited in the earlier part of the chapter
is partly made up from figures on the consumption of certain important raw
materials.
[49] By consumption is meant here, and in the sequel, delivery to the final con-

measured in physical rather than value units) which this would normally necessitate was more than compensated by the receipts from the sales of currency never redeemed. Statistics on general consumption ought therefore to check fairly closely with those on production, 1913 being taken as a base in both cases.

Most of the available statistics on consumption, however, apply to foodstuffs. A large part of the consumption of foodstuffs ordinarily takes place within the confines of the middle-income class. But this was the very class which was brought to ruin by the depreciation of the currency. It is not to be expected that the prosperous group which was benefiting at the expense of the middle-income class would expand its consumption of foodstuffs in anything like the same measure as the latter class was forced to cut it down. The *type* of consumption, rather than its total volume, was entirely changed by the phenomena of inflation and this change is not reflected in the statistics available. There was a showy but probably not absolutely very large expenditure on luxuries by the "profiteers." A considerable share of this expenditure was made outside of Germany and the foreign journals of the day are full of references to the objectionable display, by certain classes of Germans, of their new-found wealth. German newspapers mark the same tendency at home though the total *import* of luxuries greatly declined. Consumption of domestically produced luxuries is very inadequately reported.

Of much greater absolute importance than this luxury expenditure, however, were the outlays, on capital account, of funds which would ordinarily have accrued to the population at large and have been spent, at least in part, on consumable goods. The volume of new industrial building, of renewal, repair, and expansion of equipment in manufacturing, transportation, agriculture, and mercantile life was large, especially when currency depreciation became so rapid as to make outlays on capital almost the sole means of preserving the substance of profits. These investments were for the most part made directly from undistributed profits. Under stable monetary conditions the funds thus

sumer of the commodity in question whether it is a producers' good or a consumers' good. Similarly, production is whatever is delivered. In any one year goods may be fabricated in excess of the deliveries to the final consumer, or there may for that year be a deficiency made up out of stocks, but such differences are negligible where the margin of error in the statistics is certainly much greater than the change in unsold stocks from year to year. After the occupation of the Ruhr, accumulation of stocks was great enough to exert a considerable influence on the figures, since a large number of concerns then worked only for stock. No reliable figures, however, are available as to the volume of goods so accumulated.

employed would have first gone to private individuals who would have exercised their volition as to whether they would invest them or use them for immediate consumption and would in many, and perhaps in the majority of cases, have decided for the latter.

The expenditures for improvements in productive equipment[50] of course lowered the ratio of immediate final consumption to total production. Further than this, in the relationship between production and consumption, it should not be forgotten that domestic consumption was diminished relatively to output by the payment of reparations both in cash and in kind. While cash reparations were of greater import in wrecking the exchange value of the mark, the payments in kind involved a larger sum of values and were consequently more significant in reducing home consumption below the level of production. Large deliveries of goods were required, in addition, to cover the costs of the armies of occupation and the restitution of Allied nationals' property seized during the war. In the three years, 1920 to the end of 1922, *goods* to a total value of about 9 billion gold marks were delivered to the Allies out of current production[51] in addition to total cash payments of approximately 2 billion. Such deliveries amount to more than 25% of the total German monetary income in 1913[52] or, if allowance be made for the higher gold price level in post-war times, to some 17% of the total *real* income in 1913. They were spread over a period of four years and therefore average yearly between 4% and 5% of the 1913 income. Insofar, however, as the total German output was less in the period of inflation than in 1913, these deliveries to the victors would represent a larger share of the post-war production and would correspondingly lower the relation of domestic consumption to output. Quite apart then from the question of the relative division of output between producers' and consumers' goods, indices of per capita consumption of commodities, other than

[50] The forced conversion of many plants from war to peace purposes must be regarded as an increase in true productive equipment. Much labor, however, was expended, at the behest of the Allied powers, in mere destruction of potential war equipment. This of course lowered production and domestic consumption coincidently. It should also be noted that, though industrial building was more than usually active, residential building was very slack.

[51] This estimate is derived from German sources (*Germany's Economic and Financial Situation*, Statistisches Reichsamt, Berlin, 1923), but unlike the property delivered under the armistice agreement, as to the value of which a huge difference exists between the estimates of the Germans and of the Reparations Commission, these deliveries from current production are valued at current world prices. The estimates may therefore be regarded as substantially accurate.

[52] According to Karl Helfferich's estimate in his *Deutschlands Volkswohlstand 1888-1913*, Verlag von Georg Stilke, Berlin, 1914, p. 97.

raw materials of industry, might therefore reasonably be expected to run some 6% or 7% below indices of production.

§ INDICES OF CONSUMPTION

Table XXXIV gives indices of per capita consumption of certain important foodstuffs (the only available data which seemed relevant to the purpose in hand) as compared with indices of production.

TABLE XXXIV

INDICES OF PER CAPITA CONSUMPTION OF CERTAIN FOOD PRODUCTS COMPARED WITH
INDICES OF PRODUCTION; 1920/21–1924/25

(1913/1914 = 100)

YEAR JULY 1– JUNE 30	CONSUMPTION OF					AGRICUL- TURAL[55] PRODUCTION	INDUS- TRIAL[55] PRODUCTION
	WHEAT	RYE	POTATOES	MEAT[53]	SUGAR[54]		
1913/14	100.0	100.0	100.0	100.0	100.0	100.0	100.0
1920/21	—	—	—	—	88.4	63	62
1921/22	79.4	65.6	47.3	—	108.9	64	78
1922/23	48.5	58.6	79.9	66.1	102.6	71	89
1923/24	59.9	68.9	61.9	59.7	70.0	72	56

[53] Figures for consumption of meat refer to calendar years, 1913, 1922, 1923.

[54] Figures for consumption of sugar refer to years from Sept. 1–Aug. 31.

[55] The indices of production are for the calendar years 1913, 1920–1923, and are the Dessirier indices weighted for changes in population. Whatever differences may from year to year appear in the indices of agricultural and industrial production should not greatly affect consumption of foodstuffs since, in short crop years, imports of foodstuffs would tend to rise.

Source of data: *Statistisches Jahrbuch* 1924/25, 1926.

It should be noted that, on a diminution of income, the consumption of basic foodstuffs will not be curtailed in anything like the same measure as consumption in general. The use of non-essential foods and drinks, for instance, fell off to a much greater degree than did that of the commodities shown above. If the figures here given therefore seem low relative to the indices of production this is probably due to the defects of an index of the consumption of foodstuffs as a criterion of general output under the circumstances to which it here applies. In view of what has already been said as to the general relation between production and consumption in Germany in the period under review, and as to the peculiar conditions affecting the consumption of foodstuffs, it may perhaps be asserted that the indices of consumption and of production corroborate one another reasonably well. This assertion is in some degree supported by such fragmentary evidence as is at hand on the output of producers' goods.

§ OUTPUT OF PRODUCERS' GOODS

The share of total production which took the form of producers' rather than consumers' goods, and its relation to the pre-war division of total output between these two groups, is far from being an open book but it seems probable that a somewhat larger proportion of total output went into capital goods in the inflation years than was the case before the war. Consumption of consumers' goods was necessarily reduced *pro tanto*. Saving, in the old manner, was destroyed by the depreciation of the currency but this was replaced by the ardor for investing in durable commodities which possessed the mind of every holder of any surplus in the monetary form. It is by no means certain that there was not more actual saving than there would have been under a stable monetary régime but it was done by direct investment rather than through financial institutions. The bulk of the population no doubt spent on immediate consumption a larger proportion of their incomes than in former times but a much smaller share of the total national income came into their hands. Final consumption relative to output was thus considerably reduced. It will be worth while to consider some forms of capital accumulation for which usable figures are available.

(1) *The Mercantile Marine.*

The mercantile marine, which had been almost completely confiscated by the Allies, was by the end of 1923 more than half rebuilt. Activity in this line was stimulated by the governmental policy of reimbursement of the shipowners for their losses to the Allies, on the condition that the funds so received go into new construction. In this way the administration was imposing upon the people a forced saving since the money paid to the shipowners was taken from consumers through the inflation process in precisely the same manner as would have occurred under orderly arrangements in public finance had taxes been levied to the required amount. New construction in German yards for the years 1921-1923 as compared with the average of 1909-1913 was as follows:

SHIPBUILDING IN GERMAN YARDS

TONNAGE OF MERCHANT VESSELS LAUNCHED

(*Average of* 1909-1913; *annually,* 1921-1923)

YEAR	THOUSAND TONS*	YEAR	THOUSAND TONS*
Average 1909-1913	272.8	1922	525.8
1921	509.1	1923	345.1

*Vessels of less than 100 tons gross omitted.

Source of data: *Documents of the International Economic Conference,* League of Nations Publications, C.E.I. 8., Geneva, 1927, p. 8.

The high output of this type of capital good during inflation is obvious. Even in the disastrous year 1923 the tonnage produced was considerably above that of the annual average of the quinquennium immediately preceding the war.

(2) *Railroad Equipment.*

As with the mercantile marine so with the railroads reconstruction was vigorously pushed in the inflation years. Here, as elsewhere, monetary statistics are a very uncertain guide but in Table XXXV expenditures for new installations out of the ordinary railroad budget (that is without emission of new capital) are expressed not only as absolute sums but also as a percentage of total expenditures and so, to some degree, avoid the difficulty inherent in the use of data in monetary form.

From one-fifth to one-fourth of total working expenditures in the inflation years were outlays for new installations whereas in 1913-1914 only one-eighth of the total was so spent. On the other hand, expenditures made out of the proceeds of new capital issues were much less in the later years than in 1913-1914: inflation was leading to the making of the greater share of improvements out of current income. Taking the two items together the total expenditures (in terms of real purchasing power) were undoubtedly larger than in pre-war years.[56]

The conclusion that the capital equipment of the railroads was being more than ordinarily extended and improved is confirmed by statistics on the number of locomotives put into service and by those on rolling stock in general. Of the locomotives in operation in Germany in 1925 there were put into service in the designated years the following numbers:

NUMBER OF LOCOMOTIVES IN USE IN 1925 PUT INTO SERVICE IN THE YEARS 1910-1925[57]

YEAR	NUMBER	YEAR	NUMBER	YEAR	NUMBER	YEAR	NUMBER
1910	859	1914	1150	1918	1132	1922	1454
1911	766	1915	1259	1919	1716	1923	1302
1912	878	1916	1246	1920	1986	1924	657
1913	1321	1917	1114	1921	2170	1925	126

[57] cf. *Statistik der im Betriebe befindlichen Eisenbahnen Deutschlands*, Reichsverkehrsministerium, Vol. 46, Berlin, 1926, p. 151.

Practically all locomotives put into service later than 1913 were still in operation in 1925. The figures here given therefore closely represent the number of new locomotives acquired by the railroads in the years

[56] The assertion here made might not be warranted if paper mark outlays should be converted into gold at current rates of exchange. But the exchange rate is not appropriate for this conversion. The wholesale price index is much better and, using this index, the assertion made in the text is true.

TABLE XXXV

EXPENDITURES FOR PROFIT-YIELDING INSTALLATIONS CONTAINED IN THE ORDINARY BUDGET OF THE GERMAN STATE RAILWAY (AMORTIZATION) AND THEIR SHARE IN THE TOTAL WORKING EXPENSES

| | FINANCIAL YEARS | | | | | | | | 1923 APRIL 1—OCTOBER 31 | |
| EXPENDITURE FOR: | 1913/14 | | 1920/21 | | 1921/22 | | 1922/23 | | | |
	GOLD MARKS	IN PERCENTAGE OF THE TOTAL WORKING EXPENDITURE	PAPER MARKS	IN PERCENTAGE OF THE TOTAL WORKING EXPENDITURE	PAPER MARKS	IN PERCENTAGE OF THE TOTAL WORKING EXPENDITURE	PAPER MARKS	IN PERCENTAGE OF THE TOTAL WORKING EXPENDITURE	BILLIONS OF PAPER MARKS (ESTIMATED)	IN PERCENTAGE OF THE TOTAL WORKING EXPENDITURE
New fittings and installations	112,245,080	4.78	909,365,950	2.93	1,252,907,970	2.56	56,471,101,210	2.36	58,600	3.42
Machinery and cars	181,984,590	7.76	3,377,837,330	10.87	5,363,437,170	10.95	265,358,945,680	11.10	175,100	10.18
Reparation of damage suffered during the war	—	—	3,299,684,160	10.62	4,566,306,380	9.32	196,100,990,900	8.20	123,400	7.18
Total	294,229,670	12.54	7,586,887,440	24.42	11,182,651,520	22.83	517,931,037,790	21.66	357,100	20.78

cf. *Germany's Economy, Currency and Finance*, p. 101.

after 1913 to which they refer. The additions in the inflation years are markedly greater than at any other period and, to the extent of the difference, capital equipment was more than ordinarily extended. Furthermore, the quantity of locomotives under repair fell from 43.2% of all locomotives on April 1, 1920 to 27.2% on January 1, 1924, and the number of freight cars from 100,010 on August 1, 1920, to 45,400 on January 1, 1924.[58] The quality of the existing equipment was thus being constantly improved in the period under review.

Except for locomotives no figures on the additions to rolling stock in 1920 are available. The gap left by the Allies' sequestration of railroad property was, however, rapidly mended in that year and the increase in equipment was undoubtedly large. By 1921 the rolling stock had been brought fairly well up to the volume requisite for the existing traffic though there were some additions in the next two years. Table XXXVI shows the weight in tons of certain classes of rolling stock from 1921 to 1926.

TABLE XXXVI

WEIGHT (IN TONS) OF CERTAIN CLASSES OF ROLLING STOCK ON
GERMAN RAILROADS; 1921–1926

FISCAL YEAR	PASSENGER CARS	FREIGHT CARS	BAGGAGE CARS
1921/22	1,307,104	5,717,593	290,305
1922/23	1,356,319	5,825,697	312,194
1923/24	1,368,710	5,998,695	313,942
1924/25	1,365,313	6,017,822	315,886
1925/26	1,294,074	6,595,652	304,943
1926/27	1,292,386	6,632,415	301,670

Source of data: *Statistik der im Betriebe befindlichen Eisenbahnen Deutschlands,* Reichsverkehrsministerium, Vols. 44, 47, Berlin, 1925, 1927, *passim.*

The fact that the total weight of passenger and baggage cars in operation showed a declining tendency after the currency was stabilized would seem to indicate that these types of rolling stock had been somewhat overbuilt during the inflation years. Though the total weight of freight cars markedly increased in 1925 and 1926, this was due to increased need in those years rather than to any shortage in 1922 and 1923 relative to the freight then being carried. By 1923 the deficiency, which was acute immediately after the war, had apparently been made up. On the whole, in spite of inadequate statistics, there can be little doubt that the restoration of the railroads from the bad shape into which they had fallen during the war[59] necessitated and called forth an unusu-

[58] *Germany's Economy, Currency and Finance,* p. 104.
[59] *cf.* "German Railway System After the War," G. Francke, *Manchester*

ally heavy outlay on improvements and extensions in the inflation years and inflation appears to have been a distinctly facilitating factor.

(3) *Industrial Building.*

The capital outlays on transportation were paralleled in other branches of industry though for this it is difficult to cite chapter and verse. The area of industrial constructions is said to have increased by 25% from 1920 to 1923.[60] The vast amount of reconditioning carried out in these years is noted in foreign official reports[61] and the German Under-Secretary of State in the Ministry of the Interior, Dr. Julius Hirsch, is quoted as follows: "Until the Ruhr conflict. . . . the income of Germany's work showed a slow but fairly steady increase, whereas direct consumption, although it also was again growing, was growing somewhat more slowly,"[62] the implication being that a larger share of production was going into capital expenditures.

Industrial building statistics are meager. All that is available in the official statistics is the total number of new buildings put up within the year, with the number of dwellings stated separately. The difference between the two totals would no doubt consist largely of industrial and commercial building but the mere number of erections for business purposes is of no great significance without some indication of the size of the individual units. The data on non-dwelling constructions are, however, set forth in Table XXXVII for whatever value they may have.

The steady growth throughout the inflation period in the number of business buildings constructed, the substantial margin by which the figures for 1921, 1922, and 1923 overtop those of 1913, which was itself a very active business year, and the decline in activity with the coming of currency stabilization as shown by the figures for 1924, furnish at least some statistical verification for the assertion that in the years of currency depreciation a much larger than usual share of total output took the capital form.

(4) *Industrial Equipment.*

Evidence that investment in equipment other than buildings was active is also meager but goes to show that here too a relatively large

Guardian Commercial, Reconstruction Supplement, Section VIII, Manchester, September 7, 1922, p. 405.

[60] *Mythology of Reparations,* Robert Crozier Long, London, Duckworth, p. 106.

[61] *cf.* British Dept. of Overseas Trade; *Report on Economic and Financial Conditions in Germany,* London, 1924, p. 129. The reference is to the metallurgical industry but the condition is, elsewhere in the report, assumed to have been general.

[62] *Mythology of Reparations,* R. C. Long, p. 125.

TABLE XXXVII

CONSTRUCTION OF NEW BUILDINGS OTHER THAN DWELLINGS; 1913, 1920-1924[63]

(*Number of buildings*)

YEAR	TOTAL FOR 31 DISTRICTS	TOTAL FOR 72 DISTRICTS
1913	3,307	—
1920	3,075	4,660
1921	4,303	6,267
1922	4,764	6,645
1923	5,184	7,069
1924	4,821	6,316

[63] Statistics for only 31 districts are available throughout the period covered but figures for 72 districts from 1920 on are at hand. Each of the several districts represents, in the main, one of the largest cities so that the figures practically present industrial and commercial building in the cities. The table nowhere appears in this form in official statistics but is compiled from data in: (1) *Statistisches Jahrbuch* 1921/22; (2) *Vierteljahrshefte zur Statistik des Deutschen Reichs*, 1920, IV; 1922, I; 1923, I; 1924, I; 1925, I.

share of total output was producers' goods. The number of workmen employed in the construction of machinery, instruments and apparatus in 1913 and in 1920 to 1922 was, in thousands:[64]

YEAR	1913	1920	1921	1922
Workers employed on Machinery, Instruments, and Apparatus	1173	1420	1462	1654

These figures cover iron works, shipbuilding, and vehicle manufacture as well as the more strictly engineering trades. In the engineering industry proper the number of persons employed is estimated at five to six hundred thousand in 1913 and seven to seven hundred and fifty thousand in 1922.[65] Since productivity per worker in these lines seems to have been at least as great as in 1913 the output in the inflation years was in all likelihood not less than in proportion to the number of workers engaged. It is significant that, after stabilization of the currency, the number of workers in these industries declined from 700 to 750 thousand in 1922 to about 550 thousand in 1924 and 1925.

(5) *Agricultural Equipment*.

Investment in agricultural machinery probably kept pace with that in industrial equipment, though the only evidence at hand is very incon-

[64] *Documents of the International Economic Conference*, League of Nations Publications, C.E.I. 15, Vol. I., Geneva, 1927, p. 85. Figures derived from the *Jahresberichten der Gewerbe-Aufsichtsbeamten und Bergbehörden*.

[65] *ibid.*, according to data compiled by the *Verein deutscher Maschinenbau-Anstalten*.

clusive. Figures have been compiled showing the machine equipment of German farmers in 1924/25 in contrast with that of 1906/07. The increase during these years is remarkable and a sizable share of this increase must, it would seem, have occurred in the inflation period since equipment was neglected during the war. It cannot be alleged that the data provide any assurance on this point but they are given for what they may be worth. See Table XXXVIII.

TABLE XXXVIII

NUMBER OF MACHINES OWNED BY GERMAN FARMERS; 1906/07 AND 1924/25
Post-war Territory (Less Saar Basin)

Type of Machinery	1906/07	1924/25
Power ploughs	304	8,552
Mowing machines	307,454	1,023,381
Machine hoers	14,633	145,638
Potato planting machines	1,986	47,837
Potato digging machines	10,064	173,703
Power threshers	732,772	1,055,151
Rough grinding mills	25,588	319,670
Cream separators	293,795	1,415,699

Source of data: *Wirtschaft und Statistik*, 1927, p. 764.

(6) *Activity in Industries Manufacturing Producers' Goods.*

It may be of interest to present the number of workers employed in various branches of production in order to note the relative growth of industries producing capital and consumers' goods respectively. Table XXXIX shows the number of persons employed in the several industries for the years 1913, 1919, 1922, and 1923 and the percentage of workers in each of the industries in 1922 in relation to the situation in 1913. The year 1922 was chosen for comparison with 1913 as being most representative of the effects of inflation since production in 1923 was greatly influenced by non-monetary causes. The industries are ranked according to their relative status in 1922 as compared with the pre-war and pre-inflation period. It will be noted that all the industries which show a large relative growth are producers of capital goods.[66] The building, and stone and earth, industries, it is true, bring up the rear but this was due to the falling off in the construction of dwellings rather than in industrial building. Dwelling construction was not checked by inflation, as such, but by rent limitation laws which rendered it impossible to build new houses to rent on a competitive basis with the old.

[66] The chemical industry is a partial exception but a large part of the increase in output of this industry was in artificial fertilizers, a capital good for agriculture.

TABLE XXXIX

NUMBER OF WORKERS EMPLOYED IN VARIOUS INDUSTRIES; 1913, 1919, 1922, 1923

INDUSTRY	1913	1919	1922	1923	1922 AS A PER CENT OF 1913
Chemical	358,442	392,517	512,288	466,278	142.9
Machine	2,337,055	2,274,521	2,958,673	2,664,416	126.6
Metal working	680,107	660,427	827,516	—	121.7
Mining	918,805	967,962	1,073,754	885,461	116.9
Wood	491,963	433,357	529,956	430,514	107.7
Leather	96,384	71,635	102,448	87,511	106.3
Paper and manifolding	464,364	387,260	486,620	412,899	104.8
Clothing and cleaning	358,879	276,163	374,034	334,301	104.2
Foodstuffs	923,419	699,627	885,914	673,494	95.9
Textile	986,586	559,222	938,549	744,954	95.1
Building	1,766,083	1,060,135	1,488,944	1,225,667	84.3
Stone and earth	859,733	500,065	714,176	589,743	83.1
Total	9,561,986	7,622,473	10,065,360	8,515,238	105.3

Source of data: *Wirtschaft und Statistik*, 1926, p. 171. The figures are derived from the annual reports of the Berufsgenossenschaften except for the metal-working industry where they come from the reports of the Gewerbeaufsichts-behörden.

With the single exception of 1923, a year in which all production was low, it is clear that in most branches of capital accumulation progress was comparatively rapid during all the years of currency depreciation. This does not mean that the country was prosperous, even if the great distress caused by inequity in the distribution rather than insufficiency in the total amount of income, be left out of account. Total production was much below the ante-bellum level and consumption was curtailed in a still greater degree. But the reasons for this are to be traced to the war rather than to the currency. Restoration of capital equipment used up during the period of hostilities was not checked by inflation but went on more rapidly than would have been likely to have occurred under a stable monetary standard. The accessions to capital, as always, were at the expense of current consumption, which would in any case necessarily have been low, and the relative growth of capital explains part of the discrepancy between production and immediate standards of living. The remainder of such discrepancy as exists was presumably due to exactions under the Treaty of Versailles.

4. INDIRECT ESTIMATES OF PRODUCTION. REAL WAGES

§ SPECIAL FACTORS AFFECTING WAGES IN GERMANY

The bulk of the total income of an industrial country like Germany takes the form of wages and even the stupendous shift in distribution which currency depreciation brought about did not alter this situation very profoundly. Real wages ought, therefore, to furnish still another check on the figures of production. The statistics on wages as a criterion of production are, however, open to the same objections as apply to the available figures on consumption. They show only the returns to the middle and lower classes, not those to the classes which benefited from inflation. For a given volume of production they also tended to be low relative to the pre-war situation in the degree to which capital was saved through unusually large direct investment of profits and to the extent that the burden of reparations payments fell on the worker. In addition to this, other government outlays, financed by inflation, were being met by a form of taxation which came out of wage and other incomes before, rather than after, those incomes were received, since, with every rise in prices attendant upon new issues of currency, a given payment in marks represented lower real wages. Taxes were thus levied at the source with a vengeance.[67] On all these grounds real wages tended to be comparatively smaller than production, 1913 being taken as a standard in both cases. On the other hand, governmental control of prices, particularly rents, may have operated to raise real wages. It is indeed probable that the practical confiscation of the property of house owners enured almost wholly to the benefit of industrial entrepreneurs who offered proportionately lower money wages than they would otherwise have been forced to pay. So far, however, as the worker derived any advantage therefrom, his real wages, reckoned on the basis of cost of living (including rent), would on this account tend to be higher than current general productivity would warrant.[68]

Statistics of real wages, moreover, are appropriate indices of production only so far as the classes of the population to which they refer secured an unvarying proportion of the total national output. There is no probability of any strict constancy in this matter but it is probable that the proportionate share of unskilled laborers in the total income did not

[67] As inflation progressed, the worker, it will be remembered, also paid a larger and larger share of the standard taxes since the income tax on wages was deducted at the source and therefore when it meant something in purchasing power. Although the total receipts from the income tax fell far, the worker paid as much as 10% of his wage in some months of 1922 and 1923. High surtaxes were levied on the larger incomes. Even a bare cost of living worker's income became nominally large, however, with the progress of inflation. The worker could not postpone payment and consequently bore a heavy burden. cf. *Deutschland und Frankreich*, edited by R. Kuczynski, Verlag von R. L. Prager, Berlin, 1924, p. 27.

[68] Measured, that is, by pre-war standards.

fall very greatly and that the aggregate income of the industrial population was not much below its pre-war percentage of production.

The best study of wages in Germany in the inflation period is that of the International Labor Office. Their estimate of aggregate real income of the German industrial population,[69] relative to 1913-14, is as follows:[70]

INDEX OF AGGREGATE REAL INCOME OF GERMAN INDUSTRIAL
POPULATION, 1920-1923[71]

YEAR		APPROXIMATE INDEX NUMBER (1913-1914 = 100)
Yearly average	1920	60-85
" "	1921	75-105
" "	1922	70-90
Jan. to August	1923	58-76
November	1923	36-47

These figures are expressly declared to be but very rough approximations from which conclusions should be drawn only with the greatest caution. But there is no doubt that the real income of the working class in Germany rose greatly in 1921 while it fell heavily in almost every other country, that the decline in 1922 was due to a smaller share in the total national income rather than to a falling off in the national output,[72] and that the low yield for 1923, especially in the first half, is in large measure due to the effects of the Ruhr invasion.

Except in 1922 there is a fairly good correlation between this index of the aggregate real income of the industrial population and the production indices presented earlier in this chapter. All the indices of production which have been examined do, in fact, square fairly well with one another. The most comprehensive are those of agricultural yields, of general industrial output, of transportation, and of aggregate income

[69] Aggregate real income is a combination of money wages, cost of living, and volume of employment.

[70] See Workers Standard of Life in Countries with Depreciated Currency, International Labor Office, Series D., No. 15, Geneva, 1925, p. 25.

[71] It should not be forgotten that the social insurance provided for the German worker has been much more extensive since the war than in 1913.

[72] The extraordinary degree of activity in German industry in 1922 has already been noted. But this was the year in which the rate of depreciation of the currency began to rise with extreme speed. Wages lagged far behind prices. In 1923, however, the lag was reduced, and the wage figure in that year therefore corresponds more closely with production.

CHART XXXIV

LINK RELATIVES OF THE INDEX NUMBERS OF AGRICULTURAL PRODUCTION, INDUS-
TRIAL PRODUCTION, TRAFFIC ON RAILROADS AND INLAND WATERWAYS, AND
AGGREGATE REAL INCOME OF THE INDUSTRIAL POPULATION; 1920-1923

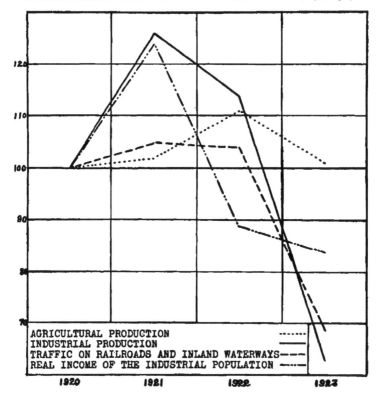

of the working classes. Chart XXXIV shows the relation between these
four indices.[78] The correspondence is sufficiently close to warrant the use
of the general indices of production (agricultural and industrial) as fairly
representative of the actual situation. All the indices are rough, of course,
but corroboration of the general indices comes from the similar results
obtained through the several methods of approach. It would therefore
seem that the margin of error involved in the direct estimates of production is not unduly wide.

[78] For the index of aggregate real income of the industrial population the
mean of the yearly estimates of the International Labor Office has been taken.
The 1923 figure is based on the estimate for the eight months January to August.

§ CONCLUSIONS AS TO THE EFFECT OF INFLATION ON
DOMESTIC PRODUCTION

Most authorities would readily concede that inflation in its early stages exercises a stimulating influence on business activity, and might increase production, but they would be loth to admit that this effect could be more than temporary. In the German case, however, there is little evidence up to the end of 1922 or, indeed, till late 1923, to show that the stimulus was losing its power. As contrasted with business activity production can, it is true, be increased by inflation only up to the point at which unemployment practically disappears. After this point is reached any further fluctuation in production, so far as it is affected by inflation, must, in the first instance, be downward. Opinion is unanimous that in the final weeks of inflation in Germany the depreciation of the currency was, to say the least, a deterrent to productive effort. The turning point came with the refusal of the employed classes to suffer further losses and with the demand for stable value payments in every type of transaction, that is, with the repudiation of the mark. The inability of entrepreneurs further to exploit the situation to their own advantage came quite suddenly. A fair index is furnished by

TABLE XL

UNEMPLOYMENT AMONG TRADE UNION MEMBERS, BY MONTHS; 1922–1923[74]

DATE		PERCENTAGE WHOLLY UNEMPLOYED	PERCENTAGE PARTIALLY UNEMPLOYED
1921: yearly average		2.8	5.4
1922	Jan.	3.3	1.6
	April	0.9	0.6
	July	0.6	0.8
	Oct.	1.4	4.7
1923	Jan.	4.2	12.6
	Feb.	5.2	14.9
	Mar.	5.6	23.6
	April	7.0	28.5
	May	6.2	21.7
	June	4.1	15.3
	July	3.5	14.5
	Aug.	6.3	26.0
	Sept.	9.9	39.7
	Oct.	19.1	47.3
	Nov.	23.4	47.3
	Dec.	28.2	42.0

[74] cf. *The Workers Standard of Life in Countries with Depreciated Currency*, p. 21.

monthly statistics on unemployment in the unoccupied part of the country. It was not until the first of September, only ten weeks before the introduction of the rentenmark, that the number of people entirely out of work began rapidly to increase, though partial unemployment had risen a month earlier. The degree of unemployment is indicated by the preceding Table XL, the figures of which, though referring only to trade unionists, nevertheless cover a large portion of the population and include all the principal industries.

Since the increase in the numbers of unemployed had already begun in October 1922, it is probable that some part of the depression in the early months of 1923 was directly due to the dislocation issuing out of the immense acceleration in the rate of currency depreciation (which began in the fall of 1922 and was almost uninterrupted thereafter), rather than to the Ruhr invasion. But, though this may possibly be true, the recovery in the summer of 1923 does not offer any corroboration of such a view. Not until the final three months of the paper mark régime can a deleterious effect on industry be clearly traced to the collapse of the currency. Something between a quarter and a third of the decline in output in 1923 (estimated at 37% lower than 1922) should therefore be assigned to monetary disturbances with the probability running toward the lower rather than the higher figure.[75] The fall in 1923 production which was due to inflation may thus be fairly put at about 10% of a normal year's output at that time.

If the conclusion just reached as to the effect of inflation on production in the final year of life of the old mark is justified, it follows that, so far as the total of domestic production goes, the gains from the employment of inconvertible and depreciating currency more than outweighed the losses. Counting in both the two post-inflation crises, for

[75] To assign to inflation even as much as a quarter of the decline may perhaps be too much. The evil effects of the Ruhr occupation ran throughout that year and into 1924. Though the policy of passive resistance was officially abandoned on October 6, and though the German government announced on October 24 that it was ready, in principle, to resume the payment of reparations after impartial examination of Germany's capacity had been made, there was no immediate relaxation of the grip of the occupying powers. After the rentenmark had been introduced an agreement was reached between the German industrialists and the Mission Interalliée de Controle des Usines et des Mines (under which the so-called "Micum" contracts were negotiated) which restored control of their properties to the German industrialists on condition that they deliver a sizable proportion of their output to the occupying Powers. (The German government was to reimburse the industrialists.) Activity in the Ruhr then began slowly to pick up. The crippling effect of the invasion, however, lasted well beyond the inflation period.

which inflation can with some reason be held responsible, and the falling
off in production in late 1923 attendant upon the dying throes of the
old currency, the reduction in output can scarcely have exceeded the
benefits which inflation seems to have brought in 1921 and 1922. The
decline in production due to the stabilization crises in 1924 and 1926
has been set at 10% and 5%, respectively, of a normal year's output
at that time.[76] The decline due to the phenomena of complete currency
collapse in late 1923 has just been estimated at perhaps 10% of the
output which might have been realized in that year had a stable monetary
standard been in operation. A rough notion of the extent of all of these
losses, measured in current gold values, may be obtained from the following computation:

ACTUAL AND POTENTIAL OUTPUT IN GERMANY IN 1923, 1924, AND 1926

(*Millions of gold marks*)

YEAR	APPROXIMATE TOTAL GERMAN OUTPUT[77]	APPROXIMATE POTENTIAL OUTPUT (ASSUMING THAT INFLATION HAD NEVER TAKEN PLACE)[78]	LOSSES DUE TO INFLATION
1923	30,240	33,600	3,360
1924	43,200	48,000	4,800
1926	48,600	51,158	2,558
Total	122,040	132,758	10,718

[76] See *supra*, p. 291.

[77] Helfferich's estimate of 42 billion gold marks *total income* in 1913 is first
reduced to 36 billion in order to apply to post-war territory only and to eliminate
the computed difference in the return on foreign investments in 1913 and in
the years here considered. This 36 billion is converted to post-1920 gold values
(approximate index of gold prices on a 1913 base = 150). The resulting 54
billion gold marks is then multiplied for each year by the appropriate index
(Dessirier's index weighted for changes in population) of industrial production
(1923 = 56; 1924 = 80; 1926 = 90). The final figure should approximate the
gold value of the total output of the German economy for the year to which
it applies. The index of gold prices used for conversion is that of the United
States Bureau of Labor Statistics. Since all other calculations of gold values are
based on prices in the United States this seemed the best index to use, though
gold prices in Germany were somewhat lower. The estimates of German income
here made check fairly closely with computations otherwise derived. Thus the
Institut für Konjunkturforschung, on the basis of income tax returns, estimated
the German income in 1925 at 50 to 55 billion marks. (*Vierteljahrshefte*, 1926, I.)
According to the method here used the 1925 income works out at approximately
51 billion marks.

[78] Actual production has been estimated as being less than potential production in 1923, 1924, and 1926 by 10%, 10% and 5% respectively.

Total losses in domestic production traceable to inflation in the years when its influence was adverse, may thus be set, in round figures, at 11 billion gold marks. These losses are much more than offset by the presumable gains from inflation in the year 1921 alone. Estimating in the same manner as above, the industrial output of the German economy in that year was raised over that of 1920 by nearly 10 billion gold marks,[79] whereas, if a gold standard had prevailed, a sharp drop, perhaps equal to the 25% fall in industrial production which occurred in the gold standard United States[80] or the 31% of Great Britain, would have been almost certain. If a 25% fall had occurred, the net loss, as compared with the situation which in fact eventuated, would have amounted to about 19 billion gold marks. As for 1922, it has already been pointed out that it is most improbable that production in Germany, where industrial activity was at its maximum, would have been as great under stable monetary conditions as it actually proved to be under the stimulus of currency depreciation since this was a year of but slow recovery from the depression of 1921 in all countries where prices were kept on an even keel.[81]

So far as output is concerned there is therefore little support in actual statistics for the contention that the evils of inflation were other than evils of distribution. Domestic production seems on the whole to have been greater than would have been attained if the currency had been solidly based on gold. Taking the nation as a unit, the collapse of the currency was thus far from being an unmixed curse.

[79] The 1920 income works out at 36.6 billion gold marks and the 1921 at 46.0 billion.

[80] 25% according to the index corrected for changes in population, 22% for the uncorrected index.

[81] Business cycles do not, of course, show the same pattern synchronously in all parts of the world. But the depression of 1921 was evident in all countries in which prices followed the movement in the value of gold.

CHAPTER XIII

CONCLUSION

§ SUMMARY OF RESULTS

IF THE computations in the immediately preceding chapters may be trusted, the balance of *material* gains and losses, attributable to inflation, is distinctly on the side of gains. The returns from the sale of money abroad much more than balanced the losses on international trade in merchandise and capital items, and domestic production seems, on the whole, to have been substantially greater than would presumably have been achieved under a stable monetary standard. One is inclined to shrink from drawing the seemingly inevitable conclusion that the depreciation of the currency, nationally considered, was a benefit. The immense injustices consequent upon extreme depreciation are no doubt, in themselves, enough to damn the practice of inflation. Yet one would like to find a buttress for the policy of stable money in a demonstration that, just as in ethics, so also in the realm of economics, abuse of the currency could work nothing but ill. The facts however lie the other way.[1] It is true that such gains as accrued to the German economy were due to special factors which are unlikely to recur. Part of these gains arose from the fact that a smaller total of reparations was paid than would, in all likelihood, have been exacted if a stable domestic monetary standard had been maintained. It is, however, to be hoped that the world has seen the last of intolerably severe punitive damages under the name of reparations, and that so dubious an opportunity of "gain" will, in consequence, not again be open to any nation. Such "gains" as the Germans may have attained on this score have not, in any event, here been taken into account. The receipts from the foreign sales of German currency, moreover, were on a scale which will perhaps never be repeated. The confidence of the outside world in German recuperative capacity after the war was nothing short of pathological. Prior to and during the war the Germans had been widely regarded as diabolically efficient and a world which was ignorant of the first principles

---

[1] It is possible that the mere shift in wealth and income may have involved an economic loss through the operation of the law of diminishing utility. But, if this occurred, it is too intangible for measurement.

of monetary matters bought marks in enormous volume on the assumption that a mark represented a definite share in the economic structure and must grow in value as German economic life revived.[2] Such an illusion is not apt to be indulged again so long as the memory of what happened in the German case remains at all green. In the absence of any opportunity to exploit foreign buyers of currency, the almost inevitable losses in the international commodity transactions of a country which abandons a metal, and abuses a paper, standard will probably eliminate any future chance of a net national gain from inflation.

Even in the German case the gain may possibly have been apparent only. In the preceding chapter German production has been measured in relative terms. It is possible, however, that disturbed monetary conditions in any one important country may have such ramifications as to cripple trade all over the world. The relative status of production in the country of inflation would then furnish no reliable criterion of the absolute effect of the lapse from monetary stability. While it is impossible to appraise such imponderables, the writer is of the opinion that, except where international trade forms a very large part of the total commerce of any given political unit and where trade relations with the country of depreciated paper are very close, the repercussions of a monetary explosion, in their adverse aspects at any rate, are chiefly confined to the country in which the explosion takes place. No convincing evidence can be brought to show that the widespread depression of 1920-1921, for instance, was due to depreciation of any currency. On the contrary it was tied up with the almost universal *appreciation* of monetary units. In 1919 and the fore-part of 1920, on the other hand, when all of the important currencies were falling in value, world trade was extremely active. Furthermore, though it was not until late 1926 that practically all the important monetary units were stabilized relative to gold, world trade and production cannot be shown to have suffered unduly in the years 1922 to 1926. With some slight reservations, arising from an unproved but perhaps real adverse influence of German monetary phenomena on world economic activity, production in the Reich, as it developed up to 1924 in relation to that in other countries, may therefore be assumed to have measured the absolute effect of currency depreciation.

One or two other facets of the matter should, however, be considered. German inflation transformed the machinery for accumulation of capital

[2] It should be noted to the credit of German private business men that practically no losses were sustained during the inflation period by foreign creditors of German *business* concerns provided the debts were denominated in foreign currencies.

goods and, though it does not appear that the collapse of the currency led to any reduction in the amount of real capital annually added to the wealth of the Reich, there may have been a decline in its quality. Especially in the later stages of inflation, investment in durable goods took on a bizarre aspect. Little effort was made to distinguish between such extensions of plant and equipment as would justify, in future yield, the present outlay, and those which would merely prevent the complete evanescence of the monetary values involved. The progress of inflation increasingly induced capital expenditures which had no prospect of showing a long-run profit. If, as seems to have been the case, the net effect of inflation was to divert a larger than usual share of production from immediate consumption to investment, the sudden reversion to a stable monetary standard was almost sure to lead to some dislocation. When monetary stability was restored there was no longer any strong tendency toward capital accumulation and the industries producing capital goods were therefore subjected to a sudden shrinkage in demand. Further than this, equipment which may have been well suited to the production of commodities for which there was a ready market when money was rapidly depreciating, was superfluous, or very ill-adapted, to the conditions prevailing from the beginning of 1924 onward. Much of the apparatus installed in the years 1920 to 1923 was therefore scrapped in the reconstruction of industry which, under the name of "rationalization," has been something of a fetich to the post-inflation German economy. The contraction of consumption essential to the accumulation of such equipment as had to be scrapped was, of course, a useless sacrifice and the marked improvement in German output in recent years is probably mainly due to real, instead of illusory, industrial betterments the introduction of which was retarded by inflation.[3]

The habit of individual saving, moreover, which for the time being had been destroyed by currency depreciation, was slow to revive when it once more became other than folly. The post-stabilization German economy has therefore continued to be saddled with high interest rates especially since its capital requirements are no longer being supplied through

[3] cf. The Recovery of Germany, James W. Angell, Yale University Press, New Haven, 1929. Some of the immense properties acquired through inflation, particularly the ponderous acquisitions of Hugo Stinnes, proved to be white elephants when order in currency matters had been reestablished. Professor Angell seems to be of the opinion that *most* of the capital investments of the inflation years were wasted. This seems to the present writer to be an exaggeration. In general, he is of the opinion that Professor Angell overstates the evil effects of inflation.

the inflationary stimulus to direct investment.[4] Though the situation has been markedly alleviated by large draughts of capital from abroad the cost of capital has no doubt been greater than it would have been had German thrift been present in its old-time intensity. This development is not to be counted as direct loss. If the German people prefers to spend rather more and save rather less, and is ready to pay the high interest charges which such a preference, in part, imposes,[5] the relatively small savings are compensated by relatively large immediate consumption. High interest rates are, nevertheless, an undesirable aftermath of inflation and should be given some place in the summation of its adverse effects. With all these reservations taken into account, however, it cannot but be asserted that, considering only the material aspects of the matter, the Germans, *as a nation*, profited rather than lost through the collapse of their currency. The adverse effects on the national psychology were no doubt of import, but they cannot be measured, and these effects will perhaps more quickly disappear than is ordinarily supposed. In foreign countries there is no disposition to recognize any decline in the German economic virtues. Germany's credit abroad is excellent, the inflation episode is properly regarded as due to such temporarily invincible circumstance as not at all to reflect upon the essential business integrity of the nation, and the events of the past five years have fully demonstrated the economic vitality of the Reich.

§ INFERENCES FOR THE FUTURE

The burden of reparations is still heavy, but the elasticity of demand for both exports and imports, convincingly demonstrated in the inflation years,[6] leaves small room for the opinion that the necessary increase in the export-import ratio will not occur. The national economic structure was not impaired seriously, if at all, by the currency *débâcle;* the terrific external pressure which, in the years 1920-1923, led to aberrations even from the ordinarily erring course of exchange rates, prices, and international trade under depreciated paper monetary standards has been withdrawn; the requisite price adjustments are proceeding slowly and surely toward a new equilibrium in international transactions in which reparations payments will play a normal and undisturbing rôle. As yet

---

[4] Deposits in savings banks, however, within a couple of years began to grow surprisingly. The height of interest rates marks the hunger for capital rather than its absolute shortage.

[5] The imposition is relatively light since foreign capital may be obtained at rates not greatly above those prevailing on similar investments in the country from which the capital comes.

[6] *cf. supra,* Chap. VIII.

the easing of the credit situation which the adoption of the Dawes Plan occasioned, and the facilities for borrowing abroad thus opened up, have had the effect of postponing the actual impact of reparations on German national income while readjustment to the new international economic position is going forward. It cannot definitely be concluded, even with the revision of the Dawes Plan carried out in 1929 under the chairmanship of Owen D. Young, that no further troubles will eventuate. But the loans already floated have operated to bring about a status analogous to that which would have obtained if reparations payments had been graded upwards from a low level at the start, while experience since 1924 has tended to show that, provided a rational method is pursued, the reparations obligations now laid upon the Germans can be met without serious difficulty.[7] The ethics of reparations will perhaps always be an open question but, on the possibility of payment and transfer, indisputable fact is laying an ardent controversy quietly to sleep. Nor is there any reason to suppose that the interest charges on the private debt obligations incurred by the Germans since 1924, or those which may hereafter be assumed, will obstruct the machinery of international finance. Oiled with credit at appropriate times, and operated with some circumspection, that machinery will function indefinitely under any load likely to be put upon it by commercial transactions. Properly invested, all borrowings will yield, within the borrowing country, at least enough to pay interest, and the possible range of expansion of exports and contraction of imports of any given country over an extended period, is so great as to ensure the transfer to the lender of any excess of interest on old borrowings over the borrower's receipts from current loans. No transfer problem has ever arisen out of *commercial* transactions in the past and there is no reason to believe that any such problem will appear in the future. The older theories of money and of foreign exchange failed to take into account the possible effects of enormous absolute burdens imposed without regard for economic realities, and certain modifications which the German experience suggests have been set forth above. But those older theories were fundamentally sound and the policy of *laissez-faire* to which they point is valid still. The play of prices brings about, under our very eyes, the adjustments which we are prone to believe can never be effected, and the secular growth of international trade, in spite of all obstacles thrust in its way by mercantilistic governments, gradually

[7] For a detailed discussion of this question the reader is referred to an article by the present writer entitled "Germany's Capacity to Pay and the Reparation Plan," *American Economic Review*, Vol. XV, No. 2, June 1925, pp. 209-227.

reduces the problems of the present to the commonplaces of the future. The mills of international finance grind slowly but their capacity is great. It is also flexible. The one condition is that the hoppers be not unduly loaded in the effort to get the whole grist from a single grinding. So much for the economics of the question. What politics has in store is, however, an inscrutable mystery. It can only be said that such financial difficulties as may occur will almost certainly arise from political rather than from economic sources.

BIBLIOGRAPHY

BIBLIOGRAPHY

OFFICIAL OR QUASI-OFFICIAL PUBLICATIONS

Statistisches Reichsamt (Current publications).
   Statistik des deutschen Reichs.
   Statistisches Jahrbuch für das deutsche Reich.
   Monatliche Nachweise über den auswärtigen Handel Deutschlands.
   Wirtschaft und Statistik.
   Vierteljahrshefte zur Statistik des deutschen Reichs.
   Statistik der Güterbewegung auf deutschen Eisenbahnen.
Statistisches Reichsamt (Special publications).
   Zahlen zur Geldentwertung in Deutschland 1914 bis 1923. Berlin,
      Reimar Hobbing, 1925.
   Germany's Economic and Financial Situation. Berlin, Zentralverlag
      G.m.b.H., 1923.
   Germany's Economy, Currency and Finance. Berlin, Zentralverlag
      G.m.b.H., 1924.
   Konzerne, Interessengemeinschaften und ähnliche Zusammenschlüsse
      im Deutschen Reich Ende 1926. Berlin, Carl Heymann, 1927.
Institut für Konjunkturforschung.
   Vierteljahrshefte zur Konjunkturforschung. Berlin, Reimar Hobbing,
      1926—.
Auswärtiges Amt.
   Gutachten der internationalen Finanzsachverständigen über die
      Stabilisierung. Berlin, Carl Heymann, 1922.
Reichsverkehrministerium.
   Statistik der im Betriebe befindlichen Eisenbahnen Deutschlands.
      Berlin, Reichsdruckerei, 1882—.
Reichsministerium des Innern.
   Reichsgesetzblatt. Berlin, 1871—.
Reichsarbeitsverwaltung.
   Reichsarbeitsblatt. Berlin, 1903—.
Reichstag.
   Referentenentwurf einer Denkschrift über die Aufwertung. Verf. im
      Reichsfinanzministerium. Berlin, Carl Heymann, 1925. (Denk-
      schriften des Deutschen Reichstags, 1925, No. 4.)

Denkschrift über die Ablösung der Markanleihen des Reichs. Berlin, Carl Heymann, 1928. (Denkschriften des Deutschen Reichstags, 1928, No. 6.)

Reichsbank.

Die Reichsbank 1901-1925. Berlin, Druckerei der Reichsbank, 1926.

Annual reports. Berlin.

Commercial banks. Annual reports of:

Berliner Handels-Gesellschaft, Berlin.

Commerz- und Privatbank Aktiengesellschaft, Hamburg and Berlin.

Darmstädter und Nationalbank, Berlin, Bremen and Darmstadt. (Established 1921 by an amalgamation of the Bank für Handel und Industrie and the Nationalbank für Deutschland—see these two banks for earlier reports.)

Deutsche Bank, Berlin.

Diskontogesellschaft, Berlin.

Dresdner Bank, Berlin and Dresden.

Reichsverband der deutschen Industrie.

Deutsche Wirtschafts- und Finanzpolitik. Berlin, 1925. (Veröffentlichungen des Reichsverbandes der deutschen Industrie, No. 29.)

League of Nations.

Currencies After the War. London, Harrison & Sons, 1920.

International Economic Conference, Geneva, May 1927, Documentation. Geneva, 1927.

Memorandum on Balance of Payments and Foreign Trade Balances 1910-1923 et seq. Geneva, 1924-1926.

Memorandum on International Trade and Balances of Payments, 1912-1926 et seq. Geneva, 1927—.

Memorandum on Currency 1913-1921 et seq. Geneva, 1922-1924.

Memorandum on Central Banks 1913 and 1918-1921 et seq. Geneva, 1924-1925.

Memorandum on Currency and Central Banks 1913-1924 et seq. Geneva, 1925—.

Monthly Bulletin of Statistics. Geneva, 1919—.

International Labour Office.

Enquête sur la production. Rapport général. Paris, Berger-Levrault, 1923-1925.

European Housing Problems Since the War, 1914-1923. Geneva, 1924. (Studies and Reports, Series G, No. 1.)

Wage Changes in Various Countries, 1914 to 1925. Geneva, 1926. (Studies and Reports, Series D, No. 16.)

Workers Standard of Life in Countries with Depreciated Currency. Geneva, 1925. (Studies and Reports, Series D, No. 15.)

Unemployment, 1920-1923. Geneva, 1924. (Studies and Reports, Series C, No. 8.)

Reparation Commission.

The Experts' Plan for Reparation Payments. Paris, The Reparation Commission, 1926.

Execution of the Experts' Plan: Reports of the Agent General for Reparation Payments and the Commissioners and Trustees. Berlin, The Office for Reparation Payments, 1925 *et seq.*

Official Documents. London, His Majesty's Stationery Office, 1922 *et seq.*

Cunliffe Committee on Currency and Foreign Exchanges After the War. (Great Britain.)

First Interim Report. London, His Majesty's Stationery Office, 1924.

Department of Overseas Trade. (Great Britain.)

Report on the Economic and Financial Conditions in Germany to March 1922, *et seq.* London, His Majesty's Stationery Office, 1922-1925.

United States Federal Reserve Board.

Prices in the United States and Abroad 1919-1923. Special Bulletin. Washington, Government Printing Office, 1924.

United States Senate Commission of Gold and Silver Inquiry.

European Currency and Finance. Washington, Government Printing Office, 1925. (Serial 9, 2 vols.)

United States Tariff Commission

Depreciated Exchange and International Trade. Washington, Government Printing Office, 1922.

Haut Commissariat de la République Française dans les provinces du Rhin.

Bulletin d'informations économiques. Mainz, 1923-1926.

Bulletin financier. Mainz, 1922-1925.

Bulletin d'informations économiques et financières. Paris, 1926-1927.

Mission Interalliée de Controle des Usines et des Mines.

Dix ans du Développement industriel allemand 1914-1924. (Vol. 1.)

Questions économiques diverses: 1. Le commerce extérieur de l'Allemagne. 2. Les dettes obligataires et hypothécaires de l'industrie allemande avant la guerre. 3. Les propriétés en France de la grosse métallurgie allemande en 1913. 4. La stabilisation de la monnaie allemande. (Vol. 8.) Brussels, Dewaricht, 1924.

International Chamber of Commerce.
Progress in Public Finance of the Principal European Countries Since 1920. Germany. Brochure No. 38, Pt. 1, pp. 54-79.
International Federation of Trade Unions.
The Position of the Workers in Germany. Amsterdam 1923.

BOOKS

Abramovici, Arthur
Etude sur les transformations du systeme monétaire allemand de 1919 à 1923 et ses consequences economiques. Paris, Jouve et cie., 1926.
Aftalion, Albert.
Monnaie, prix et change: expériences récentes et théorie. Paris, Recueil Sirey, 1927.
Albers, Edgar.
Die Entstehungsgeschichte und der Streit um den wirtschaftlichen Charakter der deutschen Rentenmarkwährung. Berlin, Industrie-verlag Spaeth und Linde, 1928.
Amonn, Alfred, and Bernatzky, M. von.
Währungsreform in der Tschechoslowakei und in Sowjet Russland, München and Leipzig, Duncker und Humblot, 1924.
Anders, Ferdinand.
Der Stand der Aufwertung. Eine imparteiische Untersuchung ihrer volkswirtschaftlichen Grundlagen und Voraussetzungen. Berlin, Dohrn, 1924.
Anderson, Benjamin M., Jr.
The Value of Money. New York, The Macmillan Company, 1917.
Angas, L. L. B.
Germany and her Debts. A critical Examination of the Reparation Problem. With an Appendix on Exchange Stabilisation. London, Simmonds, 1923.
Reparations, Trade, and Foreign Exchange. London, P. S. King & Son, Ltd., 1922.
Angell, James Waterhouse.
The Recovery of Germany. New Haven, Yale University Press, 1929.
The Theory of International Prices; history, criticism and restatement. Cambridge, Harvard University Press, 1926.
Ansiaux, Maurice.
Principes de la politique regulatrice des changes. Brussels, Misch & Thron, 1910.
Aupetit, A.
Théorie générale de la monnaie. Paris, Guillaumin et cie., 1901.

Auspitz, Rudolph, and Lieben, Richard.
Untersuchungen über die Theorie des Preises. Leipzig, Duncker und Humblot, 1889.

Bastable, C. F.
The Theory of International Trade. London and New York, The Macmillan Company, 1903.

Baumgartner, Wilfrid.
Le rentenmark (15 octobre 1923—11 octobre 1924). Paris, Les Presses universitaires de France, 1925.

Becher, Carl.
Kommentar zu den Gesetzen und Verordnungen gegen die Steuerflucht und Kapitalflucht. Köln, O. Schmidt, 1924.

Behnsen, Henry, and Genzmer, Werner.
Die Folgen der Markentwertung für uns und die andern. Leipzig, Felix Meiner, 1921.
Valuta-elend und Friedens-vertrag. Leipzig, Felix Meiner, 1921.

Bendixen, Friedrich.
Geld und Kapital. Jena, Gustav Fischer, 1922.
Das Inflationsproblem. Stuttgart, Ferdinand Enke, 1917. (Finanz- und Volkswirtschaftliche Zeitfragen, No. 31.)
Währungspolitik und Geldtheorie im Lichte des Weltkrieges. München and Leipzig, Duncker und Humblot, 1919.

Bergmann, Carl.
History of Reparations. London, Ernest Benn, Ltd., 1927.

Beusch, Paul.
Währungszerfall und Währungsstabilisierung. Berlin, Julius Springer, 1928.

Billaudot, Maurice.
La politique monétaire de l'Allemagne depuis la fin de la guerre. Paris, Jouve et cie., 1923.

Bissing, Frh. von.
Inflation und Besteuerung in Deutschland von 1914-1923. Berlin, 1924.

Bonn, Moritz Julius.
Der Neue Plan als Grundlage der deutschen Wirtschaftslage. München, Duncker und Humblot, 1930.
Stabilization of the Mark. Chicago, First National Bank of Chicago, 1922.

Bonnet, George Edgar.
Les expériences monétaires contemporaines. Paris, A. Colin, 1926.

Brauer, Karl.
Die Anpassung der Löhne und Gehälter an die Lebenskosten, mit besonderer Rücksicht auf die deutschen und englischen Verhältnisse. Dresden, v. Zahn und Jaensch, 1922. (Veröffentlichungen der sächsischen Landesstelle für Gemeinwirtschaft, No. 18.)

Bressfeld, Friederich.
Die notwirtschaftliche Gesetzgebung. Stuttgart, Hess, 1923.

Bücher, Hermann.
Finanz- und Wirtschaftsentwicklung Deutschlands in den Jahren 1921 bis 1925. Berlin, Carl Heymann, 1925.

Büscher, Gustav.
Die Inflation und ihre Lehren. Zürich, A. Rudolf, 1926.

Cannan, Edwin.
An Economist's Protest. London, P. S. King & Son, Ltd., 1927.
The Paper Pound of 1797-1821. London, 1919. (A reprint of the Bullion Report of 1810, with comments.)

Cassel, Gustav.
Money and Foreign Exchange After 1914. New York, The Macmillan Company, 1923.
Post-War Monetary Stabilization. New York, Columbia University Press, 1928.
The World's Monetary Problems. London, Constable & Co., Ltd., 1921.

Clare, George.
A. B. C. of the Foreign Exchanges. London and New York, The Macmillan Company, 1893.

Cohen, Arthur.
Besteuerung und Geldentwertung. München and Leipzig, Duncker und Humblot, 1924. (Schriften des Vereins für Sozialpolitik, Vol. 168, Part 2.)

Cross, Ira B.
Domestic and Foreign Exchange. New York, The Macmillan Company, 1923.

Dalberg, Rudolf.
Banko-Mark im Aussenhandel? Die Entwicklung einer neuen stabilen Geldeinheit aus der Erkenntnis von Triebkräften und Auswirkungen des Währungsverfalls. Berlin, Reimar Hobbing, 1922. (Handbücher der Industrie- und Handels-Zeitung, Vol. 3.)

Deutsche Währungs- und Kreditpolitik, 1923-1926. Berlin, Reimar Hobbing, 1926.

Die Entthronung des Goldes. Aus den Erfahrungen des Wirtschaftskriegs. Stuttgart, Ferdinand Enke, 1916. (Finanz- und Volkswirtschaftliche Zeitfragen, No. 30.)

Die neue deutsche Währung nach dem Dawesplan. Berlin, Carl Heymann, 1924.

Dane, E. Surrey.

What is Germany Doing? A Report on the Economic Conditions Prevailing in Germany. London, Simpkin, 1922.

Dawson, Sir Philip.

Germany's Industrial Revival. London, Williams and Norgate, Ltd., 1926.

de Bordes, J. van Walré.

The Austrian Crown. London, P. S. King & Son, Ltd., 1924.

Dernis, Georges.

La renaissance du crédit en Allemagne. Paris, Les Presses universitaires de France, 1927.

Diehl, Karl.

Über Fragen des Geldwesens und der Valuta während des Krieges und nach dem Kriege. Jena, Gustav Fischer, 1921.

Diehl, Karl, and Mombert, Paul.

Valuta. Karlsruhe, G. Braun, 1925.

Dub, Moriz.

Katastrophenhausse und Geldentwertung. Stuttgart, Ferdinand Enke, 1920. (Finanz- und Volkswirtschaftliche Zeitfragen, No. 65.)

Duboin, Jacques.

La stabilisation du franc. Paris, M. Rivière, 1927.

Dulles, Eleanor Lansing.

The French Franc, 1914-1928. New York, The Macmillan Company, 1929.

Ebel, Martin.

Das Reichsmietengesetz (vom 24 März 1922) und die preussische Ausführungsverordnung. (Dritte Auflage.) Berlin, Carl Heymann, 1922. (Wohnungsnotrecht, Vol. 1.)

Elster, Karl.

Die deutsche Not im Lichte der Währungstheorie; gesammelte Aufsätze. Jena, Gustav Fischer, 1921.

Die deutsche Valutapolitik nach dem Kriege. Stuttgart, Ferdinand Enke, 1919. (Finanz- und Volkswirtschaftliche Zeitfragen, No. 59.)

Die Seele des Geldes. Jena, Gustav Fischer, 1923.

Von der Mark zur Reichsmark; die Geschichte der deutschen Währung in den Jahren 1914 bis 1924. Jena, Gustav Fischer, 1928.

Enke, Alfred.

Der bargeldlose Zahlungsverkehr nach Stabilisierung der deutschen Währung. Borna-Leipzig, Universitätsverlag, Robert Noske, 1927.

Escher, Franklin.

Foreign Exchange Explained. New York, The Macmillan Company, 1917.

Eucken, Walter.

Kritische Betrachtungen zum deutschen Geldproblem. Jena, Gustav Fischer, 1923.

Eynern, Gert von.

Die Reichsbank, Probleme des deutschen Zentralnoteninstituts in geschichtlicher Darstellung. Jena, Gustav Fischer, 1928.

Feilen, Josef F.

Die Umlaufsgeschwindigkeit des Geldes. Berlin and Leipzig, W. de Gruyter & Co., 1923.

Feldmann, Grégoire.

Le franc français depuis 1914. Paris, E. Figuière, 1926.

Fischer, Julius.

Das Steuerwesen des deutschen Reiches. Stuttgart, W. Kohlhammer, 1924.

Fisher, Irving.

The Purchasing Power of Money. New York, The Macmillan Company, 1911.

Flux, Alfred W.

The Foreign Exchanges. London, P. S. King & Son, Ltd., 1924.

Fourgeaud, André.

La dépréciation et la revalorisation du mark allemand et les enseignements de l'expérience monétaire allemande. Paris, Payot, 1926.

Frayssinet, Pierre.

La politique monétaire de la France, (1924-1928). Paris, Recueil Sirey, 1928.

Fritz, Jakob.

Finanzierung und Steuer in der Goldmarkeröffnungsbilanz unter besonderer Berücksichtigung der angrenzenden Bilanzen. Berlin, Industrieverlag Spaeth und Linde, 1925. (Betriebs- und Finanzwirtschaftliche Forschungen, Series II, No. 17.)

Frommer, H., and Schlag, H.
Die Gesetzgebung über die Rentenmark mit ausführlichen Erläuterungen. Mannheim, J. Bensheimer, 1924.

Furniss, Edgar S.
Foreign Exchange. Boston and New York, Houghton Mifflin Company, 1922.

Gaertner, Friedrich.
Vom Gelde und der Geldentwertung. München, Drei Masken Verlag, 1922.

Gallatin, Albert.
Credit, Currency, and Banking: Considerations on the Currency and Banking System of the United States. Philadelphia, Carey and Lea, 1831.

Geiler, Karl.
Goldmarkbilanz und Goldmarkumstellung unter besonderer Berücksichtigung des Bewertungsproblems. Mannheim, Berlin and Leipzig, J. Bensheimer, 1924. (Wirtschaftsrechtliche Abhandlungen, No. 2.)

Germain-Martin, Henry.
La réglementation des opérations de change. Exportation des capitaux. Importation des valeurs mobilières. Paris, Jouve et Cie., 1926.

Geyer, Curt.
Drei Verderber Deutschlands. Berlin, J. H. W. Dietz Nachfolger, 1924.

Giustiniani, Gaston.
Le Commerce et l'industrie devant la dépréciation et la stabilisation monétaire; l'expérience allemande. Paris, Félix Alcan, 1927.

Gooch, G. P.
Germany. New York, Charles Scribner's Sons, 1925. (The Modern World, ed. by H. A. L. Fisher. Vol. 2.)

Goschen, George J. G.
The Theory of the Foreign Exchanges. London, E. Wilson, 1898.

Gregory, T. E.
The First Year of the Gold Standard. London, Ernest Benn, Ltd., 1926.
Foreign Exchange Before, During, and After the War. London, Humphrey Milford, 1921.

Grube, Harry.
Privatversicherung und Geldentwertung. Berlin, Industrieverlag Spaeth und Linde, 1923. (Betriebs- und Finanzwirtschaftliche Forschungen, Series II, No. 7.)

Grünfeld, Ernst.
Die deutsche Aussenhandelskontrolle. Bonn and Leipzig, Kurt Schröder, 1922. (Bonner Staatswissenschaftliche Untersuchungen. No. 2.)

Haber, Franz.
Untersuchungen über Irrtümer moderner Geldverbesserer. Jena, Gustav Fischer, 1926.

Haberland, Gunther.
Elf Jahre Staatlicher Regelung der Ein- und Ausfuhr, eine systematische Darstellung der deutschen Aussenhandelsregelung in den Jahren 1914-1925. Leipzig, Universitäts Verlag, R. Noske, 1927.

Hahn, L. Albert.
Geld und Kredit: gesammelte Aufsätze. Tübingen, J. C. B. Mohr, 1924.

Hantos, Elemér.
Das Geldproblem in Mitteleuropa. Jena, Gustav Fischer, 1925.

Harburger, W.
Gleitende Währung. München and Leipzig, Duncker und Humblot, 1923.

Harris, S. E.
The Assignats. Cambridge, Harvard University Press, 1930. (Harvard Economic Studies, Vol. 33.)

Hawtrey, Ralph George.
Currency and Credit. London and New York, Longmans, Green & Co., 1923.
Monetary Reconstruction. London and New York, Longmans, Green & Co., 1923.

Heichen, Arthur.
Deutschlands Zahlungsbilanz, 1925. Leipzig, B. G. Teubner, 1926.

Helfferich, Karl.
Deutschlands Volkswohlstand 1888-1913. Berlin, Georg Stilke, 1914.
Das Geld. Leipzig, C. L. Hirschfeld, 1923.

Hermberg, Paul.
Volkswirtschaftliche Bilanzen, Handels- Zahlungs- und Wirtschaftsbilanz als Massstab volkswirtschaftlicher Erfolgsrechnung. Leipzig, Akademische Verlagsgesellschaft, 1927.

Herzfelder, Edmund.
Die volkswirtschaftliche Bilanz und eine neue Theorie der Wechselkurse; die Theorie der reinen Papierwährung. Berlin, Julius Springer, 1919.

Heymann, Elsa.
Die Stellung der deutschen Sozialdemokratie zur Inflation. Charlottenburg, Gebrüder Hoffmann.

Heyn, Otto.
Über Geldschöpfung und Inflation. Stuttgart, Ferdinand Enke, 1921.
(Finanz- und Volkswirtschaftliche Zeitfragen, No. 73.)

Hildebrand, Richard.
Die Theorie des Geldes. Jena, Gustav Fischer, 1883.

Hirsch, Julius.
Die deutsche Währungsfrage. Jena, Kommissionsverlag von Gustav
Fischer, 1924. (Kieler Vorträge, No. 9.)
Der Moderne Handel. Tübingen, J. C. B. Mohr, 1925. (Grundriss der
Sozialökonomik, Section V, Part 2, 2nd edition.)

Hobson, C. K.
The Export of Capital. London, Constable and Co., Ltd., 1914.

Hoffmann, Hans Ludwig.
Die Antidumpinggesetzgebung des Auslandes und ihre Anwendung.
Berlin, Reichsverband der deutschen Industrie, 1925. (Veröffent-
lichungen des Reichsverbandes der deutschen Industrie, No. 26.)

Hofrichter, Helmut.
Über die Devisenpolitik der Reichsbank nach dem Kriege bis zur
Neuordnung des deutschen Währungswesens durch die Gesetze
vom 30. August 1924 zur Durchführung des Sachverständigen-
Gutachtens. Berlin, Ebering, 1926.

Horten, Alfons.
Erfassung der Sachwerte und Reparationsproblem. Berlin, Hans
Robert Engelmann, 1922.

Huas, René.
La valorisation des obligations industrielles en Allemagne. Ses rap-
ports avec la réforme monétaire. Paris, Librairie générale de droit
et de jurisprudence, 1928.

Jack, Daniel Thomas.
Restoration of European Currencies. London, P. S. King & Son, Ltd.,
1927.

Jaeger, Ruth Muller.
Stabilization of the Foreign Exchanges. New York, 1922.

Jankovich, Bela von.
Beiträge zur Theorie des Geldes auf Grund der Erfahrungen in den
Jahren 1914 bis 1925. Wien, Manzsche Verlags und Universitäts
Buchhandlung, 1926.

Jessen, Arnd.
  Die deutsche Finanzwirrnis. Berlin, Julius Springer, 1924.
  Finanzen Defizit und Notenpresse 1914-1922. Berlin, Julius Springer, 1923.
Jevons, W. S.
  Money and the Mechanism of Exchange. London, H. S. King & Co., 1875.
Katzenellenbaum, P. S.
  Russian Currency and Banking. London, P. S. King & Son, Ltd., 1925.
Kellenberger, Eduard.
  Geldumlauf und Thesaurierung. Zürich, Orell Füssli, 1920.
Kemmerer, E. W.
  Modern Currency Reforms. New York, The Macmillan Company, 1916.
  Money and Credit Instruments in their Relation to General Prices. New York, Henry Holt & Co., 1907.
Kerschagl, Richard.
  Die Geldprobleme von heute. München and Leipzig, Duncker und Humblot, 1922.
  Theorie des Geldes und der Geldwirtschaft. Jena, Gustav Fischer, 1923.
Keynes, John Maynard.
  Indian Currency and Finance. London, Macmillan & Co., Ltd., 1913.
  Monetary Reform. New York, Harcourt, Brace and Company, 1924.
  A Revision of the Treaty. London, Macmillan & Co., Ltd., 1922.
Knapp, Georg Friedrich.
  Staatliche Theorie des Geldes. München and Leipzig, Duncker und Humblot, 1921.
Knies, Karl G. A.
  Geld und Kredit. Berlin, Weidmannsche Buchhandlung, 1873-1879. 2 vols.
Koch, Erwin.
  Devisengesetzgebung und Ablieferungspflicht mit allen Ausfuhrungsbestimmungen nach den Stand von Ende September 1923. Stuttgart, J. Hess, 1923.
Koch, Richard, and Schacht, Hjalmar.
  Die Reichsgesetzgebung über Münz- und Notenbankwesen. Berlin and Leipzig, Walter de Gruyter & Co., 1926.

Koeppel, William.
Die Gesetzgebung gegen die Kapitalflucht. Berlin, Industrieverlag Spaeth und Linde, 1923.

Kraus, Emil.
Inflation. Valuta, Preis, Lohn 1914-1924. Kritische Gedanken zur gegenwärtigen Wirtschaftskrise. Mannheim, Berlin and Leipzig, J. Bensheimer, 1924.

Kuczynski, Robert René.
Lebenshaltung und Löhne. Berlin and Stuttgart, J. H. W. Dietz Nachfolger, 1923. (Jahrbuch der Finanzpolitischen Korrespondenz, 1922, Part 2.)

Kuczynski, Robert René, editor.
Deutschland und Frankreich; ihre Wirtschaft und ihre Politik, 1923-1924. Berlin, R. L. Prager, 1924.

Lachapelle, Georges.
Les batailles du franc; la trésorerie, le change et la monnaie depuis 1914. Paris, F. Alcan, 1928.

Lansburgh, Alfred.
Die Massnahmen der Reichsbank zur Erhöhung der Liquidität der deutschen Kreditwirtschaft. Stuttgart, Ferdinand Enke, 1914. (Finanz- und Volkswirtschaftliche Zeitfragen, No. 8.)
Die Politik der Reichsbank und die Reichsschatzanweisungen nach dem Kriege. München and Leipzig, Duncker und Humblot, 1924. (Schriften des Vereins für Sozialpolitik, Vol. 166, Part 2.)

Lehfeldt, Robert Alfred.
Restoration of the World's Currencies. London, P. S. King & Son, Ltd., 1923.

Leitner, Friedrich.
Finanz- und Preispolitik bei sinkendem Geldwert. Frankfurt-am-Main, Sauerländer, 1923.

Leurence, Fernand.
La stabilisation du franc. Paris, Marcel Giard, 1926.

Lewinsohn, Richard.
Die Umschichtung der europäischen Vermögen. Berlin, S. Fischer, 1925.

Liefmann, W. Robert.
Von Reichtum der Nationen; Untersuchungen über die sogenannten Reparationsfragen und die internationalen Verschuldungs- und Währungsprobleme. Karlsruhe, G. Braun, 1925.

Long, Robert Crozier.
Mythology of Reparations. London, Duckworth, 1928.

Lotz, Walther.
  Die deutsche Staatsfinanzwirtschaft im Kriege. Carnegie Endowment
    for International Peace. Berlin, Deutsche Verlagsanstalt, 1927.
  Valutafrage und öffentliche Finanzen in Deutschland. München and
    Leipzig, Duncker und Humblot, 1923. (Schriften des Vereins für
    Sozialpolitik, Vol. 164, Part 1.)
Luther, Hans.
  Feste Mark—Solide Wirtschaft. Berlin, Otto Stollberg & Co., 1924.
Mahlberg, Walter.
  Bilanztechnik und Bewertung bei schwankender Währung. Leipzig,
    G. A. Gloeckner, 1922. (Betriebs- und Finanzwirtschaftliche Forsch-
    ungen, No. 10.)
  Goldkreditverkehr und Goldmarkbuchführung. Berlin, Julius
    Springer, 1923. (Betriebswirtschaftliche Zeitfragen, No. 4.)
Marshall, Alfred.
  The Fiscal Policy of International Trade. London, Printed for H. M.
    Stationery Office by Eyre and Spottiswoode, 1908. (Memorandum
    to the House of Commons.)
  Memorandum on the Effects of Differences in Currencies. Submitted
    to the Gold and Silver Commission of 1888. 1888 Parliamentary
    Papers, Vol. 45.
  Money, Credit and Commerce. London, Macmillan & Co., Ltd., 1923.
Martin, Pierre-Georges.
  La stabilisation et la retour à la monnaie or (Pologne, Allemange,
    Territoire de Dantzig.) Paris, R. Guillon, 1925.
Maus, Josef.
  Anleiheformen unter dem Einfluss der Geldentwertung. Leipzig, G. A.
    Gloeckner, 1925. (Ergänzungsbände zur Zeitschrift für Handels-
    wissenschaftliche Forschung, Vol. 4.)
Meyer, Lothar.
  Die deutsche Landwirtschaft während der Inflation und zu Beginn
    der Deflation. Tübingen, S. C. B. Mohr, 1924.
Meynial, Pierre.
  La balance des comptes de quelques grands pays industriels, Angle-
    terre, France, Etats- Unis, Allemagne &c. Paris, Dalloz, 1926.
Mills, Frederick C.
  The Behavior of Prices. New York, National Bureau of Economic
    Research, Inc., 1927.
Mises, Ludwig von.
  Theorie des Geldes und der Umlaufsmittel. München and Leipzig,
    Duncker und Humblot, 1924.

Mises, Ludwig von, and Klein, Franz.
Die geldtheoretische und geldrechtliche Seite des Stabilisierungs-
problems. München and Leipzig, Duncker und Humblot, 1923.
(Schriften des Vereins für Sozialpolitik, Vol. 164, Part 2.)

Mitchell, Wesley C.
Business Cycles: the Problem and Its Setting. New York, National
Bureau of Economic Research, Inc., 1927.
International Price Comparisons. Washington, Government Printing
Office, 1919. (War Industries Board, Price Bulletin, No. 2.)

Moldenhauer, Paul.
Die Regelung der Aufwertungsfrage. Köln, P. Neubner, 1925. (Kölner
Industriehefte, No. 2.)

Moll, Bruno.
Die modernen Geldtheorien und die Politik der Reichsbank. Stuttgart,
Ferdinand Enke, 1917. (Finanz- und Volkswirtschaftliche Zeit-
fragen, No. 45.)

Morgain, Georges.
La couronne autrichienne depuis le traité de Saint-Germain. Paris,
L. Tenin, 1927.

Moriès, Valéry de.
Misére et splendeur des finances allemandes. Paris, Société d'edition
"Les Belles-Lettres," 1925. (Les Cahiers Rhénans, No. 5.)

Moulin, Gustav.
Les réformes du régimes des assurances sociales en Allemagne depuis
la révolution de 1918. Paris, Les Presses universitaires de France,
1925.

Moulton, H. G.
The Reparation Plan. Institute of Economics. New York, McGraw-
Hill Book Company, 1924.

Moulton, H. G., and McGuire, Constantine E.
Germany's Capacity to Pay. Institute of Economics. New York, Mc-
Graw-Hill Book Company, 1923.

Mügel, Oskar.
Die Aufwertung. Überblick über die Entwicklung. Berlin, Gersbach,
1926. (Schriften der Vereinigung für staatswissenschaftliche Fort-
bildung, No. 14.)

Muhs, Karl.
Preispolitik und Preiskalkulation unter den Einwirkungen der Geldentwertung. Jena, Gustav Fischer, 1923.

Nadler, Max.
Grundbuch- und Aufwertungsfragen. Berlin, Sack, 1926.

Naphtali, Fritz von.
    Im Zeichen des Währungselends. Frankfurt-am-Main, Franfurter
    Societäts-Druckerei G.m.b.H., 1923.
    Währungsgesundung und Wirtschaftssanierung. Frankfurt-am-Main,
    Frankfurter Societäts-Druckerei G.m.b.H., 1925
National Industrial Conference Board.
    Cost of Living in Foreign Countries. New York, National Industrial
    Conference Board, Inc., 1927. (Research Report, No. 119.)
    The Inter-Ally Debts and the United States. New York, National
    Industrial Conference Board, Inc., 1925.
    Wages in Great Britain, France and Germany. New York, National
    Industrial Conference Board, Inc., 1921. (Research Report, No. 40.)
Neckarsulmer, Ernst.
    Der alte und der neue Reichtum. Berlin, F. Fontane & Co., 1925.
Neumark, Fritz.
    Begriff und Wesen der Inflation. Jena, Gustav Fischer, 1922.
Nogaro, Bertrand.
    Finances et politique. Paris, Marcel Giard, 1927.
    Modern Monetary Systems. London, P. S. King & Son, Ltd., 1927.
Nordmann, Georges.
    Exportation de capitaux et evasion fiscale. Paris, Les Presses universi-
    taires de France, 1927.
Oelenheinz, Theodor.
    Spiegel der deutschen Inflation. Dokumente, Berichte, Urteile. Leipzig,
    "Volks-Recht," 1928.
Palyi, Melchior.
    Der Streit um die staatliche Theorie des Geldes. München and Leipzig,
    Duncker und Humblot, 1922.
    Das Wesen der Inflation. München and Leipzig, Duncker und Hum-
    blot, 1923. (Hauptprobleme der Soziologie; Erinnerungsgabe für
    Max Weber, Vol. 2, pp. 339-352.)
    Zur Frage der Kapitalwanderungen nach dem Kriege. München
    and Leipzig, Duncker und Humblot, 1926. (Schriften des Vereins
    für Sozialpolitik, Vol. 171, Part 3.)
Pfeifer, Bruno.
    Der Schriftwechsel im Bankgeschäft. Leipzig, A. Gloeckner, 1925.
Pfeifer, Kurt.
    Die Einwirkung des Weltkriegs und der Nachkriegszeit auf die
    deutsche Effektenbörse in wirtschaftlicher und rechtlicher Bezie-
    hung. Landau (Pfalz), Kaussler, 1926.

Pohle, L.

Geldentwertung, Valutafrage und Währungsreform; kritische Betrachtungen über die gegenwärtige Lage der deutschen Volkswirtschaft. Leipzig, Deichert, 1920.

Pommery, Louis.

Changes et monnaies. Paris, Marcel Giard, 1926.

Prochownik, Martha Eva.

Die wirtschaftliche Lage der geistigen Arbeiter Deutschlands. Berlin, Reimar Hobbing, 1925. (Schriften der deutschen Gesellschaft zur Bekämpfung der Arbeitslosigkeit, No. 8.)

Raffegeau, P. C. and Lacout, A.

Établissement des bilans-or. Paris, Payot, 1926.

Ramhorst, Friedrich.

Die Entstehung der deutschen Rentenbank. Berlin, Reichsverband der Deutschen Industrie, 1924. (Veröffentlichungen des Reichsverbandes der Deutschen Industrie, No. 20, March, 1924.)

Ramstein, Adolf.

Das Verhältnis der Notenbanken zur Kriegsfinanzierung in England, Frankreich, Deutschland, und der Schweiz. Bern, P. Haupt, 1923.

Rasin, Alois.

Financial policy of Czecho-Slovakia during the first year of its history. London, Humphrey Milford, 1923.

Reinhold, Peter P.

The Economic, Financial, and Political State of Germany since the War. Institute of Politics. New Haven, Yale University Press, 1928.

Renell, Erich.

Der Warenwechsel in Deutschland in der Geldentwertungszeit, 1919-1923. Charlottenburg, Gebrüder Hoffman.

Ricardo, David.

The High Price of Bullion. London, J. Murray, 1810.

Riss, Hans.

Leitfaden durch das Aufwertungsrecht. Gladbach, Volksvereins-Verlag, 1926. (Staatsburger-Bibliothek Part 137/138.)

Rist, Charles.

La déflation en pratique. Paris, Marcel Giard, 1924.

Les finances de guerre de l'Allemagne. Paris, Payot, 1921.

Robert, Jean Maxime.

Dépréciation de la monnaie et équilibre budgétaire, étude sur les finances allemandes, 1922-1923. Paris, Les Presses universitaires de France, 1926.

Robertson, Dennis H.
  Money. London, Nisbet & Co., Ltd., 1922.
Rogers, James Harvey.
  The Process of Inflation in France, 1914-1927. New York, Columbia
  University Press, 1929.
Rogowski, Erich.
  Das deutsche Volkseinkommen. Berlin, E. Ebering, 1926.
Rosendorff, Richard.
  Die Goldmarkbilanz. Berlin, Otto Stollberg & Co. (Verlag für Politik
  und Wirtschaft), 1924.
Sachs, Carl L.
  Die deutsche Währungslage. Freising-München, F. P. Datterer & Cie.,
  1924.
Sacy, Jacques S. de.
  Conséquences économiques et sociales du retour de l'Allemagne à
  l'étalon-or. Paris, Les Presses universitaires de France, 1927.
Sancery, Jean.
  Le retour à l'or dans les régimes monétaires après la guerre. Paris,
  Jouve et Cie., 1925.
Schacht, Hjalmar.
  Eigene oder geborgte Währung. Leipzig, Quelle & Meyer, 1927.
  (Schriftenreihe der Weltwirtschaftlichen Gesellschaft zu Münster,
  No. 16.)
  Stabilization of the Mark. London, George Allen and Unwin, Ltd.,
  1927.
Schaefer, Carl A.
  Klassische Valuta-Stabilisierungen und ihre Lehren für Mark-
  stabilisierung. (3. Auflage.) Hamburg, C. Boysen, 1922.
Schaeffer, Karl, and Keidel, Fritz.
  Die Hauptfragen der Geldentwertung und Aufwertung nach bürger-
  lichem Recht. (3. Auflage.) Leipzig, Hirschfeld, 1925.
Schmalenbach, Eugen.
  Goldmarkbilanz. Berlin, Julius Springer, 1923. (Betriebswirtschaft-
  liche Zeitfragen, Vol. 1.)
  Grundlagen dynamischer Bilanzlehre (3. Auflage.) Leipzig, G. A.
  Gloeckner, 1925.
Schmalenbach, Eugen, and Prion, Willi.
  Zwei Vorträge über Scheingewinne: Die steuerliche Behandlung der
  Scheingewinne. Die Finanzpolitik der Unternehmung. Jena, Gustav

Fischer, 1922. (Mitteilungen der Gesellschaft für wirtschaftliche Ausbildung, Frankfurt-am-Main, Sonderband 1, Parts 1 and 2.)

Schmidt-Essen, Alfred.

Devisenkurse und Devisenpolitik. (3. Auflage.) Gladbach, Volkvereins-Verlag, 1922. (Staatsburger-Bibliothek, Part 75.)

Währungsfragen der Gegenwart. Jena, Gustav Fischer, 1922.

Schoenthal, Justus.

Papiermark, Rentenmark, Reichsmark. Ein Beitrag zur jüngsten Entwicklungsgeschichte der deutsche Währung. Leipzig, Stein und Kroll, 1925.

Rentenbank und Rentenmark. Berlin, Carl Heymann, 1924.

Schramm, Albert.

Deutsches Notgeld 1914-1919. Leipzig, Deutscher Verein für Buchwesen und Schrifttum, 1920.

Schultz, Hans-Otto.

Devisenhandelspolitik. Stuttgart, Ferdinand Enke, 1918. (Finanz- und Volkswirtschaftliche Zeitfragen, No. 55.)

Schultzenstein, Siegfried.

Anleiherecht. Reichsschuldwesen, Reichsschuldbuch, Anleiheablösung, Anleihen auf Grund des Dawes-Plans, Anleihen der Reichspost und Anleihen der Schutzgebiete. Berlin, Sieben Stäbe-Verlag, 1929. (Die deutsche Reichsgesetzgebung.)

Schwartz, Arnold Richard.

Die deutsche Ausfuhrkontrolle nach dem Kriege. Greifswald, L. Bamberg, 1923. (Griefswalder Staatswissenschaftliche Abhandlungen, No. 21.)

Schwiedland, Eugen.

Geld und Währung. Stuttgart, W. Kohlhammer, 1923.

Sering, Max.

Germany Under the Dawes Plan. London, P. S. King & Son, Ltd., 1929.

Shaw, William Arthur.

Currency, Credit and the Exchanges during the Great War and Since (1914-1926). London, G. G. Harrap & Co., Ltd., 1927.

Singer, Kurt.

Staat und Wirtschaft seit dem Waffenstillstand. Jena, Gustav Fischer, 1924.

Soecknick, Margarete.

Die Entwicklung der Reallöhne in der Nachkriegszeit, dargestellt an typischen Thüringer Industrien. Jena, Gustav Fischer, 1927.

(Abhandlungen des wirtschaftswissenschaftlichen Seminars zu Jena, Vol. 18, Part 1.)

Sontag, Ernst.
Hypothekengläubiger und Anleihebesitzer im Kampf um ihr Recht. Eine Kritik des Entwurfes eines Gesetzes über der Aufwertung von Hypotheken und anderen privatrechtlichen Ansprüchen sowie des Entwurfes eines Gesetzes über der Ablösung öffentlicher Anleihen. Berlin, Sack, 1925.

Stein, Wilhelm.
Valuta-Risiko und Sicherung der Unternehmung. Berlin, Industrie-verlag Spaeth und Linde, 1924. (Betriebs- und Finanzwirtschaft-liche Forschungen, Series II, No. 11.)

Stenger, Hermann.
Die Aufwertung von Hypotheken und anderen Ansprüchen und die Ablösung öffentlicher Anleihen. (In 3 Lieferungen.) München, Bayer. Kommunalschriften-Verlag G.m.b.H., 1925-1926.

Taussig, F. W.
Free Trade, the Tariff and Reciprocity. New York, The Macmillan Company, 1920.
International Trade. New York, The Macmillan Company, 1927.

Terhalle, Fritz.
Das deutsche Bankwesen. Berlin, Zentralverlag G.m.b.H., 1922. (Staat und Wirtschaft, Einzeldarstellungen in Grundrissen, Vol. 16.)
Währung und Valuta. Jena, Gustav Fischer, 1922.

Tross, Arnold.
Der Aufbau der Eisen und eisenverarbeitenden Industrie Konzerne Deutschlands. Berlin, Julius Springer, 1923.

Viner, Jacob.
Canada's Balance of International Indebtedness, 1900-1913. Cambridge, Harvard University Press, 1924. (Harvard Economic Studies, Vol. 26.)

Wächter, Siegfried von.
Der Kampf um die Währung: die wichtigsten Währungsreformen der letzten Jahrzehnte und das Valutaproblem der Gegenwart. Berlin-Grünewald, Walther Rothschild, 1922.

Wagemann, Ernst F.
Allgemeine Geldlehre. Berlin, H. R. Engelmann, 1923.

Wagemann, Gustav.
Aufwertung und Geldentwertungsausgleich nach der dritten Steuer-notverordnung vom 14. Februar 1924. Berlin, Carl Heymann, 1924.

Wagner, Adolf H. G.
Die russische Papierwährung. Riga, N. Kymmel, 1868.

Wahle, Karl.
Das Valorisationsproblem in der Gesetzgebung und Rechtsprechung Mitteleuropas. Wien, Rikola Verlag, 1924.

Walter, Hubert Conrad.
Foreign Exchange and Foreign Debts. London, Methuen & Co., Ltd., 1926.

Warneyer, Otto.
Geldentwertung und Vertragserfüllung nebst anderen wichtigen, die Geldentwertung betreffenden Fragen. Berlin, Industrieverlag Spaeth und Linde, 1923.

Wernlé, Gabriel.
La balance commerciale et la politique économique de l'Allemagne. Paris, Imprimerie de la Société d'études et d'informations économiques, 1924.

Whitaker, Albert C.
Foreign Exchange. New York and London, D. Appleton & Company, 1920.

Williams, John H.
Argentine International Trade, 1880-1900. Cambridge, Harvard University Press, 1920. (Harvard Economic Studies, Vol. 22.)

Willis, H. P., and Beckhart, B. H., Ed.
Foreign Banking Systems. New York, Henry Holt & Co., 1929.

Winnewisser, Georg.
Die Aufwertung der Industrie-Obligationen. Eine wirtschaftliche Untersuchung. Karlsruhe, G. Braun, 1927. (Wirtschaftsstudien, No. 9.)

York, Thomas.
International Exchange, normal and abnormal. New York, Ronald Press Company, 1923.

Yves-Guyot.
Les problèmes de la déflation. Paris, Felix Alcan, 1923.

Yves-Guyot and Raffalovich, Arthur.
Inflation et déflation. Paris, Felix Alcan, 1921.

Zehnder, Alfred.
Die inländische und ausländische Kaufkraft des Geldes in den Jahren 1914 bis 1922. Weinfelden, A. G. Neuenschwander, 1923.

Zeiger, Philipp.
Das deutsche Geldwesen. Leipzig, G. A. Gloeckner, 1925.

Zimmermann, Heinrich.
  Die deutsche Inflation. Berlin, Emil Ebering, 1927.

                    PERIODICAL ARTICLES
Amonn, Alfred.
  Das Ziel der Währungspolitik. Zeitschrift für Volkswirtschaft und
  Sozialpolitik, N.F. Vol. 1, No. 7/9, pp. 401-430.
Anderson, Benj. M.
  German Business and Finances under the Dawes Plan. Chase Eco-
  nomic Bulletin (Chase National Bank, New York), Vol. 6, No. 1,
  April 2, 1926.
Andreack, Ernst.
  Die gleitende Lohnskala als Mittel zur Erhaltung des Arbeitfriedens.
  Arbeit und Beruf, Vol. 1, No. 3, pp. 105-107.
Angell, J. W.
  Equilibrium in International Trade: the United States, 1919-1926.
  Quarterly Journal of Economics, Vol. 42, pp. 388-433, May 1928.
  International Trade under Inconvertible Paper. Quarterly Journal
  of Economics, Vol. 36, pp. 359-412, May 1922.
  Monetary Theory and Monetary Policy. Quarterly Journal of Eco-
  nomics, Vol. 39, pp. 267-299, February 1925.
Anonymous.
  Currency Reorganization in Germany. Federal Reserve Bulletin, Vol.
  10, pp. 36-37, August 1924.
  The Foreign Borrowing of Germany. Economist (London), Vol. 105,
  No. 4400, pp. 1135-1137, December 24, 1927.
  The Influence of a Falling Exchange on the Wealth of a Country.
  By a German Economist. Economist, Vol. 95, No. 4139, pp. 1165-
  1166; No. 4140, pp. 1213-1214, December 23-30, 1922.
  An Official Explanation of the German Law for the Revaluation of
  Öld Mark Bonds and Debts. Economic World, N.S., Vol. 30, pp. 449-
  450, September 26, 1925.
Beckmann, F.
  Die Wiederherstellung der deutschen Währung. Zeitschrift des Vereins
  deutscher Ingenieure, Vol. 66, No. 25, pp. 637-641, June 24, 1922.
  Inlandpreis und Weltmarktpreis für Getreide; Getreideeinfuhr und
  Mehleinfuhr. Schmollers Jahrbuch, Vol. 48, pp. 871-896, 1924.
Bell, John.
  Germany's Trade War and After. Fortnightly Review, N.S., Vol. 116,
  No. 696, pp. 763-772, Dec. 1, 1924.

Bente, Hermann.
   Die deutsche Währungspolitik von 1914 bis 1924. Weltwirtschaft-
      liches Archiv, Vol. 23, No. 1, pp. 117-191, January, 1926.
Berliner, Ludwig.
   Die Aufwertung der privaten Versicherungsverträge. Versicherungs-
      praxis, Vol. 24, No. 6, pp. 78-82.
Bernhard, Georg.
   Die Geldklemme. Plutus, Vol. 19, No. 8, pp. 141-145.
   Reichsbankkredit. Plutus, Vol. 19, No. 25, pp. 469-472.
   Rettung der Währung. Plutus, Vol. 19, No. 22, pp. 417-422.
Bickerdike, C. F.
   Internal and External Purchasing Power of Paper Currencies. Eco-
      nomic Journal, Vol. 32, No. 125, pp. 28-38, March 1922.
Bonn, M. J.
   Die Kapitalflucht aus Deutschland. Plutus, Vol. 21, No. 3, pp. 36-45,
      February 1, 1924.
   Les leçons de l'inflation allemande. Europe nouvelle, Vol. 9, No. 411,
      pp. 8-11, January 2, 1926.
Breska, Herbert v.
   Die Aufwertung der industriellen Obligationen. Gruchots Beitrage
      zu Erläuterung des deutschen Rechts, Vol. 68, No. 2/3, pp. 129-181.
Buxton, D. F.
   The Position of the German Working Classes. Foreign Affairs, Vol.
      5, No. 3, p. 56, September 1923.
Cassel, Gustav.
   Downfall of the Mark. Living Age, Vol. 315, pp. 395-398, November
      18, 1922.
   Problem of the Under-valued Currencies. Bankers Magazine, Vol.
      106, pp. 523-539, March 1923.
Clemen, Rudolf A.
   Germany's New Financial System. Economic World, N.S., Vol. 29,
      No. 23, pp. 798-801, June 6, 1925.
Commons, John R.
   Inflation and Deflation of Currency. La Follette's Magazine, Vol. 15,
      No. 10, pp. 157-158.
D'Abernon, Viscount.
   German Currency: Its Collapse and Recovery, 1920-1926. Journal
      of the Royal Statistical Society, Vol. 90, Part 1, pp. 1-40, 1927.
Dalberg, R.
   Diskontpolitik und Kreditkontingentierung. Zugleich eine Unter-

suchung zur Höhe des Reichsbankdiskontsatzes. Bank-Archiv, Vol. 25, No. 4, pp. 51-54.

Davies, G. R.

The Quantity Theory and Recent Statistical Studies. Journal of Political Economy, Vol. 29, No. 3, pp. 213-221. March 1921.

Décamps, Jules.

La Crise financière allemande. Revue de Paris, Vol. 6, pp. 180-197, November 1, 1922.

Dell, R.

The Causes of German Currency Inflation. Foreign Affairs, Vol. 4, No. 8, pp. 163-164; No. 11, pp. 231-232; February, May, 1923.

Dessirier, Jean.

Indices comparés de la production industrielle et de la production agricole en divers pays de 1870 à 1928. Bulletin de la statistique générale de la France, Vol. 18, section 1, pp. 65-110, October-December 1928.

Düring, Carl Frhr. von.

Die gleitende Lohnskala in Flensburg. Schmollers Jahrbuch, Vol. 46, pp. 121-150, 1922.

Edwards, G. W.

Financial Status of Germany: 1) Fall of the mark and its causes; 2) Effects of the price revolution on Germany; 3) How business is conducted under a depreciated currency; 4) The financial crisis in Germany; 5) What the future holds; 6) Foreign credits to Germany. Annalist, Vol. 20, pp. 535+, 565+, 598-599, 630-631, November 20-December 11, 1922; Vol. 21, pp. 13+, 253-254, January 1, February 12, 1923.

Eldridge, Richard.

The Balance Sheet of German Industry: Reduced Earnings, Low Capitalization and Bonded Indebtedness, Financial Reorganization. Commerce Reports, 1926, No. 35, pp. 528-530, August 30, 1926.

Cartels in Germany. Commerce Reports, 1926, No. 3, pp. 123-124, January 18, 1926.

Elsas, Moritz.

Die innere Kaufkraft der deutschen Mark. Jahrbücher für National-ökonomie und Statistik, 3. F., Vol. 62, pp. 503-515, 1921.

Eulenberg, Franz.

Die sozialen Wirkungen der Währungsverhältnisse. Jahrbücher für Nationalökonomie und Statistik, 3. F. Vol. 67, pp. 748-794, 1924.

Fillman, Heinrich.
Valutaschwankungen und Exportpreisgestaltung. Deutsch-Nordisches Jahrbuch, 1923, pp. 24-29.

Foth, Fritz.
Tatsächliche und gleitende Löhne. Reichs-Arbeitsblatt, 1922, No. 4, Nichtamtlicher Teil, pp. 131*-133*, February 28, 1922.

Glasenapp, von.
Die Tätigkeit der Reichsbank vor dem Kriege—während des Krieges —nach dem Kriege. Deutsche Wirtschafts-Zeitung, Vol. 19, No. 6, pp. 125-127.

Gottschalk, Alfred.
Geldentwertung und Versicherung. Hanseatische Rechtszeitschrift, Vol. 6, No. 15/16, pp. 569-582, 1923.

Graham, F. D.
Germany's Capacity to Pay and the Reparation Plan. American Economic Review, Vol. 15, No. 2, pp. 209-227, June 1925.
International Trade under Depreciated Paper: the United States, 1862-1879. Quarterly Journal of Economics, Vol. 36, pp. 220-273, February 1922.
Self-limiting and Self-inflammatory Movements in Exchange Rates; Germany. Quarterly Journal of Economics, Vol. 43, pp. 221-249, February 1929.

Guébhard, Pierre.
Le problème monétaire allemand. (Address before La Société d'Économie Politique de Paris.) L'Économiste Français, 1922, Vol. 1, No. 16, pp. 485-490, April 22, 1922.

Günther, Ernst.
Die Anpassung der Sozialversicherung an die Geldentwertung und Lohnsteigerung. Jahrbücher für Nationalökonomie und Statistik, 3. F. Vol. 66, pp. 1-54, 1923.

Hahn, L. Albert.
Kapitalmangel. Bank-Archiv, Vol. 25, No. 6, pp. 91-96.

Heilfron, Eduard.
Die Aufwertung von Versicherungsansprüchen. Versicherungspraxis, Vol. 23, No. 12, pp. 162-165.

Hirsch, Julius.
Le miracle du rentenmark et l'avenir de la monnaie allemande. Europe nouvelle, Vol. 8, No. 369, pp. 361-364, March 14, 1925.

Hobson, J. A.
Germany facing dissolution. The Nation and Athenaeum (London), Vol. 32, pp. 188-190, November 4, 1922.

Hokamp, W.
Die Aufnahme langfristiger Anleihen in der Zeit der Geldentwertung. Deutsche Gemeinde-Zeitung, Vol. 61, No. 13, pp. 195-196.

Jenny, Frédéric.
Le mark et les réparations. Revue politique et parlementaire, Vol. 113, No. 336, pp. 161-230, November 1922.

Kemény, Georg.
Zur Kreditpolitik der Reichsbank. Wirtschaftsdienst, Vol. 8, No. 32, pp. 776-777.

Keynes, J. M.
Financial Reconstruction of Germany. New Republic, Vol. 53, pp. 276-277, January 25, 1928.

King, W. I.
Why Monetary Inflation Cannot Continue Indefinitely: an Explanation of the Passing of the Mark. Annalist, Vol. 22, pp. 629+, November 12, 1923.

Kuczynski, R. R.
Elimination of the Paper Mark as Standard of Value. Quarterly Journal of Economics, Vol. 37, pp. 761-769, August 1923.

Lamoy, Ch. de.
Un exemple de la grande concentration industrielle: les konzerne de Hugo Stinnes. Révue Économique Internationale, 1926, Vol. 1, No. 2, pp. 328-349, February 1926.

Landauer, C.
Wert, Preis und Zurechnung, Betrachtungen zu Robert Liefmanns Aufsatz: Zurechnung und Verteilung. Schmollers Jahrbuch, Vol. 49, pp. 805-833, 1925.

Lane, Clayton.
Foreign Loans to Germany during past Four Years. Commerce Reports, 1928, No. 12, pp. 723-724, March 19, 1928.

Lansburgh, Alfred.
Die Dynamik des Währungsverfalls. Die Bank, 1923, No. 6, pp. 337-347, June 1923.

Geldknappheit. Die Bank, 1922, No. 7, pp. 537-545, July 1922.

Der Niedergang der Mark. Die Bank, 1922, No. 9, pp. 647-657, September 1922.

Die Opfer der Inflation. Die Bank, 1922, No. 3, pp. 255-264, March 1922.

Die Rückkehr zur Goldwährung. Die Bank, 1921, No. 12, pp. 673-683, December 1921.

Die Verankerung der Mark. Die Bank, 1923, No. 1, pp. 1-17, January 1923.

Laughlin, J. L.
The German Problem. Fortnightly Review, N.S., Vol. 114, No. 679, 153-156, August 1922.

German Monetary Situation. Review of Reviews, Vol. 65, pp. 504-508, May 1922.

Leyland, John.
The German Problem. Fortnightly Review, N.S., Vol. 114, No. 679, pp. 17-28, July 2, 1923.

Liefmann, R.
Zurechnung und Verteilung. Schmollers Jahrbuch, Vol. 48, pp. 439-471, 1924.

Liesse, André.
L'Assainissement du régime monétaire allemand. La "dévaluation" du mark. L'Économiste Français, 1922, Vol. 2, No. 42, pp. 513-515, October 21, 1922.

La baisse du mark et la situation économique de l'Allemagne. L'Économiste Français, 1921, Vol. 2, No. 47, pp. 641-643, November 19, 1921.

Long, Robert Crozier.
Letters from Berlin. Fortnightly Review, N.S., Vol. 107-116, March 1920-November 1924.

Manchester Guardian Commercial.
Supplement on Reconstruction in Europe. Manchester 1922-1923.

Martin, Rudolph.
Die grossen Vermögen vor und nach dem Kriege. Westermanns Monatshefte, Vol. 146, I, No. 873, pp. 256-260, May 1929.

Meneau, J.
Conséquences de l'inflation et de la dépréciation monétaire pour l'économie générale de l'Allemagne. Revue Économique internationale, 1922, Vol. 1, pp. 130-146, January 1922.

Menger, Carl.
Die Valutaregulierung in Österreich-Ungarn. Hildebrands Jahrbuch, 1892.

Mertens, A.
   Le commerce extérieur et la politique commerciale de l'Allemagne depuis l'armistice. Revue Économique internationale, 1927, Vol. 1, No. 3, pp. 532-552, March 1927.
Meuren, J.
   Die Aufwertung von Industrieobligationen und Pfandbriefen nach der Durchführungsverordnung zum Aufwertungsgesetz vom 29. Nov. 1925. Westdeutsche Wirtschafts-Zeitung, Vol. 3, No. 46, pp. 2-4.
Moeller, Hero.
   Die Diskontpolitik der Reichsbank und der valutarische Kreditgewinn. Bank-Archiv, Vol. 22, No. 20, pp. 243-248.
Morley, Felix.
   Unemployment in Germany (3 Articles). The Nation and Athenaeum (London), Vol. 30, pp. 137-138, 206-208, 337-338; October 22, November 5, November 26, 1921.
Münch, Georg.
   Die Diskontpolitik der Reichsbank. Deutsche Stimmen, Vol. 34, No. 36, pp. 572-575.
Naphtali, Fritz.
   Bankbilanz und Liquidität. Wirtschaftsdienst, Vol. 7, No. 18, pp. 419-420.
Nathan, Otto.
   Über die Berechnung von Indexzahlen für die Lebenshaltungskosten. Jahrbücher für Nationalökonomie und Statistik, 3. F., Vol. 65, pp. 573-581, 1923.
Nöllenburg, Wilhelm.
   Ausverkauf oder Überfremdung? Die Glocke, Vol. 7, No. 38, pp. 1031-1040.
Patterson, E. M.
   Why the Mark Sank. New Republic, Vol. 35, pp. 148-150, July 4, 1923.
Pigou, A. C.
   The Foreign Exchanges. Quarterly Journal of Economics, Vol. 37, pp. 52-74, November 1922.
   Some Problems of Foreign Exchange. Economic Journal, Vol. 30, No. 120, pp. 460-472, December 1920.
Prion, W.
   Auslands-Kredite und Inflation. Bank-Archiv, Vol. 25, No. 5, pp. 69-74.

Deutsche Kreditpolitik 1919-1922. Schmollers Jahrbuch, Vol. 47, pp. 163-205, 1924.

Zinspolitik und Markstabilisierung. Schmollers Jahrbuch, Vol. 48, pp. 843-869, 1924.

Raape, Leo.
Die Aufwertung der Hypotheken. Gruchots Beitrage zu Erläuterung des deutschen Rechts, Vol. 68, No. 2/3, pp. 181-260.

Saupe, Paul.
Lohnpolitik nach dem Stande der Valuta! Konsumgenossenschaftliche Rundschau, Vol. 18, No. 51, pp. 548-550.

Schmitt, Carl L.
Die Probleme der Bankgewinne. Die Bank, 1922, No. 1, pp. 19-25; No. 2, pp. 96-102; January, February, 1922.

Schulz, Paul.
Die Stützungsaktion der Reichsbank. Jahrbücher für National-ökonomie und Statistik, 3. F., Vol. 66, pp. 68-76, 1923.

Silberling, Norman J.
Financial and Monetary Policy in Great Britain during the Napoleonic Wars. Quarterly Journal of Economics, Vol. 38, pp. 214-233, 397-439, February, May, 1924.

Strauss, Walter.
Das Aktienwesen und die Inflationzeit. Recht und Handel, Vol. 1, No. 4, pp. 267-274.

Taussig, F. W.
International Trade under Depreciated Paper. Quarterly Journal of Economics, Vol. 31, pp. 380-403, May 1917.

Théry, René.
La vie des grandes banques allemandes de 1914 à 1925. L'Économiste européen, Vol. 70, No. 1798, pp. 115-116; No. 1799, pp. 131-132; No. 1800, pp. 147-149, August 1926.

Williams, J. H.
German Foreign Trade and the Reparation Payments. Quarterly Journal of Economics, Vol. 36, pp. 482-503, May 1922.

Yves-Guyot.
Aberrations germanophiles et dévaluation du mark. Journal des Économistes, Vol. 73, pp. 129-151, October 1922.

Zahn, Friedrich.
Die innere Verflechtung der deutschen Volkswirtschaft. Jahrbücher für Nationalökonomie und Statistik, 3. F., Vol. 69, pp. 286-304, 1926.

INDEX

Lightning Source UK Ltd.
Milton Keynes UK
UKHW022050140223
417031UK00021B/232